WAA MAR 2 6 2003

D0080932

796.082 Ede

Edelson, Paula.

A to Z of American women
in sports /

DISCARDED:
PALM BEACH COUNTY
LIBRARY SYSTEM
3650 SUMMIT BLVD.
OUTDATED, REDUNDANT,
WEST PALM BEACH, FLORIDA 33406
MATERIAL

A TO Z OF WOMEN

A TO Z OF
AMERICAN WOMEN
IN
SPORTS

PAULA EDELSON

Facts On File, Inc.

For Cliff, with Love

A to Z of American Women in Sports

Copyright © 2002 by Paula Edelson

All rights reserved. No part of this book may be reproduced or utilized in any form or by any means, electronic or mechanical, including photocopying, recording, or by any information storage or retrieval systems, without permission in writing from the publisher. For information contact:

Facts On File, Inc.
132 West 31st Street
New York NY 10001

Library of Congress Cataloging-in-Publication Data

Edelson, Paula.
    A to Z of American women in sports/Paula Edelson.
        p. cm.
    Includes bibliographical references and index.
    ISBN 0-8160-4565-8
    1. Women athletes—United States—Biography—Encyclopedias. 2. Sports for women—United States. I. Title.

    GV697.A1 E28 2002
    796'.082'092273—dc21
    [B]   2001054735

Facts On File books are available at special discounts when purchased in bulk quantities for businesses, associations, institutions, or sales promotions. Please call our Special Sales Department in New York at (212) 967-8800 or (800) 322-8755.

You can find Facts On File on the World Wide Web at http://www.factsonfile.com

Text design by Joan M. Toro and Cathy Rincon
Cover design by Cathy Rincon

Printed in the United States of America

VB Hermitage 10 9 8 7 6 5 4 3 2 1

This book is printed on acid-free paper.

CONTENTS

■ ■ ■

AUTHOR'S NOTE

■ ■ ■

Choosing the people to profile in this volume was a difficult endeavor. Any woman who has attempted to play sports, and done so with some success, has almost certainly encountered and overcome challenges. Under that criterion alone, dozens of women are worthy of mention; much to my regret, I could not include all of them. In making my final selections, I set up the following parameters:

1) The Greatest Athletes: I chose the best athletes in a given sport—virtually every world record holder and multiple Olympic champion has been included. In addition, I gave preference to participants—several coaches and administrators and journalist/broadcasters have been profiled, but I have devoted the great majority of entries to the athletes themselves.

2) The Most Significant Trailblazers: I tried to include as many true pioneers as I could find in this book, to underscore the importance of these courageous people to all female athletes—and indeed to all women.

3) Diversity: I included a vast array of sports (although the high-profile events do have more entries), races, and chronological periods.

Even with these categories in place, making my final decisions was extremely challenging. I offer a sincere apology to those worthy women who were not profiled in this book. In addition, I suggest that all interested readers consult the sources cited in the bibliography at the end of the volume, not only to find out more about the figures profiled here, but to learn about some of the women who were not.

I end this author's note with true regret: There were several people who were highly deserving of inclusion in this book, but whom I did not include because research regarding their lives was scant and sketchy. It is my great hope that at a future time I can find more resources on these individuals and include them in an upcoming edition.

INTRODUCTION

■ ■ ■

The story of American women in sports is an epic of struggle, of inequity, of frustration, and of triumph. There is no doubt that women in every field have had to fight for recognition and opportunity; but if there is one profession that has been owned and dominated by men throughout American history, it has been athletics. Back in Senda Berenson's time, it was thought that athletics were beyond the female capacity, and indeed dangerous for the body. Against the backdrop of these limitations, Berenson organized the first women's basketball contest in 1892. Since that era, women in sports have pushed the boundaries of rules, beliefs, and prejudices to succeed on their own terms and to pave the way for contemporary female athletes.

Breaking societal rules requires courage and dedication, for it often has consequences. Babe Didrikson Zaharias, arguably the finest athlete of the first half of the 20th century, excelled in both individual and team sports. After starring on a corporate basketball team in 1930 and 1931, Didrikson turned to track and field and went on to win two gold medals at the 1932 Olympics. Two decades later, she became the finest golfer on the women's circuit. But in addition to her triumphs, Zaharias suffered her share of taunting. Members of the media constantly commented on her less-than-feminine appearance; one columnist even ventured to say that he "didn't know what to call her—Miss, Mr., or It."

Zaharias was one of the earlier women athlete pioneers, but she was far from the only one. Katherine Switzer, who yearned to run in the 1968 Boston Marathon—then strictly a men's-only event—registered in the race as "K. Switzer," and joined the other racers on the starting line. But about halfway through the race, Switzer, running without a hood or a cap to hide her gender, was spotted by the race director. The business suit–clad executive scooted through the Mass of runners to Switzer and then tried to yank off her race number. Switzer's boyfriend, a competitive hammer thrower who was running with her, pushed the director away from Switzer, who managed to finish the race.

Then there was Ann Meyers, who became the first woman to attend a Division I program on a basketball scholarship when she went to the University of California at Los Angeles (UCLA) in 1974. Meyers was one of the early beneficiaries of Title IX, the federal legislation that compelled all universities receiving federal funding to offer equal opportunities to male and female students. A star athlete at UCLA, Meyers set another precedent five years later when she was invited to try out for the Indiana Pacers of the National Basketball Association (NBA). Meyers showed up for a Pacers practice, in spite of reproaches from Pacers coach Bob Leonard, who insisted that women were better off in the kitchen than on the basketball court. And perhaps most celebrated of all, Billie Jean

King withstood microscopic public attention and pressure when she played Bobby Riggs in the famed 1973 "Battle of the Sexes" tennis match. Up against not only Riggs, who was favored to win the match despite being almost 30 years older than his 26-year-old opponent, but the prejudice of many Americans, who agreed with Riggs that women were inferior competitors, King whipped her rival in straight sets.

Most of the athletes profiled in this book managed to succeed in the face of criticism. Bernice Gera, the first woman to umpire a professional men's baseball game during the modern era, was not quite as fortunate. After battling her way into an otherwise all-male umpiring school, where she was ostracized by her classmates, Gera had to sue for the right to umpire in the men's minor league. Finally, in 1972, the Class A New York–Pennsylvania League followed up on a court order and hired her. Working her first game, Gera, who was stationed at second base, called a runner safe and then reversed her call. The runner's manager flew out of the dugout hurling every known epithet at Gera and then told her that she stood have "stayed in the kitchen, peeling potatoes." Worn out from her years of struggle, an exhausted Gera broke down after the game and resigned from the league, never to umpire again.

In fairness to Gera, she chose to participate in what many people believe is one of the most chauvinistic of sports. True, dozens of women played baseball in the Bloomer League years of the early 20th century, and during World War II, with the majority of male baseball players in the service, All-American Girl's Baseball League drew thousands of fans. Even so, men in baseball have never welcomed women. Back in the 1930s, a barnstorming pitching star named Jackie Mitchell was signed by a minor-league team, but her contract was terminated at the insistence of the Major League Baseball commissioner, Kenesaw Mountain Landis, who insisted that women did not belong on the diamond. More than 50 years later, Julie Croteau filed a suit to play baseball for her high school team. Although she lost her case,

Croteau did go on to become the first woman to play on a men's collegiate baseball team; she resigned from the squad after her sophomore year, however, weary of being ostracized by her teammates. And Pam Postema, who took up where Bernice Gera left off, umpired hundreds of minor-league baseball games during the 1970s and 1980s. But although she was clearly qualified, she was never asked to work a major league game. Postema retired from the diamond after suing Major League Baseball in 1989. (The case was settled out of court.)

Clearly, some sports were more welcoming to women than others. In contrast to baseball, figure skating embraced its female champions. Sonja Henie, who won gold medals in three consecutive Olympic games while a citizen of Norway, moved to the United States and promptly became a successful film star. Henie was undoubtedly one of the most important pioneers in the history of women's figure skating; unlike so many of the other female barrier breakers, she was beloved by both fans and media from the moment she set foot on the ice. Perhaps one reason society has had an easy time accepting women figure skaters is that skating requires, not only strength and athleticism, but finesse and beauty—two traditionally feminine characteristics—as well.

The dynamic between femininity and athleticism has in fact played a major role in the history of women in sports. Aside from the comments the press made about Babe Didrikson Zaharias, such athletes as Dawn Riley, who sailed an all-women's crew in the 1995 America's Cup, and Martina Navratilova, who brought a new standard of power into women's tennis, endured negative comments and publicity during their careers. Riley's boat challenged the ship sailed by the erstwhile America's Cup champion Dennis Connor, and Connor made disparaging remarks about Riley and her crew's sexuality. And Navratilova, who was open about her homosexuality, struggled to win fan support and land endorsement deals in a country that was much more comfortable hailing the more traditional Chris Evert.

A to Z of American Women in Sports is full of brave pioneers, but perhaps the most courageous are the women who fought not only gender battles but racial ones as well. Consider Alice Coachman, who traveled to London in 1948 to become the first African-American woman to win an Olympic gold medal. Coachman, who took top honors in the high-jumping competition, returned to her native Georgia, in the heart of the racially segregated Jim Crow South. Coachman was feted in an elaborate ceremony, during which she was required to sit quietly on the stage of a segregated auditorium. The mayor of her hometown spoke of Coachman's achievement but did not look at her or shake her hand.

It was hardly a hero's welcome, but at least Coachman did compete in the 1948 games. The first two African-American women to qualify for an Olympic team, Tidye Pickett and Louise Stokes, both ran fast enough at the 1932 Olympic trials to earn places on the U.S. track team. In the weeks leading up to the games, which took place that year in Los Angeles, Stokes and Pickett practiced with their teammates during the day, but they were stranded each night in their rooms as the other runners gathered to eat in the whites-only dining room. On the train to California, Pickett and Stokes suffered a rude awakening when their teammate Babe Didrikson hurled ice water on them as they were sleeping. But the greatest indignity occurred at the games themselves, when officials from the U.S. Olympic Committee notified Pickett and Stokes that they were no longer team members; the committee had decided that two white runners (who had been beaten by Pickett and Stokes at the trials) would take their places.

Then there was Ora Washington, rumored to be the finest women's tennis player of her time—an era that included the great champion Helen Wills—but whose race prevented her from playing in any American Lawn Tennis Association–sanctioned events. Washington's travails provided added incentive for tennis player Althea Gibson, who smashed the color barrier in the early 1950s and then went on to win consecutive Wimbledon and U.S. championships in 1958 and 1959. Other African-American pioneers included Ann Moore Gregory, an orphan who grew up working as a maid in an affluent Mississippi home and later became the first of her race to compete in a Ladies' Professional Golf Association (LPGA) tournament, and Toni Stone, the only woman to play baseball in the legendary Negro Leagues.

Women athletes all had their own reasons to participate in their chosen sports, but rarely has that incentive been financial. Some of the finest female athletes in history struggled financially for much of their careers. The skater Peggy Fleming, whose family pooled their resources and made great sacrifices in order to finance her training, turned professional after the 1968 Olympics, specifically to pay her family back. Before the days of the Women's National Basketball Association (WNBA), women basketball players who had excelled in college, such as Cheryl Miller and Cynthia Cooper, headed to Europe in order to earn money at their sport. And Wilma Rudolph, who shattered the Olympic mark in the 100-meter race at the 1960 Rome games, returned after her glorious summer to Tennessee—and to her job at the post office. The gold medal had made Rudolph a national celebrity, but it did not pay the rent.

The profiles of women athletes are often tales of triumph over tribulation. Rudolph, the swimmer/diver Ethelda Bleibtrey, and the figure skater Tenley Albright, all became Olympic champions—the latter two at the 1920 Summer and 1956 Winter Games, respectively—after battling cases of polio during childhood. They are frequently stories with legendary aspects: Gertrude Ederle caused a media frenzy in 1926 when she became the first woman to cross the English Channel—in a time faster than that of any male swimmer. In 1932, Babe Didrikson set the pattern for her larger-than-life career when, as the only member of her team, she singlehandedly defeated a 22-member squad at an intercompany track meet. And Jackie Mitchell made front-page news when she struck out Babe Ruth and Lou Gehrig at a 1931 exhibition game—a stunt that might or might not have been authentic. Every once in a while, a bizarre twist might occur, such as in the almost farcical story of Nancy Kerrigan and Tonya Harding, and the stranger-than-fiction tale of Helen Stephens and Stella Walsh.

But most emphatically, the story of women in sports is a telling of history in the making. Female athletes have made tremendous strides since the days of Senda Berenson. Once confined to modest outfits and meager salaries (if any), their stories told (if at all) on the back pages of newspapers, contemporary women sports figures dazzle fans and media alike with their dedication and talent. At one time, those who made money in sports were the few—such as Sonja Henie, Esther Williams, and Eleanor Holm, who were able turn their athletic talent into an entertainment enterprise.

Today, women in sports can make money both on the field—soccer and basketball now have professional leagues for women—and through endorsements. At one time, the notion that a team of sweating women athletes could hold the nation breathless for more than three hours was about as realistic as finding humans on Mars. But in 1999, the U.S. National Women's Soccer Team did just that. Michelle Akers, Brandi Chastain, Mia Hamm,

and company battled the Chinese squad through two scoreless overtimes before winning a battle of penalty kicks to take the Women's World Cup at a sold-out Rose Bowl—and before a television audience of more than 3 million.

Even so, women athletes have a way to go in their quest to even the playing field. Women professional tennis players have battled for many years to earn pay equal to that of their male counterparts, and today, three out of four Grand Slam events (the exception is Wimbledon) pay their women and men champions the same amount. But women basketball players make only a fraction of the money that men earn in the NBA, and women baseball players, such as Ila Borders, still harbor dreams of playing in the major leagues but are confined to minor league teams.

Nevertheless the strides made by women athletes in the last century are not to be underestimated. Each woman chronicled in this book has made a memorable contribution to this overall achievement. These figures have paved the way for future women athletes. More important, they have redefined gender roles in the United States, thereby pushing American society farther forward.

A

ACKERMAN, VALERIE
(1959–   )   *President of the Women's*
National Basketball Association (WNBA)

After the failure of three professional women's basketball leagues, few ever thought that one day there would be a league of women players that would thrive in the United States. But Val Ackerman, who is the president of the Women's National Basketball Association (WNBA), thought differently. And so far, no one has proven her wrong.

Valerie Ackerman was born on November 10, 1959, in Pennington, New Jersey. Her father, Randy, was the athletic director at Hope Wells High School in Princeton, New Jersey. It was from her parents that Val and her two siblings learned not only the skills to play sports but the discipline to excel, both on the field and off. "Whatever it was Valerie did, she did it with great intensity, dedication, and integrity," said Debbie Ryan, who had graduated from Hope Wells a few years before Ackerman. Ryan had been a basketball standout herself at Hope Wells and had turned to coaching after graduating from the University of Virginia.

During Ackerman's senior year in high school, she received a phone call from Ryan, who was about to become the head coach at Virginia. After the passage of Title IX in 1972, universities were required to offer scholarships to female athletes as well as men. Those scholarships were few and far between, however, and in 1977, Virginia had only one to offer. Ryan told Ackerman that she could have half the scholarship if she agreed to come to Charlottesville (where the University of Virginia is located). Ackerman agreed. She later joked that while the university paid her tuition, it paid room and board to her roommate, who had received the other half of the scholarship. "I didn't have to pay for classes," she said, "and my roommate didn't have to pay to eat."

Ackerman excelled at Virginia. Majoring in social and political studies, she was a two-time academic All-American. She also performed impressively on the basketball court, and after graduating in 1981, decided to play professionally in France. After a year on the European circuit, however, Ackerman returned to the United States to attend law school at the University of California at Los Angeles (UCLA). After graduating, she took a job at a Wall Street law firm, where she met her future husband, Charles Rappaport. Ackerman and Rappaport married in 1988 (the couple has two daughters). That same year, Ackerman left the firm to work as an attorney for the National Basketball Association (NBA).

It was during her tenure as an NBA lawyer that Ackerman began discussing a possible women's league with league president David Stern. Ackerman, who served as Stern's special assistant from 1990 to 1992 (she was then promoted to director of business affairs and then vice president of business affairs), believed that with the right amount of marketing and exposure, an all-women's league would work. "It would require television coverage, advertising, and the proper backers," she said later. The proper backing was, of course, the NBA.

In 1995, the NBA financed a nationwide tour by the U.S. Olympic women's basketball team. The team played exhibition games against top university squads. With the help of a tremendous marketing effort by the NBA, the games were well-attended and often sold out. As important, they were televised. By the time the team played in the Atlanta Olympics in the summer of 1996, many of the players had become household names. The team swept to gold in Atlanta. Carried live on NBC, the final game garnered one of the highest television ratings ever for a women's sporting event.

It was a perfect way to usher in the brand-new WNBA, which premiered in the summer of 1997. Top collegiate players, as well as those who had recently graduated and were playing professionally in Europe, flocked to enlist in the draft. Interestingly, the WNBA was not the only league to open operations for professional women's basketball in 1997. The American Basketball League (ABL) also premiered that year, giving talented players a choice of leagues.

Both the ABL and the WNBA enjoyed successful first seasons, but at the end of its second year, in 1998, the ABL folded. The WNBA, however, continued to thrive. In 1999, two new franchises joined the original 14 teams, and the league enjoyed a sold-out all-star game at Madison Square Garden. Sitting in the president's box was New Jersey's own Val Ackerman, who has offered a new generation of women the opportunity to play professional basketball in the United States. Ackerman has remained at the helm of the WNBA, which continued to thrive during the 2001 and 2002 seasons.

Further Reading

"An Interview with WBNA President Val Ackerman," NBA Online. Available online. URL: www.nba.com/heat/july_ackerman_interview.html. Downloaded on January 24, 2001.

Lannin, Joanne. *A History of Basketball for Girls and Women: From Bloomers to Big Leagues.* Minneapolis, Minn.: Lerner Sports, 2000.

NBA Staff Member Biographies. "Val Ackerman," NBA Online. Available online. URL: http://www.nba.com/Basics/00421429.html. Downloaded on January 24, 2001.

Sports Profiles. "Val Ackerman," FoxSports Online. Available online. www.foxsports.com/business/trends/z000524 valerie_ackermanl.sm. Downloaded on January 24, 2001.

AKERS, MICHELLE
(1966–) *Soccer Player*

A five-foot-10-inch tall midfielder, Michelle Akers endured three knee surgeries, two knocked-out teeth, and countless other injuries—as well as a debilitating chronic disease—on her way to leading the U.S. women's soccer team to two World Cup championships and an Olympic gold medal.

Born in Santa Clara, California, on December 1, 1966, Michelle Akers began playing soccer when she was eight. Her mother, whom Michelle described as "no June Cleaver," was her first coach. The team lost every game, and Michelle, the goalkeeper, cried after each defeat.

The Akers family moved to Seattle when Michelle was 10, and she quickly joined two soccer teams. When she was 12, Michelle's parents divorced. The marital breakup was hard on both Michelle and her brother, Mike. To cope with her anguish, Michelle spent most of her time on the soccer field, practicing and playing. The hours of experience helped her to deal with her family situation. It also honed her extensive natural athletic gifts, turning Michele into a premier soccer player.

After graduating from high school, the three-time All-American Akers went to the University of

Central Florida (UCF) on an athletic scholarship. During her sophomore year at UCF, Akers joined the newly formed national soccer team. The year was 1985. For the next 15 years, Akers would form the foundation for that team, serving as valued player, captain, and mentor to such future stars as MIA HAMM, BRANDI CHASTAIN, and Julie Foudy.

Akers graduated from UCF in 1985 and began playing soccer full time. Once an obscure sport in the United States, women's soccer was beginning to gather momentum, not only at home, but internationally. In 1991, the Fédération Internationale de Football Association (FIFA), the organization that runs the men's World Cup soccer championships, decided to organize a World Cup tournament for women.

The inaugural Women's World Cup was held in China, and the United States was one of six nations participating. The U.S. team won its early-round matches with ease. But the team was to face Norway in the final. Norway was a strong team, and it had been playing together for as long as the U.S. national team.

Once on the field, however, the Norwegians were no match for Akers and the U.S. team. Akers scored two goals as the United States claimed the first Women's World Cup title. The Americans were ecstatic to be world champions, but back in the United States, their feat was little known. The match had taken place in a faraway country, and it had received very little press coverage at home. Akers later recalled sitting next to an older American woman on the flight home from China.

"So what were you doing in China?" the woman asked. "Well, I was playing in the Women's World Cup soccer championships," Akers replied. "Oh," said the woman. "And how did you do?" "We won," answered Akers. The woman hesitated for a moment. "Well that's nice, dear," she said.

But even if the public at large was unaware of the national team's achievement in the 1991 World Cup, the victory in China did do a great deal for women's soccer in the United States. The team, which had had a lot of trouble attracting media attention before 1991, now had a regular, if small,

press following. More important, the victory impressed thousands of young female soccer players, who now had an inspiration—and a goal.

For Akers, the 1991 World Cup was a thrilling victory, but it also marked the beginning of a devastating time. Shortly after returning from China, she began experiencing severe flu-like symptoms. Over the next few months, the symptoms got worse; Akers was unable to sleep at times, and at other times was so exhausted that she could not leave her bed. Her appetite had diminished dramatically, and perhaps most frightening of all, she was experiencing memory loss.

It took Akers three years to get a diagnosis. Finally, she learned that she was suffering from an illness called chronic fatigue and immune dysfunction syndrome (CFIDS). After the diagnosis, Akers spoke in front of a congressional committee about the disease. "It was the first time I said out loud, 'I can't beat this,'" she remembered later.

But Akers was not about to let the disease beat her, either. After the national team finished a disappointing third in the 1995 World Cup, the team began training for the 1996 Olympics. It would be the first time that women would play soccer in the Olympics. Moreover, the U.S. team would be playing on their own home turf; the game was to take place in Atlanta, Georgia.

At the Olympic final game, 78,000 people jammed the Georgia Bowl to watch the United States defeat China to take the gold medal. For Akers, it was a victory to savor. "I remember standing on the podium looking up to heaven," she said of the gold medal ceremony. "I could see all my friends and family from where I stood. It was a moment I will always remember."

The rest of the country remembered the moment as well. Although the final game of the Olympics was not televised, millions of Americans watched the highlights. It was enough to convince them that women's soccer was a thrilling game and that the U.S. team boasted superlative athleticism and grace.

The timing of the Olympic victory could not have been better for the U.S. team. The next

Women's World Cup was in the United States in 1999, and all of a sudden, the national soccer team became the target of a media blitz. The press coverage began in 1998, when the team began playing preparation matches. Each of the exhibition games held in the United States drew thousands of fans; in May 1999, the women's team played at a sold-out Meadowlands Arena in Rutherford, New Jersey. That the soccer team could draw a capacity crowd in one of the largest football stadiums in the nation made a huge statement about women in sports: People will come to watch them play.

The Women's World Cup began in June 1999, and the early-round matches, played in different cities, all sold out when the U.S. team played. Akers and her teammates were thrilled by the fans' enthusiasm, and they did not hesitate to return the affection. Akers even suffered a minor injury when a fan tugged too hard on her arm as she ran around the stadium exchanging high-fives and handshakes with the spectators.

The 1999 World Cup championships culminated with a riveting game at the Rose Bowl in Pasadena, California. After playing to a scoreless tie with China during regulation play and two overtime periods, the U.S. team won the cup in a thrilling shoot-out. Akers, however, had to watch the end of the game from the locker room. Halfway through the first overtime, she had collapsed on the field, suffering from severe fatigue and dehydration so severe she was given fluids intravenously.

But Akers did return to the field after the game ended. Watching Brandi Chastain's game-sealing score from the locker room, Akers ripped the intravenous device from her arm and ran on to the field to join her ecstatic teammates as they received their medals and the cup. It was the crowning achievement of this soccer warrior's career.

Early in 2000, Akers retired from the national team. She had helped take the team to three international championships, but more important, she had helped raise awareness and appreciation for women's soccer in the United States to new heights. Akers always knew the game was worth the attention it was suddenly receiving. "To those who say we couldn't deliver the goods," she said after the 1996 Olympic victory, "I simply said, 'Just watch me play.'"

Further Reading

Akers, Michelle. *The Game and the Glory*. Grand Rapids, Mich.: Zondervan Publishing House, 2000.

Longman, Jere. *The Girls of Summer: The U.S. Women's Soccer Team and How It Changed the World*. New York: HarperCollins, 2000.

Miller, Marla. *All-American Girls: The US Women's National Soccer Team*. New York: Archway Paperbacks, 1999, pp. 7–20.

ALBRIGHT, TENLEY
(1935–)   *Figure Skater*

Since the modern Winter Olympic Games began in 1908, seven U.S. women have brought home gold medals in singles figure skating. Tenley Albright, the first U.S. woman skater to take an Olympic gold medal, won the prize at the 1956 games in Cortina, Italy.

Born in Newton, Massachusetts, on July 18, 1935, Tenley began skating early in her childhood. Her father, a surgeon, flooded the backyard of their property every winter, and by the time she was nine, young Tenley was cutting accurate figures on her home skating rink. Two years later, however, Albright's skating future came close to ending permanently. At the age of 11, she contracted polio. Although she was never paralyzed, her body was severely weakened by the disease. "For a time it was quite scary," Albright remembered later. "I didn't have full use of my leg, neck, and back."

Luckily for Albright, she slowly regained her strength, and eventually her doctor recommended that she return to skating as a form of physical therapy. Albright heeded her physician's advice, and by the time she was 13, she was skating in competitions. At the age of 14, Albright won her first skating tournament, taking top honors at the U.S. Eastern Junior Championships. It was the first of a long string of skating victories for Albright, who would win her first of five consecutive U.S. titles in 1952.

That same year, Albright competed in the Oslo Olympic Games. The eventual gold medalist, Jeanne Altweg, built up a large lead in the compulsory figures portion of the competition, and then she barely held off a brilliant free-skating performance by Albright, who ended up winning the silver. Interestingly, Albright would have taken the title had the rules at the 1952 games been what they are today. At that time, however, the compulsory figures accounted for a full 60 percent of the final score. Today the compulsory figures are no longer a part of the Olympic skating competition, and the free-skating portion accounts for two-thirds of the final tally.

In 1953, Albright became the first U.S. woman to win the gold medal at the World Championships. After finishing second at the same event in 1954, she reclaimed the title in 1955. That achievement was all the more remarkable given the fact that Albright had entered the premed program at Radcliffe College in the fall of 1953. She carried a full course load at Radcliffe, but was able to stay in top skating form by training every morning from 4 to 6 A.M.

With two World Championships under her belt, Albright emerged as the favorite to win the

Tenley Albright took time off from her studies at Radcliffe College to train for the 1956 Olympic Games. She returned to college after winning the gold medal in figure skating, and she eventually became a doctor.
(Library of Congress)

gold medal at the 1956 Olympic Games. She took a semester off from college in order to train full time for the event, and when she arrived in Cortina, Italy, a few weeks before the game, she was relaxed and confident. Barring serious injury, she knew she had an excellent chance of becoming the first U.S. woman to win the Olympic skating title.

But two weeks before the competition began, Albright did indeed suffer an injury She was practicing her free-skating routine when her skate hit a rut in the ice. The blade on her left skate cut through her right boot, cutting her foot almost to the bone. Bleeding profusely and in terrible pain, Albright called her father, who immediately few to Cortina to tend to his daughter. Although Dr. Albright was able to stitch up the wound, his daughter was unable to put much weight on her injured foot for several days. Less than a week remained before the games were to begin, and Albright sat on the sidelines, waiting for the day that she could spin and jump again. Happily, that day occurred—the very same day that the skating competition began.

Albright skated a strong compulsory program, and going into the free-skating portion of the event, she held a slight lead over her closest competitor—her teammate CAROL HEISS. Heiss skated a superb free-skating routine, and Albright, still feeling some pain from her injury, skated to the center of the ice, about to begin her routine.

"I remember waiting for the music to begin," Albright said of that moment. "Suddenly I heard singing. I knew my music was just orchestral, but now I heard singing . . . what happened is that the thousands who were watching were humming and singing with the music."

Swept away by the crowd, Albright forgot about her injury and skated an exuberant program. Using elegance and strength, she jumped and spun to the resounding roar of the spectators, who erupted into wild applause when Albright concluded her routine. Minutes later, the crowd roared again. Albright had been awarded first place by 10 of the 11 judges. (The U.S. judge cast his vote for Heiss.) She had accomplished her goal and won Olympic gold.

At the end of 1956, Albright retired from competitive skating. Three years later, she graduated from Harvard Medical School. Dr. Tenley Albright became a sports physician, and in 1976 she was the chief doctor for the U.S. Winter Olympic team. Albright married Gerald Blakely in 1958, and the couple has three children. Albright continues to practice medicine in a suburb of Boston, Massachusetts.

Further Reading

Greenspan, Bud. *Frozen in Time: The Greatest Moments at the Winter Olympics.* Santa Monica, Calif.: General Publishing Group, 1997.

Layden, Joe. *Women in Sports: The Complete Book on the World's Greatest Female Athletes.* Santa Monica: General Publishing Group, 1997, pp. 15–16.

ALI, LAILA
(1977–) *Boxer*

Laila Ali, a professional woman boxer who is still early in her career, deserves notice not for what she has already achieved but for her future potential. The daughter of legendary boxer Muhammad Ali, one of the most recognized athletes in the world, can bring the sport of women's boxing to new heights in regard to media and fan attention.

The eighth child of Muhammad Ali, born in Los Angeles on December 30, 1977, Laila did not grow up close to her father. Her mother, Veronica, had divorced Ali when Laila was eight, and she had moved with her two daughters to Malibu, California. As a teenager, Laila was defiant and difficult. At the age of 16, she was arrested for shoplifting, and she then served a three-month term in prison for another, unpublicized offense. But if Laila was at times angry (she got into numerous street fights during her youth), she was also resilient and ambitious. She finished community college and then managed her own beauty salon.

In the meantime, she had discovered boxing—not the unofficial street type but the sanctioned sport that had brought her father fame and fortune. Ali found her groove when she was looking for a way to exercise during her off hours. In 1998 she decided to turn professional. Making the choice to do so was easy; breaking the news to her father was not. "He doesn't want me to get hurt, but he's going to support me 100 percent as a father," she told the Associated Press. No doubt the senior Ali's own medical condition made it harder for him to accept his daughter's decision. Muhammad Ali suffers from Parkinson's disease, a progressive disease of the brain and spinal cord. Ali's condition was caused, at least in part, by the severe head injuries he received during his ring career.

Pursuing her new career in earnest, Laila Ali hired a trainer and began working out for three hours a day, six days a week. Her daily regimens included running three to four miles, jumping rope, hitting punching bags, and sparring. She developed a lethal combination that began with a right-hand jab and ended with a left hook.

After several months of training, Ali was ready for her first bout. That match took place on October 8, 1999, in Verona, New York. But this was no ordinary professional debut. Media from around the world came to witness the daughter of "The Greatest" (as Muhammad Ali had labeled himself years before) enter the ring for the first time. Laila's opponent was April Fowler, but both boxers were overshadowed by a surprise guest. "Ladies and gentlemen," the ring announcer boomed over the arena's public address system: "a man who needs no introduction. . ." The rest of his speech was lost in the din; the fans in the arena were chanting "Ali, Ali," as Laila's father made his way to ringside.

It took Laila Ali a mere 31 seconds to win her first fight, as she knocked out the hapless Fowler in champion fashion. Ali also won her next two bouts, triumphing both times by technical knockouts (TKOs), which are victories awarded when the referee determine that the opponent is too injured to continue the bout. After a third consecutive TKO, over Crystal Arcand in March 2000, Laila began reaping praise as well as inevitable comparisons to her father. "I've never experienced a woman with the kind of power she has," Arcand

Laila Ali in action. The ninth child of the champion boxer Muhammad Ali, Laila is the only one of his children to follow in his footsteps.
(Tom Hauck/Getty Images)

said of her defeater. "You can see some of her dad's moves," the referee, Fern Chretien, added.

Ali won her fifth consecutive match the following month, but she suffered the first knockdown of her career, when her opponent, Karen Bill, landed several blows in the first round. After exchanging several combination punches, Ali finally emerged victorious with a third-round TKO.

After taking time off to get married in October 2000, Ali returned to the ring in early 2001. After winning her first three bouts of the year, Ali traveled to Verona, New York, in June 2001 to participate in what would thus far be her most publicized bout: Laila Ali would be fighting Jackie Frazier, the daughter of Joe Frazier, the first man to defeat Muhammad Ali. The notion of "Ali-Frazier IV" (their fathers fought one another three times in their careers; Ali won two of them in convincing fashion) fascinated boxing fans of both genders. As a delirious sold-out crowd changed "Ali! Ali!" Muhammad's daughter forced Joe's daughter into the ropes time and time again. Frazier managed to go the full distance against Ali, who won a unanimous decision for her ninth win. To date, she has never lost a fight.

Laila Ali continues to train, and she continues to fight. The road she has chosen is not an easy one; following in a legendary parent's footsteps has its own set of pitfalls. Moreover, being an ambassador for a sport is never an easy task; only time will tell if Laila Ali has the talent and the attitude to carry it off. But with a thus-far undefeated career, she is off to a terrific start.

Further Reading

"Laila Ali: Daughter of Boxing Legend Brings Instant Recognition to the Sport," Women's Boxing Page. October 2000. Available online. URL: http://www.geocities.com/Colosseum/Field/6251/lali.htm. Downloaded on February 16, 2001.

"Laila Ali: She Bee Stinging," Laila Ali. Available online. URL: http://www.lailaali.net/bg_centa.htm. Downloaded on February 16, 2001.

Waters, Mike. "Laila Ali Boxing in the Shadow of the Greatest: Legend's Daughter, 'Madame Butterfly,' Vows to Sting Like a Bee at Turning Stone," Syracuse Online. © 1999 The Herald Company. Available online. URL: http://www.syracuse.com/sports/stwednesday/19991006_apnsc.html. Downloaded on February 16, 2001.

ANDERSEN, LISA
(1969–) *Surfer*

Ever since she was a young girl, Lisa Andersen's goal was to become a world champion surfer. Eventually she did just that—a record four times. But her ride to the top was not an easy one.

Born in Ormond Beach, Florida, on March 8, 1969, Lisa had a difficult time at home. Her parents had a deeply unhappy marriage that affected Lisa profoundly. When she was a teenager she spent most of her time on the beach, where she learned to surf. The harder things became at home, the more time Lisa spent surfing.

When Lisa was 16, she took her surfboard and clothes and ran away from home. She hitchhiked across the country and settled in Huntington Beach, California. Lisa supported herself by waitressing and working as an ice cream scooper, and she spent every moment of her spare time on her surfboard. Although there were some women surfers in California, Lisa spent most of her time surfing with men. To keep up with her surfing pals, she learned to ride waves aggressively. Later, Andersen's surfing would be noted for its assertive style—a feature she would attribute to her training with men.

In 1987 Andersen began entering surfing tournaments. Relatively unknown in the competitive world, she upset a field of much more established surfers to take top honors in the U.S. Amateur Championships. Later that year she beat a group of professional surfers to win another high-profile event, the Katin Challenge. With two major tournament wins under her belt, Andersen decided to turn professional at the end of 1987.

But although Andersen was named Professional Rookie of the Year in 1987, she found life on the professional tour difficult and tiring. She struggled to find her form, and she failed to win any major events during her first couple of years on the tour. Then in 1992, Andersen came back with a roar, winning three Association of Surfing Professionals titles.

Andersen was a favorite to win the 1992 women's world championships, but when she discovered she was pregnant, she took a leave of absence from the tour. She gave birth to a daughter, Erica, in 1993, and the following year, she won her first world championship.

Andersen repeated as world champion in 1995 and 1996. During that time she set new records for women surfers in endorsements and prize money. In search of greater competition in 1997, she became the first woman to compete in the men's world surfing championships. She was eliminated in an early heat, but she came back later that year to capture her fourth consecutive women's world championship. Andersen, who reconciled with her parents in 1995, continues to compete on the women's professional tour. Now the most prolific champion of all women surfers, she continues to win tournaments around the world.

Further Reading

Greenberg, Judith E. *Getting into the Game.* Danbury, Conn.: Franklin Watts, 1997, p. 118.

Hill, Jim. "Surf's Up for Gender Equality," US News Story Page, August 8, 1997. Available online. URL: http://www.cnn.com/US/9708/08/female.surfer. Downloaded on February 13, 2001.

SI for Women: 100 Greatest Athletes of All Time. "Lisa Andersen." Available online. URL: http://sportsillustrated.cnn.com/siforwomen/top_100/76/. Posted on November 29, 1999.

⊞ ASHFORD, EVELYN
(1957–   ) *Sprinter*

Evelyn Ashford, a sprinter who competed in three Olympic Games and won four gold medals, could have been one of the most decorated athletes in history. In her athletic prime in 1980, however, she was unable to compete in Moscow because the United States boycotted the games that year.

Evelyn Ashford was born in Shreveport, Louisiana, on April 15, 1957. She has a brother and three sisters. Her father was a sergeant in the air force, and the family moved several times during her childhood. By the time Evelyn was in high school, her family had settled in Roseville, California.

Ashford had always been athletic, but when she was a senior in high school her running so impressed her math teacher that he suggested that she participate in track. Because there was no girls' track team in Ashford's high school, she competed on the boys' team. Ashford was so quick that she regularly beat the school's star football running back every time they raced the 50-yard dash.

She was also fast enough to earn a track-and-field scholarship to the University of California at Los Angeles (UCLA). During Ashford's freshman year at UCLA, a volunteer coach named Pat Connolly asked Ashford to run a timed 100-yard dash. Ashford's time on the sprint was so quick that Connolly thought she had misread her stopwatch and asked the young athlete to run it again. After Ashford's second dash, Connolly, a former Olympic sprinter herself, told the freshman that she had a good chance of making the 1976 Olympic team. Ashford was flattered but skeptical. "I thought the lady was nuts," she said later.

But Ashford did indeed qualify for the 1976 Olympic track-and-field team in Montreal. Competing against a field of experienced world-class athletes, Ashford finished fifth in the 100-yard dash, beating her more seasoned teammate Chandra Cheeseborough, as well as a young East German runner named Marlies Gohr, who became her chief rival.

After the games, Ashford decided to pursue what had become an obsessive dream of winning an Olympic gold medal. She dropped out of UCLA in 1979 to devote more time to her training, and Connolly continued to coach her, even though she was no longer on the university track team. But later that year, Ray Williams, a basketball coach whom Ashford had married the year before, replaced Connolly as Ashford's coach.

Ashford put the sprinting world on notice at the Montreal World Cup meet in 1979. In a stunning performance in the 100-meter race, Ashford beat Gohr, the world-record holder who was the hands-down favorite to capture gold at the Olympics the following year. But Ashford ran an impressive string of races during the 1979–80 track and field season, and in early 1980 it was she whom most people favored to win gold in Moscow.

But then something happened that would become a pivotal event in Ashford's life. Citing the Soviet Union's invasion of Afghanistan in 1979 as reason to protest, President Jimmy Carter announced in February 1980 that the United States would boycott the Moscow games. For such athletes as Ashford, who were in their athletic prime, it was a devastating blow. Ashford was shattered when the announcement came—winning gold in Moscow had been her sole goal for the past four years—and she considered leaving the sport altogether. But she and Williams embarked on a cross-country trip that summer, and Ashford used the time to ponder her career and her goals. By journey's end she had decided to continue to train and to pursue Olympic gold.

In 1981 Ashford won the 100-meter and 200-meter events at the World Cup, and in 1983 she was favored to capture another pair of gold medals at the International Amateur Athletic Federation World Championships, but she pulled a hamstring muscle in a preliminary heat and had to pull out.

The sprinter Evelyn Ashford won a total of four gold medals in three Olympic Games.
(Steve Powell/Getty Images)

The next year, back at full strength, Ashford qualified to compete in her third consecutive Olympic Games.

This time, Ashford was not going to be denied. She set an Olympic record of 10.97 seconds in the 100-meter dash, and she anchored the 4 × 100 U.S. relay team to a first-place finish. At last Ashford had her prized gold medals. The victory, however, was somewhat diminished by the fact that Ashford's chief rival, Gohr, was on an East German team that boycotted the Los Angeles games along with the rest of the Soviet bloc, and therefore did not compete against Ashford in the 100-meter competition.

Nevertheless, Ashford was now an Olympic champion. With that achievement behind her, she took time off from training in 1985 to start a family. She and Williams became parents on May 30 of that year, when their daughter, Raina Ashley, was born. The following year, Ashford was back in racing form and proved that she was a world-champion sprinter with a win over, not only Gohr, but a talented East German athlete named Heike Drechsler as well.

In 1988, Ashford prepared for her third Olympic competition with slightly different goals in mind. With the emergence of FLORENCE GRIFFITH JOYNER, Ashford was no longer the world's fastest woman. Even so, Ashford competed successfully in Seoul, finishing second to Griffith Joyner in the 100-meter dash, and then anchoring the U.S. 4 × 100 relay team to win the a gold. Although the spotlight at the Seoul games shone mostly on Griffith Joyner, Ashford's third career gold medal put her in elite company; only WYOMIA TYUS and WILMA RUDOLPH (and, in 2000, MARION JONES) join Ashford as U.S. women sprinters who have won three Olympic gold medals.

In 1992, Ashford competed in her fourth and final Olympics, this time in Barcelona. She made history there when she won an unprecedented fourth gold medal, as her performance helped the U.S. team capture the 4 × 100 relay. Since retiring from track and field following the Barcelona games, Ashford has made occasional appearances as a television commentator, and she has also served as cochairperson of Athletes for Literacy.

Ashford's four gold medals have set a standard for Olympic track-and-field excellence. As important, her durability—she competed in four Olympic games over the course of three decades and would have competed in a fifth if the United States had not boycotted the Moscow games—shine as an example of dedication that endures.

Further Reading

Davis, Michael D. *Black American Women in Olympic Track and Field: A Complete Illustrated Reference.* Jefferson, N.C.: McFarland, 1992.

Layden, Joe. *Women in Sports: The Complete Book on the World's Greatest Female Athletes.* Santa Monica, Calif.: General Publishing Group, 1997, pp. 19–20.

▦ AUSTIN, TRACY
(1962–)   *Tennis Player*

Tracy Austin, the youngest U.S. player ever to win a Grand Slam event, won two U.S. Opens before the age of 20 and was the youngest person ever voted into the Tennis Hall of Fame when she was inducted at the age of 29, in 1992.

Born in Redondo Beach, California, on December 12, 1962, Tracy Austin was swinging a tennis racket by the time she could walk. The youngest of four children born to John Austin, an insurance salesman, and his wife, Debbi, Tracy loved to play against her older siblings. When they were unavailable, she would happily pass the hours hitting ground strokes against a wall. One day, doing just that at the neighborhood tennis club, she was spotted by the club coach, who began teaching her private lessons on the spot. Young Tracy, the coach predicted, would one day be a champion.

It did not take Tracy long to prove her first teacher right. She won the 12-and-under national title in 1974, and she then took top honors at the indoor singles championships for girls 16 and under in the spring of 1976. One year later, in England, 15-year-old Austin made her major tour debut, at Wimbledon, the world's most prestigious

championship. After surviving her opening round match at Wimbledon, Austin played on Centre Court against the world's top-ranked player, CHRIS EVERT. Austin lost in straight sets, curtsied to the queen side-by-side with Evert, and left the court with a smile.

Austin continued to play, and she improved quickly. One year after turning professional in 1978, she won her first major championship when she took top honors at the 1979 Italian Open. Four months later, she avenged her Wimbledon loss when she defeated Chris Evert in the championship match at the U.S. Open. In December 1979, Austin gained the top ranking in women's tennis—the youngest player up to that point to have that honor.

Although Austin played solid tennis in 1980, she did not win a Grand Slam tournament that year. She did, however, take her second U.S. Open title when she beat MARTINA NAVRATILOVA in a three-set final in 1981. But although Austin was on top of her game once again, she was beginning to suffer physical problems. At the age of 19, her body, pushed for so long, started to betray her. From 1982 until 1989, she endured a series of debilitating injuries and conditions, including pulled hamstrings, ankle problems, tendinitis, and sciatica.

Then, in 1989, Austin was driving her car when she was hit by a van. The accident shattered Austin's kneecap. She underwent a five-hour operation and was told at the end of the procedure that she would never play professional tennis again. Austin returned home and underwent a rigorous physical therapy regime. After several months she was walking without a limp, and a year later she was back on the court practicing volleys and serves.

But although Austin did attempt a comeback on the professional tour, she never completely regained her old form. Austin found a second profession in the broadcast booth, where she shares her extensive knowledge of and passion for the game of tennis during Wimbledon, U.S. Open, and French Open coverage for various networks.

Married to Scott Holt since 1993, she has three sons, Dylan (born in 1997), Brandon (born in 1999), and Sean (born in 2001).

Further Reading

Feinstein, John. *Hard Courts.* New York: Random House, 1993.

Johnson, Anne Jarette. *Great Women in Sports.* Detroit: Visible Ink Press, 1996.

Layden, Joe. *Women in Sports: The Complete Book on the World's Greatest Female Athletes.* Santa Monica, Calif.: General Publishing Group, 1997, pp. 20–21.

B

BABASHOFF, SHIRLEY
(1957–) *Swimmer*

Although Shirley Babashoff never won an individual gold medal, she is one of the most decorated U.S. swimmers in the history of the Olympics. With a career total of eight medals, Babashoff is second only to JENNY THOMPSON, a swimmer who won 10 Olympic prizes.

Shirley Babashoff was born on January 31, 1957, in Vernon, California. Her parents, Jack, a machinist, and Vera, a homemaker who handled the family finances, made it a priority to have the money to pay for swimming lessons for their athletic children. Vera and Jack's investment paid off; in addition to Shirley's success, Jack Babashoff Jr. won a silver medal at the 1976 Olympics, Billy Babashoff became a top collegiate swimmer at the University of California at Los Angeles (UCLA), and Debbie Babashoff won a national championship in the 1,500-meter freestyle event in 1989.

The most talented swimmer in the family, though, was Shirley, who began racing when she was 10. After winning several junior championships, Babashoff became one of the youngest swimmers in history to compete in the Olympics, when she qualified for the U.S. team in 1972. By that time, she had already broken a world record with a time of 2:05:21 in the 200-meter freestyle race. She was favored to win the gold in that race for that reason, and she swam brilliantly, lowering her own mark by nearly a second and finishing the race in 2:04:33. Unfortunately for Babashoff, however, a young Australian named Shane Gould swam even faster, clocking a 2:03:56 in the final, and leaving Babashoff with a silver medal.

Babashoff got some revenge against Gould in the 100-meter freestyle, beating the Australian to win silver as her fellow U.S. swimmer Sandra Neilson took the gold. But Babashoff's finish was astonishing, considering the fact that she got off to a horrendous start. Swimmers competing in a 100-meter event swim the length of the pool, then turn and swim back to finish where they began. Because of the short distance, it is crucial that the swimmer leave the blocks fast and get a good start in the water. But Babashoff had trouble leaving her block, and swam poorly during the first half of the race. She found herself in seventh place at the race's halfway mark. Swimming swiftly and strongly, Babashoff overtook five swimmers in the second half of the race and was gaining steadily on Gould as well. Shortly before the finish, Babashoff passed Gould and touched the wall before her. Two days later, Babashoff won her first Olympic gold medal, when she swam the anchor leg of the 4 × 200 meter freestyle relay.

Four years later, 19-year-old Babashoff traveled to Montreal to compete in her second Olympics. Once again she was a favorite to win gold, having captured world championships in both the 200-meter and 400-meter events in 1975. As in 1972, she led the U.S. team to a gold medal in the 4 × 100 meter event and to a silver in the 4 × 200 meter race. But in the individual races, gold once again eluded her. Babashoff took silver medals, once again, in both the 100-and 200-meter freestyle events.

Babashoff was beaten in both races by East German swimmers. During the 1976 games, rumors abounded about illegal steroid use among swimmers from East Germany. For the most part, these rumors circulated among athletes and coaches, but they were not made public. Babashoff, however, did not keep her suspicions to herself. She told the media that she believed the East Germans had won the gold medals illegally. But none of the accused racers tested positive for steroid use, and Babashoff won the moniker "Surly Shirley" for her efforts.

In the early 1990s, however, coaches and athletes from East Germany, which by then had unified with West Germany to form one country, admitted that there had been "heavy doping" among East German skaters in the 1970s. When Babashoff heard about the confession, she responded sharply: "What is the statute of limitations on cheating?"

After the 1976 games, Babashoff enrolled at UCLA. She swam competitively there but decided that she had lost a great deal of her passion for the sport. She left UCLA after her freshman year and worked first as a swimming instructor and then for the U.S. Postal Service.

Further Reading

Layden, Joe. *Women in Sports: The Complete Book on the World's Greatest Female Athletes.* Santa Monica, Calif.: General Publishing Group, 1997, pp. 22–23.

Sports Biographies. "Shirley Babashoff." Hickok Sports Online. Available online. URL: http://www.hickoksports. com/biograph/babashof.shtml. Downloaded on February 9, 2001.

BAUER, SYBIL
(1903–1927)   *Swimmer*

Sybil Bauer, the finest backstroker of her day, led a brief but glorious life. By the time she was 21, she was a world record holder and an Olympic champion. Tragically, she was stricken with cancer two years later, and she died at the age of 24.

Born in Chicago in 1903, Sybil Bauer was a natural all-around athlete from a young age. While a student at Northwestern University, she played field hockey and basketball, and she also swam competitively. Although Bauer swam the freestyle well, her specialty from the start was the backstroke. In 1921, the 20-year-old Bauer traveled to Bermuda, where she swam the 440-yard backstroke in 6:24:8—four seconds faster than the men's world record at the time. Unfortunately, the Bermuda tournament was not a sanctioned event, so Bauer did not get credit for the race.

Later that same year, however, Bauer captured the first of her national championships when she took top honors in the indoor 100-yard backstroke race. (She would go on to win six consecutive indoor championships in that event.) In 1922, Bauer won the outdoor national championship in the 100-yard race. She would go on to take outdoor national titles in the 150-meter backstroke race in 1923 and in the 220-yard event in 1924 and 1925.

In 1924, Bauer traveled to Paris, France, to compete in the Olympics. Because there was only one backstroke event for women, the 100-meter race, Bauer had the opportunity to win just one gold medal. This she did with great aplomb, defeating the second place finisher by a full 20 seconds.

At the age of 21, Bauer was an Olympic champion. At this point she met a New York City–based sportswriter named Ed Sullivan. The two became engaged to be married, but in 1926, Bauer was diagnosed with cancer. That same year, she swam to her last national championship, in the indoor 100-meter backstroke, but deteriorated quickly after that. On January 31, 1927, she died of the disease. She was 24 years old. Years later, Sullivan gained national prominence as the host of the Ed Sullivan Show, one of the most successful programs in television history.

Bauer, who swam competitively for six years, set a total of 23 world records, all in the backstroke. No one swimmer ever dominated one stroke as completely as Bauer did during her brief career.

Further Reading

Hickok Sports, "Sybil Bauer," Hickok Sports Online. Available online. URL: http:www.hickoksports.com/biograph/bauer.shtml. Downloaded on June 10, 2001.

Markel, Robert, Susan Wagoner, and Marcella Smith. *The Women's Sports Encyclopedia.* New York: Henry Holt, 1995, pp. 43–44.

⊞ BELL, JUDY
(1935–) *Golfer, President of the U.S. Golfing Association (USGA)*

Although Judy Bell never won a national golfing tournament, her contributions to the sport rival those of the most prolific women champions. In 1996, Bell was elected president of the United States Golf Association (USGA), and she became the first woman to head one of the most prestigious organizations in all of sports.

Born in Wichita, Kansas, in 1935, Judy Bell spent her childhood summers in the Colorado mountains. She first began playing golf at the Broadmoor Club, near Colorado Springs, and fittingly, she won her first tournament there, in 1957. Soon after, Bell enrolled at Wichita State University, where she played competitive golf and was twice the runner-up in the National Collegiate Athletic Association (NCAA) golfing championships. She graduated from Wichita State in 1961.

Bell's illustrious amateur career included two stints on the U.S. Curtis Cup team (the Curtis Cup is an amateur team championship that is played every year between American women and women from Great Britain and Ireland), in 1960 and 1962. Although she failed to win a major title, she played impressively at the U.S. Women's Open in 1964, when she shot a record 31 during a nine-hole stint. Three years later, she excelled at the same tournament by shooting a 67 during one of the rounds— a record that would stand for 30 years.

Although Bell could easily have turned professional, she chose instead to remain on the amateur circuit. She also began a new career as a store owner, opening her own clothing store at the Broadmoor Club. Bell gained good business experience during this stint, but she never left competitive golf completely, playing in several national tournaments each year.

In 1976, Bell was asked to serve on a committee at the USGA—"I stupidly said 'yes,'" she said with a laugh years later—and steadily worked her way up the executive ladder. In 1981, she became chairwoman of the Women's Committee, and in 1986, she became the first woman to serve on the USGA Executive Committee.

In the meantime, Bell served as captain of the Curtis Cup team in 1986 and 1988. She would later become the first person to serve as captain for both a men's and women's World Amateur Team, leading the women's squad in 1988 and the men's team in 2000.

In 1991, Bell became treasurer of the USGA Executive Committee, and then served a two-year stint as secretary, in 1992 and 1993. In 1994, Bell was appointed vice president of the committee. At the same time, she was given the chairmanship of the Competition Committee—a symbolic move on the part of the USGA, given the fact that traditionally, the chairman of the Competition Committee eventually assumed the role of USGA president.

As it happened, that is exactly what occurred in 1996. Reg Murphy, the USGA president, announced his resignation from the post and recommended that Bell be elected as his successor. "She's a born leader," Murphy said of Bell before her election. "She brings a perspective to the game as a player, which is very important."

Bell served a two-year term as president and led the USGA through some of its most prosperous years. Golf in the late 1990s and early 2000s reached a new height of popularity, as such charismatic players as Tiger Woods and Kari Webb began drawing greater numbers of spectators, sponsors, and media attention than ever before. After stepping down as president, Bell remained a member of the executive committee. She also became a partner in Bell Retail Group, a company that specializes in consulting and management.

Further Reading

Golf Online. "Judy Bell to Receive PGA First Lady of Golf Award," Golfonline.com. Available online. URL: http://www.golfonline.com/new/2001/awards/firstladyof-golf0306.html. Posted on March 6, 2001.

Purkey, Mike. "First Lady," *Golf Magazine,* vol. 38, no. 1 (January 1996): 58–59.

Smith, Lissa, editor. *Nike Is a Goddess: The History of Women in Sports.* New York: Atlantic Monthly Press, 1998, pp. 79–81.

⊞ BENOIT SAMUELSON, JOAN
(1957–) *Marathon Runner*

When Joan Benoit won the gold medal in the marathon at the 1984 Summer Olympics, it was truly a double victory. For the rest of the world, Benoit would always be known as the victor of the first women's marathon in Olympic history. And for Benoit personally, it was a triumph over the recurrent physical maladies that would often plague her brilliant career.

Joan Benoit was born on May 16, 1957, in Cape Elizabeth, Maine. The only daughter in an athletic family, Joan was an avid skier who also loved to play basketball and tennis with her three brothers. Although Joan sometimes ran on the neighborhood track, she did so only as a way to stay in shape in between sports seasons.

When Joan was 15, she broke her leg while skiing down a slalom course. She began running more regularly as part of her physical therapy, and she ended up falling in love with the track. Joan elected

to go to college close to home, enrolling at Bowdoin College, in Brunswick, Maine. During her first few months at Bowdoin she competed in both track and field and field hockey. Realizing that she had only a limited future in field hockey, Benoit decided to make a full-time commitment to running. By the end of her freshman year, she had become such an accomplished long-distance runner that she qualified for the 1976 Olympic trials.

Benoit did not make the Olympic team that year, but she came away from the trials with a new goal in mind—to win the Boston Marathon. She immediately began a grueling training regimen, logging long hours on the track as well as on the road. Three years and hundreds of miles later, she entered the 1979 Boston Marathon. Few had heard of Joan Benoit at the beginning of that April day in Boston, but by the end of the day she had made headline news. "I wanted to see how well I could do in a race I was prepared for," she told the press after her victory. Not only had Benoit won the race, but she had set a new U.S. record of 2 hours, 35 minutes, and 15 seconds in the process.

By the early 1980s, Benoit was considered one of the elite runners in the nation. But she was also beginning to fight what would become a consistent battle against physical ailments and injuries. In 1981, Benoit had an appendectomy and had to miss the Boston Marathon. The next year, she underwent surgery to repair an Achilles tendon and to remove bone spurs from both of her feet. The road back to competition was a long and difficult one for Benoit, who trained endlessly on a stationary bicycle until she was back at full strength.

Some doubted that Benoit could come back to full form a mere year after major surgery, but she proved the cynics wrong in dramatic fashion. Not only did Benoit win the 1983 Boston Marathon, but she set a world record in the process, finishing the historic course in 2:22:43.

In 1984, Benoit once again qualified for the Olympic trials, and this time she made the national team. But Benoit suffered another injury only three weeks before the games were to begin in Los Angeles. In August 1984—a mere 17 days before the

Olympics—she underwent arthroscopic surgery on her knee. This time she had only weeks for rehabilitation, and even she had doubts that she could return to top form in time to win her event.

The day of the marathon was hot and humid. Benoit jogged around the starting line, testing her knee. "I honestly didn't know if I could manage the race," she said later. Benoit knew that she would have to be at her best in order to challenge her top rival, Grete Waitz of Norway. Waitz, who had beaten Benoit in 10 of 11 races, had won every Boston Marathon she had ever entered—a total of seven.

When the starting gun sounded, Waitz and Benoit kept pace with each other through the first parts of the course. But at the three-mile mark, Benoit made her move, and ran ahead of Waitz and the rest of the pack. At the 15-kilometer mark, Benoit was a full minute ahead of Waitz; at the 25-kilometer mark, she was nearly two minutes ahead. By the end of the race, Benoit was racing against only herself. The last part of the race took place inside the Olympic stadium, where the finish line—and more than 100,000 spectators—awaited the victor. "When I saw the stadium and saw all the colors and everything, "she said later, "I said 'listen, just look straight ahead, because if you don't you're probably going to faint.'" Benoit kept her eyes on the prize and won the race.

Two weeks after the Olympics, Benoit married Scott Samuelson. A year after that, Benoit Samuelson, took top honors at the Chicago Marathon, setting another U.S. record in the process, and she won several other prestigious long-distance races. These accomplishments helped Benoit Samuelson win the Sullivan Award as the outstanding amateur athlete in the United States.

Benoit Samuelson continued to suffer injuries, not only to her legs and feet but to her back as well. In the late 1980s Benoit Samuelson took time off the track to have two children, Anders and Abigail. She attempted a comeback in the mid-1990s, but she failed to make the Olympics in 1996 when she finished 13th in the marathon race at the trials. The Samuelsons remain in Benoit Samuelson's hometown in Maine, where the 1984

Olympic champion continues to run, train, and on occasion, to compete.

Further Reading

Hickok Sports.com, Biography, "Joan Benoit Samuelson." Available online. URL: http://www.hickoksports.com/ biograph/benoitjo.shtml. Downloaded on March 30, 2001.

Layden, Joe. *Women in Sports: The Complete Book on the World's Greatest Female Athletes.* Santa Monica, Calif.: General Publishing Group, 1997, p. 213.

Woolum, Janet. *Outstanding Women Athletes: Who They Are and How They Influenced Sports in America.* Phoenix: Oryx Press, 1998.

BERENSON, SENDA (Senda Valvrojenski)
(1868–1954)   *Founder of Women's Basketball*

In the fall of 1892, Senda Berenson, a physical education teacher, introduced the game of women's basketball to her students at Smith College. Later that year Berenson's students played one another in the first game of collegiate women's basketball in history.

Senda Berenson was born Senda Valvrojenski on March 19, 1868, in Biturmansk, Lithuania. In 1875, her parents, Albert and Julia Valvrojenski, immigrated to Boston, where the family name was changed. Settled in Massachusetts with his wife and three children, Albert Berenson earned a meager living as a peddler of pots and pans. Although they were poor, the Berensons always stressed education for their children. Senda's brother Bernard, in fact, would grow up to become one of the leading art historians of his time.

A frail and sickly child, Senda attended the Boston Latin School for several years, but was never able to complete a full term there. She excelled at both music and art, but because of her health—she had a back condition that prevented her from sitting up for long periods of time—she was not able to practice either one regularly. In 1890 a doctor persuaded her to attend the Boston Normal School of Gymnastics. Although Senda initially disliked the program, after a few months, she changed her attitude completely. The regular, regimented exercises had cured her back ailment, and she became convinced that physical activity could help other women as well.

Berenson left the Boston Normal School in 1892 and took a job as a teacher of physical education at Smith College in Northampton, Massachusetts. For the next 20 years, Berenson served as one of the nation's major advocates for women's sports; during her tenure at Smith she introduced gymnastics, fencing, folk dancing, and field hockey to the college. But it was Berenson's innovation on the basketball front that remains her greatest contribution to women's sports. After reading about the invention of the game by Dr. James Naismith, Berenson decided that with some alterations, basketball could be suitable for women as well as men.

The original game of women's basketball was dramatically different from today's sport. Berenson's version had nine players crammed onto the court, which was divided into thirds. Each player was designated to a specific area and was not allowed to cross the lines from one third to another. Moreover, Berenson's rules prevented players from stealing the ball, dribbling the ball more than three times, or holding it more than three seconds. Little wonder that the score of the first collegiate basketball game, which took place between the teams representing the freshman and sophomore classes at Smith, was a paltry 4 to 3 (in favor of the freshmen). But although Berenson might have believed that women should not exert the same energy that men did while playing sports, she lived during a time when many people believed that women should not exert themselves *at all*. For that reason, Berenson's game was groundbreaking.

In 1911, Berenson married Herbert Vaughn Abbot, an English professor at Smith. Later that year she resigned from the college to take a job as director of physical education at the Mary Burnham School, which was also in Northampton. When Herbert Abbot died in 1929, she moved to Santa Barbara, California, where she lived with her sister until her death in 1954. An inaugural member of the Women's Basketball Hall of Fame, she

was also among the first women to be inducted into the Naismith Memorial Hall of Fame, when she was posthumously honored in 1974.

Further Reading

"Berenson Abbott Biography." Basketball Hall of Fame. Available online. URL: www.hoophall.com/hallof famers/BerensonAbbottt.htm. Downloaded on March 27, 2002.

Lannin, Joanne. *A History of Basketball for Girls and Women: From Bloomers to Big Leagues.* Minneapolis, Minn.: Lerner Sports, 2000.

Woolum, Janet. *Outstanding Women Athletes: Who They Are and How They Influenced Sports in America,* Phoenix, Ariz.: Oryx Press, 1992.

BERG, PATTY (Patricia Berg)
(1918–)   *Golfer*

It is memorable enough that golfer Patty Berg was the leading money winner among women in her sport. Add to that the fact that she was one of the founding members of the Ladies' Professional Golf Association (LPGA) and its first president, and she becomes even more impressive. But it is Berg's sheer longevity in golf—she has been a presence on the green for an astonishing seven decades—that completes her résumé as one of the greatest sports figures in history.

Patty Berg's story began on February 13, 1918, when she was born in Minneapolis, Minnesota. A natural athlete, Patty grew up playing virtually every competitive sport imaginable. By the time she was a teenager, she had become a top-notch speed skater and a standout in track and field. Considering Berg's lifelong dedication to golf, it is interesting to note that her first passion was not for the links, but for the gridiron. At the age of 15 she was the starting quarterback for the 50th Street Tigers, an otherwise all-boy team, in her neighborhood.

But it was golf that turned Patty's head for good. When she was 14, her father had bought her a secondhand set of clubs and a membership at the local golf course. One year later, she won the Minneapolis city championship, and the year after that she took top honors at the state amateur tournament. Over the next seven years, Berg would win 29 titles, including the nation's most prestigious championship, the U.S. Amateur. By the time she was 22, in 1940, Berg was the most famous woman golfer in the United States. That year, she turned professional.

In 1941, Berg was injured in a serious automobile accident. After missing 18 months of golf, she began competing again in 1943 and won the Western Open that year. In 1944, Berg joined the U.S. Marines and served as a lieutenant during World War II. She returned to the links after the war ended and took top honors at the 1946 U.S. Women's Golf Open.

At this point, Berg had won virtually every professional women's tournament in the sport. Frustrated that there was no tour for professional golfers, she decided to take matters into her own hands. In late 1946, she became one of the founders of the Women's Professional Golf Association, which would become the LPGA in 1948. The following year, Berg became the association's first president. At age 30, Berg was not only the leader of the major professional women's association in the sport of golf, but she was the dominating player as well. In the 1950s she won 11 major titles and was the LPGA's leading money winner in 1954, 1955, and 1957. In 1959, Berg marked another first: playing at the U.S. Women's Open, she became the first woman to score a hole in one at a United States Golf Association (USGA) competition. Berg won several major sporting awards during her playing years, including the Associated Press Athlete of the Year in 1938, 1943, and 1955. In 1978, the LPGA named an annual prize after her: the Patty Berg Award, presented to a person who had made outstanding contributions to women's golf.

In addition to her stellar play on the links, Berg is a first-rate ambassador for her sport. She has given thousands of clinics and exhibitions, and she has worked for various charitable organizations. In 1963 she was given the Bob Jones Award for her humanitarian achievements, and in 1976, she received the Humanitarian Award from the Cerebral Palsy Foundation.

Although Patty Berg's first love was football, she would go on to become one of history's most prolific golfers, competing on the links for more than seven decades.
(Library of Congress)

Berg stopped competing in LPGA tournaments in the mid-1960s, but that did not mean she has stopped playing golf. In addition to writing three successful books on golf and continuing her humanitarian activities, she has remained an active presence on the links. Playing in an exhibition tournament in 1993, the 71-year-old Berg showed she still had her touch: She hit a hole in one.

Further Reading

Hickok Sports Biographies. "Patty Berg," Hickok Sports Biographies Online. Available online. URL: http://www.hickoksports.com/biograph/bergpatt.shtml. Posted on June 21, 2000.

Layden, Joe. *Women in Sports: The Complete Book on the World's Greatest Female Athletes.* Santa Monica, Calif.: General Publishing Group, 1997, p. 29.

⊞ **BLAIR, BONNIE (Bonnie Kathleen Blair)**
(1964–) *Speed Skater*

The woman with the most individual gold medals in U.S. Olympic history is not a runner, a figure skater, or a swimmer. The honor goes instead to Bonnie Kathleen Blair, a speed skater who competed in three Olympic competitions and took home five top prizes, along with a host of world records.

It might be said that Bonnie Blair, the sixth child of Eleanor and Charlie Blair, was born with speed skating in her blood. On March 18, 1964, Eleanor gave birth to Bonnie in Cornwall, New York. That day, Charlie, a civil engineer who officiated at speed skating matches as a hobby, was timing a match in Yonkers, New York. In the middle of the race, an announcement came over the public-address system in the arena: "Looks like Charlie's family has just added another skater."

Not just another skater, as it turned out, although for the Blair family, Bonnie was, for her entire childhood, just one of the bunch. Five of the six Blair children were ardent speed skaters. Bonnie first strapped on a pair of skates at the age of four, and she began racing with her brothers and sisters at a local ice-skating rink in Champaign, Illinois, where the Blair family had moved in 1966.

Bonnie quickly became a fast skater, but her specialty as a teenager was in short-track skating—a sport not recognized as an Olympic event at the time. Most North American speed skaters have trained and raced on short tracks, which are circuits of 111 meters. In short-track skating, the skaters race against each other, and in simple terms, the first one to cross the finish line wins. The long-track event, in contrast, is held on a 400-meter oval. Skaters line up on different parts of the oval, two at a time, and rather than racing against one another, they race against the clock. Short-track racers master different strategies—they have to turn often and have a rival to beat head to head—from long-track racers, who mainly strive for endurance and balance as well as speed.

It was in short-track racing that Bonnie Blair first made her mark; by the time she was 16, she was one of the top short-track skaters in the United States. But Blair knew that in order to compete in the Olympics she would have to master the long-track method. With that in mind, she decided to go to Europe in 1980 to begin training on long tracks. (In 1980 there were only two long-track speed skating facilities in all of the United States.) The Blairs did not have the money to send their youngest child abroad, but Bonnie was able to find funding from the Champaign Police Department in Champaign, which held a variety of bake sales and other fund-raisers in order to raise money for the cause.

Once in Europe, Blair began training in earnest for long-track skating. She was most comfortable with the 500-meter sprint event, and she also became a proficient skater in the 1,000-meter race. But in the early 1980s the sport of speed skating—in the women's field—was completely dominated by East Germany. Blair prepared for the 1984 Olympic games in Sarajevo knowing that her top competitors had grown up training on long-track rinks. In contrast, Blair had been training for long-track events for only four years. Hardly anyone in Europe had heard of her, and she herself was in awe of the top East German skaters, Christa Rothenburger and Karen Kania.

Blair made her Olympic debut in the 500-meter race. She finished a respectable eighth, well behind the gold-and-silver-winning Rothenburger and Kania. No one could know it at the time, but that would be the last 500-meter Olympic race that Blair would ever lose. After the 1984 games, Blair returned to full-time training, in both the short-track and the long-track events. In 1985 she took top honors at the U.S. indoor championships, and in 1986, she won the short-track title at the world speed skating championships in Chamonix, France.

In 1987, Blair made her first serious mark in the long-track speed skating events when she set a world record in the 500-meter race. Two months later she broke her own world record, and speed skaters around the world began to take note of the small (five feet, three inches tall) but determined athlete from Illinois.

The following year, Blair traveled to Calgary, Alberta, Canada, to compete in both the 500-meter and 1,000-meter events. At 23, Blair had become much stronger in both races, and she was much more confident than she was in 1984, although she faced the same competitors. "I had been looking up to Christa Rothenburger and Karen Kania for a long time," Blair remembered later, "and now, all of a sudden, I was skating on their level. Now that I was where they were, I had to stop being in awe of them."

Even so, Rothenburger was a formidable presence on the ice. Two months before the Calgary games, she had broken Blair's record in the 500-meter event. And in Calgary, it was Rothenburger who made a statement first. Skating in the second pairing, Rothenburger broke her own world record, finishing the 500-meter race in 39.12 seconds.

Blair remained calm in the face of Rothenburger's achievement. She figured that if she started strong, she would have a good chance of besting the East German's time. At the sound of the starting gun, Blair sprinted the first 100 meters. After crossing the finish line, she then heard her time over the loudspeaker. It was $^2/_{100}$ of a second quicker than Rothenburger's. Although there were several competitors remaining, Blair knew she had won the gold. Four days later, Blair took a bronze in the 1,000-meter race, finishing behind Rothenburger and Kania.

When the Calgary games ended, Blair returned to Champaign and was the toast of the nation. The story of local police funding her training in Europe had brought national attention to her quest for gold. In addition, her mother had gathered a group of more than 40 friends and family to watch Bonnie compete; christened "the Blair Bunch," they traveled with Bonnie to each Olympic competition. This fan club—and, of course, her double-medal performance—earned her admiration across the country.

In 1989, Charlie Blair died after a long bout with cancer. Grieving for her father, who was her original skating mentor, Bonnie decided to take a break from the ice. She hung up her skates and

began cycling, with the hope of competing in the sport someday. Blair was not the first speed skater to be enticed by cycling; in the 1970s, SHEILA YOUNG had won world championships in both speed skating and cycling. But Blair was not as successful in the saddle as she was on the ice, and she soon returned to her original sport.

Blair began training in earnest for the next Olympics, held in Albertville, France, in 1992. Now 28, Blair had hit her prime as a skater. She had become extremely consistent, and her technique was flawless. Blair crouched down extremely low and was able to keep her position during turns and at high speeds. As important, she was able to

Bonnie Blair stands on the medal podium at the 1994 Olympic Games. Blair's total of five Olympic gold medals makes her the most celebrated Olympic woman athlete in history.
(Chris Cole/Getty Images)

keep her strides in an even rhythm throughout an entire race. Those skills—along with the hoarse cheers of the Blair Bunch—accompanied Blair to Albertville, and led her to two more gold medals; she defended her championship in the 500-meter race and won the 1,000-meter event as well.

After the Albertville games, many expected Blair to retire, but she decided that she had one more Olympic competition left in her, and she continued to train. Olympic officials had made the decision to move the Winter Olympics to non-leap even years after 1992 (up to that point both the summer and winter games were held during leap years), meaning that the next Olympics would take place in 1994.

The year 1994 may be remembered by many sports fans as the worst year in the history of American sports. In figure skating, Tonya Harding helped plan an attack on her rival NANCY KERRIGAN to keep her from winning the national championship. In basketball, Michael Jordan unexpectedly retired (he would return the following year) to try his hand at baseball. And Major League Baseball went on strike, causing the first cancellation of the World Series in history.

But at the Olympics in Lillehammer, Norway, the Bonnie Blair story continued to impress Americans. Once again, Blair sped to victory in the 500-meter race. She competed in the 1,500-meter event for the first time and scored a bronze medal. And in front of a sold-out arena that included (once again) the smiling, cheering Blair Bunch, she took her fifth and final gold of her stellar Olympic career, winning the 1,000-meter race.

Blair was awarded the *Sports Illustrated* "Sportsperson of the Year" award in 1994 (she shared the prize with Norwegian speed skater Johann Olav Koss). "She stands as a . . . rebuke to every slob who said he would play for free but wouldn't suit up for less than $68 million . . ." the magazine said of Blair ". . . just win, baby, is all she does." In April 1995 Blair retired permanently from speed skating. The next year she married a fellow Olympian, speed skater Dave Cruikshank and moved to Milwaukee. The couple have two children. After leaving sports, Blair became a motivational speaker and started her own foundation, where she continues to work.

Further Reading

Greenspan, Bud. *Frozen in Time: The Greatest Moments at the Winter Olympics.* Santa Monica, Calif.: General Publishing Group, 1997.

Hickok Sports Biographies. "Bonnie Blair." Hickok Sports Biographies Online. Available online. URL: http://www.hickoksports.com/biograph/blairbon.shtml. Downloaded on January 18, 2001.

Wolf, Steve. "Bonnie Blair: Sportsperson of the Year," *Sports Illustrated* (December 14, 1994), p. 70.

BLAZEJOWSKI, CAROL
(1956–)   *Basketball Player*

The best pure shooter in the history of women's basketball was a determined New Jerseyite named Carol Blazejowski. Playing in the early days of Title IX (the legislation passed in 1972 that compelled universities to provide the same opportunities for male and female students), when women's sports garnered little fan response and even less media attention, Blazejowski posted the highest scoring average of any collegiate basketball player when she scored 38.2 points per game during her senior season.

Carol Blazejowski was born on September 29, 1956, in Cranston, New Jersey. A basketball enthusiast from the start, young Carol consistently showed up at the local playground, eager for a chance to play. The neighborhood boys were anything but eager to include Carol in their games—she was the last one chosen for a team and often was not selected at all. But Carol kept coming to the playgrounds, and she would remain there after everyone went home, working on her shots. Self-coached and supremely motivated, Carol learned her technique from watching basketball games on television and then endlessly practiced what she learned. Finally, the neighborhood kids began to notice her talent, and she became a regular fixture at the playground pickup games.

Although Carol longed to play high school basketball, there were no girls' sports teams at Cranston High School during her first three years there. Fortunately, during her senior year the school did form a girls' basketball squad, and Carol quickly became the star player. Scoring an average of 25 points per game, she led her team to an undefeated season and to the finals of the state championships.

After graduating from Cranston, Blazejowski chose to attend a college close to home, and entered Montclair State University in the fall of 1974. In her four years at Montclair State, Blazejowski simply rewrote the record books. Named an All-American three times, she set single-season records during her senior year for total points (1,235), and points-per-game average (38.6). Her scoring average during her college career of 31.7 points per game remains the highest score for any collegiate player; her career point total of 3,119 is the highest tally ever for a woman player and second in collegiate history only to Pete Maravich. In 1978 Blazejowski became the first recipient of the Wade Trophy, which is now given every year to the finest collegiate woman basketball player in the nation.

With her college days behind her, Blazejowski found few opportunities for her basketball talents. She played for the U.S. national team in 1979, helped the United States win a silver medal in the Pan American Games, and then easily qualified for the 1980 Olympic team. When her hopes for Olympic gold were shattered by the U.S. boycott of the 1980 Moscow games, Blazejowski signed a contract later that year to play for the New Jersey Gems in the newly formed Women's Basketball League (WBL). Blazejowski commanded the highest salary of all WBL players, but the league was short-lived, folding after only one season.

Blazejowski left professional basketball after the demise of the WBL, and she took a job as a promotional representative for a major athletic shoe company. In 1990, she was hired by the National Basketball Association (NBA) to work in its Consumer Products Group, where she stayed until 1997, when she found out that the NBA was involved in the formation of a brand-new basketball league for women. Blazejowski asked her employers for a position in the Women's National Basketball Association (WNBA), and soon afterward she took the job of general manager of the New York Liberty, helping to make it one of the most successful franchises in the league.

Further Reading

Hickok Sports Biographies, "Carol Blazejowski," Hickok Sports Biographies Online. Available online. URL: http://www.hickoksports.com/biograph/blazejow.stml. Downloaded on April 3, 2001.

Kallom, Clay. "A Blaze of Glory," Fullcourt Press. Available online. URL: http://www.fullcourt.com/people/blaze96.html. Posted on June 25, 1996.

Layden, Joe. *Women in Sports: The Complete Book on the World's Greatest Female Athletes.* Santa Monica, Calif.: General Publishing Group, 1997, pp. 35–36.

New York Liberty online. "Blazing Ahead," WNBA.com. Available online. URL: http://www.wnba.com/liberty/mail_blazejowski_resp.html. Downloaded on April 3, 2001.

▦ BLEIBTREY, ETHELDA
(1902–1978) *Swimmer*

The first woman to win an Olympic gold medal in swimming was an 18-year-old American named Ethelda Bleibtrey. More accurately, Bleibtrey won three gold medals at the games in Antwerp, Belgium, in 1920, in the 100-meter and 300-meter freestyle individual races and in the 100-meter freestyle relay.

Ethelda Bleibtrey was born on February 27, 1902, in Waterford, New York. When she was 16, Ethelda, who had always been an active and athletic child, contracted polio. Her case was a mild one, yet it left her weakened and sickly. The following year, her doctor suggested that she try swimming for its therapeutic and soothing effects. Ethelda took to the water immediately; not only did she regain her strength, but she quickly became a world-class swimmer. Initially hesitant to put her face in the water, Ethelda concentrated most of her time and energy on the backstroke. She won several regional championships and enthusiastically trained to earn a place on the U.S. Olympic team. Bleibtrey was disappointed to learn that the backstroke race would not become a women's event until 1924, but rather than losing heart, she simply changed her focus and began training for the freestyle races.

In the summer of 1919, Bleibtrey, always a bit of a free spirit, had decided to swim at New York City's Manhattan Beach without her stockings on. It may seem silly by today's standards, but in the early years of the 20th century, rules regarding outfits for swimmers—particularly females—were quite strict. The New York law forbade a woman swimmer from any "baring of the lower female extremities for public bathing." Aware of the rule but tired of swimming in soaked leggings, Bleibtrey rolled her stockings off and went for her swim. When she returned to shore, she was met by authorities with a warrant for her arrest. Bleibtrey briefly went to jail for her crime, but the incident aroused a tremendous amount of public sympathy. Several hours after her arrest, not only was Bleibtrey released from prison, but the ordinance demanding stockings was rewritten.

Unfazed by her brush with the law, Bleibtrey returned to her training, and earned a place on the U.S. Olympic team. When they arrived in Antwerp, Bleibtrey and her cohorts surveyed the location for the swimming races with some dismay. Less than two years after World War I, Belgium, along with the rest of Europe, was in a state of disrepair. There were no decent pools, either indoor or outdoor, for the swimmers, so the races were delegated to a tidal estuary.

Although Bleibtrey found the conditions difficult—she later said that swimming in the estuary was like swimming in mud—she plowed through her qualifying heat for her first race, the 100-meter freestyle, in a world-record time of 1:14:4. One day later, she did even better, winning the final with a mark of 1:13:6 to become the first woman Olympic swimming champion of the modern age. Two days later, she took top honors in the 300-meter freestyle race and then capped her victorious week by swimming the anchor, or final, leg for the U.S. team's winning effort in the 100-meter freestyle race.

Bleibtrey returned to the United States and proceeded to win every event in which she competed between 1920 and 1922. During that time span, her titles included two U.S. outdoor championships in the 100-yard freestyle, the 440-yard freestyle, and the 880-yard freestyle, and two indoor championships in the 100-yard freestyle. She also won national titles in the 1-mile freestyle outdoor race in 1920, the 100-yard backstroke in 1920, and the 3-mile outdoor race in 1921.

In 1928 Bleibtrey once again challenged authority when she decided to take a swim in the Central Park Reservoir—a gesture she made as part of a campaign for better public swimming facilities for New York City residents. Bailed out by Mayor Jimmy Walker, Bleibtrey was once again a successful revolutionary when the city council voted to open a public swimming pool the following year. Bleibtrey lived in New York City until her death, at the age of 76, in 1978.

Further Reading

Hickok Sports Biography, "Ethelda Bleibtrey," Hickok Sports Biographies Online. Available online. URL: http://www.hickoksports.com/biograph/curtisan.shtml. Downloaded June 10, 2001.

USA Today.com Sports: "1920: First Swimming Gold for a US Woman." Available online. URL: http://www.usatoday.com/sports/century/082599.htm.

Woolum, Janet. *Outstanding Women Athletes: Who They Are and How They Influenced Sports in America.* Phoenix, Ariz.: Oryx Press, 1992.

BORDERS, ILA
(1975–) *Baseball Player*

Ila Borders is the contemporary U.S. version of JACKIE MITCHELL. Although Borders has never had the opportunity to strike out Major League Baseball stars, as Mitchell did in the 1930s, she made just as impressive a statement for women in baseball by becoming both the first woman to pitch on a men's collegiate team and the first woman to pitch in a men's minor league team in the modern era.

Born in La Mirada, California, on February 18, 1975, Ila Borders learned the game of baseball from her father. Phil Borders clearly recognized his young daughter's talent; by the time she was 10, he had taught her how to pitch overhand. By this time, Ila had already logged three years in the "Little Miss" Softball League in La Mirada. Because she was the only player on the team who could make the long throw from third to first on a ground ball, she played third base during those early years.

Ila's life took a twist at the age of 10, when her parents took her to see a Los Angeles Dodgers game. After watching the Los Angeles outfielder Dusty Baker belt a home run, she turned to her parents and announced that she never wanted to play softball again. Baseball had entered her blood.

In 1986, 11-year-old Ila played her first full season of Little League baseball. Although her team-mates and opponents initially made fun of her (she was hit on the head during her first at-bat, and singled her next time up) they soon learned to respect, and then admire, her talent. Ila was chosen for the All-Star team in each of the three years she played in the league.

At the age of 15, Ila attended Whittier Christian High School, a private school her father had chosen for her because officials there had promised to give Ila a chance to play for the all-boys' baseball team. Once again, Ila had to cope with ridicule, and once again, she turned her tormentors into fans. She made the freshman team with ease, and by midseason was pulled up to junior varsity. By the end of the year, she was starting for the varsity.

By this time, Ila had dedicated her skills to pitching, and she boasted not only a high-paced fastball but an effective curveball, split-finger, and

The first woman ever to pitch in a men's collegiate game, Ila Borders fell in love with baseball at the age of 10, when she went to her first Dodgers game.
(Elsa Hasch/Getty Images)

screwball as well. She used these skills to lead Whittier Christian to an undefeated season in her senior year. With a four-year win-loss record of 16-7 and a 2.37 earned run average, Borders was named most valuable player of the team. At this time, she was also busy making a decision: although her life's goal was to play Major League Baseball (and most players on that level opt not to go to college but instead play minor league ball), she also cared about her own education. Borders ended up enrolling at Southern California College, on a scholarship—to play baseball in the men's league.

As always, Borders's presence caused a media frenzy. But her college coach, Charlie Phillips, shook off reports that he had signed his newest recruit merely as a public relations stunt. "People think I took her for the publicity," he told the media. "I don't need the publicity. I took her because she can pitch and because she can help this team." By this time Borders was accustomed to the additional pressure and attention she regularly received, so it was with grace that she became the first woman to pitch on a men's college team. During her first outing she pitched a complete game victory, and during the next, gave up only one unearned run.

After Southern California College switched coaches, Borders transferred to Whittier College for her senior year. During her final season, a scout for the St. Paul Saints, a minor-league franchise, saw her pitch. Impressed with Borders's repertoire and talent, he decided to sign the 21-year-old to a contract. Several weeks later, Borders made her minor-league debut—another first for women athletes. Although her first game as a Saint was a difficult one for Borders—she was replaced on the mound after allowing five runs in two innings—she did pitch effectively in a game several nights later.

After two years with three minor-league clubs—she was traded first to the Duluth Saints and then to the Zion (California) Pioneerzz, Borders decided to retire from competitive baseball in July 2000. Borders left the diamond for the broadcast booth, signing with ESPN to work as a commentator at collegiate baseball games. Although Borders made a significant mark as a pioneer of women's sports, she does not consider herself a major advocate for the feminist cause. "I'm not trying to prove anything about women," she said before her first collegiate game. "This has nothing to do with women's rights. I love the game, nothing else."

Further Reading

Borders, Phil. "Who Is Ila Borders?" Mirada Information Services. Available online. URL: http://www.ilaborders.com/. Downloaded on May 8, 2001.

"Ila Borders to Make History Again with 1st Start in Northern League," Associated Press, 1998. Available online. URL: http://www.sportserver.com/newsroom/ap/bbo/1998/min/min/feat/archive/070898/min6560.html. Downloaded on May 8, 2001.

Layden, Joe. *Women in Sports: The Complete Book on the World's Greatest Female Athletes.* Santa Monica, Calif.: General Publishing Group, 1997, p. 36.

Warren, Justine, "High and Tight: Ila Borders Retires," e-sports.com. Available online. URL: http://www.e-sports.com/article.asp?Article_Id=4588&Category=Baseball. Posted on July 5, 2000.

▦ BRISCO-HOOKS, VALERIE
(1960–   )   *Sprinter*

Valerie Brisco-Hooks won three gold medals at the 1984 Olympic Games in Los Angeles and was the first athlete, male or female, to win gold medals in both the 200- and 400-meter events at the same Olympiad. She was also the first American to win three gold medals in one Olympic competition since WILMA RUDOLPH did it in 1960.

Born in Greenwood, Michigan, on July 6, 1960, Valerie was the sixth of 10 children in the Brisco family. Her parents, Augustus and Guitherea, moved the Briscos to Los Angeles when Valerie was five. When Valerie was 14, her brother Robert, who was four years older than Valerie, was killed when he was hit by a stray bullet while running on a high school track near Watts, an area of Los Angeles. The loss of her brother, who was her athletic role model, had a lasting effect on Valerie, who had practiced on that same track many times herself.

In high school, Valerie Brisco was a natural athlete who loved competing but was not as wild about training. "In high school, workouts weren't the thing for me," she said later. "I'd just jog and go home—that was it." Even so, Brisco turned in some outstanding performances in the 400-meter event while still in high school. During her senior year, she ran the event in 52.08 seconds, which remained her best time until the 1984 Olympic trials.

After graduating from high school in 1979, Brisco joined the World Class Track Team and met Bob Kersee, who would become her coach. Kersee encouraged Brisco to take training more seriously, reminding her that "lazy athletes do not win gold medals." Perhaps because of Kersee's words—and perhaps because as a member of the World Class Track Team she was training alongside such elite athletes as JACKIE JOYNER-KERSEE and FLORENCE GRIFFITH JOYNER, Brisco changed her work ethic completely. Working with Kersee, Brisco logged long days of practice, training seven hours a day, then lifting weights for two or three more hours.

Despite the amount of time she spent on the track and in the gym, Brisco managed to have a personal life. In 1982 she married Alvin Hooks, a wide receiver for the Philadelphia Eagles. One year later the couple had a son, Alvin Hooks Jr. Brisco-Hooks enjoyed motherhood immensely. In fact, shortly after Alvin Jr. was born, she seriously considered retiring from track completely. She had gained 50 pounds during her pregnancy, and she dreaded the amount of work it would take to shed the weight. But Kersee persuaded her to continue training. Brisco-Hooks lost the weight and returned to her grueling schedule.

Brisco-Hooks's goal was to compete in the 200- and 400-meter events at the Los Angeles Olympic games in 1984. Ironically, Brisco-Hooks, who was not an especially disciplined athlete, had chosen as her specialty the 400-meter race, known as the most grueling of the sprint events. The 400-meter race tests the endurance and strength of its runners. The first 200 meters must be run quickly, but the last half of the race is arduous and often painful. Athletes struggle against stiffening joints

Valerie Brisco-Hooks exults after winning the 200-meter race at the 1984 Olympic Games. After having a baby in 1983, Brisco-Hooks almost retired from sprinting. Instead, she became the first woman to win gold medals in the 200-meter and 400-meter events at one Olympiad.
(Tony Duffy/Getty Images)

and severe fatigue as they race for the finish line, and they often collapse once they have crossed it. Knowing this about her event, Brisco-Hooks never complained about her torturous, seemingly endless days of training with Bob Kersee.

And her work paid off in the summer of 1984. Not only did Brisco-Hooks gallop to victory in both the 200-meter and 400-meter events, but she did so in style, setting U.S. and Olympic records in the process. Brisco-Hooks added a third gold medal when she ran the starting leg of the U.S. team's victorious 4 × 400 relay.

But all of her Olympic victories aside, perhaps Brisco-Hooks's finest moment came at the Pan-American games in 1987. She had just won a gold medal in the 4 × 400 relay, when a deaf and legally blind teenager approached and asked her if she would pose for a photograph with him. Brisco-Hooks not only obliged the boy's request, but she gave him her gold medal as a memento. "It's not that the medal didn't mean anything to me," she said later, "but it meant more to him."

Brisco-Hooks, who retired from competition in 1988, has continued to serve as a role model to young children, appearing in several public-service films stressing good health and education.

Further Reading

Davis, Michael D. *Black American Women in Olympic Track and Field: A Complete Illustrated Reference.* Jefferson, N.C.: McFarland, 1992.

Layden, Joe. *Women in Sports: The Complete Book on the World's Greatest Female Athletes.* Santa Monica, Calif.: General Publishing Group, 1997, pp. 39–40.

⊞ BROUGH, LOUISE (Althea Louise Brough, Louise Clapp)
(1923–) *Tennis Player*

Louise Brough was one of the most successful American tennis players of the 1940s. She won six major singles titles over a seven-year span, and her total of 21 Grand Slam doubles crowns make her one of the most successful tennis champions in history.

Althea Louise Brough was born in Oklahoma City, Oklahoma, on March 11, 1923. When she was four her parents separated, and her mother, Althea, moved with Louise and her brother J. P. to Beverly Hills, California. Althea Brough was a strong-willed woman with definite ideas for her children. Although she was not interested in sports herself, she thought it was important that both her daughter—whom she had named after herself and her sister Louise—and her son learn to participate and compete. Louise did not oppose her mother's desire; she was an enthusiastic athlete from an early age. She also did not object when her mother suggested she learn the game of tennis. She did take issue, however, when her Aunt Louise declared that her niece wear a white school dress on the court. "I was hating every minute of it," Brough wrote later, "because I was in the white dress. I didn't play for a long time."

But when she was 13 Brough was given a tennis racket, and she began playing again, taking lessons from the renowned coach Dick Skeen. Within several months, Brough was one of his best players. During Brough's training she was driven not only by Skeen, but by her mother, who became a dedicated, and often emotional, observer. Althea was thrilled when Louise, who began competing at the age of 15, would win a match, but she would often despair deeply when her daughter lost. Her mother's reactions put a great deal of additional pressure on Louise. Although there were times when Althea's emotions angered her, on the whole Louise was able to cope with her mother's intensity; she had a great deal of her own as well. With dedication and disciplined playing, she eventually developed powerful ground strokes, as well as a deceiving, twisting serve.

As a teenager Brough had a great deal of determination and, clearly, a great deal of energy. When she was 16, Louise pulled off the impressive feat of competing in two tournaments—in two cities 90 miles apart—simultaneously. Because of an extensive rain delay, the 1939 national junior championship in Philadelphia began a week later than usual, which meant that it coincided exactly with the U.S. women's national championships at the West Side Tennis Club in Forest Hills (Queens) New York. Chauffeured by her game Aunt Louise, Braugh commuted back and forth. She never missed a match; when a tire on her aunt's car blew out en route to Philadelphia, Brough hopped out of the automobile, hitched a ride with a truck driver, and an hour later was courtside, warming up for her match.

Brough won her first major title when she took top honors at the U.S. championships in 1947. It would be her only U.S. championship title, although she would reach the finals of the tournament four more times. Brough had much better luck on Centre Court at Wimbledon, in England, where she won four singles titles, including three consecutive ones in 1948, 1949, and 1950. Asked why she had an easier time at Wimbledon than at Forest Hills, Brough replied that the British championship site, with its high, enclosed, and darkened walls, was much less distracting than the more exposed courts at the West Side Tennis Club.

If Brough played her best tennis at Wimbledon, she also was virtually always at the top of her game whenever she opposed Margaret Osborne. The two Americans, best friends off the court, played in several terrific matches. In 1948, Osborne overcame a match point against Brough in the U.S. tournament final, and she eventually prevailed by a final score of 4-6, 6-4, 15-13. Brough returned the favor the following summer, defeating Osborne in another three-set marathon, 10-8, 1-6, 10-8.

One reason the two women might have played such close matches is that they were extremely familiar with each other's game. Apart from being singles rivals, they were an extremely successful doubles team. The partnership of Brough and Osborne won nine consecutive U.S. Open doubles titles from 1942 to 1950, and altogether they took home 21 Grand Slam doubles titles.

Perhaps Brough's most memorable victory came in the singles final of the Wimbledon championships in 1955, which represented a comeback of sorts. She had suffered some problems with her technique several years before, when she began having trouble with her toss. In 1950, she was playing in the gusty winds of Australia, and making every effort to compensate for her poor toss by hitting her serve in an awkward position. By the time she returned to the United States, she had developed a bad case of tennis elbow, which plagued her on and off for many years.

Brough advanced through the early rounds of the 1955 Wimbledon tournament, although she

was still struggling mightily with her serve. She found herself at center court, up against a young and talented U.S. player named Beverly Baker Fritz.

An ambidextrous player who would switch the racket from her right to left hand to make every shot a forehand, Fritz had advanced to the finals by dismissing former champion Doris Hart in straight sets. Brough decided she would play defensively against Fritz, forcing her opponent to establish both the rhythm and the pace of the points. The match was long and difficult, and Brough trailed Fritz almost as often as she led. Yet she prevailed in straight sets, by a score of 7-5, 8-6.

Brough would never again win a major title, but she continued to play for many years. Some of her peers questioned her willingness to keep competing when she was so clearly past her prime, but Brough loved the tournaments, especially the one in Great Britain. "You win Wimbledon and you don't want to quit," she said later.

Eventually Brough did stop competing, but she did not leave the game completely. She married Alan Clapp, a dentist, in 1958, and became a tennis teacher. She continued to play and teach her beloved sport until her retirement in the early 1990s.

Further Reading

King, Billie Jean, and Cynthia Starr. *We Have Come a Long Way: The Story of Women's Tennis.* New York: McGraw-Hill, 1977, pp. 47–49.

Layden, Joe. *Women in Sports: The Complete Book on the World's Greatest Female Athletes.* Santa Monica, Calif.: General Publishing Group, 1997, p. 59.

BUTCHER, SUSAN
(1954–)   *Dogsled Racer*

Susan Butcher was not the first woman to win the grueling and prestigious Iditarod Trail Sled Dog Race, but she is its most prolific female champion and one of the best competitors of either gender to race the course. Butcher won the Iditarod, a trek of some 1,000 miles through the wilderness that begins in Anchorage and ends in Nome, Alaska,

Four-time Iditarod champion Susan Butcher in action in Alaska. In 1986, Butcher gave a T-shirt to President Reagan that read, "Alaska: Where men are men, and women win the Iditarod."
(Paul Souders/Getty Images)

four times, and in 1986 she broke the world record for completing the race—by 31 hours.

Born in Cambridge, Massachusetts, on December 26, 1954, Susan Butcher could not have chosen a less appealing location to spend her childhood. From an early age she recognized her feelings; in first grade, she wrote a story called "I Hate Cities." As soon as she was old enough—at the age of 17—she fled the cafés and cobblestoned streets of Cambridge for Colorado, where she attended Colorado State University.

Butcher studied veterinary medicine at Colorado State and worked as a veterinary technician for three years. In the meantime, Butcher found her true passion. She became entranced with the sport of dogsled racing. Always more comfortable with animals than people, Butcher had found her perfect team sport. In 1975, at the age of 19, Butcher decided to pursue dogsled racing full time. She moved to Eureka, a minuscule town in the Wrangell Mountains of Alaska, and built a compound for herself and her 150 dogs.

Soon after settling in Alaska, Butcher began preparing for competition. For Butcher, this meant training 12 to 16 hours a day, running, cycling, and weight lifting, as well as "mushing," or sledding with the dogs, which in Alaska is possible to do nine months out of the year. By 1978, Butcher felt ready to compete in the Iditarod. This trek may well be the most grueling event in athletic competition. Competitors stock their sleds with a sleeping bag, an ax, a proper supply of food, ski poles, and snow shoes, and booties for their dogs. Accompanying the racers are 16 dogs, some are at the tow line, while others rest on the sled. During her training, Butcher not only got into top shape physically, but she learned ways to survive a race that can take as long as three weeks, traveling through open wilderness, to complete. She also learned how to manage her dogs—how to tell if one of them was tired or absolutely exhausted and how to keep the entire team calm and focused.

Butcher had learned her lessons well. She ably completed the Iditarod course, not only in 1978, but the following six years as well. By 1985, Butcher was considered one of the favorites to win the course. But during that year's race she ran into trouble. Butcher described her experience this way: "I was traveling alone at night in the lead of the race and ran into an obviously crazed moose. She was starving to death. There was something wrong with her. She was just skin and bones. And rather than run away, she turned to charge the team. I thought she would just run through me. I stopped the team, threw the sled over. She had plenty of room to pass us along the trail. She came into the team and stopped. She just started stomping and kicking the dogs. She charged at me. For twenty minutes, I held her off with my ax and with my parka, waving it in her face." Another racer came along and shot the moose, but not before the crazed animal had killed two of her dogs. Butcher suffered a severe shoulder injury and was not able to finish the course. The victory went to another woman racer, LIBBY RIDDLES.

But the following year a fully healed Butcher rode her dogs to a resounding victory. Her racing time of 11 days, 15 hours, and six minutes set a new world record for the course. Butcher repeated as champion in 1987 and 1988, and then, in 1990, she won her fourth Iditarod, once again in record-breaking fashion, with a time of 11 days, one hour, 23 minutes, and 23 seconds.

Butcher, who married David Monson, a fellow musher, in 1985, has cut back on her competing, although she still races occasionally. She breeds and trains racing dogs professionally, and she gives several motivational speeches a year. She and Monson have a daughter, Marguerite, and continue to live in Eureka, Alaska.

Further Reading

Layden, Joe. *Women in Sports: The Complete Book on the World's Greatest Female Athletes,* Santa Monica, Calif.: General Publishing Group, 1997, p. 45.

"Susan Butcher," InterSpeak Inc. Featured Speakers. Copyright 1996–1999, Interspeak, all rights reserved. Available online. URL: http://interspeak.com/butcher.htm. Downloaded February 17, 2001.

"Susan Butcher," Keppler Associates Inc. Online. Copyright 2001, Keppler Associates Inc. Available online. URL: http://www.kepplerassociates.com/butcher.htm. Downloaded February 17, 2001.

"Susan Butcher, 1986, 1987, and 1988 Winner of the Iditarod," Copyright 1997, Elizabeth Becker and Sarah Teel. Available online. URL: http://library.thinkquest.org/11313/Iditarod/susan.html. Downloaded February 17, 2001.

C

CAPRIATI, JENNIFER
(Jennifer Marie Capriati)
(1976–) *Tennis Player*

At one point, Jennifer Capriati's story read like a lesson in morality. This is what happens, pundits wagged, when you force a child to turn professional at an early age. But the story of Capriati, who turned professional to great media fanfare at the age of 14, and left the sport three years later depressed and burned out, has an eloquent epilogue.

Jennifer Marie Capriati was born on March 29, 1971, in Long Island, New York. Her father, Stefano Capriati, a self-taught tennis player as well as a movie stuntman, knew his daughter was a tennis player before she was born. "I could tell just by the way Denise carried her," he claimed. Denise Capriati, a former flight attendant, had played tennis every day of her pregnancy with Jennifer until she went into labor. Once Jennifer was born, however, Stefano took over. When Jennifer was a baby, Stefano would do daily calisthenics with her, propping her up with pillows and helping her do sit-ups. The workouts evidently paid off: by the time she was four, Jennifer could rally up to 100 shots with a ball machine.

By this time, Stefano had moved his family to Fort Lauderdale, Florida. Eager to further his daughter's tennis career, he invited Jimmy Evert, CHRIS EVERT's father as well as a coach, to see Jennifer play. Evert was not eager to take on a four-year-old student, but when he saw Jennifer play, he changed his mind. Evert coached Jennifer until she was nine. At the age of 10, she played under another coach, Rick Macci, and three years later, she entered the Hopman Tennis Academy and studied under yet another coach, Tim Gullickson. But it was Stefano who was her guiding force during her early years, and Stefano who urged her to compete.

Her father was her inspiration, but it was clear that Jennifer Capriati was a natural competitor as well. She won her first junior competition at the age of 12, and one year later, in 1989, took top honors at the junior competitions at both the U.S. and the French Opens. At this point, Stefano was eager for Jennifer to turn professional, but the United States Tennis Federation, which had strict rules regarding juniors playing tennis, required a minimum age of 14 for every professional player. The Capriatis waited for their moment, and in March 1990, it finally arrived.

Capriati turned pro and promptly became America's newest sweetheart. Featured on countless magazine covers and touted as the next great tennis legend, she also signed countless endorsement packages, making her the third-highest-paid woman player in the United States—before she had even played a tournament. Capriati was appealing on the court, entering with a smile and chatting amicably with her opponent, then showing little intimidation during the match. Whether opponent was "a lege," as she called the legendary MARTINA NAVRATILOVA, or a contemporary such as Gabriela Sabatini, Capriati appeared relaxed and happy on the court.

She was also winning her share of matches. In 1991, she reached the semifinals at both Wimbledon and the U.S. Open, and in 1992, she took the gold medal in singles at the Barcelona Olympic Games. But slowly, Capriati's smile on the court began to fade. The pressure seemed to overcome her joy and, in time, cut into her enjoyment of her game. Followed virtually everywhere by the press, she became sullen and irritable. Capriati reached a low point at the 1993 U.S. Open, when, after losing in the first round, she frowned and fought her way off the court and into the locker room.

By this time, Capriati had already announced that she would be taking a leave from tennis in order to finish high school. During this hiatus, she returned to Florida, where she began experimenting with drugs and alcohol. In May 1994, a night of partying led to an arrest in Coral Gables. Capriati was charged with marijuana possession; one of her companions claimed that she had also smoked crack. Two days after the arrest, the tennis prodigy entered a drug rehabilitation program in Miami.

The Capriati saga could have ended there. But Capriati never completely lost her competitive fire. Out of shape both mentally and physically for several months after her arrest, Capriati eventually returned to the practice court and began playing again. In the fall of 1996, now coached exclusively by her father, she came back to the tour. This time, Capriati was greeted with little fanfare. Her first tournaments were unremarkable, but she kept playing and slowly worked her way back up the rankings.

Capriati entered the Australian Open seeded number 12. Even so, few fans anticipated her dominant play in Melbourne. Capriati would lose only one set as she dismantled opponent after opponent. Finally, facing Martina Hingis in the championship match, Capriati cracked winner after winner against the Swiss former prodigy to take her first Grand Slam victory. Four months later, Capriati took top honors at the French Open with a five-hour, three-set victory over Kim Clijsters, a young Belgian player. At the age of 25, Jennifer Capriati had at last reached her potential. She remains one of the most competitive and exciting players on the tennis tour. Capriati captured her third Grand Slam in January 2002 when she won her second consecutive Australian Open Championship.

Further Reading

Biography Resource Center, "Jennifer Capriati," *Encyclopedia of World Biography,* 2nd edition, 17 vols. Detroit: Gale Research, 1998.

Biography Resource Center, "Jennifer Capriati," *Great Women in Sports.* Detroit: Visible Ink Press, 1996.

Layden, Joe. *Women in Sports: The Complete Book on the World's Greatest Female Athletes.* Santa Monica, Calif.: General Publishing Group, 1997.

Smith, Lissa, editor. *Nike Is a Goddess: The History of Women in Sports.* New York: Atlantic Monthly Press, 1998, p. 75.

CARILLO, MARY
(1957–)   *Tennis Player, Broadcaster*

John McEnroe may be the most famous tennis player ever to emerge from Douglaston, New York, but he is by no means the only one. McEnroe's neighbor and one-time mixed doubles partner, Mary Carillo, has done her Long Island neighborhood proud, not only by winning a Grand Slam title during her playing days, but by serving as one of the most knowledgeable and articulate sports broadcasters on television.

Mary Carillo was born in Douglaston in 1957. She met McEnroe for the first time when they were both tennis pupils at the community tennis club. The two became fast friends, as well as a lethal team on the court. Carillo entered St. John's University in 1976, but a year later, she left college to join the Women's Professional Tennis Tour. Playing in her first international tournament, Carillo teamed up with McEnroe to take top honors in the mixed doubles event at the 1977 French Open.

Although her career began promisingly, Carillo never enjoyed a tremendous amount of success as a tennis player. She did win a singles tournament in 1979 when she took the crown at the Trophée Pernod Masters championship, and she rose as high as number 34 in the national rankings, but for the most part she was plagued by injuries. After undergoing three knee operations in less than 12 months, Carillo retired from competition in 1980.

For many people, injury has marked the end of a sports career. But for Carillo, it served as a beginning. Noting her articulate and intelligent manner, USA Network asked Carillo to provide tennis commentary in 1980. Soon afterward, *World Tennis Magazine* hired her to write a column. A gifted writer, Carillo went on to write a major book about tennis and served as coauthor of MARTINA NAVRATILOVA's memoirs.

Carillo began broadcasting the U.S. Open for CBS in 1985. That same year, the network hired her to provide commentary during its 1988 Winter and Summer Olympic Games coverage, where she broadcast skiing and gymnastics competitions, and she also sat in the broadcast booth during the 1989 women's basketball Final Four collegiate basketball championships.

By 1995, Carillo had expanded her broadcasting umbrella even farther. Too hotly pursued to be confined to one network, she has provided coverage for NBC during the 1996 Olympic Games in Atlanta, has also covered several ski championships for CBS, and has hosted several sports documentaries for HBO. In 1996, Carillo and McEnroe had a brief falling out when McEnroe complained that no woman, including Mary Carillo, had the

proper experience or knowledge to broadcast men's tennis. Carillo never issued a public reaction to McEnroe's comment, and the occurrence eventually blew over.

Carillo's first love continues to be tennis. She provides expert commentary—with McEnroe, for both women's and men's matches—for CBS during the U.S. Open, and she also serves as the lead broadcaster for TNT during Wimbledon. She lives in Naples, Florida, with her husband and two children.

Further Reading

Layden, Joe. *Women in Sports: The Complete Book on the World's Greatest Female Athletes.* Santa Monica, Calif.: General Publishing Group, 1997, p. 122.

Women's Sports Legends, "Mary Carillo," Women's Sports Legends Online. Available online. URL: http://www.wslegends.com/legends_Mary_carillo.htm. Downloaded July 10, 2001.

CARPENTER-PHINNEY, CONNIE
(1957–)   *Speed Skater and Cyclist*

When Connie Carpenter-Phinney won the gold medal in the 79.2-kilometer bike race at the 1984 Olympic Games in Los Angeles, she became the first U.S. cyclist of either gender to win a gold medal in that sport. That achievement alone is impressive enough, but what makes Carpenter-Phinney a truly extraordinary athlete is that she was competing in her second games and in her second sport. Eight years earlier, Connie Carpenter came in seventh in the 1,500-meter speed skating race at the 1972 Games in Sapporo, Japan.

Born in Madison, Wisconsin, on February 26, 1957, Connie Carpenter was a natural athlete who dabbled in different sports during most of her childhood. When she was 12, she became interested in speed skating, and decided to train for what appeared to be a long shot: competing in the 1972 Olympic Games.

To many people's surprise, Carpenter, at the age of 14, made the U.S. Olympic team and traveled to Japan to compete. Carpenter finished a respectable seventh in the 1,500-meter race and was expected to win a medal at the 1976 games. Unfortunately, she suffered a serious ankle injury weeks before the Olympics and had to give up speed skating.

Later that year, Carpenter's brother suggested that she take up cycling. Aware that SHEILA YOUNG, a fellow speed skater, had also become a competitive cyclist, Capenter began spending several hours a day on her bike. In 1977, Carpenter entered her first two national cycling competitions and won them both. That same year she took a silver medal in her first international race, and in 1978, she won two more national titles.

By 1983, Carpenter was one of the top cyclists in the world. In eight years of competitive racing, she had won 12 titles, including four national championships and one world championship. Later that year she married Davis Phinney, also a world-class cyclist. The following year, Carpenter-Phinney prepared to compete in the women's cycling event at the 1984 Olympics in Los Angeles. It would be the first time women would be competing in the sport, and Carpenter was, along with her fellow American Rebecca Twigg, favored to win a medal.

The race was close from start to finish, as Twigg and Carpenter-Phinney traded leads several times over the course of the race. Finally, trailing Twigg by several meters with 200 meters to go, Carpenter-Phinney pushed her bike in a final sprint, edging her wheels slightly in front of Twigg's to cross the finish line first. It was a triumphant ending for Carpenter-Phinney, who had announced that she would retire after the Olympic Games, and it was an equally auspicious beginning for U.S. women cyclists, who grabbed the first gold and silver Olympic medals ever offered in their sport.

After retiring from competitive racing, Carpenter-Phinney remained involved in the sport, providing written commentary for several cycling magazines and doing work on behalf of cyclists for both the U.S. Olympic Committee and the U.S. Cycling Federation. In addition, Carpenter-Phinney and her husband, who settled in Boulder, Colorado, established a successful bicycle camp for competitive cyclists.

Further Reading

"About Davis Phinney and Connie Carpenter." Carpenter/Phinney Bike Camp. Available online. URL: www.bikecamp.com/connie.html. Downloaded on March 27, 2002.

Layden, Joe. *Women in Sports: The Complete Book on the World's Greatest Female Athletes.* Santa Monica, Calif.: General Publishing Group, 1997, pp. 34–35.

CAULKINS, TRACY
(1963–) *Swimmer*

If there is one woman who could be called the best U.S. female swimmer of all time, the honor may well go to Tracy Caulkins, a master of all strokes who won three gold medals in the 1984 Olympics in Los Angeles.

Tracy Caulkins was born in Winona, Minnesota, on January 11, 1963. Her older brother and sister were also swimmers, and when she was eight, Tracy found herself being coaxed by her siblings to join the neighborhood swim club. Tracy finally agreed, on one condition: She would swim only the backstroke. Young Tracy Caulkins hated getting her face wet.

Soon enough, though, it was hard to drag Tracy Caulkins's face out of the water. "I used to cry when my parents couldn't take me to practice," she recalled later. As a teenager, Tracy felt most comfortable swimming. Thin and tall, the five-foot-eight, 108-pound adolescent felt awkward out of the water, but once in the pool she was able to use her long arms and big hands to propel through the water at astonishing speeds.

At the age of 12, Caulkins qualified for her first national seniors competition. And two years later, at age 14, she won her first national titles, winning both the 100- and 200-meter breaststroke races. One year later, in 1978, she won five gold medals at the world championships in Berlin. Unlike most swimmers, who specialize in one stroke—or at the most two strokes—Caulkins was equally dominant in the backstroke, freestyle, breaststroke, and butterfly events. And she used her formidable skills in all

Perhaps the greatest American all-around woman swimmer in history, Tracy Caulkins won three gold medals at the 1984 Olympic Games.
(Tony Duffy/Getty Images)

of these strokes to set 63 U.S. records and five world records during her career.

In 1978, Caulkins received the James Sullivan Award as the year's outstanding athlete—the youngest person ever to win that honor. Swim experts predicted that she would dominate the 1980 Olympics in Moscow and Caulkins continued to train with that purpose in mind.

At the age of 17, Caulkins was in her swimming prime in 1980. She entered the United States Olympic Trials having dominated the Pan American Games the year before, winning five gold medals. As expected, Caulkins breezed through the trials and earned a place on the Olympic team. But then the U.S. boycott occurred, and instead of traveling to the Soviet Union, Caulkins and her teammates stayed at home.

Caulkins was disappointed to miss the Olympics, but rather than retiring from the sport—as several

of her 1980 teammates did—she decided to set her sights on the 1984 Olympic Games. She enrolled at the University of Florida and continued to compete, but the constant training took a toll on Caulkins. She endured a slump in 1982, when she swam at the World Championships but left with only two bronze medals, and some in the swimming world began to wonder if she would be able to regain her edge and her focus.

But Caulkins did recover her old form, and she proceeded to win the Broderick Award for outstanding female swimmer in 1982, 1983, and 1984. Caulkins was also a first-rate student, earning All-American academic honors during her last two years at the University of Florida.

In 1984, Caulkins once again qualified for the Olympic team. This time, with the games being held in Los Angeles, the United States was certain to compete. And Caulkins, at 21 and still in her prime, would be competing in three events, including the 200-meter and 400-meter individual medleys, arguably a swimmer's most difficult races. Unlike other events, where the swimmer dives into the pool and performs one stroke from the beginning of the race to the end, participants in the medley competition use all four strokes. When the starting gun sounds, the racers dive in the pool and swim two lengths (or, in the 400-meter race, four lengths) of the butterfly. Then, the swimmers turn over and swim two backstroke lengths. Next comes two lengths of the breaststroke, and finally, the swimmers break into freestyle to end the race. Medley participants need to have strength, endurance, and tremendous versatility.

Caulkins had all three qualities, and she used them to plow her way to gold medals in both the 400-meter and the 200-meter races. She broke a U.S. record in the 400-meter event, and several days later, won a third gold when she swam the breaststroke length of the 4×100 medley relay. Her masterful performance in Los Angeles led to more accolades, and Caulkins was named Sportswoman of the Year for 1984 by the U.S. Olympic Committee.

Shortly after the Los Angeles Olympics, Caulkins retired from competitive swimming. She returned to the University of Florida, from which she had taken a leave in 1984 to train full time, and completed her degree in 1985. Caulkins married Australian Olympic swimmer Mark Stockwell in 1993 and moved to Brisbane, Australia. The mother of twin boys, Caulkins has worked for the Australian Olympic Committee and has also served as president of Womensport Queensland, an association that promotes women's sports.

Further Reading

Hickok Sports Biographies. "Tracy Caulkins." Hickok Biographies Online. Available online. URL: http://www.hickoksports.com/biograph/caulkint.shtml. Downloaded on November 16, 2000.

Layden, Joe. *Women in Sports: The Complete Book on the World's Greatest Female Athletes.* Santa Monica, Calif.: General Publishing Group, 1997, pp. 52–53.

CHADWICK, FLORENCE
(1917–1995) *Swimmer*

The United States has had its share of female pioneers in the sport of long-distance swimming. GERTRUDE EDERLE was the first woman to swim the English Channel, and DIANA NYAD became the first female to swim the long passage between Cuba and Miami, Florida. Joining Nyad and Ederle as nautical trailblazers is Florence Chadwick, the first woman to swim the English Channel in both directions.

Florence Chadwick was born on November 9, 1917, in San Diego, California. She began swimming at the age of six and immediately became a long-distance expert. When Florence was 10, she became the first child to swim the San Diego Bay Channel. She also excelled at shorter distances; in 1930, at the age of 13, she finished second to ELEANOR HOLM in the backstroke event at the National Championships.

Although Chadwick clearly had the talent to be an Olympic champion, she remained more devoted to the lower-profile sport of long-distance swimming and pursued her passion ardently. In one 14-year span, between 1929 and 1943, Chadwick won the 2.5 mile race in La Jolla, California—one of the most competitive long-distance races in the nation at the time—on 10 occasions. But Chadwick had other passions as well. Twice she put her swimming career completely on hold: in the early 1930s Chadwick went to college and seriously considered a career as an attorney. Although Chadwick decided to return to the water instead, she left competition briefly again in 1945 to appear in aquacade entertainment events alongside ESTHER WILLIAMS. Chadwick would also appear in *Bathing Beauties,* one of Williams's Hollywood movies.

Chadwick returned to long-distance swimming in the late 1940s, and she began to train seriously for her life's goal: to swim the English Channel. Employed at the time as a statistician for an overseas oil company, Chadwick would leave the office and train each day in the waters of the Persian Gulf.

Florence Chadwick could have been an Olympic champion. Instead, she became the first person to swim the English Channel in both directions.
(Library of Congress)

At last, Chadwick felt ready to pursue her goal. On August 8, 1950, on her first attempt she successfully navigated the English Channel from Dover, England, to Cape Gris-Nez, France, in 13 hours, 20 minutes. Not only was her time a new women's record for the channel, but Chadwick felt so strong at the end of the swim that she announced, "I feel fine. I'm quite prepared to swim back."

It did not quite happen that way, of course, but 1951 Chadwick did swim the channel from France to England. Swimming from east to west in the Channel meant battling against the current, and that was considered a far more difficult course. Chadwick battled against seasickness and fatigue, but she successfully navigated the distance in 16 hours and 22 minutes. The following year, she blazed another trail when she became the first woman to swim the 21-mile distance between

Catalina Island and the California mainland, in record-setting time. In 1953, the English Channel beckoned again, and Chadwick once again swam from France to England, this time in 14 hours and 42 minutes. Later that year she successfully crossed three more channels—the Strait of Gibraltar, the Bosporus, and the Dardanelles.

Chadwick's final swimming triumph came in 1955. At the twilight of her career, she once again crossed the English Channel from East to West. And she did so in the remarkable time of 13 hours and 55 minutes—a new record for that direction, not only among women, but among men as well.

After retiring from long-distance swimming, Chadwick worked as a stockbroker on Wall Street. She died in 1995.

Further Reading

Hickok Sports Biographies. "Florence Chadwick," Hickok Sports Biographies Online. Available online. URL: http://www.hickoksports.com/biograph/chadwicf.shtml. Downloaded May 4, 2001.

Layden, Joe. *Women in Sports: The Complete Book on the World's Greatest Female Athletes.* Santa Monica, Calif.: General Publishing Group, 1997, pp. 54–55.

CHASTAIN, BRANDI
(1968–) *Soccer Player*

The image most soccer fans have of the 1999 Women's World Cup final game is that of Brandi Chastain, who had just scored the winning goal for the United States in a shootout against China. In a fittingly exuberant gesture, Chastain whipped off her shirt and sank to her knees in triumph. The victory became one of the pivotal events for women in sports.

Brandi Chastain was born in a suburb of San Francisco on July 21, 1968. Her father, Roger, was a corporate marketing manager, and her mother, Lark, was a homemaker. During her childhood, Brandi would later say that she played with two kinds of friends. First there were the girls her own age, who would play imaginary games such as "house." Then there were the younger kids, mostly

Brandi Chastain drops to her knees in exultation after scoring the winning goal in the 1999 Women's World Cup. Five years earlier, Chastain had been cut from the national team. She returned in 1996 to help the United States win the Olympic gold medal.
(Jed Jacobsohn/Getty Images)

Brandi. The following year, 12-year-old Brandi began playing soccer for the Olympic Development Program, where she played on state and regional teams. Four years later, at the age of 16, she was invited to play at the junior soccer national camp.

Chastain enrolled at the University of California at Berkeley in 1986, and it was there that her problems with injuries began. During the spring of her sophomore year, she tore a ligament in her knee during a game and missed the rest of the season. Chastain also struggled academically at Berkeley, and in 1988, she left the university and joined the national soccer team. But during her first international appearance with the team, she suffered another knee injury. Chastain came back to California and enrolled at Santa Clara University. Once her knee had healed, she joined the Santa Clara soccer team and led it to two Final Four appearances in the National Collegiate Athletic Association (NCAA) soccer championships.

In 1991, Chastain graduated from Santa Clara and rejoined the national soccer team. Her timing was perfect; shortly after her return, the national team traveled to China to play in the first Women's World Cup. Chastain did not play a great deal during the tournament; she was on the sidelines in the waning moments of the final game, when the United States beat China for the championship. Even so, Chastain had contributed to the national team's winning efforts. She accepted her gold medal with pride. But two years later, national team coach Anson Dorrance decided to drop Chastain from the squad. Devastated, but determined to continue playing soccer, Chastain moved to Japan and competed in the national leagues there.

In 1996, Chastain married Jerry Smith, her head soccer coach at Santa Clara. Shortly before their wedding, the new coach of the national team, Tony DiCicco, contacted Chastain and told her he wanted her to return to the team, which was training for the upcoming Atlanta Olympic Games. Chastain married Smith as scheduled, but skipped the honeymoon in order to begin Olympic training.

When she rejoined the national team in 1996, Chastain had switched positions. Originally a for-

boys, who were the friends of her brother, Chad. After a quiet afternoon with her own friends, Brandi would often rush home to play baseball with the younger set.

When she was eight, Brandi joined her first soccer team. She loved the game immediately, but then, Brandi Chastain always thrived when she played sports. And the rougher things got on the field, the more she liked it. When she was 11, she played noseguard on a neighborhood flag football team. One of her proudest memories from her football days was the day she sacked the opposing quarterback—a boy who was somewhat bigger than ward, she made the change because DiCicco though she would be more effective in the defender's position. In soccer, the forwards are the main offensive threat for the team. They are positioned closest to the opponent's goal, and therefore have the opportunity to score the most often. Defendants, on the other hand, are, as Chastain puts it, the team's "safety valve"—often the last resort between an opposing player trying to score and the goalkeeper. The United States took top honors in Atlanta, and this time, Chastain played every minute of every game. After the United States defeated China in the gold medal game, DiCicco called Chastain "a world class defender and one of the best players in the world, period."

Following the Olympics, Chastain remained with the national squad. With her teammates, she traveled for the next three years to train and practice for the 1999 World Cup, which would be held in the United States. The 1999 World Cup was a breakthrough event for Chastain. One of the most vivacious and outgoing members of the team, she appeared on several television talk shows during the weeks leading up to the tournament and promoted the event. Her efforts paid off and helped persuade thousands of viewers to watch the games. As the tournament progressed, the audience for the games, both in the stadiums and at home, increased, and the final game, played at the sold-out Rose Bowl, garnered the highest ratings ever for a women's sports event.

Chastain had also distinguished herself on the field. Playing with energy and enthusiasm, she was an entertaining presence whenever she had the ball. At times she might have been a bit too entertaining; during the semifinal game against Germany, Chastain opened the scoring by inadvertently knocking the ball backward with her foot, then watched in horror as the ball squirted into the U.S. goal. She saved face later in the game, however, scoring two goals for the United States. But Chastain saved her finest moment for the shoot-out at the end of the final game of the tournament. The United States and China had played to a scoreless tie during both regulation periods and two 15

minute "golden goal" sudden-death overtimes. International soccer rules call for tied games to be determined by a "shoot-out," in which five players from each team, playing one at a time, challenge the opposing goalkeeper with a shot on goal.

One by one, the U.S. and Chinese players took their shots. The first U.S. and Chinese shooters both scored. Then the second U.S. shooter scored, but then Brianna Scurry, the U.S. goalkeeper, blocked the next Chinese player's kick. The U.S. team now had a lead, but they had to score all their remaining goals to clinch the World Cup.

The U.S. and Chinese players exchanged successful scoring kicks, until there was one player left. Chastain stood facing the goalkeeper. The score was tied; a successful kick would win the championship outright for the United States. Chastain hesitated before beginning her assault on goal; earlier in the year, she had been in a similar shoot-out situation with the goalkeeper, and her kick had been blocked. This time, however, Chastain dribbled the ball toward the goal, and then booted a powerful kick with her left foot. The ball shot past the diving goalkeeper and into the net. Chastain had scored—the United States had won. The crowd erupted, and Chastain, preparing to celebrate, spontaneously grabbed her shirt. The rest is history.

Chastain continued to play with the national team after the World Cup victory. In the 2000 Olympic games in Sydney, the team won the silver medal, falling to Norway in a hotly contested final match. One year later, play began for the WUSA, the first professional women's soccer league in the United States. Chastain was drafted by the San Jose Cyber Rays. In typical fashion, she led her team to the first WUSA championship in August 2001.

Further Reading

Longman, Jere. *The Girls of Summer: The U.S. Women's Soccer Team and How It Changed the World.* New York: HarperCollins, 2000.

Miller, Mark. *All-American Girls, The US Women's National Soccer Team.* New York: Archway Paperbacks, 1999, pp. 21–34.

CLEMENT, AMANDA
(1888–1971)   *Baseball Umpire*

Amanda Clement was the first woman to umpire a men's baseball game. A sought-after and respected referee who made a decent living in the Midwestern semipro leagues, she used the money she had earned calling balls and strikes to send herself to college.

Amanda Clement was born on March 20, 1888, in the Dakota Territory. Her mother, Harriet Clement (Amanda's father died when she was quite young), settled with her two children in the town of Hudson, South Dakota, and supported Amanda and her brother, Hank, by cooking and serving meals to railroad workers. Hank and Amanda both loved baseball and spent much of their spare time playing in the town baseball field, Hudson Park. Being a girl, Amanda was not always allowed to play with the neighborhood boys, but when she did not play, she was the umpire.

The Clements moved to Hawarden, Iowa, when Amanda 17. Hank had become a semipro pitcher there, and his family made the move with him. One day, Hank was playing in an amateur game, and the umpire did not show up. Hank suggested that his sister, sitting in the stand, call the game instead. Amanda did such an impressive job in the field that she was immediately recruited to umpire a game between the Hawarden and Renville semipro teams the following day. And so, on that early spring day in 1904, when Amanda stepped behind the pitcher's mound and assumed her stance, she became the first woman ever to umpire a professional baseball game.

In the early days of baseball, umpires had an even heavier workload than their contemporary peers. Only one referee judged a game, and that person would stand behind the pitcher's mound, in a proper position to call not only the balls and strikes, but also to judge close calls on the bases and fair or foul drives to the outfield. It was a hefty load for one person, but Amanda Clement, who stood nearly six feet tall, was a commanding presence on the field, with her hair tucked under her cap and the hemline of her long blue skirt tucked into her socks. She had a fair and discerning eye for balls or strikes, and she put up with very little abuse from players or managers; she did not hesitate to eject anyone who argued too strenuously.

Slowly but surely, word of Clement's talents spread. She became a regular presence on the baseball diamond, first in Iowa, and then in such neighboring states as Minnesota, Nebraska, and the Dakotas. From 1904 to 1908 Clement umpired dozens of games and was often the first umpire requested by teams and fans alike. Toward the end of her tenure, her reputation was so stellar that, in one tempestuous baseball tournament played in the upper Midwest, fans were so fed up with the errant calls by the hired umpire that they took up a collection to hire a driver to fetch "the lady umpire," Amanda Clement.

By 1908, Clement, who was paid between $15 and $25 for the games she called, had collected enough money to send herself through college. She enrolled at Yankton College in South Dakota, but she continued to umpire throughout her years there. After graduating from Yankton in 1911, Clement attended the University of Nebraska to study physical education. Although she had retired from full-time baseball umpiring when she left Yankton, she continued to make occasional appearances to call games.

In her later years Clement taught physical education at schools in North and South Dakota as well as in Wyoming. She also managed several Young Men's Christian Associations (YMCAs) and went on to become a police matron, a typesetter, and a justice of the peace. Clement was also a loving aunt to her brother's children; she taught her nephews to play baseball, and reportedly threw the ball so hard (while in her 40s) that the boys had to put sponges in their gloves in order to catch her throws without wincing.

In 1929 Clement retired from her various jobs and moved back to South Dakota, where she cared for her sick mother. After Harriet Clement died in 1934, Amanda Clement moved to Sioux Falls and became a social worker. Tireless and enthusiastic to the end, she died in 1971, at the age of 83.

Not only was Clement a talented and respected umpire, but she used her fame to serve as an advocate for her gender. In 1906, she wrote a column for the *Cincinnati Enquirer* in which she argued fiercely that women make better umpires than their male counterparts. "Can you suggest a single reason why all the baseball umpires should not be women? Of course you can't," she wrote. "Do you suppose any ballplayer in this country would step up to a good-looking girl and say to her "you color-blind pickle-brained, cross-eyed idiot, if you don't stop throwing the soup into me I'll distribute your features all over your countenance! Of course he wouldn't."

Further Reading

Gregorich, Barbara. *Women at Play: The Story of Women in Baseball.* New York: Harcourt Brace, 1993, pp. 17–21.

Kratz, Marilyn. "Amanda Clement: The Umpire in a Skirt." Available online. URL: http://www.nagb.org/pubs/reading/rgrade4.html. Downloaded December 5, 2000.

COACHMAN, ALICE
(1923–   )   *High Jumper*

A high jumper and sprinter from Georgia, Alice Coachman went to London in 1948 and became the first African-American woman to win an Olympic gold medal. Then after being feted for her winning efforts and hobnobbing with royalty and celebrities in London, she returned to her segregated Jim Crow homeland.

The third of seven children born to Fred and Evelyn Jackson Coachman, Alice Coachman was born on November 9, 1923, in Albany, Georgia. When she was a very small child she wanted to be a famous star like Shirley Temple, but she also was a tomboy—so much so that her father whipped her for not being ladylike enough. A fast runner who enjoyed competing against other children, Coachman became a standout in both basketball and track and field at Madison High School.

But Coachman's career really went into high gear when she enrolled at the Tuskegee Institute.

In 1948 after Alice Coachman became the first African-American woman to win an Olympic gold medal, she returned to her native Georgia, where she was not allowed to speak at her own celebration ceremony.
(Library of Congress)

An oasis for African-American athletes of both genders, Tuskegee dominated U.S. women's track and field for many years. While at Tuskegee, Coachman became one of the premier track-and-field athletes in the United States. She was a world-class sprinter, winning the outdoor 50-meter national championship five years in a row. But her real specialty was as a high jumper.

Between 1939 and 1948 Coachman won 10 consecutive outdoor high-jumping championships. It was unfortunate for Coachman that she was in her athletic prime during the early 1940s; both the 1940 and 1944 Olympic Games were canceled because of World War II. Even so, Coachman continued to compete on the national level, and in 1946, after winning national championships for the Tuskegee team in the high jump, the 50-meter race, and the 100-meter race, she was chosen for the U.S. track-and-field team in a meet against Canada.

Coachman was the only African-American woman on the team that year, and she was scrutinized very carefully by the national Amateur Athletic Union (AAU) committee before she was selected. Fortunately for Coachman, the committee found her to be, according to one newspaper, "quiet, ladylike, reserved, and most desirable."

Two years later, at the age of 25, Coachman at last had the chance to compete at the Olympics. At the Olympic trials in the spring of 1948, Coachman had to wait to compete in the high jump, which was the final event of the day. By the time Coachman got ready to jump, evening had fallen, and in an era before stadium lights, officials had to light matches so the athletes could see. Coachman tied a white handkerchief on the high-jumping bar to keep her bearings. Then, with no further ado, she cleared the lighted rail, setting an Olympic-trial record that was not broken until 1960s.

Those Olympic trials were notable not only for Coachman's achievement, but for the fact that an unprecedented nine African-American women made the 11-member U.S. Olympic women's track-and-field squad. African-American women would represent the majority of every Olympic track-and-field team from that year forward.

It was an exciting time for Coachman but a frightening one as well. Aboard the SS *America,* on her way to the London games, Coachman, the veteran and leader of the U.S. women's track-and-field team, looked around her cabin and promptly burst into tears. Perhaps she cried because, like many of her teammates, the London trip marked Coachman's first time away from North America. In addition, Coachman might have realized that there was a tremendous amount of pressure on the mostly African-American women's team to prove themselves at the Olympic games. They would need to win at least one gold medal to prove themselves, not only to the world but to their segregated nation.

Sadly for the U.S. team, they had sound competition in London. In particular, a 30-year-old Dutch athlete named Fanny Blankers-Koen was virtually unbeatable. A mother of two children, Blankers-Koen showed that a woman can indeed be both a parent and a fierce competitor, winning individual gold medals in the 100-meter and 200-meter events and in the 800-meter high hurdles, and taking a team gold in the 4×100-meter relays. Meanwhile, the U.S. athletes were running poorly; most were eliminated in the trial heats, and the players managed only one third-place finish, as Audrey Patterson took a bronze in the 200-meter event. U.S. women fared no better in the field events, as Europeans dominated the javelin, broad jump, shot put, and discus events. There was only one event left, and that was the high jump.

Coachman had spent much of her time in London seeing the sights, riding on a double-decker bus, and traveling to small towns outside the city limits. Now she was back at Wembley Stadium, the only U.S. woman left with an opportunity to bring home a gold medal. The British fans were cheering on their home athletes, who had also thus far failed to win gold. The last hope for the British women was Dorothy Tyler, a high jumper who had competed in the Berlin Olympics in 1936.

The competition proved long and grueling. By late afternoon, the bar reached five feet, three inches, and with 50,000 fans rooting for Tyler in the Wembley stands, the field had narrowed to three jumpers—Coachman, Tyler, and Michelline Ostermeyer of France, who had already won two gold medals. Ostermeyer was eventually eliminated, but with the bar set at five feet, six and one-half inches, both Coachman and Tyler were able to clear it. At this point, according to the Olympic rules, Coachman was declared the winner, because she had missed fewer times during the course of the competition. "I didn't know who had won until I saw my name on the board," she would later say.

But she had indeed won the event, giving the U.S. women's track-and-field team its one and only gold medal of the games. Coachman was immediately hailed by U.S. citizens living in London; she was given numerous receptions at expatriates' homes and was invited to a tea party by Lady Nancy Astor. When Coachman returned to the United States, she went to a White House reception, where she was personally congratulated by President Harry Truman. Then it was time to go back to Georgia.

Coachman returned to her native state a hero. Her victory had brought honor and pride to her hometown of Albany, which immediately planned an Alice Coachman Day. The celebration began promisingly, with a motorcade that carried Coachman from Atlanta through several small Georgia towns, as thousands of people lined the streets to hail the first African-American Olympic champion. But once the motorcade reached Albany, reality set in.

At the official celebration for Coachman, she sat on the stage of a segregated auditorium. Along with a number of African-American dignitaries, Coachman sat on the platform, separated from the mayor and the white dignitaries by a black grand piano. The mayor spoke at great length about the white male champions of the Olympics. He mentioned Coachman's achievement but did not shake her hand or look at her. Coachman sat silently throughout the celebration in her honor; she was not given the chance to speak.

But Coachman's Olympic achievement remains a major statement and a tremendous milestone for African-American athletes. After the London games, Coachman returned to the Tuskegee Institute where she majored in education. Following her retirement from competition, she became a coach and teacher, and then she devoted a great deal of her time to activism. In the late 1950s and early 1960s she traveled across the South to denounce segregation, as well as discrimination against women. She still lives in her hometown of Albany, Georgia, and remains an outspoken advocate for women's rights.

Further Reading

Davis, Michael D. *Black American Women in Olympic Track and Field: A Complete Illustrated Reference.* Jefferson, N.C.: McFarland, 1992.

Layden, Joe. *Women in Sports: The Complete Book on the World's Greatest Female Athletes.* Santa Monica, Calif.: General Publishing Group, 1997, p. 60.

Plowden, Martha Ward. *Olympic Black Women.* Gretna, La.: Pelican Publishers, 1996.

CONNOLLY, MAUREEN
(Maureen Connolly Brinker)
(1934–1969) *Tennis Player*

The first woman to win the four major tennis championships in one calendar year—known as the Grand Slam—was a Californian named Maureen Connolly. Her career was brief, as she retired from her sport at the age of 19 following a horseback riding accident, but during her tenure on the court she dominated tennis like no champion before or since.

Maureen Connolly was born on September 17, 1934, in San Diego, California. Her parents divorced when Maureen was three years old, and she was raised by her mother and her aunt. Her mother recognized Maureen's extraordinary athleticism early on, and she decided to steer her daughter toward a dancing career. Maureen starting taking tap dancing lessons at the age of five, but it was also at an early age that Maureen's strong will emerged; she behaved so poorly during a dance tryout, disrupting her fellow dancers as well as the judges, that her mother decided to pull her out of dancing altogether.

Connolly's first passion was horseback riding. As a child she longed for a horse of her own, but knew that her mother could never afford it. Instead, she turned to tennis at the age of nine, and she was soon playing in a San Diego playground under the guidance of a local coach named Wilbur Folsom.

Although Connolly was left-handed, Folsom persuaded her to play with her right hand, claiming that there were no left-handed champions. (Of course, that has changed today—MARTINA NAVRATILOVA and MONICA SELES are among the many left-handed women who have won major titles—but a left-handed woman did not win a grand slam championship until 1969, when Ann Jones captured the Wimbledon title.) He also encouraged Connolly to dedicate time to her game, and young Maureen did just that, practicing three hours a day, five days a week.

At the age of 12, Maureen Connolly met one of the most pivotal people in her life. Teach Tennant was a seasoned tennis coach who had guided ALICE MARBLE to championships in the 1930s. Tennant recognized a rare talent in Connolly—a natural athleticism combined with a determination to succeed. Tennant set out to mold Connolly into a champion. And she succeeded, but at some cost.

In 1949, when Connolly was 14, she won the national girls' 18-and-under championship. She was the youngest ever to win that tournament, and she repeated as champion the following year. It was in 1950 that Connolly was nicknamed "Little Mo," inspired by the World War II battleship *Missouri,* which was known as "Big Mo." Then, in 1951, Connolly won her first major title when she won the U.S. championship.

But Connolly lost an important friendship during the process. Connolly had grown up idolizing Doris Hart, a player 10 years older than she. Much to the younger player's delight, Hart befriended her during the 1950 U.S. tournament. But in 1951, Connolly's coach Tennant decided that it was not a good idea for Connolly to be close friends with a fellow competitor. So a day before the semifinal of the 1951 U.S. championship, when Connolly was slated to play Hart, Tennant took Connolly aside and told her that Hart had said she was a "spoiled little brat."

The accusation was untrue, but Connolly, who believed it, was shattered, angry, and filled with a new-found emotion—hatred. She focused her anger on the court the next day, when Hart was leading in the first set by a score of 4-0, and a light rain began to fall. Hart, who had lost great mobility in her legs owing to childhood illness, asked for a rain delay, fearing injury. But when the officials refused her request, Connolly took advantage of her opponent's lack of concentration to seize the first set, 6-4. The match was indeed suspended

after the first set, but the next day Connolly won the second set by a score of 6-4, and ran off the court weeping with happiness, as Hart, who had yet to win a major tournament, followed in despair. Connolly later said that when she met Hart in that semifinal match, that she "saw blinding red . . . I never hated anyone more in my life!"

It was that kind of emotion—pure passion, fueling intensity and excellence—that spurred Connolly on to win a total of three U.S. championships, three Wimbledon championships, two French championships, and one Australian championship, in a mere three and a half years. During that time, Connolly lost only five matches. She did it with a game that featured powerful and precise ground strokes; Connolly was once hit in the head by an overhead while standing at the net during her childhood, so she spent the rest of her career as far away from the net as she could manage to be. But patrolling the baseline was her specialty, and she was able to wear down her opponents by her tireless movement, fierce determination, and fearsome shots.

Shortly before the 1952 Wimbledon championships, Connolly discovered that Tennant had lied to her about Hart's remark during the 1951 U.S. championship, and the two tennis players were able to resume their friendship. But Tennant and Connolly were heading toward the end of their relationship; they bickered about whether Connolly should continue to play after suffering a minor injury early in the Wimbledon tournament (Connolly wanted to continue playing, but Tennant begged her to default, fearing serious injury), and then Connolly heard that Tennant had expressed a wish to be "through with" her young protégée. Then, in an unprecedented move, Connolly called her own press conference right after winning an early round match. Without informing her coach beforehand, Connolly stood before the assembled journalists and fired Tennant on the spot.

Connolly went on to win Wimbledon that year and then hired a new coach, Harry Hopman. It was Hopman and his wife, Nell (whom Connolly credited with teaching her to win without hating her opponents), who steered Connolly to many of her triumphs, including her Grand Slam achievement in 1954. It was Connolly's greatest ambition to become the first player since Don Budge to win all four major championships in one year. And in the winter of 1954, she began her quest by beating Julie Sampson to take the Australian title. She added the French championship in May of that year, besting Doris Hart to take those honors.

Then came her third consecutive Wimbledon title. The final of that tournament pitted Connolly and Hart against each other yet again, and although Connolly triumphed in straight sets, the match is remembered as one of the greatest in Wimbledon history. After topping Hart by a score of 8-6, 7-5, Connolly set her sights on the fourth and final tournament—the U.S. championship. One more time, Connolly would play Hart for top honors. And once again, Connolly outplayed her opponent, winning 6-2, 6-3, in 45 minutes. Connolly's Grand Slam achievement would not be matched until Martina Navratilova would win four straight major opens in 1983–84, and she remains one of only three players (Steffi Graf is the third) to reach that milestone. Interestingly, although Connolly had made tennis history with her win at the U.S. championship, it was the men's winner, Tony Trabert, who graced the front page of the *New York Times* after the tournament ended. Grand Slammer Connolly was shown on the first page of the sports section.

After winning the Grand Slam, Connolly would play another year, but she was losing incentive to continue playing in a sport that did not pay its champions well. During Connolly's career, all tennis players had to maintain amateur status in order to participate in the major tournaments—professionals were not allowed to compete. So while Connolly could lay claim to some of the most prestigious titles in sports, she took home no money for her efforts.

It could be that lack of financial reward that contributed to Connolly's diminishing interest in the game after 1953. With the Grand Slam achievement, Connolly had reached the pinnacle of success in her field. She went on to win the 1954 French and Wimbledon titles, then went to San Diego to

The first woman to win all four tennis Grand Slam events in one year, Maureen Connolly dominated her sport until her retirement, at the age of 19. Although she was born left-handed, Connolly learned to play the game with her right hand after being told that there were "no left-handed champions."
(Library of Congress)

take time off. During her vacation there, Connolly went horseback riding—her old childhood passion. Riding her own horse, Colonel Mayberry, Connolly was grazed by a cement truck and thrown to the ground. Connolly broke her right leg severely in the accident and tore several muscles below the knee.

As severe as Connolly's accident was, it is quite possible that she could have made a return to competitive tennis after undergoing rehabilitation. But Connolly chose instead to retire. "I really don't enjoy playing tennis anymore," she said when she made her announcement. Whether it was because she realized she would never be the player she was before the accident, or because Connolly had simply grown disillusioned with the long hours of training that tennis demanded, was never clear. But Connolly had made her choice and moved on with her life.

That new life included marriage to Norman Brinker, a British Olympic equestrian, in 1954, and the birth of two daughters, Cindy and Brenda. Connolly also kept active on the tennis scene, playing for fun and coaching the British Wightman Cup team during the 1960s. Then, when she was 29, Connolly was diagnosed with stomach cancer. She fought the disease for five years and was in attendance when she was elected into the International Tennis Hall of Fame in 1968. One year later, at the age of 34, Connolly died.

On the court Connolly was relentless, dominating the game with intensity and focus rarely seen in athletes of her era. But away from the game she was gracious and generous. Toward the end of her life Connolly established the Maureen Connolly Brinker Tennis Foundation, an organization dedicated to promoting junior tennis. Connolly brought women's tennis to new heights during her career, which, like her life, was glorious but too brief.

Further Reading

King, Billie Jean, and Cynthia Starr. *We Have Come a Long Way: The Story of Women's Tennis.* New York: McGraw-Hill, 1988, pp. 82–89.

Layden, Joe. *Women in Sports: The Complete Book on the World's Greatest Female Athletes.* Santa Monica, Calif.: General Publishing Group, 1997, pp. 63–64.

⊞ COOK, WILLA McGUIRE
(1928–   )   *Water-skier*

Arguably the most talented person ever to strap on a pair of water skis is Willa McGuire Cook, winner of 18 national titles. Aside from her excellence in competition, McGuire combined balletic moves with athletic excellence to become a successful freestyle skier—the first of her kind.

Ironically, Willa McGuire, who was born in Lake Oswego, Oregon, in 1928, was not interested in waterskiing as a young child. Her first love was diving. But her father, Wally, owner of a local marina, noticed that his 14-year-old daughter enjoyed riding an aquaplane at high speeds over the water. Rather than cringing in terror at this sight, he insisted that Willa try waterskiing. His instincts were on the money—from the first time Willa glided over the water, she was completely hooked.

Three years later, in 1945, the waterskiing pioneer Don Ibsen brought his traveling show to Lake Oswego. Ibsen noticed McGuire immediately and suggested that she compete in the National Water Ski championships, which were held that year in Holland, Michigan. McGuire entered the tournament, and she breezed to first-place finishes in the slalom and tricks categories, as well as the overall title. The 1945 nationals would prove to be the beginning of a tremendously successful competitive career for McGuire, who would triumph in eight of the nine National Championships she would enter. In 1949 and 1951 McGuire won those titles in style, scoring "clean sweeps"—or first-place finishes in all three categories, the slalom, tricks, and jumping.

In the meantime, McGuire, who loved the freestyle aspects of her sport most of all, became a featured performer at Cypress Gardens, a show that showcased water-skiers, in 1948. McGuire would star at the gardens for 10 years; during that time, she not only entertained thousands with her swivels and jumps but invented several new moves. These innovations included the back jump—which skeptics had claimed could not be done—and the 360 spin, moves that are now regular parts of freestyle waterskiing competitions.

Possibly the highlights of McGuire's competitive career were the four world tournaments in which she competed for the United States. Skiing against the world's best in 1949, 1950, 1953, and

1955, McGuire won the overall title three times and scored five world event victories. She recalled later that her proudest moment was when she carried the U.S. flag during the playing of the national anthem at the 1953 event in Beirut.

Not only was McGuire a splendidly gifted skier, but she was a talented teacher of her sport as well. For virtually her entire career, she worked tirelessly with younger skiers, training them in the skills that came so naturally to her. Her formula was simple: "My theory is that if you feel it, ski it," she said later. McGuire taught dozens of young skiers, many of whom grew up to become champions in their own right.

McGuire married Bob Cook in the late 1950s. The couple has remained intensely involved in the sport of waterskiing. Bob Cook serves as a member of the board of trustees for the American Water Ski Education Foundation, and Willa McGuire Cook heads the foundation museum committee. She focuses much of her creative talent as an artist and designer of the exhibits at the National Water Ski Museum in Winter Haven, Florida.

Further Reading

Layden, Joe. *Women in Sports: The Complete Book on the World's Greatest Female Athletes.* Santa Monica, Calif.: General Publishing Group, 1997, pp. 65–66.

"Willa Worthington McGuire Cook," American Water Ski Education Foundation. Available online. URL: http://www.usawaterski.org/pages/HoF/Bios/Willa%20Cook.htm. Downloaded May 8, 2001.

⊞ COOPER, CYNTHIA
(1963–) *Basketball Player*

The Women's National Basketball Association (WNBA) is one of the newest professional leagues in the United States, but it has already had one legendary superstar. She is Cynthia Cooper, who led the Houston Comets to four consecutive championships during the league's first four years of existence.

Cynthia Cooper was born on April 14, 1963, in Chicago, Illinois. The youngest of eight children born to Mary Cobb, a single mother, Cynthia moved with her family to the Watts section of Los Angeles, when she was a very young girl. Unlike many of her fellow professional basketball players, Cynthia did not grow up playing pickup ball on neighborhood courts. In fact, she did not even play the game until she was in ninth grade.

But once she did begin playing, she quickly became obsessed. Eager to escape the rough street life of her Watts neighborhood, Cynthia spent as much time as she could on her high school court. And her effort paid off. During her senior season at Locke High School in 1981, she averaged an astonishing 31 points a game. It was good enough to land her Los Angeles player-of-the-year honors and good enough to earn her an athletic scholarship to the University of Southern California (USC).

Although Cooper was thrilled to win the scholarship, it took her a while to adjust to life on the USC campus. "I don't think I was ready to juggle schoolwork, practice games, and time for myself," she said later of those first weeks at USC. But Cooper soon got used to her new life and began excelling on the basketball court. At the end of her freshman year, Cooper, who had averaged 14.6 points a game for the season, was named a Freshman All-American. That was just the beginning of a terrific collegiate career for Cooper. The following two years she and her teammate CHERYL MILLER led the USC Trojans to consecutive National Collegiate Athletic Association (NCAA) championships.

After graduating from USC in 1986, Cooper headed to Italy to play professional basketball. Unlike many of her contemporaries, who returned to the United States overcome by homesickness, Cooper had a successful career overseas. She played for teams in Italy and Spain, and she won the European league scoring championship eight times. During that time span, Cynthia returned to the United States to play for the U.S. women's basketball team in two Olympic Games. Her sparkling play on the court helped the U.S. women win a gold medal in 1988 in Seoul, Korea, and a bronze medal at the 1992 games in Barcelona, Spain.

Cooper left Europe for good in 1997, when she was recruited by a new professional league in her

Cynthia Cooper handles the ball for the Houston Comets. Cooper led the Comets to the first four championships in WNBA history.
(Todd Warshaw/Getty Images)

home country. The Houston Comets, of the WNBA, drafted the 34-year-old Cooper in the first round of the draft. Although she was one of the older players in the league, Cooper quickly showed that she had lost none of her speed—and none of her scoring touch—over the years. In the first year of WNBA play, Cooper led the league in scoring and took the Comets to a dominating win in the league championship series. She was rewarded for her efforts by seizing both season and championship most-valuable-player (MVP) honors.

Most sports pundits realize the truth of the statement "how hard it is to repeat." And yet for Cooper, it was as natural as one of her patented scoring layups. In 1998, still with the Comets, Cooper led them once again to the league championship. And sure enough, when the dust from the season and championship season had settled, Cooper had won her second consecutive double-MVP award.

In 1999, Cooper once again played an integral role for the Comets, who galloped to their third consecutive WNBA title. Cooper was a "three-peater" as well, gathering her third straight championship MVP as the Comets beat the New York Liberty for the crown. The following year, the 38-year-old Cooper announced that she would be hanging up her sneakers after the 2000 season ended. Cooper went out with style, leading Houston to its fourth league title, and gathering her fourth consecutive championship MVP in the process.

WNBA fans were sad to see Cooper depart from the court, but in early 2001 they were delighted to find out that she would be returning. Her playing days were over, but she had accepted the head coaching job for the Phoenix Mercury. Echoing her college playing days, Cooper was asked to fill the shoes of Cheryl Miller, who had coached the Phoenix Mercury for the first four years of its existence and then had resigned in late 2000. "I am looking forward to being a part of bringing a championship to the city of Phoenix," Cooper declared at the press conference announcing her hire. In 2001, the Mercury finished in fifth place of the WNBA's western division, with a 13–19 record.

Further Reading

Associated Press. "Mercury Names Cynthia Cooper As Coach." Total Sports Network. Available online. URL: http://aol.totalsports.net/news/20010108/bko/010108.0404.html. Downloaded February 27, 2001.

CNN.SI for Women, 100 Greatest Female Athletes. "Cynthia Cooper," *Sports Illustrated for Women.* Available online. URL: http://sportsillustrated.cnn.com/siforwomen/top_100/90/. Posted November 29, 1999.

Cooper, Cynthia. *She Got Game: My Personal Odyssey.* New York: Warner Books, 1999.

Rutledge, Rachel. *The Best of the Best in Basketball.* Brookfield, Conn.: Millbrook Press, 1998, pp. 15–18.

CROTEAU, JULIE
(1970–) *Baseball Player*

The first woman to play college baseball, Julie Croteau, got there not by being in the right place at the right time or through the kindness of strangers. Instead, Croteau became the first woman on a men's collegiate baseball squad through persistence, courage, and passion, as well as sheer athletic talent.

Julie Croteau was born on December 4, 1970, in Prince William County, Virginia. Enamored with baseball from the start, Julie began playing T-ball when she was six years old. Her parents, Ray and Nancy Croteau, were not baseball fans themselves, but they were pleased that their daughter had such an interest and encouraged her to play. Two years later, she joined the neighborhood Little League team, where she started at first base. In 1974, when Julie was four years old, women's organizations had successfully sued Little League, demanding that girls be allowed to play. Julie benefited from that court case, and she remained involved in youth baseball leagues, including the Major Leagues (for 13- to 15-year-olds) and the Babe Ruth Leagues (for 16- to 18-year-olds) until she was a young woman.

Although Julie remained eligible for those leagues, her quest to join her high school junior varsity baseball team was quite a different story. She first tried out for the team at Osbourn Park High when she was a ninth grader, and the coach took her aside and suggested politely that she try softball. Julie was not interested and returned the following year to try for the hardball team once again. And once again, the coach told her to try softball and Julie refused. Julie tried out to no avail during her junior year in high school, and yet again her senior year. When the coach of the junior varsity team cut her during her fourth and final attempt to play, Julie's parents, who were both lawyers, decided to take legal action.

The Croteaus' law case made national headlines. Witnesses from Julie's Major League team testified on her behalf, stating that she was as talented a baseball player as most of the boys and that she had earned her starting position on the team. On the other side, 17 players for the Osbourn Park High junior varsity team appeared in federal court to back their coach's decision, and the court received affidavits from several others who stated that Julie Croteau was cut from the team not because of her gender, but because of a lack of talent. At the end, the courts ruled in favor of Osbourn Park High.

Although she had lost the case, Julie Croteau had gained a following, who were now curious as to what her next move would be. She ended their suspense when she was accepted for admission at St. Mary's College in Maryland, where she was informed that she was welcome to try out for their National Collegiate Athletic Association (NCAA) Division II baseball team. At around the same time, the manager of the Fredericksburg Giants of the semipro Virginia League invited Croteau to try out for his team. In the summer of 1988, Croteau made the Giants roster and played several summers of semipro ball.

In the fall of 1988, Croteau entered St. Mary's, and several months later she tried out for and made the baseball team. In so doing, she became the first woman ever to play for a men's college team, and the media took notice. Unfortunately for Croteau and the team, her first season on the diamond was a difficult one. She struggled at the plate, hitting only .222, and the team hacked its way to a paltry 1-20-1 record.

After that first season, the media attention Croteau had initially received disappeared. The team was no longer the "First Team to Include a Woman Player," but merely a mediocre Division II squad. And Croteau herself slowly became disillusioned with the sport she so adored. She came to realize during the season that baseball was first and foremost a men's sport, and she tired of being the only woman on the diamond. She had no friends on the team; in fact, the players often went out of their way to avoid her. By the end of the 1990 season, she had lost most of her initiative to play on the St. Mary's squad. Wary of being labeled a quitter, she came back for her junior season, but after the 1991 season ended, she left the team.

After graduating from St. Mary's in 1991, Croteau continued to play semipro ball with the Fredericksburg Giants and then, in 1993, with the Colorado Silver Bullets. In 1995 she blazed another trail when she accepted a one-year coaching post at the University of Massachusetts, thus becoming the first woman ever to serve as a coach for a Division I baseball program. Croteau aimed to become a lawyer like her parents, with the hope of helping other women trying to make their way in an all-men's sport.

Then in 1997, Croteau found a new vocation when she began broadcasting Pac 10 (Pacific 10, a college sports league) baseball games on television. Croteau, who was hired only one week after ANN MEYERS became the first woman hired to broadcast a National Basketball Association (NBA) basketball game, was once again a pioneer. She continued to serve as a part-time broadcaster for collegiate baseball and has also done work for the Women's Sports Foundation, helping future trailblazers break boundaries and play with the boys.

Further Reading

Burton Nelson, Mariah. "Julie Croteau: Breaking Down Barriers," *Women's Sports and Fitness,* vol. 13 no. 6 (September 1991): 54–55.

Gregorich, Barbara. *Women at Play: The Story of Women in Baseball.* San Diego: Harcourt Brace, 1993, pp. 253–257.

Slusser, Susan. "Croteau to Broadcast Baseball," *San Francisco Chronicle.* Available online. URL: http://www.sfchronicle.com. Posted March 1, 1997.

CURTIS, ANN
(1926–) *Swimmer*

Ann Curtis, one of the finest freestyle middle-distance swimmers in history, has won more national Amateur Athletic Union (AAU) gold medals than any swimmer. In addition, Curtis won two golds in the 1948 Olympic Games in London and quite possibly would have won more if there had been as many events for women then as there are now.

Born in Rio Vista, California, on March 6, 1926, Ann Curtis learned how to swim as a young student at the Ursuline Convent School in Santa Rosa. Her first swimming teachers were the nuns at the convent, but she eventually joined the Crystal Plunge Club in San Francisco and trained with its coach, Charlie Sava.

In 1937, Ann won her first AAU crown, in the girls' freestyle event. Because she was only 11, she was not allowed to swim the senior races until 1943. As soon as she qualified for those senior events, Ann began dominating them. Over the six-year period 1943 through 1948, Curtis would win nine outdoor titles and nine indoor championships at the AAUs. She had a particularly stellar season in 1944, when she took top honors in the 100-meter, 800-meter, and 1-mile outdoor events, and in the 220-yard and 440-yard indoor races. As a result of those performances, Curtis became the first woman, as well as the first swimmer of either gender, to win the Sullivan Award, given each year to the outstanding amateur athlete in the United States.

Curtis could have easily been an Olympic champion in 1944 as well, but World War II prevented the games from occurring. Four years later, she traveled to London as the favorite to win gold in the 400-meter freestyle event. Curtis had dominated this event during her career—she had never lost the event in the years preceding the Olympics and would go on to win a total of nine national titles. So few were surprised when the Californian touched pool's edge for the gold in London. Two days later, Curtis swam a strong anchor (final lap) to help the U.S. team win the 4×100 relay event for her second gold. That Curtis swam anchor for that race was alone testament to her remarkable talent. A middle-distance swimmer rather than a sprinter, she nevertheless posted the fastest time of all Olympic swimmers during her 100-meter leg of the relays. Curtis also swam in the 100-meter individual race and won a silver medal, coming in second to Denmark's Greta Anderson. Unfortunately for Curtis, the 1948 Olympics did not feature races in the 800-meter and 1,500-meter distances. If they had (as Olympic games now do) there is little doubt that Curtis would have swept those events as well.

Retiring from swimming after the 1948 games, Curtis moved back to California and opened her own swimming school. She continued to teach swimming until the mid-1970s.

Further Reading

Hickok Sports Biographies. "Ann Curtis," HickokSports.com. Available online. URL: http://www.Hickoksports.com/biograph/curtisan.shtml. Downloaded on May 23, 2001.

Stories about USMS Swimmers. "Ann Curtis," United States Masters Swimming. Available online. URL: http://www.swimgold.org/ttsto/cuo26cf.htm. Downloaded on May 23, 2001.

Woolum, Janet. *Outstanding Women Athletes: Who They Are and How They Influenced Sports in America.* Phoenix, Ariz.: Oryx Press, 1992.

D

DECKER SLANEY, MARY (Mary Decker)
(1958–   ) *Long-Distance Runner*

Mary Decker Slaney, one of the most successful performers in track-and-field history, will be remembered not only for her athletic talent and endurance, which helped her overcome injury to become a world-champion middle-distance runner, but also for her unfortunate entanglement with the South African runner Zola Budd at the 1984 Olympic Games. Decker and Budd collided with one another in the middle of the race, and Decker a favorite to win the race, tripped and fell painfully to the track.

The story of the greatest U.S. runner never to win an Olympic medal began on August 4, 1959, when Mary Decker was born in Bunnvale, New Jersey. Mary fell in love with cross-country running at an early age; she began to compete when she was only 10. The next year she won her first race, and at the age of 12, she ran a marathon, along with four other middle and long-distance races, in the space of one week. At the end of the week, she was rushed to the hospital with appendicitis.

In a way, that week in Decker's life epitomized her early career on the track. Always pushing herself

for faster times, longer distances, and better finishes, it seemed as though her greatest challenge was the limit of her own body. At four feet, 10 inches tall and 108 pounds, 15-year-old "little Mary," as the teenaged Decker became known, set the running world on its ear when she took top honors in the 800-meter race at a 1973 track meet between the Soviet Union and the United States in Minsk, USSR. One year later, Mary owned world records in the 1,000-meter, 880-yard, and 800-meter events. But in 1974, Decker suffered the first of what became a long list of injuries that, in effect, kept her off the track for the better part of three years.

Decker's troubles began with a stress fracture in her ankle. The fracture did not heal properly, partially because Decker had suffered a series of shin splints as well. Adding to her physical problems, Decker had a dramatic growth spurt in late 1974; she grew six inches and gained 25 pounds in just a few months. Decker suffered compartment syndrome as a result of the spurt, meaning that her calf muscles became too large for the outer sheaf that contains them.

In 1977, Decker had surgery to correct the compartment syndrome. The operation was successful, and soon afterward she was back on track,

Although she has never won an Olympic medal,
Mary Decker Slaney is one of the top
middle-distance runners in history, competing in the
sport for more than three decades.
(Allsport Photography)

literally and figuratively. The following year she lowered her own world record in the 1,000-meter race by $^3/_{10}$ of a second. And in 1980, after overcoming yet another condition—tendinitis—she added three new world records to her résumé, setting new marks in the outdoor mile, the indoor 1,500-meter event, and the outdoor 880-yard run.

Injuries had prevented Decker from competing for a spot in the 1976 Olympics, but she was intent on participating in the 1980 games. Decker finished first in the 1,500-meter event at the Olympic trials in the spring of 1980, which assured her a place on the Olympic team. But then the United States boycotted the Moscow Games, and Decker and all the U.S. athletes were denied the opportunity to compete.

Decker continued to battle injuries in the early 1980s. She was sidelined for the entire 1981 season with a torn Achilles tendon, and she also battled chronic tendinitis and sciatica. But in 1982, a relatively healthy Decker returned to competition and enjoyed her greatest success on the track. She set new word records in the mile, the 2,000-meter and 3,000-meter events, and the 5,000-meter race. That same year, she was awarded the Jesse Owens Award for top amateur athlete.

The following year, Decker won the 1,500-meter and 3,000-meter races at the World Championships in Helsinki. Also in 1983, Decker was named the Amateur Sportswoman of the Year by the Women's Sports Foundation. Now all that Decker needed was an Olympic medal to seal a legendary career. Decker was healthy and strong; nothing, it seemed, could stand between her and her goal.

Meanwhile, a young runner by the name of Zola Budd trained in South Africa, with the hopes of competing in the 1984 Los Angeles games. Budd had rarely competed in any international races; South Africa was banned from most world events because of its apartheid (legal separation of races) practices. Intent on participating in the games, Budd took advantage of the fact that her grandfather was born in Great Britain. She applied for British citizenship. In a controversial decision, her application was granted, and she eventually qualified to run the 1,500-meter race for the British Olympic team.

Budd arrived in Los Angeles amid a sea of publicity. Would she, a barefoot runner competing for a country she had lived in for only a few months, pose a serious challenge to the fan and media favorite Mary Decker? Most experts did not think so; Decker, who had decided to concentrate solely on the 3,000-meter race, was the heavy favorite for gold. Budd might score a medal, pundits predicted, but few thought her capable of beating the world record holder.

The race began, and shortly after the halfway mark, Decker took the lead. Farther back in the pack, Budd was slowly but surely working her way toward the front. With three laps to go, Budd, now in second place, made her move. She tried to pass Decker. As Budd cut in front of the American, her foot came down in front of Decker's foot. Decker landed on Budd's ankle, and both women lost their balance. Budd was able to recover, but Decker could not. She fell to the track and immediately burst into tears. Her hopes for gold had been shattered.

Later Decker claimed that Budd had cut in too quickly. "She cut in on me before she was ahead," she told the press. "I should have pushed her, but if I had, the headline would have been 'Mary pushes Zola.'" Although Budd completed the race, her collision with Decker had also foiled her medal chances. She finished seventh.

Decker retired from track for a few years after the 1984 games. The following year, she married the British discus thrower Richard Slaney, and in 1986, the couple had a daughter. Slaney returned to the track in 1987 and continued to compete. She qualified for the Olympic team in 1988, 1992, and 1996, but she failed to earn a medal. Unperturbed, Slaney continued to compete, now in masters competitions, and set a new record in the 1,500-meter event in 1997.

But Slaney, never a stranger to difficulties, had more problems in 1998, when she tested positive for steroid use. A series of court hearings ensued, and early in 1999 her name was cleared by the U.S. Track Federation, although the International Federation removed her name from records she had set after 1996. Slaney continues to compete, unabashed, and, it seems, indefatigable. "I do it because it's how I love competing," she said of her long track career in 1996. "It's as simple as that."

Further Reading

CNN/SI online. "Mary Decker," SI For Women: 100 Greatest Athletes. Available online. URL: http://sportsillustrated.cnn.com/siforwomen/top_100/31/. Posted on November 29, 1999.

Guttmann, Alan. *Women's Sports: A History.* New York: Columbia University Press, 1991, pp. 246–247.

Hickok Sports Biographies. "Mary Decker," Hickok Sports Biographies Online. Available online. URL: http://www.hickoksports.com/biograph/deckerma.shtml. Posted on January 21, 2001.

Layden, Joe. *Women in Sports: The Complete Book on the World's Greatest Female Athletes.* Santa Monica, Calif.: General Publishing Group, 1997, pp. 221–222.

DEFRANTZ, ANITA

(1952–)   *Rower, Member of the International Olympic Committee*

Anita DeFrantz was not your ordinary jock. For one thing, DeFrantz, who grew up in hoop-crazed Indiana, did not know a thing about basketball—even when she played on her college team. More important, Anita DeFrantz, who spent her competitive years on various rowing teams, became the first U.S. woman to serve on the International Olympic Committee (IOC).

In some ways, the story of Anita DeFrantz does not begin with her birth, on October 4, 1952, but several generations earlier. The descendent of slaves (and the great-granddaughter of a white plantation owner in Louisiana and his servant), DeFrantz came of age with a deep appreciation of her family's battle to survive in U.S. society. "Knowing of the struggles my parents, my grandparents and their ancestors have faced has been an important part of my life," DeFrantz would say years later. "Respect for others is something I believe in and I make part of everything I do."

Interestingly, the things Anita DeFrantz did during her early childhood did not include sports. Although her three brothers were active athletes who all played basketball in grade school and high school, there were few opportunities for girls to play sports in Indianapolis, Indiana. Even in high school, Anita did not have a chance to play sports—there were no girls' teams. Anita kept busy doing other things, however, and when she enrolled at Connecticut College in 1970 she did so on an academic scholarship.

On campus in New London, Connecticut, DeFrantz was encouraged to find a sport she liked to play. After her debacle on the basketball court, she knew she had to look elsewhere. The answer came several days later. Walking across a quad, she noticed a man hauling a thin boat on his shoulder. Intrigued by the sight, DeFrantz asked the man what he was carrying. The man, who turned out to be rowing coach Bob Gulong, told her it was a rowing shell, and then invited DeFrantz to try out for the team.

It was love at first sight for DeFrantz and rowing. She ended up rowing competitively during all four years at Connecticut College. When it came time for her to consider graduate programs, DeFrantz chose to attend law school at the University of Pennsylvania. DeFrantz's decision was based partially on Pennsylvania's excellent reputation as a law school, but she also chose Penn because of the school's top-rated rowing program.

DeFrantz trained intensely during her three years at Penn, and while at law school she tried out for and made the 1976 Olympic rowing team. She took her talents to Montreal, where the team won a bronze medal. After getting her law degree in 1977, DeFrantz began practicing at a public-interest firm in Philadelphia. Two years later, DeFrantz took a leave of absence to train, this time with her eyes on a gold medal at the Moscow Olympics in 1980. DeFrantz once again qualified to row for the Olympic team, but this time her ambitions were spoiled by the U.S. decision to boycott the games.

Virtually every athlete was distraught by the news of the boycott. Some of them complained loudly to the press, while others remained stoic and continued training with the 1984 Los Angeles games in mind. None of them, though, reacted the way Anita DeFrantz did. Incensed by the decision to boycott, DeFrantz filed a lawsuit against the U.S. Olympic Committee (USOC).

She lost the case, but DeFrantz's commitment, passion, and intelligence caught the eye of the IOC. In 1981, DeFrantz was hired by the IOC to serve as vice president of the Organizing Committee of the 1984 Olympic Games. Two years after the Los Angeles games, De Frantz was promoted, and became the first U.S. woman—as well as the

first African-American female—to become a member of the IOC.

DeFrantz has worked her way up the IOC rankings; in 1992 she became a member of its executive board, and in 1997, she was elected first vice president. Her latest ambition, announced in March 2001, was to become the first woman president of the IOC. She was not elected but stayed on the committee's executive board.

Further Reading

Layden, Joe. *Women in Sports: The Complete Book on the World's Greatest Female Athletes.* Santa Monica, Calif.: General Publishing Group, 1997, pp. 70–71.

Women's Sports Illustrated online. "Anita DeFrantz," SI for Women: 100 Greatest Athletes. Available online. URL: http://sportsillustrated.cnn.com/siforwomen/top_100/56/. Posted November 29, 1999.

U.S. News Online. "A Rower's Olympic Dream." Available online. URL: http://www.usnews.com/usnews/issue/010312/john.peo.htm. Posted on March 3, 2001.

⊞ DE VARONA, DONNA
(1947–)   *Swimmer, Commentator*

One of the true groundbreakers in women's sports is the Olympic champion swimmer Donna de Varona. An astonishing swimmer from an early age, de Varona won two gold medals at the 1964 Olympics. But aside from her competitive talent, de Varona helped blaze the trail for other women in sports by helping to form the Women's Sports Foundation and also by becoming one of the first women commentators on television.

Donna de Varona was born on April 26, 1947, in San Diego, California. Her father, Tom de Varona, was an All-American collegiate football player who encouraged his oldest daughter to compete. Donna listened to her father but had a hard time finding other girls who loved sports as much as she did. "As a kid," she remembered later, "I can still picture myself being constantly in the wrong playground. Was it my fault I was so athletic and so full of energy?"

Her athleticism and energy would serve her well when she joined a recreational swimming program

In 1960, Donna de Varona became the youngest person to compete in the Olympics when she qualified for the U.S. swim team. Four years later, de Varona won two gold medals at the 1964 Games in Tokyo.
(Getty Images)

she grew stronger and quicker, she began to dominate the pool. A strong swimmer in every stroke, de Varona won four consecutive 400-meter individual medley outdoor titles from 1960 to 1964, as well as titles in the 200-meter individual medley outdoor event in 1963 and 1964. All told, de Varona won an astonishing 37 national titles and held 18 world records.

In 1964, de Varona once again found herself competing for the U.S. Olympic swim team. This time, she traveled to Tokyo as a favorite to win gold, and she did not disappoint. In the 400-meter medley race, de Varona knifed through the water to take the championship in an Olympic record time of five minutes, 18.7 seconds. Several days later, she won her second gold, in the 4×100 freestyle relay. De Varona returned to the United States after the games to more accolades; she was named Outstanding Athlete of the Year by both the Associated Press and United Press International.

Gold medals in pocket, de Varona decided to retire from swimming—at the grand old age of 17—in the fall of 1964. But rather than disappearing from sports altogether, de Varona merely switched directions. An articulate and intelligent young woman who felt as at home in front of the camera as she did in the water, de Varona quickly landed a job providing special commentary on swimming for ABC Sports. In doing so, she became the first woman in U.S. history to work as a television broadcaster in sports. De Varona would work for 35 years at ABC, covering swimming at numerous Olympics and also working as a special assistant to the president of ABC Sports.

Never one to rest on her laurels, de Varona continued to strive for excellence, not only on her own résumé, but for all women athletes. In the 1970s she worked as an advocate for the passage of Title IX of the Equal Education Amendment Act, which ensured that female athletes receive the same collegiate opportunities as their male counterparts. From 1974 to 1976 she served as a consultant to the U.S. Senate during its preparation for the Amateur Sports Act, which would be passed in 1978. Meanwhile, de Varona had, along

at the age of 11. She so excelled at the sport that two years later, at the age of 13, she became the youngest person ever to qualify for the U.S. Olympic swim team. The press quickly picked up on the story of the swimming phenomenon from San Diego, and in the weeks proceeding the Olympic Games, de Varona found herself on the cover of *Sports Illustrated* and *Life* magazines.

Despite the media hoopla surrounding her, Donna did not earn a medal at the 1960 Rome Olympics. After the Games ended, she returned to junior high school in California and was elected president of her eighth-grade class. Meanwhile, Donna continued to train and to compete, and as with fellow Olympic champions SHEILA YOUNG, MICKI KING, and WYOMIA TYUS, and tennis player BILLIE JEAN KING, cofounded the Women's Sports Foundation in 1973. Six years later, de Varona became its first elected president—a post she held until 1989.

In 1994, the year the United States hosted the men's World Cup soccer tournament, de Varona served on the World Cup committee. Five years later, she served as a consultant to the Women's World Cup, and helped make it one of the best-publicized and most-watched events in the history of women's sports.

De Varona suffered a setback in 2000, when ABC refused to renew her contract. Angered over what she deemed unfair treatment, she sued the station for age discrimination in April 2000. As of this writing, the case is still in litigation. De Varona has continued to work during the controversy, switching stations to serve as a special commentator for NBC during the 2000 Olympic Games in Sydney, Australia. She also spends considerable time and effort working as a motivational speaker and won Gracie Allen awards from the Foundation of American Women in Radio and Television in 2000 and 2001 for her weekly radio segment "Donna de Varona on Sports," broadcast on Sporting News Radio. In 2002 she was a member of the U.S. Olympic Committee's international relations committee. Donna de Varona lives with her two children in Connecticut.

Further Reading

Conrad, Mark. "Donna de Varona Sues ABC Sports," Mark's Sportslaw News. Available online. URL: http://www.sportslawnews.com/archive/Articles%202000/De Varona.htm. Posted on April 14, 2000.

Layden, Joe. *Women in Sports: The Complete Book on the World's Greatest Female Athletes.* Santa Monica, Calif.: General Publishing Group, 1997, pp. 72–73.

Hickok Sports Biography. "Donna de Varona," Hickok Sports Biographies Online. Available online. URL: http://www.hickoksports.com/biograph/devarona.shtml. Downloaded on May 7, 2001.

Women's Sports Illustrated online. "Donna de Varona," SI For Women: 100 Greatest Athletes. Available online.

URL: http://sportsillustrated.cnn.com/siforwomen/top_100/82/. Posted on November 29, 1999.

DEVERS, GAIL (Yolanda Gail Devers)
(1966–) *Sprinter and Hurdler*

One of the fastest women in the history of track and field, Gail Devers won back-to-back gold medals in 100-meter races at the 1992 and 1996 Olympic Games. But more than being an Olympic champion, Devers is a true survivor. Stricken with Graves' disease, a serious thyroid disorder, in 1989, she overcame the illness to attain glory.

Yolanda Gail Devers was born in Seattle, Washington, on November 19, 1966. Her father, the Reverend Larry Devers, was a Baptist pastor who instilled a strong sense of faith in his three children. When she was five years old, Gail and her family moved to San Diego, where she led what she later described as a "Leave It to Beaver" life, complete with picnics, touch football games, and Bible study.

In the midst of her wholesome childhood, Gail began running competitively in high school. As a 17-year-old 12th grader in 1984, she led Sweetwater High School to the San Diego sectional track-and-field team title. At that competition she took top honors in both the 100-meter dash and the 100-meter hurdles, and she won a silver medal in the long jump.

After graduating from Sweetwater, Devers enrolled at the University of California at Los Angeles (UCLA) on a scholarship. At UCLA she began training with Bob Kersee, the husband of Olympic champion JACKIE JOYNER-KERSEE and a talented coach in his own right. Kersee put Devers on a demanding training schedule, and the hard work paid off. In 1988 she set a U.S. record of 12.61 seconds in the 100-meter hurdles, and she won the National Collegiate Athletic Association (NCAA) title in the 100-meter dash.

But just as she was hitting her peak in her sport, Devers began to suffer symptoms that left her exhausted and confused, and this condition affected her track performances profoundly. She qualified for the 1988 Olympics in the 100-meter hurdles, but she ran too slowly in the qualifying heats to make the finals. Back in the United States after the games, Devers began to suffer more serious symptoms. Her hair began to fall out, and she experienced severe memory loss. She also suffered convulsions and migraine headaches. By early 1989 Devers had lost 23 pounds; perhaps more important, she felt like she was losing her mind. "My coach would tell me to do something, and I'd walk across the field and forget what he had said," she later said of that time.

Devers saw a host of physicians, who diagnosed different problems. Some thought her training regiment was too grueling; another suggested she had diabetes. In the meantime, she began suffering vision problems. In late 1989, Devers seriously considered giving up track and field completely, but Kersee persuaded her to keep training. Finally, in early 1990, a doctor did a series of tests and informed Devers that she was suffering from Graves' disease.

Although there were medical therapies for Graves' disease, Devers could not take them and remain eligible for the Olympics. She elected instead to undergo radiation therapy. Her symptoms improved, but she suffered painful side effects from the radiation. Blood blisters appeared on the soles of her feet and between her toes, and the pain from them became so excruciating that she could barely walk. At one point her parents had to carry her around the house; at this juncture, Devers went to a doctor, who informed her that they might have to amputate her feet. Fortunately, the blood blisters disappeared soon after Devers completed her radiation therapy.

A newly healthy Devers returned to her training and made the Olympic team in both the 100-meter dash and the 100-meter hurdles. At Barcelona, Devers suffered a temporary setback when she experienced numbness in her feet, but she continued to compete and made the finals of the 100-meter dash. During the championship race, Devers ran neck and neck with four other competitors; the event was too close to call. A taped replay showed that Devers, with a time of 10.82 seconds, had broken the tape .01 seconds ahead of the second-place finisher, Julie Cuthbert of Jamaica.

Five days later, Devers tried to become the first woman since Fannie Blankers-Koen of the Netherlands to win gold medals in both the 100-meter dash and the 100-meter hurdles. But although Devers led the race from the beginning, she tripped over the last hurdle and finished fifth. Even so, Devers left Barcelona an Olympic champion.

Back in the United States, Devers decided to continue training with Kersee, who encouraged her to try for gold once more at the 1996 games in Atlanta. In the meantime, Devers cemented her standing as the fastest woman in the world with World Championship showings in the 100-meter dash and the 100-meter hurdles events at the 1993 World Championships. She won another World Championship in the 100-meter hurdles race in 1995, and then, once again, qualified to race in both events in the Olympic Games.

In Atlanta, Devers faced off in the 100-meter race against two of her top rivals: teammate GWEN TORRENCE and Marlene Ottey of Jamaica. In one of the most thrilling finals in memory, Devers and Ottey raced down the track and crossed the line, seemingly at the exact same time. Once again, the race was too close to be decided without the help of a video replay; once again, the tape proved that Devers had broken the tape .01 seconds ahead of Ottey. With that victory, Devers became only the second woman to win back-to-back 100-meter Olympic golds; the first, WYOMIA TYUS, accomplished this feat in 1964 and 1968.

Although Devers once again was favored to win a medal in the 100-meter hurdles, she got off to a poor start and finished fourth in the final. Soon after the games, she married her fiancee, Kenny Harrison, a gold-medal winner in the triple jump in Atlanta. Devers continued to train and qualified to run the 100-meter hurdles, as well as the 100-meter relay, at the 2000 Olympic Games in Sydney, Australia. Unfortunately, Devers suffered a hamstring injury shortly before the games began and had to pull out of the competition.

Further Reading

Copernicus Education Gateway. "Capture the Olympic Spirit: Gail Devers," Griffin Publishing Group, 2000. Available online. URL: http://www.edgate.com/summergames/inactive/olympic_spirit/gail_devers.html. Downloaded on June 28, 2001.

Lessa, Christina. *Stories of Triumph.* New York: Universe, 1998.

Plowden, Martha Ward. *Olympic Black Women.* Gretna, La.: Pelican Publishers, 1996.

⊞ DIDRIKSON ZAHARIAS, BABE
(Babe Didrikson, Mildred Ella Didriksen)
(1911–1956) *High Jumper, Javelin Thrower, Runner, Golfer*

No work on women in sports would be complete without a discussion of Mildred "Babe" Didrikson Zaharias. Many experts list her not only as the single greatest female sports figure in history but as one of the finest U.S. athletes—male or female—of the 20th century.

Mildred Ella Didriksen was born in Beaumont, Texas, on June 26, 1911. She was the sixth of seven children, and her parents, Ole and Hannah Didriksen, were recent émigrés from Norway. Mildred, called "Baby" or "Babe" by her family from an early age, showed passion for both athletics and showmanship from the start. At seven, she entertained her family by tap dancing and playing the harmonica. She also excelled at tumbling in the Didriksen's gymnasium, built by her cabinetmaker father to keep his children entertained.

Babe's athletic talent became her trademark at elementary school, where she was usually the first person, male or female, chosen for team games in the playground. She acquired the reputation of a bully in school; if anyone, boy or girl, gave her grief, she would challenge him or her to a fistfight and invariably emerge triumphant. She was not an academic star at any point during her schooling, but she did have a disciplined work ethic when it came to helping her parents make ends meet. At the age of 12, she began contributing to the family income, making money doing odd jobs such as picking figs for neighboring farmers.

In high school, Babe became a star athlete in every available sport. She was the star of the girls' basketball, tennis, and golf teams, and she also won local championships in swimming and diving. Babe's athletic prowess earned her the respect of her teammates, but her unorthodox (for the time) ways also made her a social outcast. Teased by the high school boys and left out of the girls' social clubs, Babe was a loner away from the athletic fields.

Even so, Babe stayed focused on sports, and if her athletic achievements did not earn her popularity at school, they did draw the attention of local newspaper writers, who charted her extraordinary high school career on a regular basis. By the time she graduated from Beaumont High, she was a local celebrity.

The newspaper articles about Didriksen's talent caught the attention of M. J. McCombs, an executive who was the head of an industrial women's basketball team sponsored by the Employers Casualty Company (ECC), an insurance company located in Dallas. McCombs came to Beaumont to watch Didriksen play basketball and offered her a job at ECC on the spot. So it happened that Didrikson (who changed the spelling of her last name around this time) left Beaumont without hesitation and moved to Dallas to become a typist. Of course, that was only her day job. During her off hours she became the star forward on the Golden Cyclones, the ECC industrial team. Didrikson's play led the Golden Cyclones to three consecutive American Athletic Union (AAU) finals and one championship.

Delighted with Didrikson's achievements, McCombs decided to find another athletic outlet for her during the basketball off-season. McCombs started an ECC women's track-and-field team, and then he entered the ECC team in the 1930 AAU national track meet.

For Didrikson, it was a tremendous opportunity. The AAU meet was a training ground for the Olympics, and Didrikson had already set an agenda for herself: She aimed not only to compete at the Olympics, but to win gold. She realized that this was her best chance to get to the Olympics; basketball was not yet an Olympic sport, and she had not swum competitively since high school. But track and field could be her ticket—so what if she had never set foot on a track before?

So what, indeed. Didrikson starred at both the 1930 and 1931 AAU track meet, setting a record in the javelin throw in the 1930 competition and winning the 80-meter hurdles, the javelin, and the baseball throwing events the following year. In 1932, McCombs, clearly one of the great public relations geniuses of his day, came up with a ploy that was sure to generate tremendous publicity for his star athlete. The ECC track team he sent to the 1932 AAU national meet in Evanston, Illinois, would be comprised of one person only: Mildred "Babe" Didrikson.

McCombs's scheme worked: the media gave full attention to the one-person ECC team, and Babe took full advantage of the publicity opportunity by announcing to her competitors, "I'm gonna lick you single-handed."

And she kept her promise. In the events Didrikson competed in, she won five outright, with world-record performances in the baseball throw, javelin toss, 80-meter hurdles, and broad jump. She tied for first in the high jump with Jean Shiley, finished fourth in the discus, and missed out on the finals of the 100-meter dash by a hair. All in all, Didrikson racked up 30 points, good for a first-place finish. Second place went to the Illinois Women's Athletic Club, whose full team of competitors still fell shy of Babe's total by eight points.

If the media had a field day with the notion of Didrikson competing single-handedly, they went ballistic when she dominated the day. "The most amazing series of performances ever accomplished by an individual, male or female, in track and field history," crowed the *New York Times*. For Didrikson, the timing was perfect. Riding a wave of tremendous publicity, she swept into Los Angeles, completely expecting to dominate the Olympics all by herself.

Didrikson's cocky attitude made her a terrific subject for the media, but it won her no popularity

A consummate athlete, Babe Didrikson Zaharias won two gold medals at the 1932 Olympics and then went on to become a champion golfer.
(Library of Congress)

contests among her fellow Olympians. Shiley, her teammate, remembered that anyone who talked about an athletic achievement of her own would get the same response from Babe—"oh, I done that, and in *half* the time." When it came time to choose the team captain, the other women got together and collectively threw their votes to Shiley—the other candidate went so far as to drop out of the running—just to ensure that Didrikson would not be elected.

But on the field, Didrikson continued to dominate. Olympic rules limited women to three events, and Didrikson had chosen the 100-meter hurdles, the high jump, and the javelin throw. In the hurdle finals, Didrikson ran a dead heat with her teammate, Evelyn Hall. They seemed to finish the race at exactly the same time—the finish tape actually left a mark on Hall's neck—but the judges ruled that Babe had won and awarded her the gold. The javelin event proved a cleaner victory for Didrikson, as she hurled the spear 43.68 meters. The throw tore cartilage in Didrikson's shoulder, but it gave her the Olympic title.

The high jump would be Didrikson's greatest challenge; once again she was competing head to head with Shiley, with whom she had tied for first at the AAU meet earlier in the year. As in the previous tournament, Didrikson and Shiley were the last two competitors in the event—all the others had been eliminated. The women were a contrast in style as well as demeanor. Shiley's high-jumping technique featured the classic scissor-kick form, in which the legs cleared the bar first. Didrikson, by contrast, talked about her "men's style" technique, in which she would leap and roll head first over the bar. Didrikson's "western roll" later became the standard technique for all high jumpers, but at the time, it cost her the gold. After both Didrikson and Shiley cleared the bar at five feet, $5^1/_4$ inch, the judges declared Shiley the winner. Didrikson, they said, "dove" over the bar, and they awarded her the silver.

Even so, Didrikson unquestionably became a celebrity during the Los Angeles games. Her feats earned her photo opportunities with the likes of Clark Gable, as well as a new round of media attention. Not all of the column inches devoted to Didrikson were flattering, however. Some writers disliked her confidence and swagger, which they considered to be masculine traits. "I don't know whether to call her Miss, Mr., or It," wrote one journalist soon after the Olympics.

For Didrikson, the Olympics marked the achievement of one goal, but on another front, the games were a tough act to follow. She returned from Los Angeles searching for more opportunities to show off her athletic gifts. Yearning to earn money playing sports, she jumped at promoter Roy Doan's offer to tour with a men's basketball team. To make things even more enticing, the team would be called "Babe Didrikson's All-Americans."

During the mid-1930s Didrikson also played professional baseball. She appeared with Doan's House of David baseball team, which barnstormed through different states, and during the off-season she traveled to Florida and pitched exhibition games against major-league teams. She failed to dominate batters during her stint in Florida. "I gave him my high, hard one," she said of her one encounter with Philadelphia Athletics hall-of-famer Jimmie Foxx, "and he hit it to the next county." Even so, Didrikson might well have been a worthy addition to a major league team. She was a top-notch hitter, and she could run from home to first base faster than most major-league players at the time. But earlier in the decade, baseball commissioner Kenesaw Mountain Landis had voided JACKIE MITCHELL's attempts to play professional men's baseball, and Didrikson knew she would meet the same fate. If she wanted to continue playing sports, she would have to find another activity—one that accepted women, and one that she could dominate.

In the late 1930s, Didrikson married George Zaharias, a former wrestler. Around this time, she made several attempts to reenter amateur sports. Signing contracts to play both professional basketball and baseball had rendered her ineligible for the 1936 Olympics, but Zaharias was determined to regain amateur status so that she could compete in future events. The battle lasted several years, and the governing boards of virtually every amateur sport, including track and field and tennis, turned down her request. At last, in 1944, the U.S. Golfing Association (USGA) granted her amateur status. The 33-year-old Zaharias was ecstatic. Here at last was another opportunity to become a world champion.

It took Zaharias a mere two years to win her first U.S. amateur tournament, and the following year she took top honors at the British amateur event—the first U.S. golfer ever to do that. Zaharias would go on to capture 31 Ladies Professional Golf Association (she had turned professional when the LPGA was founded in 1948) events in her 10-year career as a golfer. She won the last of these in 1954, one year after she had been diagnosed with rectal cancer. Two years later, she died of the disease.

In 1950, the Associated Press honored Zaharias as the finest woman athlete of the first half of the 20 century. Fifty years later, in January 2000, *Sports Illustrated* named her the top woman athlete of the entire 20th century. It can be said without hyperbole that more than any other athlete Babe Didrikson Zaharias changed the face of women's sports in this country. Not only her on-field achievements, but her willingness to promote herself—and to carry on in the face of criticism—gave credence to the idea that women can indeed be world-class athletes, and they are every bit as exciting and talented as their male counterparts.

Further Reading

Cayleff, Susan. *Babe: The Life & Legend of Babe Didrikson Zaharias.* Champaign, Ill.: University of Illinois Press, 1996.

Gregorich, Barbara. *Women at Play: The Story of Women in Baseball.* New York: Harcourt Brace, 1993, pp. 73–78.

Smith, Lissa, editor. *Nike Is a Goddess: The History of Women in Sports.* New York: Atlantic Monthly Press, 1998, pp. 9–12.

Sugar, Bert Randolph. *The Sports 100: A Ranking of the Greatest Athletes of All Time.* Secaucus, N.J.: Citadel Press, 1995.

▓ DRAGILA, STACY
(1971–)   *Pole Vaulter*

Pole vaulting did not become a sanctioned Olympic event for women until 2000. That year, a Californian named Stacy Dragila became the first woman to win a gold medal in the sport.

Born on March 25, 1971, in Auburn, California, Stacy Dragila grew up on her family's farm. During the summer she would compete in local rodeo events, excelling in such specialized sports as goat-tying. She also could run and jump, and she competed for her high school track-and-field team in the heptathlon.

Unlike the decathlon, the 10-tiered event for men, the heptathlon does not include the pole vault. Instead, each participant must run two short sprints and a long-distance race, long jump, high jump, and

throw a shot put and javelin. Dragila was a good enough heptathlete to earn an athletic scholarship to Idaho State University. At practice one day on campus, Dragila's coach, Dave Nielson, challenged all the heptathletes to try the pole vault. Like her teammates, Dragila found the pole heavy and difficult to bend. She also had a great deal of trouble clearing the bar, which was set at six feet. This height is actually quite low for experienced pole vaulters, but for Dragila and her cohorts, it seemed impossible. "The first couple trillion times going over the bar were pretty frightening to me," she remembered later.

Intrigued by the sport, Dragila knew that she had to increase her upper body strength if she wanted to improve. She began training in gymnastics and kept practicing. Soon she began to improve and then to excel. Unfortunately, Dragila had little opportunity to compete against other women, so she practiced against her own teammates instead. In 1994, Dragila, then a senior at Idaho State, vaulted 10 feet in an indoor competition. Several weeks later, she saw a copy of the *Track and Field News* and learned that her 10-foot vault had set a U.S. record.

The following year, Dragila competed in the U.S. Outdoor Championships. By this time, women's pole vaulting was becoming a fast-growing and increasingly competitive sport. Although she finished second to Melissa Price, Dragila was thrilled to be in a tournament that featured such elite athletes as JACKIE JOYNER-KERSEE and Carl Lewis. It was the first time the women's pole vault was featured at the championships, and Dragila was determined to help publicize her sport. She had the perfect opportunity to do so at the 1997 Indoor Championships, where she won the first women's pole vault title. Two years later, Dragila won the 1999 World Championships, tying Emma George's world-record vault of 15 feet, 1 inch, in the process.

Dragila was thrilled to own a World Championship title, but her greatest desire was to compete in the Olympics. She hoped that the sport would become a sanctioned event at the 2000 Sydney games, and she learned, late in 1999, that her wish would come true. Preparing for the games in the

65

May 2000, Dragila vaulted 15 feet, 1$^3/_4$ inches, at a meet in Phoenix to become the world record holder. A month later, she lowered her own record with a 15 foot, 2$^1/_4$-inch, effort at the Olympic trials.

In Sydney, Dragila prepared to compete in the track-and-field arena. Looking around the stadium, Dragila realized that thousands of fans were cheering her and her fellow competitors. Before each vault, Dragila and her rivals raised their arms above their heads and clapped, encouraging the crowd's enthusiasm. But although Dragila might have been swept away momentarily by the crowd, she was all business as she held the pole and ran toward the bar during her gold-medal vault. "I knew I had to jump within myself and keep my head on my shoulders," she told a journalist. Dragila, who had missed her first two attempts at 15 feet, 1 inch, cleared the bar on her final attempt to clinch the gold.

In 2000, Dragila set a new indoor record when she vaulted 15 feet, 2$^3/_4$ inches at the Millrose games. She broke that mark two months later with a vault of 15 feet, 5 inches at the World Indoor Championships and rounded out the year with a new outdoor mark of 15 feet, 10 inches. A true pioneer in the women's pole vault, Dragila is delighted to be a part of history in the making. "I feel like I'm living a dream," she said in 2001. "Critics said women couldn't do that, couldn't do 14 feet. Now it's 15 feet and 16 feet and you wonder, what can women really do?"

Further Reading

Cazeneuve, Brian. "On in an Off Year," *Sports Illustrated,* September 17, 2001, p. 90.

Donnelly, Sally B. "The Pioneer of the Pole Vault," *Time,* September 3, 2001, p. 66.

Layden, Tim. "Down to Earth," *Sports Illustrated for Women,* May/June 2001, p. 96.

Longman, Jere. "Women Move Closer to Olympic Equality," *The New York Times,* August 20, 2000 1, 22.

DRISCOLL, JEAN
(1966–) *Basketball Player, Racer*

Perhaps the finest athlete ever to compete in a wheelchair, Jean Driscoll holds eight Boston Marathon

Born with spina bifida, Jean Driscoll excels at both basketball and marathon racing. Here she crosses the finish line to win one of her eight Boston marathon titles.
(Al Bello/Getty Images)

titles—a record for any competitor in that event. In addition, Driscoll has won two Olympic silver medals and four gold Paralympic medals.

Born on November 18, 1966, Jean Driscoll has spina bifida, a genetic disease. Spina bifida prevents vertebrae in the spine from connecting, leaving nerves in the person's lower body unconnected. As a result of her disease, Driscoll cannot use her legs. But that has never stopped her from moving fast.

From early childhood, Jean was active and athletic. She played football, soccer, tennis, and racquetball as a child, but when she got to college at the University of Illinois at Champaign/Urbana, she fell in love with basketball. Thrilled to be in the company of athletes in a similar situation, Driscoll quickly became the leader of the Illinois team. During her college career, she captured three most-valuable-player awards for her basketball talent.

It was also at the University of Illinois that Driscoll discovered wheelchair racing. Splitting her training time between racing and basketball, Driscoll nevertheless became one of the top racers in the nation by her senior year. In 1990, Driscoll began her assault on the fabled Boston Marathon, capturing her first title there in world-record time of 1 hour, 44 minutes, and 9 seconds. (The wheelchair division of the Boston Marathon covers 26.1 miles—the same length as the regular race.) That same year, she played on the national championship wheelchair basketball team.

In 1991, Driscoll received one her greatest honors when she was named Sportswoman of the Year by the Women's Sports Foundation. Driscoll was especially delighted with the award because its previous winners include MARY LOU RETTON, JACKIE JOYNER-KERSEE, and JANET EVANS. For Driscoll, who has always aimed to be recognized as a competitor, rather than a competitor with a disability, this was a dream come true.

After playing another year on the national championship basketball team, Driscoll decided to concentrate fully on wheelchair racing in 1992. That year she won her third consecutive Boston Marathon—breaking her world record with a time of 1:36:52. She would go on to win the race in 1993, 1994, 1995, and 1996. In the 1997 marathon, Driscoll suffered a fall when the wheel of her chair snagged a trolley track at the 22-mile

mark. Then, after finishing second to Australia's Louise Sauvage in 1998 and 1999, Driscoll stormed back to take her eighth Boston Marathon crown in 2000.

Driscoll has also excelled at track racing. She entered the 800-meter exhibition events at the 1992 and 1996 Olympics, and she emerged both times with silver medals. She also helped lead the U.S. 4 × 400 meter relay team to a gold medal in the 1992 games. Driscoll continues to compete in wheelchair races, both on the road and on the track. She has also become a highly recruited motivational speaker and is a participating member of the Illinois Council of Health and Fitness.

Further Reading

CNN.SI for Women, 100 Greatest Female Athletes. "Jean Driscoll," *Sports Illustrated for Women.* Available online. URL: http://sportsillustrated.cnn.com/siforwomen/top_100/90/. Posted on November 29, 1999.

Layden, Joe, *Women in Sports: The Complete Book of the World's Greatest Female Athletes.* Santa Monica, Calif.: General Publishing Group, 1997, pp. 77–78.

1999 Women's Sports Legends. "Jean Driscoll." Available online. URL: http://www.wskgends.com/speakers_jean_driscoll.htm. Downloaded on March 15, 2001.

Women's Sports Foundation. "Jean Driscoll: On a Roll." Available online. URL: http://www.womenssportsfoundation.org/WoSport/stage/TOPISS/html/jeandriscoll.html. Downloaded on March 15, 2001.

E

EDERLE, GERTRUDE
(1906–) *Swimmer*

In 1926, an 18-year-old New Yorker named Gertrude Ederle became the first woman to swim across the body of water called the English Channel, which separates Great Britain from France.

Born in New York City on October 23, 1906, "Trudy" Ederle is the only daughter of a German butcher and his homemaker wife. Trudy learned to swim during summer trips to the seashore, and when she was 13, she joined a local swimming club in New York to learn proper technique.

She made astonishing progress at the swimming club; she was still 13 when she broke the world record in the 880-yard freestyle swim. And a mere three years later, at the age of 16, she swam in the 1924 Olympics in Paris and won three medals, including a gold in the 4 × 100 freestyle relay. By the time she was 19, Ederle was the holder of 29 world records, swimming distances ranging from 50 yards to half a mile.

With her Olympic victories, Ederle was one of the most decorated women in the history of swimming. But at 20 years of age, she longed for greater challenges. Specifically, she had her eye on the English Channel. In 1925, Ederle and her mother, borrowing money from the World Swimming Association, sailed to France, ready to challenge the channel. For the first few hours in the water, Ederle swam smoothly. But when she was a little more than halfway through the 16-mile challenge, the tide changed, and strong waves began throwing her off course. Severely seasick and only half conscious, Ederle was pulled from the water.

She had failed in her first attempt, but Ederle remained determined. The following year, Ederle took a risk and turned professional, signing a contract that would pay her passage to France, as well as training expenses. Signing the professional contract meant that Ederle could no longer swim in the Olympics, but Ederle was so completely focused on crossing the channel that she decided to give up her amateur status without a moment's hesitation.

One year later, Ederle arrived in France again. The European press remained skeptical that a woman could successfully make the crossing; "Even the most uncompromising champion of the rights and capacities of women must admit that in contests of physical skill, speed and endurance, they must remain forever the weaker sex," the London *Daily News* wrote, shortly before Ederle's attempt.

But on the morning of August 6, 1926, Ederle greased her body with her own concoction of olive oil, lanolin, and petroleum jelly, and she entered the water. Once again, at the halfway mark, the weather turned rough, and the tide began blowing Ederle off course. Ederle kept swimming, but when she had been in the water for 12 hours, she was fighting a horrendous tide that was consistently throwing her back. She was cold, nauseous, and completely waterlogged. Her companions, sitting in the warm safety of their boats, wanted her to quit but did not want to be the ones to force her to fail a second time. Finally, one of the members of her party shouted to her from his vessel: "Trudy, you must come out!" This time, the young American lifted her head out of the water and asked calmly, "What for?" The cliffs of Dover, Ederle's destination in England, were becoming more and more visible.

Two hours later, Gertrude Ederle walked out of the water and onto those cliffs. Interestingly, the first person to greet the young swimmer in Dover was an immigration officer, who asked her for her passport. Ederle, in a bathing suit and cap, did not have it in her possession (one of her companions did, and Ederle was granted entry into Great Britain). On a more serious note, Gertrude Ederle had crossed the channel in 14 hours and 31 minutes; not only had she become the first woman to swim from France to England, but she had broken the record set by the fastest man to make the journey—by more than two hours.

The U.S. media was delighted by Ederle's feat; they wanted her to come back to the United States immediately for a parade in New York City. Sponsors and promoters began peppering Ederle with personal-appearance requests; she and her agent waded through dozens of offers while she was still in England. But what Ederle wanted most of all was to visit her grandparents, who were still living in Germany. At the height of her fame, she journeyed to the Continent and spent two weeks with her family.

During Ederle's stay in Germany, another woman swam the channel. The new conqueror, Mille Gade Corson, was a Frenchwoman. And although her time was an hour slower than Ederle's, the achievement took a bit of the initial excitement away from Ederle's feat. Even so, when Ederle returned to the United States, she received the largest ticker tape parade that New York City had ever thrown. (A year later, a bigger one still would greet Charles Lindbergh after his transatlantic flight.)

But Ederle was never able to cash in on her achievement; the offers from sponsors dwindled steadily after her return, and her agent had foolishly turned down those that did come in, saying that they were not lucrative enough. In the years following her channel swim, Ederle made several promotional appearances, but she used much of the money she earned to repay the Women's Swimming Association for the loan it had made to her during her initial attempt to cross the channel in 1925.

Eventually Ederle's grueling hours in the water took a toll on her. Her hearing, which had been damaged during her channel swim, gradually diminished until she was almost completely deaf. In 1928, worn down by the sudden fame and its less-than-glamorous aftermath, she suffered a nervous breakdown. She recovered several months later, but in 1930 she hurt her back in an aquatic appearance and had to spend four years in a body cast.

Eventually she returned to the water and made a living as a swimming teacher. In 1939 she played a small role as a swimmer in producer Billy Rose's Aquacade, an extravaganza at the 1939 World's Fair in New York City. Ederle made her last public appearance in 1976, when she was invited to come to New York to mark the 50th anniversary of her channel swim.

Further Reading

Gallico, Paul. "Gertrude Ederle," *Women's Game,* edited by Dick Wimmer. Short Hills, N.J.: Burford Books, 1988, pp. 69–83.

Hickok Sports Biographies. "Gertrude Ederle," Hickok Sports Biographies Online. Available online. URL: http://www.hickoksports.com/biograph/ederlegert.shtml. Downloaded on January 28, 2001.

EDWARDS, TERESA
(1964–   ) *Basketball Player*

Women's basketball standout Teresa Edwards played in five Olympic games, spanning three decades, and took home five medals—four of them gold.

Teresa Edwards was born on July 19, 1964, in Cairo, Georgia. Her four brothers shared one room in their small house, and Teresa and her mother, Mildred Edwards, shared the other. Teresa and her mother were very close, but there was one thing they did not agree on: Mildred did not want her daughter to try out for the basketball team at Washington Middle School. She worried that Teresa would spend too much time on the court and ignore her education. Although Teresa had always been an obedient girl, this time she did not listen to her mother. She tried out for the team without telling Mildred, and her mother did not realize that Teresa was playing basketball at all until she found a pair of sneakers in their room. Mildred was angry at first, but she changed her mind when she saw her daughter play.

Mildred was not the only one impressed by Teresa's play. At the end of an All-American high school career, Teresa won a full athletic scholarship to the University of Georgia. At Georgia, Edwards quickly became the on-court leader, and she played a vital role in the Lady Bulldogs' three consecutive Southeastern Conference championships. During her junior and senior years, Edwards won All-America honors and took her team to the Final Four of the National Collegiate Athletic Association (NCAA) championships.

Edwards also achieved a personal milestone during her collegiate career. After her sophomore season, she competed for the United States at the 1984 Olympic Games in Los Angeles. At age 20, Edwards was the youngest member of the team, and she spent the bulk of the games cheering her teammates on from the bench. Nevertheless, when the games ended, Edwards had won her first gold medal.

After graduating from Georgia in 1986, Edwards decided to move to Europe, which at the

Teresa Edwards's wizardry at the point guard position led the United States to the gold medal at the 1996 Olympic Games. Edwards competed in five Olympic Games and won a total of four gold medals. *(Stu Forster/Getty Images)*

time was the only choice for women who wanted to play professional basketball. Edwards signed with an Italian team, and three years later she moved to Japan. In both Europe and Asia, Edwards performed brilliantly, averaging between 30 and 40 points per game during her seven seasons there. During her overseas career Edwards returned twice to compete in the Olympics. In 1988 she led the U.S. team to a gold medal in Seoul, Korea, with a stellar performance throughout the tournament. In 1992 she played on the bronze medal–winning U.S. team in Barcelona. That year the United States lost a close semifinal game to the newly formed united team from the former Soviet Union but then clinched the bronze by beating Cuba.

In 1995, Edwards returned to the United States to compete for the national team again. At age 31, Edwards, competing in her fourth Olympics, was now the oldest member of the team, and she remained a leader, serving as cocaptain during the 52-game national tour that preceded the Olympics. In Atlanta, Edwards, who had expected to serve as a substitute point guard behind DAWN STALEY, found herself on the starting team when Staley suffered an injury before the first game. The point guard is the quarterback of a basketball offense. She controls the ball down the floor and then usually will pass to an open player. Being a point guard takes leadership, confidence, and control. As she always had during her career, Edwards showed an abundance of all three. She guided the team through the tournament and into the final game, where the U.S. team beat Brazil soundly to win the gold.

A year after Atlanta, Edwards decided to join the American Basketball League (ABL), one of two new professional leagues that were formed in 1997 (the Women's National Basketball Association [WNBA] was the other). Returning to Georgia, Edwards became a member of the ABL's Atlanta Glory. But after her two stellar, all-star seasons in Atlanta, the ABL folded. Edwards had an opportunity to sign with a WNBA team in 1999, but she declined the offer. Instead, she decided to train for one final trip to the Olympics. When the U.S. team flew into Sydney, Australia, in September 2000 to defend its gold medal, Teresa Edwards was there, ready to play.

And play she did. Backing up Staley, Edwards made valuable plays throughout the tournament. And as the final seconds of the clock ticked down during the last game, Edwards stood on the floor, hugging her teammates. At the age of 35, she had won her fourth Olympic gold.

Edwards decided to retire from competitive basketball after the Sydney Olympics, planning to remain involved in the women's game as either a coach or an administrator. Although Edwards

applauds the way the women's game has progressed during the course of her career, she stresses that it still has a way to go. "Women are still playing basic basketball," she says. "The next level for us is to play more creative basketball, and that is where we have to learn from the men."

Further Reading

CNN.SI for Women, 100 Greatest Female Athletes. "Teresa Edwards," *Sports Illustrated for Women.* Available online. URL: http://sportsillustrated.cnn.com/siforwomen/top_100/90/. Posted on November 29, 1999.

Norwood, Robyn. "Seven Days to the Sydney Olympics," *Los Angeles Times,* September 8, 2000, n.p.

Rutledge, Rachel. *The Best of the Best in Basketball.* Brookfield, Conn.: Millbrook Press, 1998, pp. 21–24.

EVANS, JANET
(1971–) *Swimmer*

Janet Evans, a winner of four Olympic gold medals and a veteran of three Olympic games, has never looked like a swimmer. Small and lithe where most others in her sport are big and muscular, Evans nevertheless proved to be the finest long-distance swimmer of her time, and she has three world records to prove it.

Born in Fullerton, California, on August 28, 1971, Janet was walking by the time she was eight months old. Her parents, Paul, a veterinarian, and Barbara, a homemaker, noticed that Janet loved to follow her older brothers around. They also noted her immense energy levels and discovered that the best way to calm her down was to put her in the swimming pool. Janet was enrolled in swimming lessons while still a toddler, and by the time she was three, had learned to swim the breaststroke and the butterfly.

When Janet was 11, she qualified for the Junior Olympics. Over the next four years, she moved up in the rankings, and in 1986, she made the national swim team and traveled to Moscow to swim in the Goodwill Games. The other swimmers took one look at the diminutive Evans, who was swimming in her first international race, and likely decided

Although her competitors thought she did not look like a swimmer, Janet Evans dominated long-distance events in the late 1980s and early 1990s.
(Donald Miralle/Getty Images)

that she would hardly be a threat. But Evans put her rivals on notice with third-place finishes with 800- and 1,500-meter freestyle races. Evans might not have been as big as the other swimmers, but she moved her arms and legs much more quickly.

In 1987, Evans set world records in the 800- and 1,500-meter freestyle races at the U.S. Long Course Championships. A month later, at the U.S. Indoor Championships, she added another record, in the 400-meter freestyle race. Evans swam even more impressively at the 1988 Olympic trials, breaking her own world records in both the 800- and 1,500-meter freestyle events and winning the 400-meter race with ease.

At the age of 17, Evans was a triple world record holder. She was also a heavy favorite to win gold at the Seoul Olympics. She arrived in South Korea—

all five feet, 100 pounds of her—and promptly lived up to her hype. Evans won the 400-meter freestyle with ease and set a new world record in the process. A few days later she set a new U.S. record to win the 400-meter individual medley event. Then Evans added a third individual gold medal with an Olympic-record performance in the 400-meter freestyle event.

Evans was undoubtedly the star of the Olympic swim team at the 1988 games—the only woman to win a medal in an individual event. She returned to California and received a hero's welcome, and soon after, she went to the White House to meet President George H. W. Bush. Evans was a celebrity, but more than anything, she wanted a normal life. She turned down several endorsement opportunities and elected to attend Stanford University on a scholarship.

At Stanford, Evans experienced an intense physical growth spurt that added two inches and 15 pounds to her frame. She had trouble adjusting to her new size and became frustrated with her swimming for the first time in her life. She elected to transfer to the University of Texas, where she trained under Mark Shumbert, the U.S. Olympic team coach.

Evans soon returned to top form, breaking her own world record in the 800-meter freestyle at the 1989 Pan Pacific Games and winning three gold medals at the 1992 Goodwill Games. She was expected to qualify for the 1992 Olympic team in the 400-meter freestyle, the 400-meter individual medley, and the 800-meter freestyle events. But although Evans easily made the 400-meter and 800-meter freestyle squads, she swam poorly during her 400-meter medley race and failed to make the cut.

Disappointed with her performance in the 400-meter individual medley race at the trials, Evans traveled to Barcelona determined to defend her other two Olympic gold medals successfully. She did win gold in the 800-meter freestyle, and she took a silver in the 400-meter freestyle race. Evans's 800-meter gold in Barcelona made her the third U.S. woman in Olympic history to win four gold medals (PAT MCCORMICK and EVELYN ASHFORD are the others). It was a record that would stand until BONNIE BLAIR won her fifth gold medal, at the 1994 games in Lillehammer.

After the Barcelona games, Evans returned to the United States, and she decided to continue swimming and prepare for the 1996 Olympics in Atlanta. Although she could easily have retired, it was important to Evans to compete in her own country. She swam gallantly at the 1996 trials, and she qualified for both the 400-meter and 800-meter freestyle races. Evans did not win a medal at the Atlanta games, but she had a thrilling experience nevertheless when she was chosen to carry the Olympic torch around the stadium during the opening ceremony. During one of the most moving moments in modern Olympic history, Evans handed the torch to Muhammad Ali, who turned and lit the Olympic flame.

Evans retired from swimming after the 1996 games. She moved back to California, where she planned to go to law school or become a journalist. She also took up long-distance running and became a regular competitor at many national marathon races.

Further Reading

Smith, Lissa, editor. *Nike Is a Goddess: The History of Women in Sports.* New York: Atlantic Monthly Press, 1998, pp. 32–35.

Vecsey, George. "Evans Seeks a Career as a Landlubber," *New York Times,* July 18, 1996.

EVERT, CHRIS (Christine Marie Evert, Chris Evert Lloyd)
(1954–) *Tennis Player, Commentator*

Champion tennis players come and go, but never in the history of the sport was there a player with the discipline and the sheer consistency of Chris Evert. The holder of 18 career Grand Slam singles titles, Evert won an astonishing 125 consecutive clay court matches. By the time she retired in 1989, Evert, who had spent 18 years under the media glare of professional tennis, was one of the most beloved champions of all time.

Christine Marie Evert was born in Fort Lauderdale, Florida, on December 21, 1954. She was the second of five children born to Jimmy Evert, a former tennis player-turned coach, and his wife, Colette, a homemaker. Jimmy Evert, who was a ranked tennis player in the 1940s, felt strongly that his children should learn the game at an early age. As a result, all five Evert children were playing tennis by the age of six. Because they began playing at such a young age, Jimmy instructed his children to keep both hands on the racket handle when they hit backhand shots. The two-handed backhand would later become Chris Evert's trademark stroke.

Evert spent much of her childhood on the tennis court, hitting ground strokes with her father. Through his guidance she learned to hit the ball cleanly, perfectly, and consistently. So consistently, in fact, that by the time she was 15 she was playing top-caliber professionals—and making them sweat. "I had to fight for my life," Nancy Richey, at the time the second-ranked player in America, recalled after escaping with a three-set victory over the Florida teenager in 1970. "I couldn't believe a girl that young could play like that."

Playing like that did not come easily to Evert. Although she was a decent athlete with good instincts, she lacked the natural gracefulness of Evonne Goolagong, the all-court virtuosity of BILLIE JEAN KING, and the sheer athleticism of MARTINA NAVRATILOVA. But what Evert had—impeccable concentration and perhaps the most consistent ground strokes the game has ever seen—were enough to propel her to the upper echelon of the game by 1971. That year, 17-year-old Chris Evert made her first Grand Slam appearance, at the U.S. Open in Forest Hills, New York. With little on-court fanfare and frightening strokes, Evert promptly mowed down past champions Françoise Durr and then Margaret Court—the number-one player in the game—en route to the tournament's semifinals. Although Evert was dispatched in straight sets by Billie Jean King in that match, she had made her mark on the game—and on her rivals.

The year after her U.S. Open debut and at the age of 18, Evert turned professional. But her first few years on the tour were not easy ones. The early 1970s were key years for women tennis players. It was in 1970 that a group of eight players, led by Billie Jean King, had split off from the established circuit to start their own all-women's tour. Through a series of struggles, King and her cohorts had finally managed to make a name for women's tennis. But just as they were savoring their triumph, here was a new face on the scene—a young woman who had no part of their struggle, but who was threatening to steal their success. Evert, with her ribboned ponytails and feminine dresses, had quickly become a crowd and media favorite. But off the court she was often ostracized.

Evert no doubt felt tremendously isolated during those early years on the tour, but she never let her feelings interfere with her concentration or

determination on the court. She continued her assault on the tennis tour; in 1973 she reached the Wimbledon final, where once again she fell in straight sets to Billie Jean King. And the following year, Evert took the Wimbledon championship, beating Olga Marazova to take her first Grand Slam title.

The other women on the tour could easily have become more resentful still of Evert; not only was she the most photographed and popular (with fans and media) woman on the tour, but she was also a legitimate champion. At that point, Billie Jean King realized that the attention received by the golden Floridian with the blistering backhand was actually quite good for the game. King decided to reach out to Evert and asked her to be her doubles partner. The two made a successful doubles team, but more important, the partnership made Evert an accepted presence on the women's tour.

In 1974 Evert was involved in another partnership as well; after the Wimbledon tournament she and her boyfriend, gentleman's singles champion Jimmy Connors, further charmed the tennis world by announcing their engagement. Connors and Evert were an intriguing pair; both relentless backcourt players, they had each learned the game from a parent. Evert, of course, was taught by her father, and Connors learned the game from his teacher/coach/mother, Gloria. To make things even more symmetrical, Jimmy Evert and Gloria Connors had briefly dated one another during their playing days. But Connors and Evert the romantic team did not last; they broke off their engagement later in 1974 and split for good the following year.

By that time, Evert was battling King for the number-one ranking. King took top honors at Wimbledon in 1975, but Evert triumphed at both the U.S. Open and French Open. The following year Evert was even more dominating, winning at Wimbledon and repeating as U.S. Open champion. Evert was named the *Sports Illustrated* Sportswoman of the Year in 1976. She was the second woman in the history of the magazine to receive the honor; King had done it in 1972.

In 1977, Evert stumbled at Wimbledon, losing to eventual champion Virginia Wade in the semifinals, but she won the U.S. Open in the tournament's final year at Forest Hills. The next year, Evert reached the final of Wimbledon for the fourth time. Across the net from Evert stood an 18-year-old Czechoslovakian who would become Evert's friend and chief opponent for the next decade. Evert lost the 1978 Wimbledon final to Martina Navratilova in a three-set duel, and perhaps the most celebrated rivalry in the history of women's Grand Slam tennis was off and running.

Evert and Navratilova were polar opposites on the court. The cool and patient Evert patrolled the baseline and often won a majority of her points on her opponents' errors. Navratilova, by contrast, was a vastly emotional player with a powerful serve and volley. She was erratic while Evert was consistent, powerful while Evert was precise, and emotional while Evert was collected. Their differences made their matches—80 in all—fascinating to witness. The two women also developed a close friendship off the court; they would often eat a meal together before playing one another.

As Navratilova's game improved in the early 1980s, she began winning the majority of her matches against Evert. By 1982, in fact, she had replaced Evert as the world's number-one player. But although Navratilova held the number-one spot in the rankings, it was Evert who remained the crowd favorite. Navratilova was a stronger, more muscular player than Evert, but although those attributes helped her game, they were a disadvantage in her attempts to win fan and media approval in her adopted country (Navratilova had defected to the United States in 1975 and became an U.S. citizen in 1981). Evert was perceived as the more feminine—and therefore the more accepted—of the duo.

To make the distinction between the players starker still, Evert led a more traditional lifestyle off the court. Part of Evert's appeal to mainstream tennis fans was her off-court romances, not only with Connors, but with a host of different men, including such celebrities as Burt Reynolds in the 1970s. In 1981 Evert married John Lloyd, a British tennis player. When that marriage failed in 1985, she met (at a party at Navratilova's home) Andy Mill, a former Olympic skier. The two married in 1987. Navratilova, in the meantime, was outspoken about her homosexuality, making her a pioneer on a very important front, but costing her fan approval—and endorsement dollars—throughout much of her career.

In 1986, Evert scored her 18th and final Grand Slam victory. She did it in impressive style, beating Navratilova in the finals of the French Open in one of the most memorable matches ever played there. After dropping the first set to her rival, Evert came storming back, pinning Navratilova to the baseline with deep and powerful ground strokes, as well as a potent drop shot that would die on the court as Navratilova lunged in vain. At the end of the match Evert had triumphed, 2–6, 6–3, 6–3. With the victory Evert took her seventh French Open title, shattering the previous mark of six, held for six decades by the great French player Suzanne Lenglen.

By 1989 Evert knew her best playing days were behind her, and she longed for a life outside of tennis. "I'm going to be a wife and mother," she told *Sports Illustrated* when she announced her retirement. After losing to Zina Garrison in the third round of the U.S. Open in August 1989, Evert left the court—to a standing ovation—and the game. She and Mills had their first child two years later. After her retirement, Evert became a tennis commentator, calling major tennis championships for NBC. She and Mills also became hosts of the Chris Evert Pro/Celebrity tennis tournament, the proceeds of which go to various charities.

Evert was not only one of tennis's most prolific champions, but one of its most gracious ones as well. Throughout her career she never argued calls, never lost her temper or her composure, and never blamed a rare poor performance on injury or circumstance. Those qualities, along with her ability to keep winning major championships over a career that spanned almost three decades, make her one of the most successful athletes in the history of U.S. sports. She may not have been as revolutionary as King or as outspoken as Navratilova, but Evert's contributions to the sport of tennis are no less important, and just as enduring.

Further Reading

Evert Lloyd, Chris, and Neil Amdur. *Chrissie: My Own Story*. New York: Simon & Schuster, 1982.

Layden, Joe. *Women in Sports: The Complete Book of the World's Greatest Female Athletes*. Santa Monica, Calif.: General Publishing Group, Inc., 1997, pp. 86–87.

Smith, Lissa, editor. *Nike Is a Goddess: The History of Women in Sports*. New York: Atlantic Monthly Press, 1998, pp. 69–71, 150–151.

F

FERNANDEZ, LISA
(1971–)   *Softball Player*

When Lisa Fernandez was 12 years old, a softball coach advised her to give up the game. Her arms were too short, the coach observed, for her to ever be a champion pitcher. Despite that advice, Fernandez, who has powered the U.S. softball team to two Olympic gold medals, stayed with the sport and became a champion.

Born on February 22, 1971, in Long Beach, California, Lisa Fernandez inherited her parents' love for the game of softball. Lisa's father, Antonio, played semipro baseball in his native Cuba before immigrating to the United States, and her mother, Emilia, became her first coach. Lisa decided to become a pitcher when she was seven years old. A coach saw her practicing and invited her to try out for his team. Lisa made the squad, but her first game was disastrous—a 25-0 rout.

Lisa's pitching improved steadily since that rather cruel initiation, and at St. Joseph's High School, she pitched more than 65 shutout games. She then went on to the University of California at Los Angeles (UCLA) on a softball scholarship, where her brilliant pitching led the Bruins to two

Women's College World Series championships. During her four years in a UCLA uniform, Fernandez won 93 games and lost only seven. An offensive threat as well, she compiled a collegiate batting average of .382.

After graduating from UCLA in 1993, Fernandez continued to play softball for the U.S. national team, which she had joined in 1991. In 1994, the team took home the gold metal at the International Softball Federation (ISF) Women's World Championship, and the following year it took top honors at the South Pacific Classic in Sydney, Australia. Fernandez then pitched a no-hitter to lift the U.S. team to gold at the 1995 Pan-American Games. Two months later it was announced that in 1996, for the first time, the Olympics would award a medal for women's softball.

The games, which in 1996 were in Atlanta, were a triumph for the U.S. softball team. Playing in front of a highly partisan home crowd, the team scorched through the competition, losing only once on their way to the gold medal. Fernandez, who batted a stellar .348, pitched splendidly. Although she lost one game—a heartbreaker against Australia in which she had a perfect game for nine full innings before giving up one solo home run in the bottom of the 10th—she also shut out the Chinese team by a score of 1-0 in a semifinal game. Then, pitching again against the Chinese in the gold-medal contest, she earned a save with stellar hurling to seal the championship for the U.S.A. team.

After the 1996 games, Fernandez remained involved in softball, both playing and coaching. She took a job as an assistant coach at her alma mater, UCLA, and also continued to play for the national team. In 2000, Fernandez and her teammates traveled to Australia to defend their Olympic gold medal. This time the competition was tougher, and the Americans, playing on foreign soil, struggled with their game. But Fernandez shone, pitching a masterful 1-0 shutout against the hometown Australian team to put the United States in the final. One day later, she took the mound again for the gold medal game, and she allowed only three hits as the United States bested Japan by a 3–1 score.

Decorated with her second gold medal, Fernandez returned to the United States, where she continues to coach at UCLA and to play for the national team.

Further Reading

Gale Group, "Lisa Fernandez Prepares for Glory," Celebrating Hispanic Heritage. Available online, URL: http://www.galegroup.com/frerescrc/chh/fernandez.htm. Downloaded on July 11, 2001.

Smith, Lissa, editor. *Nike Is a Goddess: The History of Women in Sports*. New York: Atlantic Monthly Press, 1998, pp. 254–256.

UCLA Women's Softball. "Lisa Fernandez," UCLA Bruins Online. Available online, URL: http://www.uclabruins.com/softball/fernandezbio.htm. Downloaded July 11, 2001.

FLEMING, PEGGY (Peggy Gale Fleming)
(1948–) *Figure Skater, Commentator*

Peggy Fleming, the gold-medal winner in the ladies' figure skating event at the 1968 Olympics, was one of the United States' most graceful skaters.

Combining a lyrical artistry and a balletic elegance, Fleming brought a new level of sophistication to the sport.

Born on July 27, 1948, in Pasadena, California, Peggy Gale Fleming was nine years old when she skated for the first time. Her father, Albert, a pressman, and her mother, Doris, a homemaker, had three other children, and money was tight in the Fleming household. Nevertheless, it was clear that young Peggy was a skating prodigy, and the Flemings were willing to make the necessary sacrifices to help their young daughter become a champion. Albert worked extra hours to help make ends meet, and Doris sewed many of Peggy's ice-skating outfits herself. Their efforts paid off; by the time she was 11, Peggy was competing in national junior events and winning most of them.

But in 1961, a tragedy occurred that would test young Fleming's character and dedication. When she was 12, her skating coach, Billy Kipp, died in a plane crash. Kipp was a member of the U.S. national skating team, which had been on the way to the World Championships in Brussels. All 73 passengers on board the aircraft died, including Lawrence Owen, the young woman most experts predicted would become the next Olympic gold medalist. In the aftermath of the accident, the French skater-turned-teacher Pierre Brunet predicted that "it will take ten years for an American to again challenge for top honors."

Devastated by the loss of Billy Kipp, Peggy Fleming decided to dedicate her career to her late coach. She made it her ambition to become Olympic and world champion. Three years later, Fleming became the youngest skater to win the U.S national title when she took top honors at the age of 15. It was a championship she would win for four consecutive years. One month later, at the 1967 World Championships in Innsbruck, Austria, Fleming finished sixth—a respectable showing for such a young skater.

In 1965, the Fleming family moved to Colorado Springs, so Peggy could train with Carlo Fassi, a former European champion. Fleming had one clear goal in mind: She aimed to become the first American figure skater since CAROL HEISS in 1960 to win an Olympic gold medal. One year later, she captured her first World Championship title. But for Fleming, it was a bittersweet victory. Early in the competition, which was held that year in Dawes, Switzerland, she had learned that her father had suffered a massive heart attack and died. Overcome with grief, Fleming nevertheless continued to skate. It was her first of three consecutive World Championships.

As the 1968 Olympic Games approached, Fleming emerged as the heavy favorite to win gold. And from the moment she took the ice in Grenoble, France, the question became not whether she would win the gold, but by how large a margin. After building an insurmountable lead over the competition with a nearly flawless performance in the compulsory figures, Fleming skated exquisitely in the two-minute short program. Her final routine, a four-minute free-skating performance, included a series of extravagant moves that dazzled judges and spectators alike. At the end of her program, which ended with a spread eagle/double axel/spread eagle combination—a move that no skater, male or female, had ever mastered—one judge commented that "Peggy Fleming is the best skater to ever step on the ice." The praise was unanimous: all nine judges awarded Fleming first place.

Later in 1968, Fleming won her third straight World Championship, and she then announced her retirement from amateur skating. The time had come, she said, to pay her family back for the hard work they had done to make her a champion. Fleming appeared on a television special in November 1968 and then signed a professional contract with Ice Follies.

Fleming married Gary Jenkins, a doctor, in 1971. She retired from professional skating in 1976, and the following year she and Jenkins had the first of two children. The next challenge Fleming faced was a personal one: in the early 1990s she was diagnosed with breast cancer. She underwent radiation therapy and survived the disease, and she then became a spokesperson for breast cancer awareness. In addition, Fleming became a televi-

sion broadcaster, and providing deft and polished commentary at Olympic, national, and World Championship figure skating competitions.

Further Reading

Greenspan, Bud. *Frozen in Time: The Greatest Moments at the Winter Olympics.* Santa Monica, Calif.: General Publishing Group, 1997.

Layden, Joe. *Women in Sports: The Complete Book of the World's Greatest Female Athletes.* Santa Monica, Calif.: General Publishing Group, 1997, pp. 89–90.

FLOWERS, VONETTA (Vonetta Jeffery)
(1973-)   *Bobsledder*

In one of the most uplifting Olympic stories, Vonetta Flowers came virtually out of nowhere to become the first African American to win a Winter Olympics gold medal when she and her partner, Jill Bakken, took top honors in the women's bobsled event at the Salt Lake City games in 2002.

Vonetta Jeffery was born in Birmingham, Alabama, on October 29, 1973, the daughter of Jimmie and Barbara Jeffery. Interested in track and field from an early age, Vonetta excelled in both sprinting and long jumping events at Jackson-Olin High School in Birmingham, where she was also an All-State selection in basketball. After graduating from high school, Jeffery won a track scholarship to the University of Alabama, Birmingham (UAB). At UAB, Flowers had an impressive track career. Competing in the 200-meter sprint event, as well as in the triple jump and the long jump, she was a seven-time National Collegiate Athletic Association NCAA All-American selection and won the Great Midwest Conference (the league in which UAB competes) most valuable player award six times. It was also at UAB that Vonetta Jeffery met and married a fellow track athlete, Johnny Mack Flowers.

After graduating from UAB in 1997, Flowers took a job as an assistant coach at the University of Alabama, Tuscaloosa. In addition to her duties there, she trained ardently for a spot on the Olympic women's track-and-field team, which would compete at the Sydney games in 2000. Flowers did not perform well at the trials and failed to make the team; even so, those trials changed her destiny. As his wife was warming up for one of her events, Johnny Flowers noticed a flyer advertising a tryout for the U.S. Bobsled team. A native southerner, Flowers had rarely even seen snow. Even so, the idea intrigued her, and she decided to switch gears and try out for the team.

A strong competitor as well as a fast runner, Flowers had little trouble mastering the skills needed to be a brakeperson on the two-person bobsled crew. On these sleds, the person who is in front is known as the driver and must have superb timing and terrific technical skills. The more physically demanding position, though, is the rider in the back. The brakeperson pushes the back of the sled out of the starting gate, and then applies the brakes at the end of the run.

At the Winter Olympics bobsled trials in Park City, Utah, Vonetta Flowers and her driver, Jill Bakken, placed second, earning a place on the team. Flowers arrived in Salt Lake City amid little fanfare; rarely is a team's second sled favored to win a medal, much less gold. In addition, the number-one sled for the United States, Jean Racine and Gea Johnson, had received the lion's share of publicity after Racine had decided to split with her friend and brakeperson Jen Davidson to race with Johnson instead.

Nevertheless, Flowers was in a position to be a pioneer at the Salt Lake City games. Only one African American had ever won a medal at the Winter Olympics; Debi Thomas had taken a bronze in ladies' figure skating at the 1988 Calgary Olympics. But if Flowers felt any pressure to make history, she never let it show. It was strength, muscle, and speed all the way as Flowers and Bakken won the first heat of the women's bobsled race, and then, hours later, took the second heat as well to clinch gold.

On the podium, Flowers, a quiet and reserved presence on the athletic field, wept openly as the U.S. national anthem was played and the flag raised. "I am so blessed to be here," she said after the ceremony. "To win a gold medal for your country is simply awesome. Hopefully this will encourage other African-American boys and girls to give winter sports a try." In 2000 Flowers had returned to her alma mater, the University of Alabama-Birmingham, where she remains an assistant track-and-field coach.

Further Reading

Enslin, Paul, "As We Have Lifted Up Sarah Hughes, We Have Let Down Vonetta Flowers," *The Nando Times*, March 5, 2002. Available online, http://www.nandotimes.com/sports/story/281723p-2534327c.html. Downloaded on March 5, 2002.

"Meet Vonetta Flowers," Official Athletic Site of the University of Alabama at Birmingham. Available online, http://uabsports.fansonly.com/sports/c-track/mtt/flowers_vonetta00.html. Downloaded on March 15, 2002.

FRASER, GRETCHEN (Gretchen Kunigk)
(1919–) *Skier*

The first U.S. athlete to win an Olympic medal in skiing was a woman named Gretchen Fraser, who accomplished the feat at the 1948 Olympic Games. Fraser, who won a gold medal in the downhill event at the age of 29, could have been a much more decorated Olympic athlete had the two previous Olympic games not been canceled owing to World War II.

Gretchen Kunigk was born in Tacoma, Washington, on February 11, 1919. Both of Gretchen's parents were from Europe; her father was born in Germany, and her mother was brought up in Norway. The Kunigks owned a ski lodge on Mount Rainier, and Gretchen, a natural athlete, learned to conquer the slopes at an early age. Although skiing was her best sport, it was not her only one. By the time she was a teenager, Gretchen was an expert golfer, tennis player, and equestrian. Later in her life she learned how to fly airplanes, and she won two army jet trainer aircraft races.

In 1936, Gretchen met Don Fraser, who was a member of the U.S. ski team. The two married that same year, and they moved to Sun Valley, Idaho.

The Frasers trained intensely over the next few years, with the intention of becoming husband-and-wife Olympic skiers. When the 1940 games were canceled, Gretchen decided to concentrate on national skiing events. She took top honors at the U.S. national downhill and the Alpine combined championships in 1941, and the following year she won the U.S. national slalom championship.

Don, in the meantime, entered the naval forces in 1942, and after the 1942 season ended, Gretchen Fraser decided to retire from skiing. She spent several years teaching skiing, tennis, and swimming to war veteran amputees in army hospitals. But when the war ended, Don Fraser returned from the service and urged his wife to take up competitive skiing again. He believed she still had a chance to win an Olympic medal.

Not half as confident as her husband, Gretchen nevertheless decided, at the age of 29, to try to qualify for the 1948 Olympics. Working with her husband, who had become her coach, Fraser worked herself back into top condition and made the Olympic team.

The 1948 games were held in St. Moritz, Switzerland. Fraser, who was familiar to ski experts, quickly became a favorite with the crowds. Throughout the competition the fans rooted for Fraser, and she did not disappoint them. Fraser's first medal came when she won the silver in the Alpine combined, a double-part race that is no longer in Olympic competition. It was a groundbreaking moment for U.S. skiers—the first medal ever won by U.S. skier in an event long dominated by Europeans.

But Fraser was not finished yet. Given new confidence by her first race, she announced that she would win a second medal by capturing the slalom event. It was a bold prediction; in order to win the event, Fraser would have to beat Erika Mahringer of Austria, the top-ranked skier in Europe. At the end of the first run, Fraser was in first place, but four women, including Mahringer, were within striking distance. Fraser needed to ski a smooth final run in order to secure the gold.

Confident if a bit cold, Fraser stood in the starting gate, ready to start her second run. Suddenly the starter's race phone, which is used to signal the beginning of each run, went dead. It was a technical glitch that took 17 minutes to fix. As the telephone line was repaired, Fraser shivered in the starting gate, feeling the pressure. Finally, the delay ended, and Fraser skied a controlled and tight run to clinch the gold.

After the 1948 games, Fraser retired from skiing once again and resumed her teaching. In 1960 she was elected into the U.S. National Ski Hall of Fame. Fraser died in 1994, shortly before the Lillehammer Olympic Games began, and less than two months after the death of her beloved husband.

Further Reading

Layden, Joe. *Women in Sports: The Complete Book on the World's Greatest Female Athletes,* Santa Monica, Calif.: General Publishing Group, 1997, pp. 91–92.

Smith, Lissa, editor. *Nike Is a Goddess: The History of Women in Sports.* New York: Atlantic Monthly Press, 1998, pp. 143–144.

G

GERA, BERNICE
(1932–1992)   *Baseball Umpire*

Bernice Gera broke one of the most difficult barriers in sports when she became the first woman to become an umpire in a professional men's baseball league in 1972. But she paid a tremendous price for her pioneering; exhausted and broken, she resigned from her new post after one minor-league game.

The story of Bernice Gera began in 1932, when she was born in Ernest, a mining town in western Pennsylvania. A gifted athlete, Bernice longed to play baseball with the neighborhood boys. The boys initially scoffed at the notion of a girl playing with them, but one look at Bernice's throwing and hitting talents had them fighting with one another for the right to play on her side.

It was Bernice's bad fortune that she was born when there were no leagues for women baseball players. But the All-American Girls' Baseball League folded in 1954, and Bernice was delegated in the mid-1950s to showing off her tremendous athletic ability at amusement parks, where she would enter (and almost invariably win) throwing contests; she won so many stuffed animals at these events that several arcades banned her from participating.

By this time, Bernice had married Steven Gera, a photographer for the New York highway department. The Geras had settled in Long Island, where Bernice volunteered much of her time teaching children to play baseball. She was also able to finagle her way into competing in more exhibitions, which often featured major league baseball players. In one of these exhibitions, Gera smacked three hits off the Cleveland Indians future Hall-of-Fame pitcher Bob Feller; in another, she hit a ball farther than Yankee outfielder (and the holder of the single-season home run record at the time) Roger Maris.

Gera donated the proceeds she won at these events to charities, and she became a well-known presence on the exhibition circuit. Even so, she longed to play a more prominent role in professional baseball, and in 1967 she made the pivotal decision to become an umpire. As the judiciary branch of baseball games, which are often hotly contested, umpires are required to have extensive training. All potential referees must attend umpiring school, and with enthusiasm, Gera filled out an application to one of the most prominent of these institutes, the Al Somers Umpire School. She was accepted.

It then came as a great surprise to Al Somers when Gera called him on the phone to announce that she would be attending. Somers had mistakenly read the name "Bernie" Gera on the application and had based his decisions on the candidate's merits rather than her gender. When he realized that "Bernie" was actually "Bernice," he rescinded his offer. Gera then applied to Jim Finley's Florida Baseball Camp, and although Finley initially tried to talk her into taking a home study course rather than attending his school, he finally accepted her.

Gera had won this battle, but the men at the Finley camp had no intention of letting her win the war. Her classmates taunted her during the day, and more than once she awakened at night to the sound of beer bottles being smashed against the door of her room. "It was a horrible, lonely experience," she would say of her umpire school days. But Gera survived, and she graduated with high honors from the Finley camp in the spring of 1967.

Although Gera was now a licensed and educated umpire, she could not find employment on any level of professional baseball. And it was here that her battle truly began. Gera decided to start at the beginning; she moved back to Queens, and began working games on the high school, amateur, and semipro levels. Slowly but surely, her reputation grew, and in early 1969 she felt ready to try her luck on the professional circuit again.

Gera requested umpire application forms from every East Coast minor league organization. The only association to send her a form was the Florida Baseball League, but Gera wanted to work closer to home. She contacted Vincent McNamara, the president of the Class A New York–Pennsylvania League. McNamara told Gera that there were no dressing rooms for women in the league's ballparks, and in addition the ballplayers used foul language, which might sound shocking to a woman. Nonplussed, Gera responded, "I've umpired a lot of games and I didn't think I could hear anything new."

At this point, Mario Biaggi, a state representative from the Bronx, contacted Gera and offered her his assistance. McNamara began receiving phone calls from both Gera and Biaggi on a regular basis, and finally, in the summer of 1969, he sent her a contract. It appeared that Gera had triumphed; she received barrages of congratulatory letters, and the day after she signed her contract, newspapers nationwide ran a photograph of a beaming Gera holding the contract and giving the thumbs-up sign.

But the day before Gera was to make her minor-league umpiring debut, she received word that the president of baseball's minor-league system, Philip Piton, had decided to void her contract. Piton offered no explanation as to why he had rescinded the league's offer, but Barney Deary, the administrator of the umpire development program, stated that the league's decision had nothing to do with Gera's gender. Rather, her contract was voided because she failed to meet the National Association's height, weight, and age requirements. Indeed, Gera, at five feet, three inches tall, 129 pounds, and 38 years of age, did not come close to the league minimum standards of five feet, 10 inches, and 175 pounds, or to their age range of 24 to 35.

Unperturbed, Gera filed a complaint with the New York State Human Rights Commission, stating that her civil rights had been violated. In the wake of Gera's action, a sportswriter revealed that Vincent McNamara, who was a veteran umpire as well as the president of the Class A league, also did not fit the height or weight requirements; neither had Bill Klem, whose umpiring excellence in the major leagues had earned him a place in the Hall of Fame. The Human Rights Commission ruled in Gera's favor, and when the association, after exhausting all appeals, still refused to offer Gera a job, she filed a $25 million lawsuit. The league finally acknowledged defeat; they sent Gera a contract for the 1972 season. She was told to report to work on June 23, 1972.

If real life were a movie, Gera's story would have ended here. Sadly, reality was fast catching up with Gera; by the time she received her contract, she was mentally exhausted. Her debut was to take place on June 24; Gera was to work the second base area (two umpires work minor-league games;

Gera's partner, also a rookie, worked behind the plate) in a game between the Geneva and Auburn teams in Geneva, New York. In the weeks preceding her first game, she received dozens of threatening letters and phone calls. "Male voices would tell me not to take the field, not to take the chance," she said later. "I received threats that someone would shoot me if I took the field." In addition, Gera's peers were of little assistance. At her first league umpire meeting, Gera was ostracized and ignored. Before she took the field for her first game, Gera had already decided that she had finished with professional baseball; she would resign after the one game.

If Gera had any hesitations at all about her decision to leave baseball, they were quelled completely after her nightmarish experience in that one game. Standing behind second base, Gera made her first few calls easily and without hesitation. But in the fourth inning, an Auburn player leaning off second base hustled back to the bag after a line-drive out. The ball reached the second baseman before the runner did, but Gera signaled that the runner was safe. Then she realized that no tag was necessary, since a fly ball out means a force is in effect at every base. She reversed her call and motioned that the runner was out.

Gera's change of heart sent the Auburn manager, Nolan Campbell, running out of the dugout fuming. Campbell reached Gera and began berating her. Gera told him she had made a mistake, but Campbell, spitting tobacco as he shouted, told Gera that she should have "stayed in the kitchen, peeling potatoes." Wasting no time, Gera ejected Campbell from the game. Umpires always join forces when berated by players or managers, but Doug Hartmayer, Gera's partner, stayed behind the plate during the entire course of the argument. His indifference sent a message that was much more powerful than Campbell's: Gera was not welcome on the field, for the simple reason that she was a woman.

When the last out was recorded, Gera walked into the general manager's office and simply stated, "I've just retired from baseball." It was not the type of departure Gera had hoped for; in tears, she ran from the stadium into a waiting car. As it drove off, she wept openly in the backseat. Likewise, Gera's supporters felt that she had let them down. Some believed she left because she was intimidated by the argument with Campbell, but Gera scoffed at those charges. "I wasn't scared off. I was disgusted. I was just fed up with it."

Gera had resigned from umpiring, but she remained peripherally involved in the game for several years. In 1975 she took a job with the New York Mets, and for four years she handled the Lady Mets Club, a social association in which members met players, attended lunches, and went to games. In 1979 Gera moved to Florida with her husband, where she planned with a promoter to start a business teaching girls and boys to play baseball. But the deal fell through.

In 1992, Bernice Gera died of cancer. Her life was filled with triumphs and defeats, but she will always be remembered as one of sports' most prominent trailblazers. Her uniform, mask, and broom from her one game in the minor leagues are enshrined in the Baseball Hall of Fame in Cooperstown, and thanks in part to her legacy, opportunities for women in baseball expanded exponentially in the last part of the 20th century. Perhaps she could and should have overcome her harrowing experience during her one-game professional umpiring career; it might have helped her cause had she stayed in the league for a few more games at least. But it is easy to criticize trailblazers from the comfort of our own living rooms and to take the anguish of their battles for granted. "Bernice Gera turned out to be human," Nora Ephron wrote of the first female umpire in professional baseball, "which is not a luxury pioneers are allowed."

Further Reading

Fulton, Bob, "The Bernice Gera Story," Available online. URL: http://www.sabr.org/old/gera.htm. Downloaded on December 16, 2000.

Gregorich, Barbara, *Women at Play: The Story of Women in Baseball.* New York: Harcourt Brace, 1993, pp. 184–191.

▦ GIBB, ROBERTA
(ca. 1940–   )   *Marathon Runner*

In 1966, a woman entered the Boston Marathon. A little more than three hours later, she finished the course. But the full story is not that simple; as it happened, women were not allowed to run in the marathon at that time. Gibb, however, was not about to let a simple fact like that stop her.

Gibb does not offer details about either her age or her childhood. What is known is that she grew up in Winchester, Massachusetts, and that she attended Tufts University in the early 1960s as an art major. An impassioned runner as well as an artist, she would run 16 miles—the round-trip distance to campus from her Winchester home—every day.

Although Gibb loved to run, she had never heard of the Boston Marathon, until one day in 1964 when the father of a high school friend suggested she go see the race. She watched the event and was immediately mesmerized. "I watched people going by, and I didn't even notice if they were male or female," she said of that first experience. "I fell in love with it and the people running in it and the crowds along the way."

In February 1965, Gibb wrote to the Amateur Athletic Union to request an application for the Boston Marathon. The union rejected Gibb immediately, explaining in a letter that it was not physiologically possible for a woman to run the long distance. The rejection infuriated Gibb, but rather than frustrating her ambition to run the marathon, it only fueled her fire. "That was the first time somebody told me I couldn't be who I am because I'm a woman," she said. "To me, that was all the more reason to run. Then I had a mission."

Armed with a few running books and wearing nurse's shoes instead of sneakers, Gibb began training for the race. The night before the 1966 marathon she ate a big roast beef dinner and then retired early. The following morning, wearing a hooded sweatshirt and without an official number on her back, Gibb hid in a hollow near the starting line and waited for the gun to go off. Once it did, she jumped into the race.

It was a warm day in May, and as she continued to run, Gibb began to feel the heat. She yearned to take off her sweatshirt and sweatpants but was afraid that she would be noticed. Gibb's fellow runners, however, had already noticed that there was a woman among them. Impressed by her courage, they began shouting their support. "Some of them told me they wished their wives or girlfriends would do it," she remembered later. At their insistence, Gibb finally decided to take off the warm clothing. As she threw the sweatshirt to the side of the road, the crowds on the street took notice and cheered her.

Gibb sailed through the first two-thirds of the race, but her lack of experience and proper training began to show near the end. Gibb was under the impression that drinking water during the race would give her cramps, so she had not drunk a drop. As result, she became dehydrated. In addition, Gibb had finally tossed the nurse's shoes and bought herself a pair of boys' running shoes, but she had not broken them in before the race. Her feet developed painful blisters, which slowed her down dramatically.

It took Gibb almost a full hour to complete the final three miles of the race. When she crossed the finish line, she had completed the course in three hours and 20 minutes, well below the qualifying time for today's women racers. Even so, Gibb had done what so many had deemed impossible, and she had proven that women could indeed run a full marathon course. Gibb returned to Boston to run the race, unofficially again, the following two years. The first woman to officially win a Boston Marathon was NINA KUSCSIK, who took top honors in 1972.

Gibb continued to run for many years and entered the marathon officially more than a dozen times. She also became a professional sculptor and designed the trophies that were presented to the top three women marathon finishers at the 1984 Olympic trials. Married with children, she lives in her native Massachusetts.

Further Reading

Cimons, Marlene. "Four Who Dared," *Runner's World,* vol. 31, no.4 (April 1996) 72–78.

Docherty, Bonnie. "Roberta Gibb Paved the Way," *Middlesex News,* April 20, 1997. Available online. URL: http://www.townonline.com/marathon/race97/roberta_gibb.html. Downloaded on June 25, 2001.

▦ GIBSON, ALTHEA
(1927–   )   *Tennis Player*

In the 1950s a young African-American woman named Althea Gibson burst onto the all-white tennis scene, adding a dimension not only of diversity, but of sheer athletic excellence that changed the face of the sport forever.

Althea Gibson was born in Silver, South Carolina, on August 25, 1927. When she was three years old, her parents moved Althea, her three sisters, and brother from their failing cotton farm in South Carolina to New York City, hoping for new opportunities. The Gibson family settled in Harlem, and eventually Althea became a regular sight on the neighborhood streets and playgrounds, often skipping school to play ball. Hoping to focus his daughter's talents, Althea's father, who worked as a garage attendant, taught her how to box. But Althea much preferred playing baseball and paddle tennis on her street. Althea was such a gifted paddle tennis player that a neighborhood policeman named Buddy Walker bought her a tennis racket and told her she should try tennis sometime.

Walker taught Gibson how to practice against the wall of the playground's handball court, and he then took her to the Cosmopolitan Tennis Club in Harlem. At age 14, Gibson played so impressively at the Cosmopolitan that some of the members decided to pool their resources, and collectively they bought her a membership to the club.

For Gibson, the Cosmopolitan was a completely different world from her neighborhood streets. She learned the rules of the game as well as its very particular etiquette. "After I while," she later wrote, "I understood that you could walk out on the court like a lady, all dressed up in immaculate white, be polite to everybody, and still play like a tiger and beat the liver and lights out of the ball."

Slowly but surely, Gibson began to win tournaments, but tennis was far from her only interest. She loved playing the saxophone, bowling, and playing basketball, and to help her family make ends meet, she worked at a variety of jobs.

Then, in 1946, Gibson competed in the American Tennis Association (ATA) adult tournament for the first time. The ATA was an all–African American, national tennis organization. Gibson did not win the competition, but two ATA officials noticed her talent. These two officials, Dr. Robert Johnson and Dr. Hubert Eaton, thought Gibson had the ability to become a national champion, and they decide to help her reach that goal. Conferring with one another and with Gibson and her family, the two doctors came up with a plan: During the school year Gibson would live with Dr. Eaton and his family in North Carolina and attend high school there. During summer vacation, she would be in the care of the Johnsons, competing in tournaments around the country.

The two men became surrogate parents to Gibson over the next few years. For the rest of their lives, in fact, she called both men "dad." In 1947, at the age of 20, Gibson won the ATA national tournament—the first of 10 consecutive ATA titles she would capture. For Gibson it was a very fulfilling championship, and as she continued to improve, she became a world-class tennis player.

But although Gibson was playing competitive tennis with great success, there remained a caveat to her triumphs: The overwhelming majority of her matches were played in African-American-only tournaments. Although the competition was fierce and the matches first rate, Gibson had never played in any of the major international tennis tournaments; in fact, no African-American woman had.

It is worth noting that Althea Gibson's career coincided almost precisely with that of Jackie Robinson, who in 1947 crossed the color line in professional baseball and became the first African American to play in the major leagues. Robinson and Gibson were both tremendously talented athletes who had risen to the top of their respective leagues. Both stood on the cusp of integrating

American institutions before much of the United States itself had become desegregated; *Brown v. the Board of Education,* a Supreme Court decision that integrated public schools in the United States, would not occur until 1954, and the Civil Rights Act that abolished the Jim Crow policies of the South was still 20 years away. And both Gibson and Robinson carried, to different extents, the burden of an entire race of people as they crossed the color line; both had to excel. Nothing less would suffice.

In 1948, encouraged by the performance of Dr. Reginald Weir who competed in the formerly all-white United States Lawn Tennis Association's (USLTA) national indoor tournament, the ATA decided that Gibson would match Weir's groundbreaking appearance—and then go one huge step further. In 1949, Gibson played in her first USLTA competition, the Eastern Indoor Championships, and reached the quarterfinals. The next week, she became a quarterfinalist again, this time at the National Indoor Championships. The following winter, she played in both tournaments again, repeating as a quarterfinalist in the National Indoor Championships and taking top honors in the Eastern Indoor Championships. Gibson was eager to expand her playing résumé, but there was one major problem: Most of the outdoor tournaments sponsored by the USLTA were played at country clubs, and the 22-year-old athlete from Harlem was not receiving any invitations.

In 1950, Gibson received a boost in the form of an editorial written by a former tennis champion. "Should Althea not be given the chance to succeed or fail," ALICE MARBLE wrote in the July 1, 1950, edition of *American Lawn Tennis,* "then there is an ineradicable mark against a game to which I have devoted much of my life, and I would be bitterly ashamed."

Perhaps it was Marble's editorial that did the trick, or maybe the white tennis world was acting on an instinct that there was no stopping progress. But in late July 1950, the Orange Lawn Tennis Club in South Orange, New Jersey, invited Gibson to play in the Eastern Grass Court Champi-

onships. Gibson did what she had to do in South Orange, proving her legitimacy by winning her first match. In her next tournament, the National Clay Court Championships in Chicago, she did better, reaching the quarterfinals. Then, in mid-August, the all-important announcement came. Based on her abilities, Lawrence A. Baker, the president of the USLTA, declared that Althea Gibson was invited to compete at the U.S. championships in Forest Hills, New York.

Gibson breezed through her first-round match in Forest Hills, and then she faced the defending Wimbledon champion, LOUISE BROUGH, in the second round. The two played a fiercely aggressive, competitive match, splitting the first two sets and exchanging leads regularly in the third. Gibson, who was proving that she could hold her own against the premier tennis players in the nation, was leading Brough 7-6 (these were the days before tiebreakers), when thunder sounded and a drenching rain poured down on the court. The match was suspended until the next day. Gibson later said the delay was the worst thing that could have happened—it gave her a chance not only to think about the match but to read about it too. "By the time I got through reading the morning papers," she said later, "I was a wreck." Brough and Gibson resumed playing, and 11 minutes later Brough had broken Gibson's serve, then held her own to take the match.

Although Gibson had lost in the second match, she had played admirably and memorably. One year later, she played equally well when she became the first African American to compete in the Wimbledon championships in 1951. But it would take seven years of hard work and perseverance for Gibson to attain her ultimate goal.

Gibson continued to play tennis in the early 1950s; she also earned a college degree from Florida A&M University in 1953, and she supported herself by teaching physical education at Lincoln University, an all-black school in Missouri. Then, in 1955, Gibson decided to join the army. Gibson, whose game was rapidly improving, participated in a goodwill tennis tour in Southeast

Asia. She took the exhibition seriously, and won virtually every event she played in. The tour honed and refined her skills, as she continued to train and to play in the major tournaments.

By 1957, Gibson, recently retired from the army, had reached her peak as a player. Tall and lean, she had an aggressive game that featured a powerful serve, quick volleys, and an effective overhead. The Althea Gibson who entered the grass at Wimbledon in the summer of 1957 was a mature and confident competitor. She progressed through the tournament without incident, and after the semifinals, when she beat newcomer Christine Truman, Gibson announced to reporters, "Praise be, this could be my year."

Sure enough, Gibson triumphed in the final, beating Darlene Hart in straight sets in the cham-pionship match. What a moment it was for Gibson when Queen Elizabeth II walked on court to present her with the championship trophy. "It must have been terribly hot out there," the monarch remarked to Gibson before the ceremony. "Sure was, Madam," replied the first African American to win a Grand Slam tennis event, "I hope it wasn't as hot up there for you."

Two months after Wimbledon, Gibson added the U.S. championship trophy to her collection, beating Louise Brough in straight sets in the final. After receiving her trophy from Vice President Richard Nixon, Gibson briefly and humbly spoke to the crowd, declaring that she hoped she would wear her crown with dignity and honor. The crowd applauded, incessantly, it seemed. It was, according to the *New York Times,* "the longest

Althea Gibson broke the tennis color barrier in style, winning consecutive Wimbledon and U.S. Championships in 1957 and 1958.
(Library of Congress)

demonstration of hand clapping heard in the stadium in years."

The following year, Gibson repeated as champion at both Wimbledon and Forest Hills, and in 1959 she retired from amateur tennis. In the years that followed, Gibson played exhibition tennis during Harlem Globetrotters basketball games, something that might not appear to be a worthy successor to her past triumphs, but one that paid fairly well. Eventually Gibson began playing golf, joining the Ladies Professional Golf Associatoin (LPGA) tour, and also taught tennis in New Jersey. In 1977 she ran for state senator in the New Jersey Democratic primary, but her campaign was unsuccessful. Since that time she has continued to play golf, although not competitively, and makes occasional appearances at tennis tournaments.

Gibson gracefully broke the color barrier in tennis, blazing the trail for such future champions as Arthur Ashe and VENUS and SERENA WILLIAMS. Tennis players of all races owe her a debt of gratitude not only for breaking barriers, but for pursuing excellence relentlessly in the process.

Further Reading

Davidson, Sue, *Changing the Game: The Stories of Tennis Champions Alice Marble and Althea Gibson.* Seattle, Wash.: Seal Press, 1972.

Layden, Joe. *Women in Sports: The Complete Book of the World's Greatest Female Athletes.* Santa Monica, Calif.: General Publishing Group, 1997, pp. 95–96.

King, Billie Jean, and Cynthia Starr. *We Have Come a Long Way: The Story of Women's Tennis.* New York: McGraw Hill, 1988, pp. 74–77, 94–96.

GOLDEN, DIANA
(Diana Golden Brosnihan)
(1963–2001)   *Skier*

One of the most inspirational stories in all of sports is that of Diana Golden, who lost a leg to bone cancer as a young girl and then went on to become the most decorated U.S. skier in history.

Diana Golden was born on March 20, 1963, in Sudbury, Massachusetts. The Goldens were passionate skiers, and from the time she was five years old, Diana spent every winter weekend and holiday on the slopes with her parents. Diana clearly had an abundance of talent. More than that, she had daring.

One day in 1975, Diana's right leg collapsed while she was standing. As carefree as most preteens, she thought nothing of it. Then, a couple of weeks later, it happened again. After several more incidents, Diana and her parents went to her doctor, who ordered tests. A few days later the doctor delivered the devastating news: Diana had bone cancer. The leg would have to be amputated right away in order to keep the cancer from spreading.

The first few days after her leg was removed were difficult ones for Diana. Accustomed to an active life, she had little notion of whether she would be back on the slpes. But when she asked her doctor, he surprised her by telling her that she could ski again—she would have to relearn the sport to a certain extent, but it was possible, Diana had her doubts—not only was she nervous about getting down the mountain, but she wondered how she would even manage to get into her ski, without an extra leg for balance.

Her parents decided to invest in a special training course for their daughter. At Mount Sunapee in New Hampshire, Diana met her teacher, Kirk Baver, a Vietnam veteran who had lost a leg in combat. Under his guidance, Diana became accustomed to skiing on one leg. Several months later, back in Sudbury, Diana caught the eye of the high school ski coach. Impressed with her talent and courage, he invited her to practice with the team.

Although it was difficult at first to ski with the team, Diana loved the workouts. She gradually became stronger and faster, and when she was a senior in high school, she tried out and made the U.S. Disabled Ski Team. And at the World Handicapped Championships, she took top honors in the downhill event.

After that triumph, Golden attended Dartmouth College, and while there, she became a born-again Christian. Between her academic challenges and interest in her new religion, Golden found little time for skiing. By her junior year, she had decided to retire from the sport. She graduated from college and took a job in sales. But the slopes beckoned, and Golden started spending weekends skiing. Eventually those weekends became longer, as she decided to begin training for competitions again.

In 1986, Golden began racing again, and this time, she remained focused. Over the next four years, she would win 10 World Handicapped Championship titles and 19 National Championships. Golden received the Beck Award in 1986, a prize given every year by the U.S. Ski Team for best performance in international skiing. Two years later she won a gold medal in the disabled Giant Slalom skiing event at the winter Olympics in Calgary. She received another great honor in 1991, when she took home the Flo Hyman Award, which honors an athlete every year for courage, excellence, and dedication.

Golden retired from racing in 1991 and planned to continue working as a coach and a motivational speaker. One year later, her cancer returned, leading to a double mastectomy as well as the loss of her uterus. Devastated by the disease, Golden attempted suicide late in 1992. But Golden survived and several months later, with her cancer again in remission, she climbed Mount Rainier and returned to motivational speaking.

In 1996, Golden began dating Steve Brosnihan, a freelance cartoonist. The two had originally met years earlier, when both were undergraduates at Dartmouth. Golden and Brosnihan married in August 1996.

Sadly, Brosnihan's remission was only temporary. In 1997, the disease returned once again and spread to her lungs, pelvis, and spine. Brosnihan retired permanently from motivational speaking. She fought her cancer for the next four years but died from the illness in August 2001. She was 38. Although Broshnihan certainly epitomized bravery and fearlessness during her life, her goal as an athlete was a bit less lofty. "Athletes don't want to be courageous," Brosnihan once said. "They want to be good."

Further Reading

"Diana Golden: The Golden Skier," Women's Sports Foundation online. Available online. URL: http://www.womenssportsfoundation.org/WoSport/stage/TOPISS/html/dianagolden.html. Downloaded May 9, 2001.

Layden, Joe. *Women in Sports: The Complete Book of the World's Greatest Female Athletes.* Santa Monica, Calif.: General Publishing Group, 1997, pp. 96–97.

Litsky, Frank. "Diana Golden Brosnihan, Skier, Dies at 38." *New York Times,* August 28, 2001, p. A 17.

GRANATO, CAMMI
(Catherine Michelle Granato)
(1971–)   *Hockey Player, Commentator*

Cammi Granato, the leading woman hockey player in the United States, led the U.S. team to the first Olympic championship in women's hockey.

It could be said that Catherine Michelle Granato, whose life began on March 25, 1971, in Downer's Grove, Illinois, was born with ice in her veins. Her parents, Don and Michelle Granato, spent their first date at a Chicago Blackhawks game. Her three brothers, Tony (who would later play in the National Hockey League [NHL]), Don, and Robbie, ate dinner with their skates on so they could get back on the ice to as soon as possible. And young Cammi, whose nickname combined the first two letters of her first and middle names, was a gifted athlete whose favorite activity was endlessly hitting a puck with her brothers.

When Cammi was four, her mother, sensing that Cammi needed alternative ice activities because there were no hockey teams for girls, bought her daughter a complete ice-skating outfit and sent her to the rink for a lesson. But the moment Michelle's back was turned, Cammi had slipped out of the rink and found a television to watch the Blackhawks game. Cammi began joining her brothers and cousins for family games in the basement, where she learned the arts of puck control, passing, and cross-checking with equal fervor. In kindergarten, Cammi began playing hockey for her school, and remained the only girl on the squad through eighth grade.

In high school, Granato eagerly tried out for the varsity squad. She made the team but paid her dues in a very big fashion. By the time she was a junior, the sole female player in the state, opposing players had begun trying to intimidate her. During games they would focus on her, sometimes at the urging of their coach. "Everyone started to aim for me," Granato later said. "I had a concussion. Coaches wanted their players to injure me." Granato quit the team and focused her talents on other sports.

Granato was recruited by several colleges for her basketball and tennis skills. But her heart was still on the ice, and she decided to take a scholarship

Cammi Granato, captain and center for the U.S. National Hockey team, led the United States to the first Olympic gold in women's ice hockey at the 1998 Games.
(Al Bello/Getty Images)

from Providence College in Rhode Island—one of the few higher education institutes at the time with a women's hockey team. At Providence, Granato easily adjusted to the rules of women's hockey, which forbade fighting and cross-checking but otherwise was the same game as the men's. During her four years on the squad, she led the Providence Friars to two national championships, and she became the career collegiate scoring leader in the process.

After graduating from Providence in 1993, Granato worked as an assistant coach in the U.S. Junior Hockey League. She missed playing, though, and one year later, decided to attend Concordia University in Montreal, Canada, to pursue a master's degree in sports administration—and to play on the Concordia women's hockey team.

By this time, Granato had learned with great enthusiasm that the 1998 Olympic Games in Nagano, Japan, would feature the first medal competition in women's hockey. Granato was named the captain of the U.S. team shortly after the Olympic trials, and she eagerly traveled to Asia for the competition. The U.S. team easily advanced through the early rounds, knowing that the greatest competition would most likely come from Canada. Sure enough, the two North American squads landed in the gold medal game, and Granato led the United States to a 3–1 victory over their northern neighbors. As the final seconds ticked off the scoreboard, the U.S. players threw their gloves and sticks in the air in celebration. It was a moment Granato would never forget. "You play this game because you love it," she later said, "there's no money in it . . . and the guys tell you to get off the ice. Then all of a sudden, you're at the Olympics, and you've won. And everything you strived for has come true. And you cherish every second." Granato, who scored four goals during the tournament, was asked to carry the flag for the entire U.S. Olympic team during the closing ceremonies in Nagano.

After returning to the United States, Granato was hired to provide radio commentary for the Los Angeles Kings franchise of the NHL. In so doing, she became the second woman to broadcast NHL games (the first, Sherry Ross, called radio games for the New Jersey Devils from 1992 to 1995). She also continued to play competitive hockey and in February 2002 led the United States to a silver medal at the Salt Lake City Olympics.

Further Reading

Loverro, Thom. *Cammi Granato: Hockey Pioneer.* Minneapolis, Minn.: Lerner Publications, 2000.

Scott, David. "Golden Girl," *Sport* 90, no. 4 (April 1999): 18.

Turco, Mary. *Crashing the Net: The U.S. Women's Olympic Hockey Team and the Road to Gold.* New York: HarperCollins, 1999.

⊞ GREGORY, ANN MOORE
(1912–1990)   *Golfer*

Ann Moore Gregory, the first African-American golfer to compete nationally, had the proper tools to be a pioneer. Blessed with natural athletic talent, Gregory had the determination, the courage, and the grace to bear indignities as she blazed new trails.

Born in Aberdeen, Mississippi, on July 25, 1912, Ann Moore lost both of her parents when she was very young. A local white family agreed to raise her. They clothed her and saw that she was fed and schooled. In return, Ann served as their maid. An enthusiastic tennis player, she was interested in golf as a girl, but was unable to play often; the golf courses in Aberdeen, including the public ones, were all off-limits to African Americans.

When she was 26, Moore married Percy Gregory, and the couple left Aberdeen to live in Gary, Indiana. In Gary, Gregory began playing golf more regularly, and in 1943, she took top honors at the Chicago Women's Golf Association (CWGA) championships, which was a tournament for African-American women. Gregory continued to play for the CWGA throughout the 1940s, and in 1956, the association became the first African-American association to join the United States Golf Association (USGA). Gregory, who had yearned to play in USGA tournaments for most of her career, was at last eligible to compete. In 1956, she did just that, and entered the U.S. Amateur Championships in Indianapolis.

It was not an easy time for Gregory; she received a lukewarm (at best) welcome from officials, players, and spectators, and on the golf course, she heard a number of racial insults hurled at her. But Gregory had long ago determined that the best way to handle racism was to ignore it. She kept her head up and continued to play. Gregory won her early round matches at the 1956 tournament, but lost in the third round.

Gregory continued to play golf for several more years. She never won a USGA-sanctioned tournament, although she did finish second in the 1971 U.S. Women's Senior Amateur. Even so, Gregory has earned a place in history, as instrumental to U.S. sporting history as ALTHEA GIBSON and Jackie Robinson. Those who have shattered racial barriers stand on the highest of pedestals, regardless of the number of tournaments they have won. Gregory died in 1990.

Further Reading

Contemporary Black Biography, Volume 24, edited by Shirelle Phelps. Detroit: Gale Group, 2000.

Layden, Joe. *Women in Sports: The Complete Book of the World's Greatest Female Athletes.* Santa Monica, Calif.: General Publishing Group, 1997, pp. 99–100.

Markel, Robert, Susan Wagoner, and Marcella Smith. *The Women's Sports Encyclopedia.* New York: Henry Holt, 1995, p. 32.

⊞ GRIFFITH JOYNER, FLORENCE
(Delorez Florence Griffith, Flo-Jo)
(1959–1997)   *Sprinter*

If there is one athlete who turned the financial tide for women in track and field, that person is undoubtedly Florence Griffith Joyner. After dominating the 1988 Olympic Games in Seoul, Korea, with four gold medals and one silver, she became a media star both in the United States and abroad.

But fame and riches were in the distant future when Delorez Florence Griffith was born in the Mojave Desert in southern California, on December 21, 1959. Her mother, a seamstress, left Florence's father, an electronics technician, in 1964 and moved with her 11 children to the Watts section of Los Angeles. The years in Watts were trying ones for the Griffiths. Looking back many years later, Griffith Joyner recalled, "There were days we didn't have food, there were days when we had oatmeal for breakfast, lunch, and dinner, but my mother always figured it out."

Young Florence was a quiet child. She spent a great deal of time reading and writing, and she loved to style hair, be it her own, her siblings' or her neighbors'. She also could run. During summer visits to her father's desert home, she would race the jackrabbits and most likely gave them decent competition.

The boys in her Watts neighborhood were evidently nothing compared to the jackrabbits, for Florence used to beat them regularly in street races. At the age of seven she began competing formally, running the 50- and 70-yard dashes with the Sugar Ray Robinson Youth Foundation, a program for inner-city children. Florence continued to compete for the Robinson Youth Foundation for several years, and when she was 14, she won the annual Jesse Owens National Youth Games—an achievement she repeated the following year. As champion of the games, she got to travel to San Francisco, where she met Jesse Owens himself.

Griffith continued her winning ways at Jordan High School, where she set school records in the 100-meter and 200-meter sprints, as well as in the long jump. After graduating from Jordan, she accepted an athletic scholarship from California State University, but when her sprint coach at Cal State, Bob Kersee, accepted a position at the University of California at Los Angeles (UCLA), she transferred there—with some regret. "I had a 3.25 grade point average in business at Cal State," she said later, "but UCLA didn't offer my major—I had to switch to psychology. But my running was

starting up, and I knew that Bobby was the best coach for me. So it kind of hurts to say this—I chose athletics over academics."

During her first year at UCLA, Griffith went to the 1980 Olympic trials in hopes of making the team. But her showing there was disappointing— she failed to qualify for the squad. The United States did not compete in the 1980 games in Moscow after all, as President Carter called for a nationwide boycott to protest the Soviet invasion of Afghanistan.

Two years later, Griffith, training steadily under Kersee, became the National Collegiate Athletic Association (NCAA) champion in the 200-meter event, with a time of 22.39 seconds. The next year she took top NCAA honors in the 400-meter event, and a silver medal in the 200-meter race. Interestingly, although Griffith would later become an Olympic champion in the 100-meter race, she did not compete in that event in college; Kersee judged that she was not quick enough out of the blocks to have the exploding start sprinters need to win at that distance.

After graduating from UCLA, Griffith continued to train with Kersee, and in 1984, she won a place on the U.S. Olympic team. In the Los Angeles games Griffith took a silver metal in the 200-meter race; her time of 22.04 seconds was a quarter-second slower than that of the first-place finisher, VALERIE BRISCO-HOOKS. Even though she failed to win gold in Los Angeles, Griffith still got a lot of attention; she had by then taken to wearing brightly colored track suits and sported long, colorful fingernails. During the games, the media dubbed her "Fluorescent Flo."

Media attention aside, Griffith was disappointed that she left Los Angeles without a gold medal. She decided to cut back from her track training and took a customer-service job at a bank in Los Angeles. Griffith also worked as a beautician at night, braiding hair and painting nails. With time away from the track she began to gain weight; in 1986, 15 pounds heavier and one second slower in the 200-meter event than she was the year before, Griffith went into semiretirement.

Not only did Florence Griffith Joyner win three gold medals at the 1988 Olympic Games, but she set world records in the 100-meter and 200-meter events.
(Mike Powell/Getty Images)

But early in 1987, Griffith began to hunger for the track again. She contacted Kersee, who agreed to coach her again if she would follow his demanding training demands and work harder than she had before. Griffith began a grueling schedule of workouts; she kept both her bank and beautician jobs, so she often would not get to the track or weight room until after midnight.

Fortunately for Griffith, she had met someone who encouraged and guided her during this time. Al Joyner, a gold-medal winner in the triple jump at the 1984 Olympic Games, was the brother of JACKIE JOYNER-KERSEE, one of Griffith's training partners at Kersee's track club. (Joyner-Kersee had married Bob Kersee in 1986.) In October 1987, Joyner and Griffith were married.

By then, Griffith Joyner had slimmed down to 130 pounds and was improving not only her overall speed but her acceleration out of the blocks as well. In the summer of 1987 she had won a silver medal in the 200-meter event at the World Championships in Rome and also ran a leg of the 4 × 400 relay, won by the United States. Griffith Joyner continued to get media attention for her splashy outfits—the *Chicago Tribune* wrote that her "hooded, silver bodysuit must have been designed for the Olympic speed skating team from Pluto"—but she had no individual gold medals and no world records.

Her second-place World Championship finish lit a fire under Griffith Joyner. She began a program of daily track workouts and grueling weight

97

lifting regimens four times a week. She would leave the bank during lunch hours to work out and continued to train after midnight. Not only did she work to improve her 200-meter time, but she decided to begin competing in the 100-meter event as well.

At the 1988 Olympic trials, Griffith Joyner clocked a stunning 10.49 in the 100-meter race—a time that shocked Bob Kersee. "No one could envision a 10.49 for a woman in the 100," he said of Griffith Joyner's race. It was the first world record for Flo-Jo, as she had come to be known. Later that week, she set a U.S. record in the 200-meter race with a time of 21.77 seconds.

Griffith Joyner set the track world on its ear with her running times at the Olympic trials, but she also made some stunning statements with her appearance. Running with long fingernails (the colors of which changed by the day) and flowing long hair, she sported a one-legged blue leotard and white bikini in the 100-meter finals and a white fishnet running suit for the 200-meter event. "I came here with fourteen outfits," she told the press.

One week after the trials, Griffith Joyner decided to switch coaches. She fired Bob Kersee, who she determined was too busy coaching his other athletes—there were six Kersee-coached athletes heading to Seoul, including his wife, Jackie—and replaced him with her husband, Al Joyner. Griffith Joyner claimed she needed the individual attention, and she credited Joyner, rather than Kersee, with teaching her the fundamentals she needed to become a champion 100-meter sprinter.

The media loved the stylish runner from Watts, and they made her the cover girl for the 1988 Olympics. Her image splashed the covers of countless magazines in the weeks leading up to the Seoul games, and she was named the favorite to win gold in the 100-meter and 200-meter events. Griffith Joyner became a media celebrity abroad as well. *Paris Match* dubbed her *la tigresse noire*—the black tigress—and when she appeared in two European races in August 1988, in Malmo, Sweden, and in Gateshead, England, she earned $25,000 per appearance. Back in the United States, Hollywood produc-

ers were contacting her with film offers—and the Olympic Games were still several weeks away.

Whether or not Flo-Jo, as she was now called, felt any pressure at the start of the Seoul games is difficult to determine. Surely anyone who had gained that kind of attention would have been at least somewhat nervous that she would not perform up to expectation. Then again, at times Flo-Jo appeared to be almost superhuman—which is exactly what her performances were in Seoul. She exploded out of the blocks in the 100-meter final and left all her competitors, including EVELYN ASHFORD, the defending Olympic champ, in her dust as she galloped across the tape in an Olympic-record time of 10.54. Four days later, she broke the world record twice in the 200-meter event: first in the semifinals, with a time of 21.56, and then in the finals, when she clocked a 21.34 on her way to her second gold.

Griffith Joyner would add another gold medal when she anchored the United States 4 × 100 relay team (in 1984 she had been excluded from the relay after she refused to clip her nails, judged by her teammates to be distracting during the passing of the baton), and then helped the 4 × 400 relay team to a silver medal.

Flo-Jo's Olympic performances, along with those of her sister in-law Jackie Joyner-Kersee were called into question shortly after the games. At Seoul a total of eight athletes tested positive for using anabolic steroids, which enhance muscle development and increase speed, and they were banned from the games. Among the athletes who tested positive was Ben Johnson, a Canadian sprinter who had won the 100-meter men's event with a world record time. Johnson was stripped of his gold medal and sent back to Canada in disgrace, and the gold medal was given to the erstwhile second-place finisher, U.S. runner Carl Lewis.

Griffith Joyner had reportedly passed the steroid tests after winning her races, but then a Brazilian athlete named Joaquim Cruz told several sports writers that he suspected both Griffith Joyner and Joyner-Kersee of engaging in steroid abuse. "She

[Griffith Joyner] looks more like a man than a woman," he told reporters. "[She] must be doing something that isn't normal to get all those muscles." Griffith Joyner angrily denied the accusations, stating that she is "not into drugs." Rumors that she might have used steroids did remain—Eyelyn Ashford wrote an article for the *New York Times* in 1997 claiming that Griffith Joyner could not possibly have run the 100-meter race in that fast a time without the aid of an illegal substance—but Griffith Joyner denied all allegations, and there was never any substantial evidence or proof to the contrary.

With three golds and a silver, Flo-Jo was now a certified Olympic hero. She won the Sullivan Award, for top amateur athlete, in 1988 and the Jesse Owens Award, for outstanding track athlete, the same year. She came home, not only to a hero's welcome, but to a lucrative career. She appeared on numerous talk shows, and she became a fixture in print advertisements and television commercials.

In 1989, Flo-Jo retired from sprinting at the age of 30. She continued to work as a model and spokesperson, and she designed her own line of clothes. In 1993, she became the first woman to cochair the President's Council on Physical Fitness and Sports.

Flo-Jo's life was tragically cut short when she suffered a heart seizure and died suddenly on September 21, 1998. She was survived by her husband and their daughter, Mary.

Further Reading

Davis, Michael D. *Black American Women in Olympic Track and Field: A Complete Illustrated Reference.* Jefferson, N.C.: McFarland, 1992.

Layden, Joe. *Women in Sports: The Complete Book of the World's Greatest Female Athletes.* Santa Monica, Calif.: General Publishing Group, 1997, p. 128.

GUTHRIE, JANET
(1938–)   *Race Car Driver*

The first woman to race in the prestigious Indianapolis 500, Janet Guthrie always craved high speeds and adventure. She grew up wanting to be a fighter pilot. Happily for car racing fans, she decided instead to stay grounded.

Janet Guthrie was born on March 7, 1938, in Miami, Florida. The daughter of an airline pilot, Janet's greatest ambition as a child was to get her pilot's license and follow in her father's footsteps. By the time she had finished high school, she was flying her own plane. She studied aerodynamics and physics at the University of Michigan, and after graduating from that school in 1960, she earned a commercial pilot's license.

Degree and license in hand, Guthrie took a position as a research and development engineer for an aviation company, but found herself bored at her job. Guthrie decided to look into becoming an astronaut. A few months later, she became one of only four women to qualify for the astronaut training program at the National Aeronautics and Space Administration (NASA). Although Guthrie did well during the early rounds of training at NASA, she was later discharged from the program because she did not have a Ph.D.

After leaving NASA, Guthrie decided to change venues in her quest for speed and adventure. Using a Jaguar coupe that had been remodeled for racing, she began competing in weekend road races. Slowly but surely, Guthrie became a respected member of the racing circuit. A member of an all-woman racing team between 1966 and 1971, she won several major races and competed in such important events as the Daytona 500.

In 1976 Guthrie won the prestigious North Atlantic Road Racing championship, and later that year she decided to try her luck in the qualifying rounds (speed trials) for the Indianapolis 500 race. Guthrie did not make the cut, but she spent the rest of the year gaining experience in stock car racing. Late in 1976 she became the first woman to participate in a National Association of Stock Car Auto Racing (NASCAR) Winston Cup event.

Then, early in 1977, Guthrie once again participated in the speed trials for the Indianapolis 500 race. This time, she was successful. At the starting line for the race in May 1977, the starter's call reflected Guthrie's pioneering moment: "In company with the first lady ever to qualify at Indianapolis," the starter cried, "gentlemen, start your engines!" Guthrie's car experienced mechanical problems during the race, and she retired from the race after 27 laps, but she returned the following year and finished ninth.

After racing at Indianapolis one more time in 1979 (once again mechanical problems forced her to withdraw midway through the race), Guthrie retired from racing in 1980. That same year, Guthrie was inducted into the International Women's Sports Hall of Fame—the first automobile driver to be so honored. Since leaving the track, Guthrie has become an outspoken advocate for women's sports by serving as a tireless and inspirational public speaker.

Further Reading

Encyclopaedia Britannica, Women in American History. "Janet Guthrie," Britannica Online. URL: http://women.eb.com/women/articles/Guthrie_Janet.html. Available online. Downloaded on February 26, 2001.

Layden, Joe. *Women in Sports: The Complete Book of the World's Greatest Female Athletes.* Santa Monica, Calif.: General Publishing Group, 1997, pp. 101–102.

HAMILL, DOROTHY
(1956–)   *Figure Skater*

The greatest female skater of the late 1970s was a nearsighted, shy Connecticut resident who became one of the most popular athletes in the United States. Dorothy Hamill won Olympic gold in Innsbruck, Austria, in 1976, and then became a role model for thousands of young U.S. skaters.

Born in Chicago, Illinois, to Chalmers Hamill, a business executive, and his wife, Carol, young Dorothy grew up in Riverside, Connecticut. When she was eight years old, Dorothy received her first pair of skates—a Christmas present that had cost her parents less than six dollars. Dorothy began skating at a local pond, and then she begged her parents for skating lessons so she could learn to skate backwards—something she had watched neighborhood children do but could not master on her own.

Soon Hamill was skating backwards, spinning, and leaping her way into skating competitions. Her greatest ambition was to become an Olympic champion, and her family supported her, both financially and emotionally. "My folks said, 'If you want to skate, that's fine,'" Hamill later said. "But

they gave me stern advice. 'We're with you . . . as long as you work hard.'"

Hamill did not disappoint her parents. By the time she was 15 years old, she was practicing six days a week, seven hours a day. Eager to hire a world-class coach for their daughter, the Hamills moved to Denver, Colorado, so Dorothy could work with Carlo Fassi, who had coached PEGGY FLEMING to the Olympic title in 1968. Working with Fassi, Hamill developed a skating style that combined spins and jumps with a crisp artistic flair. Her trademark move was a standing spin that Hamill, after tapping her skate on the ice, would turn into a sitting spin. Called the Hamill Camel, it became a regular part of her routines.

A shy and insecure person off the ice, Hamill would skate to the center of the ice and wait nervously for her music to begin. That nervousness never left her, although she almost always thrived in competition. A famous example of Hamill's insecurity occurred at the 1975 World Championships in Munich, Germany. Hamill had taken the silver medal at the championships the year before, and was in second place when she skated to the center of the rink for her freestyle skating performance. Unbeknownst to Hamill, at that

Dorothy Hamill overcame a severe case of stage fright to win a figure skating gold medal—and millions of admirers—at the 1976 Olympic Games.
(Allsport Photography)

moment the scores for the previous skater, a German native, were flashed on the board above her. Disappointed in the low scores, the Munich crowd began to boo. Hamill immediately assumed the crowd was jeering her; she burst into tears and left the ice. Fortunately, Fassi caught hold of her on the sidelines and explained the situation. Laughing bashfully, Hamill returned to the ice, and skated well enough to earn her second consecutive silver.

In 1976, Hamill, the U.S. national champion since 1974, was favored to win a medal, but not necessarily the gold. The World Champion in 1974 and 1975 was a Dutch woman named Dianne de Leeyw, and many experts picked her to take the Olympic championship as well. In 1976 the Olympic ice-skating competition featured three events. To begin with, each skater would per-form compulsory figures, which were required shapes formed by the skate blades on the ice. This portion of the competition counted for 30 percent of the final score. Two days later, the skater would perform a two-minute program of mixed required and freestyle moves, which would account for 20 percent of the score. The final portion of the competition was a four-minute free-skating routine, which would show the skater's creativity, artistry, and athleticism. This portion of the competition was the most crucial; it accounted for 50 percent of the final score. Although the compulsory figures were removed from Olympic competition in 1988, they were once a pivotal part of competition. Such national U.S. champions as Janet Lynn and Linda Fratianne skated their short and long programs well enough to win gold, but less than stellar performances in the compulsory figures cost them both the first-place medal; Lynn had to settle for bronze in 1972, and Fratianne for silver in 1984.

But in 1976, Hamill, wearing thick glasses, came through the compulsory-figure portion of the competition in second place. Two days later, she skated onto the ice without her glasses (Hamill detested contact lenses) and performed a terrific short program that vaulted her into first place. Delighted already with Hamill's shy charm and perky "wedge" haircut, U.S. audiences were further charmed to watch the myopic Hamill squint at the scoreboard to read her scores.

Two days after the short program, Hamill once again took the ice, this time to skate her four-minute freestyle routine. The 14th skater of the evening, Hamill appeared to be calm and relaxed while waiting for her music to begin. But inside, she was terrified. "I was standing in the center of the ice," she wrote in her autobiography of that moment, "trying to still the thudding in my heart. My knees were trembling. I felt enormous pressure as I waited for what seemed like hours for my music to begin. Finally, I thought of Carlo Fassi's words. 'Focus your mind into the tunnel and look to the other end where the light is shining.'"

The light did shine for Hamill, as she flew through her routine with such speed and grace that she made the skaters who appeared after her look like they were skating in slow motion. Interestingly, Hamill's routine featured breathtaking footwork and dazzling spins, but no triple jumps. She incorporated two double jumps in her progam—a lutz that she performed flawlessly and a delayed axel that was another trademark moves—but no triples. She was, in fact, the last Olympic skater to win the gold medal without a triple jump.

When Hamill returned home from Innsbruck, she was an instant celebrity. Millions of girls got their hair cut in the "wedge" style that she wore, and thousands took up figure skating. The attention was not always easy for Hamill, but she handled it graciously. In the spring of 1976, she won her first and only World Championship, and then retired from competitive amateur skating to turn professional.

Hamill began skating with the Ice Capades in 1977, and later that year she married Dean Paul Martin, the son of actor Dean Martin, in a highly publicized Hollywood wedding. Two years later the couple divorced, and Hamill, still skating professionally, wed the sports physician Ken Forsythe. They had a daughter, Alexandra, and divorced in the late 1980s. In 1993, Hamill and her third husband, businessman Ben Tinsdale, bought the financially troubled Ice Capades, but they sold it a year later. She continues to tour professionally with several ice shows.

Further Reading

Greenspan, Bud. *Frozen in Time: The Greatest Moments at the Winter Olympics.* Santa Monica, Calif.: General Publishing Group, 1997.

Kaufman, Michelle. "Janet Lynn and Dorothy Hamill," *Women's Game,* edited by Dick Wimmer. Short Hills, N.J.: Burford Books, pp. 89–94.

HAMM, MIA (Mariel Margaret Hamm)
(1972–)   *Soccer Player*

Mia Hamm is the most recognizable woman athlete in contemporary America. She also may be the most gifted U.S. born soccer player—male or female—ever to grace a soccer field.

Mariel Margaret Hamm was born on March 17, 1972, in Selma, Alabama. She was the third of four daughters born to Bill Hamm, an air force pilot instructor, and his wife, Stephanie, a retired ballerina. When Mia was five, the Hamms adopted two Thai-American boys. The older of these, Garrett, was eight years old when he came to the family. Mia immediately looked up to him and followed his lead. Because Garrett loved sports, Mia began playing too. And when Garrett decided to focus on soccer, so then did Mia.

There were other factors, as well, that led to Mia Hamm's love affair with soccer. Her father, Bill, had fallen in love with the sport himself when the family lived in Italy (a military family, the Hamms lived in seven states, as well as in Italy, during Mia's childhood). When the Hamms returned to the

103

United States, Bill gave his children a choice: They could go to the field and play soccer with him, or they could go to the studio and dance ballet with their mother. Mia gallantly gave ballet a try, but she ended up on the soccer field every time.

Mia joined her first soccer team when she was 10. The family was living in Wichita Falls, Texas, at that point, and there was no girls' soccer team there. Unruffled, Mia played for the boys' team. The Hamms moved to San Antonio two years later, and Mia was able to play for a girls' team there. By the time she was 13, her soccer skills were beginning to draw notice. Although Mia never did take to ballet, she had a dancer's natural grace and moved exceptionally well with the ball, dodging defenders while maintaining control. In addition, she had an extraordinary acceleration and could speed down the field while dribbling the ball, leaving defenders in her wake.

While she was still 13, Mia was invited to join an Olympic Development Program (ODP) which was a soccer camp for young girls with extraordinary athletic talent. At the ODP she met the women who would become her teammates and closest friends: future national team members Kristine Lilly, Joy Fawcett, Julie Fowdy, and Carla Overbeck.

In 1986, Hamm, then 14, moved back to Wichita Falls with her family. This time she was able to play on a girls' team. During a tournament in New Orleans, Mia was so dominant that one of the coaches on the scene called his fiend Anson Dorrance, the coach of the University of North Carolina (UNC) at Chapel Hill who had recently formed the National Women's Soccer Team, and asked him to take a look a the 15-year old from Texas. Dorrance was skeptical; people constantly asked him to "take a look" at "exceptional" players. Rarely did those players live up to their billing. But Hamm did not disappoint Dorrance. In fact, she awed him with her acceleration and speed. After watching her play, Dorrance asked her to join the national team.

During her first year on the team, in 1987, Hamm did not score a goal. She also had some trouble relating to many of the other team members. The youngest player on the team by more than a year, Hamm was also extremely shy and very intense. She often needed to be by herself before games and would turn away from teammates who approached her.

Aware of Hamm's extraordinary skills, Dorrance also knew that she would not become a fully developed player until she learned how to be a true member of the team. He took Hamm aside and told her that she would have to work hard, not only on her game, but on her attitude if she wanted to realize her full potential. Hamm took Dorrance's words seriously, and she worked to let her guard down with her teammates. She was initially intimidated by the older members of the squad, such as April Heinrichs and MICHELLE AKERS, but she gradually learned to play next to them.

When she was 17, Hamm decided to attend UNC and play for Dorrance. Too young to be living on her own or in campus housing, Hamm moved in with Dorrance and his wife, who temporarily became her legal guardians. Hamm's national teammate Kristine Lilly also chose to attend Carolina, and during the two players' years there, the Carolina Tar Heels won four consecutive national championships. During her career at Carolina, Hamm won the Hermann Trophy, awarded each year to the top man and woman in collegiate soccer, twice—in 1992 and 1993.

In 1991 during Hamm's sophomore season at Carolina, the national team traveled to China and won the first Women's World Cup soccer competition. Although the tournament belonged to the older members of the squad, such as Akers and Heinrichs, Hamm held her own during her time on the field, playing aggressively and impressing her opponents with her speed and agility, and she scored a goal as well.

Four years later, the National Soccer Team traveled to Sweden to defend its World Cup title. In the first game, Akers left the game with an injury, and the team struggled to a 3-3 tie with China. The U.S. team won its next three matches, but in the semifinals of the tournament they were up against Norway, the team they had beaten to take the championship four years earlier. Norway took an early lead, and despite their best efforts, the U.S. players could not make up the difference.

They ended up placing third in the tournament, behind Norway and China.

But despite the disappointing finish for the U.S. team, the 1995 World Cup was a pivotal tournament for Mia Hamm. During the tournament she scored two goals—including a dazzling score after a 60-yard solo run in the final game—and had three assists. The soft-spoken Hamm had become, by the end of the tournament, the superstar of the team.

Hamm never believed that she was the best player on the U.S. squad, but she took her new role as sports spokeswoman seriously and began promoting the game with public appearances and promotional events. By 1996, the women's game had drawn a loyal following. At the final game of the Atlanta Olympics, fans jammed the Georgia Dome to watch the United States take on China. The rambunctious spectators included several men who had painted "I Love Hamm" or "Hamm Is Good" across their chests. Soccer had, at long last, arrived in the United States. The women's national team did not disappoint its fans, beating China in the final for the gold medal.

The following year, Hamm suffered an immeasurable loss when her beloved brother, Garrett, died of a rare blood disease. Hamm mourned the loss of her brother deeply. His death made her more introspective, but it also reinforced her love of soccer, something she had shared with Garrett. She threw herself into soccer more intently than ever before. Hamm had, along with her teammates, a definite goal: They wanted to win the World Cup again, and this time in front of their home country. As the soccer team toured around the nation, playing practice games for the World Cup, they received more and more attention from Americans, boys and girls alike.

Three years later, they met up with China again, this time in the final of the 1999 World Cup, in Pasadena, California. By this time, Hamm had become the biggest scorer in the history of women's soccer, with more than 100 goals in international play. It was Hamm's name that the fans at the sold-out Rose Bowl chanted most often on July 10, 1999—a day no fan of women's sports is likely

Mia Hamm handles the ball for the national women's soccer team. The leading scorer in international soccer history, Hamm has played for two World Cup champion teams.
(Aubrey Washington/Getty Images)

to forget. At the end of the scoreless game, the teams competed in a five-player shoot-out to determine the championship. The U.S. team won the shootout 5-4, to win the cup in front of a delirious crowd. Hamm dutifully scored when her turn came to take a shot on goal, then ran back to the team in delight. She later told reporters she was "relieved" that she did not miss.

It is that modesty, together with her extraordinary athletic talent and attractive appearance, that has helped Mia Hamm become the appealing superstar she is today. She had landed a host of endorsement contracts, making her one of the most affluent women in contemporary sports.

105

Hamm, who in 1994 married Christiaan Corley, a marine pilot she met while at Carolina (the two divorced in 2001), continues to play competitive soccer. The national team won a silver medal in the 2000 Olympic Games in Sydney, and many of its members, including Hamm, began playing in the WUSA, a newly formed U.S. professional women's soccer league in 2001. Hamm was drafted by, and played for, the WUSA's Washington Freedom. Mia raises money and awareness for bone marrow disease (which her brother had died of) and for the development of women's sports. She has her own foundation and also works as a volunteer coach at the University of North Carolina, assisting her mentor, Anson Dorrance.

Further Reading

Hamm, Mia, and Aaron Heifitz. *Go for the Goal: A Champion's Guide to Winning in Soccer and Life.* New York: HarperCollins, 2000.

Longman, Jere. *The Girls of Summer: The U.S. Women's Soccer Team and How It Changed the World.* New York: HarperCollins, 2000.

Miller, Marla. *All-American Girls: The U.S. Women's National Soccer Team,* New York: Archway Paperbacks, 1999, pp. 72–86.

HANSELL, ELLEN FORD
(Ellen Ford Hansell Allderdice)
(1869–1937) *Tennis Player*

Ellen Ford Hansell is an important figure in the history of women's sports for one reason: She was the first woman to win the U.S. tennis championship.

Ellen was born on September 28, 1869, in Philadelphia. Her father, Samuel Robb Hansell, was an upholstery manufacturer, and her mother, Jane Martin Hansell, was a homemaker. During her early childhood Ellen suffered from anemia, so she was pale and often sickly. She was not particularly interested in sports, but she did play tennis periodically. Her doctor suggested that exercise might help her health and advised her parents to encourage her to play tennis regularly. By the time she was 13, Ellen was playing tennis constantly.

When she turned 16, Ellen joined the Belmont Club, a tennis center in Philadelphia where such contemporary players as Louise Allderdice, Margarette Ballard, and Bertha Townsend trained and practiced. Ellen quickly befriended all three women, and the quartet soon became known as the "Big Four." Although the Belmont was not the most exclusive tennis club in Philadelphia, it was still costly for the Hansell family. Years later Ellen recalled that the yearly $10 fee "surely hurt" the family budget. To save money, Ellen always walked the mile and a half to the club rather than spend a nickel for a ride on a horsecar.

Hansell and her tennis cronies played a very different type of game from the one most of us are familiar with today. The racket, made of heavy wood, had a small face with a squared-off top. Moreover, Hansell's tennis outfit featured a full skirt that reached the ground as well as a long-sleeved, closely tailored blouse. All told, moving around the court took a great deal of time and effort; Hansell would grab her skirt in her free hand and run full force to reach a difficult shot. As she put it, "We did now and then grip our over-draped, voluminous skirts with our left hand to give us a bit more limb freedom when dashing to make a swift, snappy stroke."

The strokes Hansell and her contemporaries used were strong and sure, if not as powerful as the ones professionals use today. There was no volleying, but Hansell did have an effective slice she could place accurately, to the chagrin of her opponents, who were constantly forced to hoist their skirts and chase the shot.

Hansell's rise to prominence in the sport of tennis coincided perfectly with the ascent of women's tennis in the United States. She was 17 in 1886, the year the Chestnut Hill Tennis Club held the nation's first tournament for women. Hansell did not enter the singles portion of the Chestnut Hill tournament, but she was present the following year, when Wissahickon Inn, a posh club in the same neighborhood as the Chestnut Hill outfit, staged the first official U.S. championship for women.

Wearing her trademark red hat, Hansell swept onto the Wissahickon courts. Notably absent from the tournament was Hansell's friend and rival Bertha Townsend, who was slated to compete but withdrew after a death in her family. Townsend's absence left a total of seven women vying for the tournament title, and the ladies played their sets in front of what Hansell later described as "the most loving, openly prejudiced crowds." Those fans stood a mere two feet from the sidelines, and in addition to cheering on their local favorites, they made polite suggestions. "Place it to her left," one onlooker advised to Hansell during the final match.

Hansell emerged victorious, and she was awarded the titlist prize: a shiny, silver belt. But although Hansell was acknowledged as the winner of the Wissahickon competition, it was not until two years later that the tournament was officially known as the first U.S. championship. In 1889, the newly formed United States National Ladies Tennis Association (USNLTA) took over the event and retroactively granted national status to both the 1886 and 1887 tournaments.

Although she would play for four more years, Hansell never again won a tennis championship. She reached the finals of the 1888 tournament at Wissahickon, but was defeated. She retired from tennis in 1890 and married Taylor Allderdice, the brother of Louise Allderdice, one of her old tennis cronies. The Allderdices had six children, all of whom learned the game of tennis from their pioneer mother. Hansell died in Pittsburgh in 1937.

Further Reading

King, Billie Jean, and Cynthia Starr. *We Have Come a Long Way: The Story of Women's Tennis.* New York: McGraw Hill, 1988, pp. 20–22.

Markel, Robert, Susan Wagoner, and Marcella Smith. *The Women's Sports Encyclopedia.* New York: Henry Holt, 1999.

HAWORTH, CHERYL
(1983–) *Weight Lifter*

Cheryl Haworth is the first U.S. woman to capture an Olympic medal in the sport of weight lifting.

The 2000 games, in Sydney, Australia, was the first Olympiad to include weight lifting as a medal sport, and Haworth, a world-class lifter in both the snatch and the clean and jerk, won a bronze medal there.

Born in Savannah, Georgia, on April 19, 1983, Cheryl Haworth was a sickly toddler who had a poor appetite. Her parents, Bob Haworth, a communications consultant, and Sheila Haworth, a registered nurse, were worried about their second daughter (Cheryl has an older sister, Beth, and a younger sister, Katie). When she was four, Cheryl had surgery to remove her tonsils and adenoids, and then her appetite increased. For a time, Cheryl had normal eating habits, but by the time she was a teenager her appetite had become enormous. She gained weight rapidly—sometimes as much as 10 pounds a month. Doctors advised Cheryl's parents to put her on a diet, but they ignored these suggestions, figuring that if Cheryl wanted to eat, they should not try to stop her.

As it turned out, the weight she gained did not hinder Cheryl tremendously. A strong girl as a preteen—she could beat every boy in arm wrestling—she was also a gifted softball player. As a member of her team in middle school, in the summer of 1996, Cheryl went with some teammates to a local weight-lifting center to do some strength training. At 265 pounds, 13-year-old Cheryl caught the eye of Michael Cohen, a coach for the Savannah weight-lifting team. Cohen saw Cheryl lift a 120-pound weight without hesitation, and he realized that she could become a champion.

With Cohen's encouragement, Haworth began training at the weight-lifting center on a regular basis. Several months later, she began competing. In weight-lifting tournaments, competitors are judged on their ability to perform two kinds of lifts. The first, known as the snatch, involves lifting the weight over one's head in one single motion. The second, the clean and jerk, is a two-part lift. First the weight is brought to the chest, and then the competitor lifts the weight over the head. The contestants' scores from the two lifts are added together to determine the total score.

Haworth, an excellent competitor in both lifting categories, began setting records in 1999. At the age of 16, she established a new U.S. mark in the clean and jerk with a lift of 297 pounds. The following year she smashed that record with a lift of 319.7 pounds in the clean and jerk, and then she set a new national mark in the snatch with a lift of 264.6 pounds.

By that time, Haworth was deep into her training for the Sydney Olympics. She traveled to Australia favored to finish in the top three, and Haworth, who matched her personal bests in both the snatch and the clean and jerk, did not disappoint. She finished third, after Meijuan Ding of China, the gold-medal winner, and Poland's Agata Wrobel, who took the silver. Haworth returned to the United States to continue training. She aims to compete once again at the 2004 Games in Athens, Greece. This time, she will be shooting for gold.

Further Reading

Longman, Jere. "Women Move Closer to Olympic Equality," *The New York Times,* August 20, 2000, pp. 1, 22.

McCallum, Jack. "As Big as She Wants to Be," *Sports Illustrated,* September 11, 2000, p. 162.

Olympic Athletes. "Cheryl Haworth," NBCOlympics.com. Available online. URL: http://Sydney2000.nbco. Downloaded on July 11, 2001.

HEISS, CAROL (Carol Jenkins)
(1940–)   *Figure Skater*

When Carol Heiss won the gold medal in figure skating at the 1960 Olympics, she had fulfilled a mission—and kept a promise. Four years earlier, Heiss's mother, suffering from terminal cancer, had asked her 16-year-old daughter if she wanted to be an Olympic champion. "More than anything else," Carol had replied. "Then don't let anyone, or anything, stop you," Marie Heiss had said.

Marie was her daughter's greatest advocate and fan. Born in New York City on January 20, 1940, Carol Heiss learned to skate soon after she learned to walk. When Carol was six, her mother took her to the Skating Club of New York, where she

Four years after finishing second in figure skating to Tenley Albright, Carol Heiss struck gold at the 1960 Olympics in Squaw Valley.
(Library of Congress)

became one of several gifted young skaters taking lessons from Pierre and Andre Brunet, a husband-and-wife coaching team. The Brunets were world-champion skaters as well as teachers; they had won consecutive gold medals in the pairs events at the 1928 and 1932 Olympic Games.

To take lessons from such a high-caliber team at such a young age was impressive enough. But Carol, an exuberant and enthusiastic girl with an abundance of athletic talent, quickly became the finest skater in the Brunets' class. "I quickly recognized," Pierre Brunet said years later, "that she had immense potential and could become a champion." The Brunets told Marie Heiss in 1946 that "in ten years, Carol can become the best in the world."

Wanting her daughter to achieve her full potential, Marie decided to dedicate herself to

Carol's training. It was an expensive endeavor, honing a potential Olympic figure skating champion; Marie, a freelance fabric designer, took her drawings to the skating club and worked in the stands as Carol trained. Marie used her earnings to pay Carol's skating expenses. Marie and Carol's hard work soon began to pay dividends. When she was 11, Carol won her first title when she took top honors at the U.S. Novice Ladies' Championships. The next year, she won the Ladies' Junior Championships. Over the next five years, Carol added title after title, and Marie was always in the stands to cheer her on.

In 1953, Carol Heiss won a silver medal at the U.S. Championships. It was her first of four consecutive second-place finishes at the Nationals. The gold medal winner during those years was a skater from Massachusetts named TENLEY ALBRIGHT. Unfortunately for Heiss, she and Albright were almost contemporaries; Albright was five years older and thus more experienced. The two skaters became each another's greatest competition.

Heiss and Albright both went to the 1956 Olympic Games in Cortina, Italy, with aspirations to win gold. Although Marie Heiss had been stricken with terminal cancer, she once again accompanied her daughter. Heiss and Albright both skated magnificently, but Albright, the 1955 world champion, scored higher in the free-skating competition and took the gold. Heiss once again won silver, but her losing streak against Albright was about to end. Two weeks after the Cortina games, Heiss and Albright met once again, at the World Championships in Garmisch-Parteukirchen, Germany. This time, it was Heiss who emerged triumphant.

It was the first of five straight World Championships for Heiss; nevertheless, it was a bittersweet time for her. The 1956 World Championships was the last event that Marie Heiss attended. In October 1956 she died. Carol grieved for her mother, but focused her energy on fulfilling the dream she and Marie shared: she was intent on winning Olympic gold.

Heiss came to Squaw Valley, California, the site of the 1960 Winter Olympics, as the favorite to win gold; Albright had retired shortly after the 1956 World Championships. Skating with grace and athleticism, Heiss dominated the event completely, and she was the unanimous first-place finisher. Olympic gold in hand, Heiss returned to New York City and was given a ticker tape parade—the first Winter Olympic athlete to receive that welcome. With her mission of winning Olympic gold accomplished, Heiss was able to retire. She did so later in 1960, after winning her fifth World Championship.

In 1961, Heiss married Hayes Jenkins, a skater who had won Olympic gold in the men's event in 1960. For many years after her retirement, Jenkins remained involved in figure skating, becoming a coach and trainer. She remains a fan and viewer of competitive ice-skating today. Although her greatest triumph came at the 1960 Olympics, Jenkins was able to keep competing in perspective. "My mother and the Brunets," she later said, "gave me a fully rounded philosophy of life. An Olympic gold medal cannot give you lifetime happiness—you must go on to other things."

Further Reading

Greenspan, Bud. *Frozen in Time: The Greatest Moments at the Winter Olympics.* Santa Monica, Calif.: General Publishing Group, 1997.

Layden, Joe. *Women in Sports: The Complete Book of the World's Greatest Female Athletes.* Santa Monica, Calif.: General Publishing Group, 1997, p. 111.

HENIE, SONJA
(1912–1969)   *Figure Skater*

Long before TARA LIPINSKI, MICHELLE KWAN, NANCY KERRIGAN, and SARAH HUGHES skated to fame and glory, a Norwegian-born skater named Sonja Henie entranced the world and put the sport of figure skating on the map.

Like many Norwegians, Sonja Henie, who was born in Oslo on April 8, 1912, learned to ski at the same time that she learned to walk. Her father, Wilhelm, was not only a world champion cyclist but an accomplished skier and skater who encouraged young Sonja to learn both sports early on.

Norwegian-born Olympic champion Sonja Henie revolutionized competitive figure skating and then moved to Hollywood to become a celebrated film star. (She is shown here with former skater Artur Vieregg.)
(Library of Congress)

Sonja's mother was a homemaker and an amateur ballet dancer. Internalizing the passions of both her parents, Sonja began taking both skating and ballet lessons at the age of five.

Although the first skating tournaments Sonja entered were speed skating races, by the time she was eight she had won her first figure skating competion. Two years later, at the age of 10, she became the figure skating champion of Norway; a title she would hold for the next 14 years.

In 1924, Henie was chosen to represent her country at the very first Winter Olympic Games, which were held in Chamonix, France. At the age of 12, Henie finished fifth (out of seven) in Chamonix. Her older competitors might have skated more accurate compulsory figures on the ice—at the time a crucial part of skating competitions—but Henie's performance nonetheless drew the most attention. Never before had a skater combined the athletics of the sport with the artistry of ballet. She may not have won a medal, but Henie, with her lithe grace on the ice and her stylish costumes, had made a lasting impression.

Two years after Chamonix, Henie made her first appearance at the World Championships, where she finished second to the Olympic champion, Austria's Herma Jaross-Szabo. These championships, held in Stockholm, were significant not only because Henie placed second there at the age of 14, but because it would mark the last time in her skating career that she would not win a competition that she had entered.

At the 1928 Olympics, in Saint Moritz, Switzerland, Henie stunned the judges with a highly balletic freestyle routine. She used intricate steps and arm motions that made it appear as if she were dancing across the ice. In addition, Henie's freestyle routine featured 19 different types of spins. Using these different moves, Henie seemed to be turning incessantly; she achieved 80 complete revolutions during her freestyle routine. In addition, Henie showed up on the ice wearing a stylish satin dress that was cut above the knees. It was the first time a competitive ice skater had worn anything that revealed her legs.

By the end of the Saint Moritz Olympics, Henie had not only captured the gold medal, but she had forever revolutionized the sport of figure skating. From that time forward, figure skaters would strive to combine a dancelike grace with the athletic requirements of the sport, and a skater's artistic impression would be as important as her technical performance.

Henie successfully defended her Olympic title at the 1932 games in Lake Placid, New York. Skating in competition in the United States for the first time, Henie was the unquestioned star of the games. At the height of the Great Depression, American fans paid scalpers up to $50 for a precious ticket to the ice skating event. On the ice, Henie did not disappoint; she dazzled all seven judges as she swept to the championship. And although she had trouble with the language barrier, she also managed to charm the U.S. press, who wrote story after story about her. By the end of the games, U.S. promoters were besieging Henie with offers for personal appearances. At the age of 19, Henie had become an international star.

Shortly after the Lake Placid Games, Henie decided to skate in one more Olympics, and then retire and pursue a career in American films. The 1936 Olympics, held in the German resort town of Garmisch-Partenkirchen, proved to be Henie's most difficult games. At 23, she was one of the older women competing, a role she was not comfortable playing. Moreover, her closest competitor, the British skater Cecelia Colledge, was 15—the age Henie was when she captured her first Olympic gold, eight years earlier. Tensions were high at the compulsory figures portion of the competition. Henie, accustomed to winning by a large margin, found herself only 3.6 points ahead of Colledge at the end of the first day. Outraged by the close competition, Henie ripped the posted scores off the wall and tore them to shreds.

After her outburst, Henie pulled herself together, and in the steel-willed way that had earned her the nickname of "iron butterfly" she promised herself she would win. The freeskating program was held a week later, and Henie, the 26th and final skater, took the ice in front of a German crowd that included the nation's chancellor, Adolf Hitler. She whirled, danced, and spun through her routine with ease and grace, charming the crowd, who gave her a standing ovation. More important, her final competitive routine earned six first-place votes from the seven-judge panel (she shared the seventh vote with Colledge). Henie left Garmisch-Partenkirchen with her third Olympic gold medal, and she then retired from competitive ice-skating. During her 10-year career she had won a total of 1,473 cups, medals, and trophies.

Henie landed in Hollywood shortly after the 1936 games, and she was immediately given a contract by Twentieth Century–Fox. In the late 1930s, Henie made a host of successful movies, with such Hollywood leading men as Tyrone Power and Don Ameche. These films were so profitable that in 1938, Henie was the third leading box-office draw, behind only Clark Gable and Shirley Temple.

Interest in Henie's movies waned slightly in the 1940s, but Henie continued to draw fans to her skating routines when she launched her own traveling ice show. In 1941, Henie became a U.S. citizen. Beloved in her new nation, Henie became the subject of criticism in Norway. Many Norwegians believed that Henie was not doing enough for her native land, which was occupied by Nazi troops during the early 1940s.

Henie married three times. After two divorces, she wed her childhood sweetheart, Nils Onstad, in 1951. Henie and Onstad used her considerable funds to amass a huge collection that included not only works of art, but some of Henie's most precious skating memorabilia. In 1968, Henie and Onstad sent the collection to Norway as a gift and established a museum there to house it.

By the time Henie died of leukemia in 1969, she had a fortune worth $47 million. She remains the most successful athlete-turned-actress in history. More important, Sonja Henie completely revolutionized the sport of figure skating. During her decade-long competitive career, she introduced dance and artistry to the ice and changed the look of the skater from that of a stiff and formal competitor to a lithe and graceful artisan. Henie's influence remains today, as skaters use costumes, music, and dance in skating routines that stress artistic impression as ardently as technical performance.

Further Reading

Greenspan, Bud. *Frozen in Time: The Greatest Moments at the Winter Olympics.* Santa Monica, Calif.: General Publishing Group, 1997.

Smith, Lissa editor. *Nike Is a Goddess: The History of Women in Sports.* New York: Atlantic Monthly Press, 1998, pp. 161–165.

Sugar, Burt Randolph. "Sonja Henie," *Women's Game,* edited by Dick Wimmer. Short Hills, N.J.: Burford Books, pp. 85–88.

HILL, LYNN
(1961–   )   *Rock Climber*

Lynn Hill is one of the finest rock climbers in the world. In a sport dominated by males, she has mastered climbs once thought impossible for a woman, and she has beaten many men in the process.

Born in 1961 in Los Angeles, California, Lynn grew up in a large family. An active youngster who loved to run and jump, Lynn also tended to climb everything in sight—from trees and telephone poles to streetlights. Her parents figured that Lynn had a natural affinity for gymnastics, and when she eight, she began taking lessons.

In high school, Lynn was one of the top gymnasts in the state, but when she was about 14, she found the sport that would become her true passion. Lynn's older sister, who had become interested in rock climbing, began inviting her younger sibling to accompany her on trips to Joshua Tree National Monument and to Yosemite. Just like that, Lynn Hill became obsessed with scaling rocks, and within months, she was going on difficult climbs and mastering them.

Hill eventually quit her gymnastics team to concentrate more completely on rock climbing. A lean and muscular person with a low proportion of body fat, Hill had the perfect physique for her newfound sport. She also had the right emotional outlook. Tired of the malls and suburban sprawl of her hometown, Los Angeles, she longed to be off with just a few other people in the wild outdoors.

As Hill got more experienced in rock climbing, she became even better at it. By the late 1980s she had begun entering competitions. Although many people think of rock climbing as an outdoor activity rather than a competitive sport, there are in fact several tournaments for these athletes. In Europe, rock climbing competitions take place in front of enthusiastic fans, who often clap and chant for their favorite athlete.

At the same time, rock climbing has always been very much a men's sport. The grueling physical actions it requires are handled best by people who have little body fat and who are naturally strong. Physiologically, that is a body type that is more common in men than in women. But Hill, a five foot, two inch, woman who weighs around 100 pounds but who can bench press 150 pounds, also matches that prototype. At the age of 19, Hill easily scaled a wall named Ophir Broke in Telluride, Colorado. It was the first time a woman had ever mastered that climb, and in so doing she made a statement for female rock climbers everywhere.

In 1980, Hill, who had been doing odd jobs in order to support her rock climbing lifestyle, signed on as a contestant on a television program called *Survival of the Fittest*. Hill won the program's contest four years in a row and brought home a total of $30,000 in winnings. In the meantime, she was climbing in Europe whenever she could. In 1988 Hill suffered an injury during a climb in Buoux, France. She had forgotten to tie a safety rope around her waist and fell 85 feet from a cliff. She emerged from the accident with a broken foot and elbow but then returned the following year to take top honors in the women's division at a competition in Arco, Italy. Several months later, she landed in the record books when she became the first woman to complete a grade 5.14 climb, in Cimai, France. (A "grade" is used by rock climbers to rate the difficulty of a given climb. A grade of 5 or above means that the climb requires great expertise. The highest grade given to a climb is 5.15.)

With some money in the bank, Hill decided to move to New Paltz, New York, where in 1993 she earned a degree from the State University of New York. While living in New Paltz, Hill traveled regularly to a rock climbing region called the Shawangunk cliffs, where she trained for competitions. During one of her trips there she met Russ Raffa, a fellow climber. The two eventually married.

During her career, Lynn Hill has won more than 20 competitions in the women's division in rock climbing. More important, she has proven that women can be world-class climbers. It just takes physical muscles, mental strength, and a great deal of passion.

Further Reading

Biographical Resource Center. "Lynn Hill," *Great Women in Sports*. Detroit, Mich.: Visible Ink Press, 1996.

CNN.SI for Women, 100 Greatest Female Athletes. "Lynn Hill," *Sports Illustrated for Women*. Available online, URL: http://sportsillustrated.cnn.com/siforwomen/top_100/87. Posted on November 29, 1999.

Da Silva, Rachel. *Leading Out: Women Climbers Reaching the Top.* Seattle, Wash.: Seal Press, 1993.

⊞ HOLDSCLAW, CHAMIQUE
(1977–)   *Basketball Player*

Of all women basketball players who have competed in the Women's National Basketball Association (WNBA), perhaps the most talented is Chamique Holdsclaw. A New Yorker who played her collegiate ball under coach PAT HEAD SUMMITT at the University of Tennessee, Holdsclaw led the Lady Volunteers to three consecutive national championships and then went on to win Olympic gold as a member of the 2000 U.S. team, which took top honors at the Sydney Games.

If Holdsclaw's achievements are sparkling, her upbringing was equally humble. Born in New York City on August 9, 1977, Chamique Holdsclaw grew up in a city housing project with her parents, Bonita and Willie, and her brother, Davon. Money, tight from the start, grew even scarcer when Willie and Bonita separated. Eleven-year-old Chamique and her brother went to live with their grandmother, June, because Bonita could not afford to take care of them. Eventually Davon returned to live with his mother, but Chamique remained with June.

By this time, Chamique was not only a gifted basketball player—among the first chosen in neighborhood pickup games—but a graceful ballerina as well. Having taken dance lessons with the Bernice Johnson Dance Group, Chamique had performed at Lincoln Center at the age of 10, and she dreamed of one day dancing professionally. But at Christ the King High School, Holdsclaw completely dazzled Vincent Canizzaro, the coach of the girls' basketball team. Used to talented players—the Christ the King team was one of the most prestigious in the nation—Canizzaro was so impressed by Holdsclaw that he made her a varsity player during her freshman year.

Holdsclaw combined a confident attitude with dazzling speed and grace (picked up during her

Before she became the number-one selection in the 1999 WNBA draft, Chamique Holdsclaw led the Tennessee Lady Volunteers to three consecutive NCAA championships.
(Harry How/Getty Images)

years as a dancer) to dominate opponents on the court. She quickly became the best player on her team, and during her years in high school Christ the King won four consecutive state titles. After averaging 25 points a game her senior year, Holdsclaw sorted through dozens of scholarship offers. Her grandmother, June, was a fan of the University of Tennessee Lady Volunteers and particularly of their coach, Pat Summitt, so she urged Holdsclaw to play for the Lady Volunteers.

Heeding her grandmother's advice, Holdsclaw moved to Knoxville and quickly became Summitt's protégée. The seasoned coach was so taken with Holdsclaw's play that she told reporters the New York freshman might well be the finest player she had ever worked with. A starter from her first game, Holdsclaw averaged 18.6 points a game during her freshman year at Tennessee. Her play was so impressive that, during a late-season scoring tear, she became the first woman ever to be named player of the week by ESPN. Although she was injured during the Southeast Conference Tournament, Holdsclaw came back to help the Lady Volunteers win the National Championship.

Holdsclaw would lead the Lady Volunteers to two more National Collegiate Athletic Association (NCAA) crowns, and during her senior year, she won the Sullivan Award, given each year to the best amateur athlete in the United States. Unlike such players as LISA LESLIE, CYNTHIA COOPER, and SHERYL SWOOPES, Holdsclaw knew she had an immediate opportunity to play professional basketball after leaving college. The WNBA was beginning its third season when Holdsclaw graduated from Tennessee, and the Washington Mystics made her their first-round draft pick—the only collegiate player to be selected in the first round.

During her first years in the professional league, Holdsclaw has continued to awe fans and players alike. Named Rookie of the Year in 1999, Holdsclaw has played in the League All-Star game during each of her (as of 2002) three seasons with the Mystics. Still in the early years of what promises to be a legendary career, Holdsclaw has a simple goal for herself. "Years from now," she confided to one reporter, "I want people to say, 'that Holdsclaw kid, she really could play.'"

Further Reading

"Chamique Holdsclaw," *Contemporary Black Biography,* vol. 24, edited by Shirelle Phelps. Detroit, Mich.: Gale Group, 2000.

"Chamique Unplugged," *Sports Illustrated for Women,* May/June 2001, p. 70.

Holdsclaw, Chamique, and Jennifer Frey. *Chamique.* New York: Simon & Schuster, 1998.

HOLM, ELEANOR
(1913–) *Swimmer*

One of the most charismatic athletes of the 20th century, Eleanor Holm captured a gold in the 100-

meter backstroke race in the 1932 Los Angeles Olympic Games, and she then went on to become a national entertainer.

Holm was the finest swimmer of her time, but she was also a high-spirited woman who preferred to spend her evenings at nightclubs rather than engage in the quiet, disciplined life of the serious athlete. Born in Brooklyn, New York, on December 16, 1913, Holm won the national championship the 100-meter individual medley in 1927, at the age of 13. The following year, she swam in the 1928 Olympic Games in Amsterdam and finished fifth in the 100-meter backstroke race.

In 1929, Holm won her first national championship in the backstroke event, as well as her third consecutive national medley title. She would go on to win a total of 20 national championships—nine in the individual medley and 11 in the backstroke. Holm's athletic career culminated with her breathtaking performance at the 1932 Olympics in Los Angeles. Not only did she win the gold medal in the backstroke race, but during a preliminary heat of the event she shattered the world record by several seconds.

By 1932, Holm was also a veteran of show business. She had begun working as a showgirl at the age of 16, and between 1929 and 1932 she had divided her time between the pool, where she had set world records in the backstroke at every recorded distance, and nightclubs, where she met her first husband, musician Art Jarrett. Holm and Jarrett married in 1933.

After the 1932 Olympics, Holm was offered a contract from Warner Bros., a movie studio that wanted her to perform in swimming movies. If she had signed the contract, Holm would have become a professional swimmer, which would have prevented her from competing in future Olympic contests. She refused the offer from Warner Bros., but she did become a nightclub singer, touring and performing with Jarrett.

Holm continued to swim during this time, having set her eyes on the 1936 Olympics in Berlin, but she admitted that she hardly led the life of a typical athlete. "I train on cigarettes and champagne," she laughingly admitted. Holm's regimen seemed to work; in early 1936, she set two more world records, breaking her own marks in the 100-meter and 200-meter backstroke.

But the U.S. Olympic Committee was not amused by Holm's antics on the voyage to the 1936 Olympics. Holm's was the heavy favorite to win gold in Berlin, but on the SS *Manhattan,* the entertainer/swimmer spent her nights drinking and gambling, rather than retiring early to her cabin. When the ship landed in Berlin, Holm was informed that she was suspended from competition. The committee read her a rule in the Olympic handbook: "It is understood of course that all members of the American team refrain from smoking and the use of intoxicating drinks and other forms of dissipation in training." The committee not only prevented Holm from participating in the Olympics, but they banned her from amateur competition for the rest of her life.

Holm might have been banned from the Olympics, but she stayed in Berlin anyway; rumor had it that she cried (literally) on German chancellor Adolf Hitler's shoulder and then went on to become the life of the Berlin nightclub scene. In any event, she returned from Berlin a big celebrity and went on to tour on the vaudeville circuit.

In 1938, Holm and Jarrett's marriage ended in divorce. Later that year, Holm met and married the producer Billy Rose. She then became the first star of his swimming extravaganza, the Aquacades. Holm performed the backstroke in the Rose productions; her routine called for her to swim through large schools of minnows, and it was said that she had to swim through the fish so quickly—lest they wriggle into her swimsuits—that she likely broke many of her own world records during her performances.

After swimming in the Aquacades for two years, Holm retired from show business. She and Rose divorced in 1954, and she moved to Florida, where she worked as an interior decorator. She retired from decorating in the mid-1970s, but continues to live in Florida.

Despite her unusual lifestyle—and the ban on competitive swimming that had been imposed on her—Holm eventually received the recognition she deserved as a world-class athlete. She was inducted into the International Swimming Hall of Fame in 1966, and in 1980 she became a member of the International Women's Sports Hall of Fame.

Further Reading

Layden, Joe. *Women in Sports: The Complete Book of the World's Greatest Female Athletes.* Santa Monica, Calif.: General Publishing Group, 1997, pp. 116–117.

Smith, Lissa, editor. *Nike Is a Goddess: The History of Women in Sports.* New York: Atlantic Monthly Press, 1998, pp. 187–188.

HOUGHTON, EDITH

(1912–)   *Baseball Player, Major League Baseball Scout*

By the time she was 10, Edith Houghton was starting at shortstop on a professional women's baseball team. Years later, after a stellar career as a player on the diamond, she went on to become the first female scout in Major League Baseball.

Edith Houghton was born in Philadelphia, Pennsylvania, on February 12, 1912. The youngest of 10 children, Edith began playing baseball almost as soon as she could walk. By the age of six she was batting and throwing at neighborhood playgrounds, and when she was eight she was such a presence at Philadelphia police league baseball games that she became the official league mascot. Her duties in this role included not only sitting in the stands (decked out in her beloved uniform) but eventually giving fielding, hitting, and throwing exhibitions before games. A local favorite with both players and fans, she became known as "the Kid."

The 1920s were a positively robust time to be playing baseball. In the wake of the infamous 1919 "Black Sox" scandal, in which eight members of the Chicago White Sox were banished from the major leagues for allegedly "throwing" (deliberately losing) the World Series to the Cincinnati Reds, the major leagues had a new commissioner, Kenesaw Mountain Landis, who vowed to clean up the game. In the meantime, enthusiasm for the game soared to new heights, not only among spectators but players as well. Since the major leagues were open only to white men, those who did not fit that physical description found other opportunities for themselves. In 1920, for example, Andrew "Rube" Foster founded the Negro National League. For the next three decades, African-American players, banned from the major leagues, would find refuge and tremendous competition on the fields of the Negro Leagues.

Women also had opportunities to play professional baseball during the 1920s. The Bloomer Leagues, which had been founded during the previous decade and then developed through the playing and managing talents of MAUD NELSON and Margaret Nabel, enjoyed its pinnacle of success during the flapper age. The teams, once relegated to wearing bloomers, or short skirts with long, loose trousers, switched to legitimate uniforms, and new clubs popped up in many cities in both the Midwest and the eastern parts of the nation. Edith Houghton's hometown boasted a women's team called the Philadelphia Bobbies. Players hoping to join the team had to meet two requirements: They had to hit, throw, and catch the ball like nobody's business, and they had to bob their hair.

The Bobbies were a team of young women, supposedly ranging in age from 13 to 20. So when Edith "the Kid" Houghton showed up at a Bobbies tryout at the age of 10, she was hardly a shoo-in to make the squad. But the Kid could play. Wearing a uniform that she had to pin together to keep from falling off, Edith took the field and showed the Bobbies a thing or two about fielding and hitting. Without further ado, the 10-year-old hometown girl was named the Bobbies' starting shortstop.

Although the Bobbies, who played games against their Bloomer League rivals along the East Coast—as well as some men's semipro teams who would bat left-handed to "even things out"—did not boast a terrific record during the early 1920s, their star shortstop impressed sportswriters and fans alike with her hitting and slick fielding. Playing against an adult team from Baltimore, the 10-year-old had three hits, and in the field she handled seven chances and made only one error. After a game against a Lancaster, Pennsylvania, men's team, the local sportswriters crowed that "little Miss Houghton, ten-year-old phenom, covered the ground at shortstop for the team and made herself a favorite with the fans for her splendid field work and ability at the bat."

As Edith matured, she became an even more versatile player; during her years on the Bobbies, she played every position on the field. In 1925, she had the opportunity to show off that versatility in another part of the world; Mary O'Gara, the founder and manager of the Bobbies, arranged for the team to go on a tour of Japan. Houghton, now 13, got on a train with her fellow players and traveled across country to Seattle; along the way, the Philadelphians played local teams from North Dakota and Montana.

After picking up new uniforms—and a new manager, Eddie Ainsmith—in Seattle, the Bobbies sailed to Japan, where they embarked on a 15-game tour that pitted them against men's teams. Each player on the Bobbies received $800 a game, so it was a tremendous opportunity for Houghton and her teammates. But it was also a difficult assignment. When they first arrived in Japan, the Bobbies drew large crowds as they battled college teams and other amateur squads. Houghton, in particular, drew raves and applause with her tiny but gifted presence both at bat and on the field.

But eventually the fans and press tired of the Bobbies, who were, after all, not a field of all-star players (aside from Houghton) but just a group of enthusiastic young people. Worse, the sponsors with whom O'Gara had made the initial touring arrangement backed out of the deal; they stopped paying the Bobbies after games, and they refused to finance their trip home to the United States. After an intense argument with O'Gara, Ainsmith took his wife and a couple of players that he had recruited for the Bobbies and left Japan for Taiwan. The rest of the Bobbies stayed put, living in a Kobe hotel until the owner took pity on them and bought them ship tickets back to Seattle. The Bobbies returned to Philadelphia in December 1925.

Houghton's time with the Bobbies ended soon after their return, as the team disbanded permanently. For a while she played for the Passaic Bloomer Girls in New Jersey, and she then joined perhaps the most prestigious team in the league, the New York Bloomer Girls. Houghton played with the New York team for six years and expanded her reputation along the East Coast. In 1932 a Boston promoter wrote to Houghton and asked her to play on a touring baseball team called the Hollywood Girls. Houghton would be paid $35 a week (a good salary during the Great Depression) to play for Hollywood, which played against minor-league men's teams in western states, Texas, and Oklahoma.

After playing for the Hollywood Girls for two years, Houghton returned to Philadelphia to face a painful truth: The days of Bloomer Baseball for women were quickly ending. Told that they were not suitable to play a man's game, more and more women were turning to softball leagues in the mid-1930s. Sad but resigned to the situation, Houghton joined a softball league. At the beginning she hated the new game—the ball was heavy and much harder to hit for distance, and the sport itself was slow and hampered with unfortunate rules (runners were not allowed to steal bases, for example). But eventually Houghton mastered the game and made a living playing for the Roverettes, a New York team that played in Madison Square Garden.

During World War II, Houghton volunteered to serve in the WAVES (Women Appointed for Volunteer Emergency Service) division of the U.S. Navy. Although Houghton's official duties in the WAVES were in the supplies and accounts division, she managed to find a military women's baseball team to play for. As always, she became the star player on the field; her .800 batting average drew a write-up in the navy newsletter, which proclaimed that "Houghton . . . can play for any team in the country."

But when Houghton left the service after the war, she found employment, not as an athlete, but as a glassware buyer in Philadelphia. Then 34,

Houghton longed for baseball; if she wasn't going to play it, she was determined to stay involved any way she could. Soon after her return to Philadelphia, she called Bob Carpenter, the owner of the Philadelphia Phillies, and asked if she could work as a scout for his team. Carpenter, whose Phillies were languishing in last place, was impressed with Houghton and hired her. Just like that, Houghton had broken a barrier. The hiring of the first major-league woman scout in history made national news headlines.

Houghton scouted for the Phillies for six years and then returned to naval service during the Korean War. After her second WAVES stint, she decided not to return to baseball, and moved to Florida. Houghton had retired by this time, but she remained, then and always, a lifelong, passionate fan of America's pastime.

Further Reading

Gregorich, Barbara. *Women at Play: The Story of Women in Baseball.* New York: Harcourt Brace, 1993, pp. 52–59.

"Sports Biographies: Edith Houghton." Available online. URL: http:www.exploratorium.edu/baseball/houghton.html. Downloaded on December 2, 2000.

HUGHES, SARAH
(1985–) *Figure Skater*

In a feat unprecedented in Olympic figure skating history, young Sarah Hughes upset a field of more seasoned and polished favorites to take the gold medal in ladies' figure skating at the Salt Lake City games in 2002. Hughes bested fellow U.S. MICHELLE KWAN, as well as the Russian skater Irina Slutskaya, to become the seventh U.S. woman to wear Olympic gold.

Sarah Hughes was born on December 5, 1985, in Great Neck, New York. Her parents, John Hughes, an attorney, and Amy Hughes, a homemaker, were both passionate skaters. John, in fact, was such a good hockey player that he contemplated a professional career. Sarah began skating at the tender age of three, when she began accompanying her mother and her three older siblings to a local ice skating rink. The youngest, Sarah was invariably the first one on the ice.

Not only was Sarah a precocious skater, but she was a talented one as well. When she was four years old, she began taking skating lessons, and two years later, she was good enough to land small performance roles in skating exhibitions. When she was nine, Sarah began skating under the private tutelage of Robin Wagner, a former skater whose expertise was choreography. Wagner would become Sarah's teacher, choreographer, and, most important, her coach.

Wagner, along with Sarah's parents, decided that the local Great Neck skating rink was not the ideal practice place for the young prodigy because it lacked the proper facilities. Instead, Wagner found a good rink in Hackensack, New Jersey, that boasted four skating surfaces as well as a large studio that would enable Sarah to practice her balletic moves off the ice. Six days a week Wagner would drive Sarah to New Jersey to train, and then back to Great Neck again. It was a lot for a young girl to deal with, but Sarah was clearly not just any girl.

In 1995, Sarah began competing in regional tournaments. Two years later, she began entering junior competitions. Sarah was showing exciting progress on the ice, but at home she was facing a greater challenge. In early 1997, Amy Hughes gathered her six children and told them that she had been diagnosed with breast cancer. Sarah's mother underwent chemotherapy treatment for her disease, which left her weak and exhausted. Although Amy Hughes was in the hospital when the 1998 Junior United States National Championships began, she managed to make it to Philadelphia to watch her daughter skate in the long-program portion of the competition. Sarah made her mother's journey worthwhile by winning the gold medal with an inspiring skate.

The 1998 Junior National Championship was Sarah Hughes's first major title, and it vaulted her into the world of high-profile tournaments. All of a sudden Hughes, who had never competed anywhere outside of the United States, was invited to skate in such faraway places as Finland and Hun-

gary. In December 1998, the entire Hughes brood, including Amy, who was by then well enough to travel, flew to Zagreb, Croatia, to watch Sarah compete in the Junior World Championships. Hughes was not expected to place there, but she stunned the skating world by picking up a silver.

As Hughes was beginning to make her mark on the international skating world, two young American women were battling it out for top figure skating honors. Michelle Kwan and TARA LIPINSKI were both expected to win medals at the 1998 Olympics in Nagano, Japan. Kwan, an exquisite skater who had taken top honors at the 1998 nationals, was the odds-on favorite to win gold, while the 14-year-old Lipinski, a gifted, athletic skater, was, by most experts' account, in the hunt for the silver.

Sure enough, at the end of the first night of competition, Kwan led the field, and Lipinski was in second place. But two nights later, Kwan skated a tentative program while Lipinski flew through her jumps and spins. As a result, the gold went to Lipinski, while Kwan had to settle for silver. Kwan was gracious at the end of the competition but did state to the press that she intended to continue her pursuit for the gold medal at the Salt Lake City Olympics in 2002.

In the meantime, Hughes continued to compete and was beginning to make her mark in senior events. In 1999 she finished fourth at the nationals, and later that year, she competed in her first World Championships, where she finished seventh. The following year, Hughes picked up a bronze at the nationals, and in 2001, she won a silver at the same event as well as a bronze at the World Championships.

Hughes began the 2002 season with high expectations. Most experts predicted that she would repeat as the second-place finisher at the nationals, and that she might have a chance to win a medal at the Olympics. But at the nationals, Hughes was beaten to the silver by another young American skater, Sasha Cohen. Kwan, as expected, took the gold.

Although as the third-place finisher Hughes had earned a place on the Olympic team that would compete in Salt Lake City, she was disappointed by her placement at the nationals. She watched as the bulk of the pre-games publicity went to Kwan and Cohen, and she also realized that in order to win a medal in Salt Lake City she would be competing, not only against her two fellow Americans, but also against Irina Slutskaya, the Russian national champion.

The competition began with the short program, a two-minute routine in which the skater has to perform a group of compulsory spins and jumps. It is said of the short program, which is worth one-third of the final score, that a championship cannot be won during those two minutes, but it can be lost. Hughes was the first of the medal contenders to skate her short program, and she turned in a solid performance. Cohen, Kwan, and Slutskaya also skated fine routines, and the night ended with Kwan in the top spot, followed respectively by Slutskaya, Cohen, and, in fourth place, Hughes.

Two nights later, the tournament resumed. Shortly before their warm-up, the skaters performing in the final round—which is always the round in which the medal-contending athletes skate—drew numbers from a hat to determine the order in which they were to skate. Once again, Hughes was the first of the top four skaters to take the ice. Before skating to the center of the rink, she clasped hands with Wagner, and the two of them exchanged last-minute words. Standing near the two was Mahlon Bradley, doctor for the U.S. team. Bradley said that he saw the fire in Hughes's eyes and immediately knew: "You could tell she was going to be great," he would say later.

And, indeed, Hughes was superb. Realizing that Hughes would need a spectacular long program to beat her three competitors, Wagner had planned two triple-triple combinations. A skater performing a triple-triple jumps into the air, turns three complete rotations, lands briefly on the ice, and then jumps again for another three rotations. It is impressive enough for a skater to land one triple-triple, but to land two in one long program is extraordinary. But here was Hughes, not only landing her combinations—as well as her other jumps—but doing so with elegance, grace, and the uninhibited joy that

has always characterized her skating. When her routine was finished, Hughes looked at Wagner, who was almost jumping up and down on the sidelines as the crowd stood and roared. "Turn around and close your eyes," Wagner told Hughes. "Soak it in."

Hughes savored the moment and then went to a quiet room with Wagner, determined not to watch the rest of the skaters. Had she chosen to witness the remainder of the evening, she would have seen both Cohen and Kwan fall while attempting triple jumps, and Slutskaya stumble while skating a stiff and tenuous routine. After all four skaters had left the ice, it was time for the judges to determine the gold medalist. It was evident that Hughes had won the long program, but would it be enough to give her the gold? After a few minutes, the judges reached their decision. Kwan, it was decided, had finished third in the program, and Slutskaya second. This meant that the gold was Hughes's. A television cameraman who was backstage with Hughes and Wagner told them the marvelous news and then taped their response as the skater and her coach screamed in pure joy and then fell off the bench, wrapped in a delirious embrace.

In the course of her four-minute program at the Salt Lake City games, Hughes's life changed completely. Her living quarters just outside the Olympic village was bombarded with phone calls requesting interviews and endorsements. Hughes, who had never had an agent, let her coach and her father sift through the invitations, but did do a brief on-air visit with sportscaster Bob Costas. After congratulating Hughes on her victory, Costas asked Hughes what her next aspiration was, now that she had captured gold. Her spontaneous response served as a reminder that even ice-skating champions have lives and expectations outside of the rink. "My next goal," said the high school junior from Great Neck, New York, "is to score a 1500 on my SATs."

Further Reading

Sivorinovsky, Alina, *Sarah Hughes: Skating to the Stars*. New York: Berkley Publishing Group, 2002.

Swift, E. M., "Head Turner," *Sports Illustrated,* March 4, 2002, pp. 48–52.

⊞ HYMAN, FLO (Flora Hyman)
(1954–1986)   *Volleyball Player*

Flo Hyman was the best woman volleyball player in U.S. history. But more than that, she was a paragon of dignity, integrity, and generosity. Those qualities, along with her astonishing talent on the court, made her one of women's sports' greatest role models.

Born in Inglewood, California, on July 29, 1954, Flora Hyman grew up in an area that was passionate about volleyball. Flo's mother, a house-cleaner, and her father, a janitor, made it a priority to raise their eight children to become responsible and mature adults. Despite her happy family life at home, Flo's childhood was not always easy. Always the tallest child in her class, she made it a habit from the age of five to try to hide her size. She hunched when she walked and slouched when she sat. But her mother persuaded her to be proud of her size and to use it to her advantage.

Flo listened to her mother and found an activity that fit her physique—she began playing volley-ball. Because her two older sisters were experienced players, Flo learned the basics of the game from them. When she was 12, she began playing two-on-two tournaments on the beach, usually with her sister Suzanne as partner. By the time Flo was a senior in high school, she had developed a lethal spike. She had also grown to six feet, five inches tall, making her a dominating force both offensively and defensively.

During her last year at Morningside High, Hyman was recruited by the University of Houston, which offered her a full athletic scholarship. She spent three years there, and led the Houston Cougars to two top-five national finishes. After her junior season in 1974, Hyman left Houston to play for the national team, based in Colorado. When Hyman joined, the squad was sorely in need of leadership. Operating without a coach, it had a host of talented players with no one at the helm to guide them. Hyman could have left the squad and

returned to Houston, but she elected to stay with the team. Her dream was to play in the Olympics, and she knew that her chances lay with the national team, for better or worse.

It was a goal that would not come to fruition right away. In 1975, the U.S. team floundered through qualifying rounds for the 1976 Olympic games and failed to make the cut. Still, Hyman stayed with the team, and finally, in 1977, her dedication paid off. The team gained international respect by finishing fifth that year at the World Championships. Hyman and her teammates looked forward to qualifying for and playing in the 1980 Olympics, but their dreams were once again curtailed when the United States boycotted the Moscow games.

Another four years passed, and still Hyman stayed with the team. The heart and soul of the U.S. squad, Hyman combined power and control to intimidate opponents on offense. Playing the crucial middle hitter position, she was also a first-rate spike blocker. Opponents tried to steer the ball away from Hyman—not an easy task. By the time the 1984 Olympics got underway in Los Angeles, Hyman had turned the U.S. team into one of the premier teams in the world. They swept through the early rounds of the game, and then they beat the Soviets in the semifinal match. Hyman's dream of Olympic gold fell short when the United States lost to China in the gold-medal game, but the home team had played superbly throughout the games, and its successes ignited new excitement for volleyball in the United States.

After the Los Angeles games, Hyman decided to turn professional. Since there were no volleyball leagues in the United States, she moved to Japan in fall 1984 and quickly became a star. Hyman was so popular in Japan that she began a modeling and acting career there and was constantly in demand. Even so, she never left the game of volleyball. In addition to playing in the Japan leagues, she began coaching amateur programs there.

Flo Hyman's life was tragically cut short in 1986, when she suffered a heart attack during a volleyball match and died. She was 31 years old.

An autopsy later revealed that Hyman suffered from Marfan's syndrome, a congenital disorder that most commonly causes people to grow tall and thin. Hyman's condition was never detected during her life.

In 1987, Hyman was posthumously inducted into the Women's Sports Hall of Fame. That year, the Women's Sports Foundation honored her by establishing the Flo Hyman Memorial Award, a prize presented every year to the athlete who best demonstrates "dignity, spirit, and commitment to excellence." Throughout her short life, Flo Hyman exemplified all three of these qualities.

Further Reading

CNN.SI for Women, 100 Greatest Female Athletes, "Flo Hyman," *Sports Illustrated for Women.* Available online. URL: http://sportsillustrated.cnn.com/siforwomen/top_100/90/. Posted on November 29, 1999.

Layden, Joe. *Women in Sports: The Complete Book of the World's Greatest Female Athletes.* Santa Monica, Calif.: General Publishing Group, Inc., 1997, pp. 117–118.

INKSTER, JULI (Juli Simpson Inkster)
(1960–) *Golfer*

Juli Inkster, one of the most successful contemporary golfers, is one of only five women to win all four events on the women's tour: the Nabisco Dinah Shore, the du Maurier Classic, the U.S. Women's Open, and the McDonald's Ladies Professional Golf Association (LPGA) Championship. A member of the LPGA Hall of Fame, Inkster has taken home more than $5 million in winnings during her career.

Born on June 24, 1960, in Santa Cruz, California, Juli Simpson, her parents, and her two older brothers all lived in a house near the 14th hole of the Pasatiempo Golf Club. Even so, young Juli, a natural athlete, did not have much interest in golf as a child, preferring instead to play basketball, track, and softball in high school.

When Juli finally did yearn to pick up a golf club, at the age of 15, it was for less of an athletic reason than a social one. "A friend and I began (playing golf) together, because that's where we figured the boys are," she confessed later. When Juli started taking lessons at the Pasatiempo Golf Club at the age of 16, her teacher was Brian Inkster. Four years later, the pair got married.

Inkster attended San Jose State University, where she graduated with a degree in physical education in 1982. In the meantime, she was beginning to compete in amateur golf tournaments, and, in 1978 she qualified to compete in her first U.S. Open. She finished second among amateurs that year; two years later, she won her first amateur title.

In 1981 Inkster won her second consecutive amateur title, and sportswriters really took note in 1982, when she took her third in a row. Inkster, who depends more on arm strength than body motion to power the ball on her swings, was able to combine a strong long game with an accurate short game to dominate those tournaments. Her winning formula earned her the number-one ranking among amateurs from *Golf Digest* in 1981 and 1982.

The following year, Inkster turned professional and began competing on the LPGA tour in 1984. She won the first event she entered, the SAFECO Classic, and also took top honors at the Nabisco Dinah Shore and the du Maurier Classic. In doing so she became the first woman to capture two Grand Slam events during her rookie season.

But Inkster fell on hard times in 1985, when she had only one victory the entire season. After a fairly successful 1986 season, she had a poor year in 1987, came back to play well in 1989, and then suffered a terrible season in 1990. After having her first child, a daughter named Hayley, in February of that year, Inkster had trouble regaining her form and posted only three top-10 finishes for the season.

In 1991 Inkster recovered a bit, winning the Bay State Classic. After climbing to the number-seven ranking on the LPGA tour in 1992, when she posted her lowest season average, she slipped up once again in 1993, and by 1994 was ranked number 49. It was in 1994 that Inkster had her second child, Cori. These were difficult times for Inkster, who found herself juggling priorities between career and family. "I was trying to do too many things and do them all perfectly," she said of those times.

Nevertheless, Inkster continued playing. She climbed slowly in the rankings but failed to win a tournament during 1993, 1994, 1995, and 1996. Finally the dry spell ended in 1997, when Inkster hired a new coach, Mike McGetrick. Working daily with McGetrick, Inkster's game steadily improved. She took top honors in the Samsung World Championship of Golf in 1997—her first tournament victory in five years—and then won that title again in 1998. By 1999 Inkster was once again on top of her game, winning the U.S. Open and the McDonald's LPGA Classic to complete her Grand Slam.

Aside from her game, Inkster is admired by fans and fellow players alike for her ability to juggle family and career. "When I'm home," she said in 2000, "I'm a normal person." When she competes, Inkster is another thing completely—a force capable of dominating any tournament she enters.

Further Reading

Biography Resource Center. "Juli Inkster," *Newsmakers* 2000, Issue 2. Detroit, Mich.: Gale Group, 2000.

Glenn, Rhonda. *The Illustrated History of Women's Golf.* Dallas, Tx.: Taylor Publishing, 1991.

Langley, Dorothy. *A View from the Red Tees: The Truth about Women and Golf.* New York: Birch Lane Press, 2001.

JACKSON, NELL
(1929–1988)   *Sprinter, Track-and-Field Coach, Administrator*

The first African American to coach on Olympic track-and-field team was Nell Jackson, a talented athlete who was herself a former Olympian.

Nell Jackson was born on July 1, 1929, in Athens, Georgia. When Nell was very young, her parents, Burnette and Wilhemina Jackson, moved with their three children to Tuskegee, Alabama. A dedicated student, Nell graduated from Tuskegee High School in 1947, then went on to receive a bachelor's degree in physical education from Tuskegee Institute in 1951, and a master's degree in the same discipline from Springfield College in 1953. In 1962, Jackson completed her education by earning her Ph.D. in physical education from the University of Iowa.

In addition to her classroom studies, Jackson was a splendidly talented athlete. Her favorite track-and-field event was the 200-meter dash, and she excelled in basketball, tennis, and swimming. While in high school, she dropped her other sports to concentrate exclusively on sprinting, and her dedication paid off in 1948, when she qualified for the Olympics in the 200-meter and 400-meter relay events. Jackson did not place in either race, but the following year she set a U.S. record in the 200-meter race when she ran the distance in 24.2 seconds. She would go on to hold national championships in the 200-meter event in 1949, 1950, and 1951, and when she competed in the first ever Pan American Games in 1951, she took home a silver medal in the 200-meter race and a gold medal in the 400-meter relay.

In the meantime, Jackson had become interested in coaching. In 1954, one year after receiving her master's degree in physical education, she was hired as the head track-and-field coach at her alma mater, Tuskegee Institute. Two years later, the U.S. Olympic Committee hired her as head coach of the women's track-and-field team. Jackson took her team to Melbourne, Australia, where one of the athletes she coached at Tuskegee, Mildred McDaniels, won a gold medal in the high jump. In 1969, Jackson coached the U.S. national women's track-and-field team, and in 1972, she once again served as head coach of the Olympic women's track-and-field team, which competed that year in Munich, West Germany.

Jackson remained at Tuskegee Institute until 1960. In 1963, after she had completed her

Ph.D., she was hired as an assistant professor of physical education at Illinois State University. Two years later she took a job as an associate professor at the University of Illinois, and in 1973, she moved to Michigan State University, where she took a job as assistant athletic director—the first African-American woman to work in that capacity—as well as women's track coach and professor of physical education.

Not only was Jackson a teacher and coach, but she also served as a member of several illustrious committees. She served on the board of directors of the U.S. Olympic Committee (USOC) from 1969 to 1973, and from 1985 to 1988 she was a member of the International Relations Committee of the USOC. By that time, Jackson had moved to Binghamton, New York, where in 1981 she had become director of physical education and intercollegiate athletics at the State University of New York at Binghamton.

Jackson, who wrote a textbook for women track-and-field athletes as well as more than 20 scholarly articles on the same subject, worked steadily until she was diagnosed with cancer in early 1988. She died later that year.

Further Reading

Biography Resource Center. "Nell Jackson," *Notable Black American Women, Book 1*. Detroit, Mich.: Gale Research, 1992.

"Nell Jackson," *Contemporary Black Biography,* vol. 24, edited by Shirelle Phelps. Chicago: Gale Group, 2000.

Layden, Joe. *Women in Sports: The Complete Book of the World's Greatest Female Athletes*. Santa Monica, Calif.: General Publishing, 1997, pp. 120–122.

Plowden, Martha Ward. *Olympic Black Women*. Gretna, La.: Pelican Publishers, 1996.

JACOBS, HELEN (Helen Hull Jacobs)
(1908–1997)   *Tennis Player*

Every champion needs a top rival. The New York Yankees had the Brooklyn Dodgers; Bjorn Borg had Jimmy Connors, and MARTINA NAVRATILOVA had CHRIS EVERT. In the early days of women's tennis, HELEN WILLS MOODY, the top-rated player in the United States, had Helen Jacobs.

It is important to note that although Jacobs was never as successful as Wills, she was in her own right a supremely talented player and a national champion. She was born in Globe, Arizona, on August 8, 1908. When she was three, her father, a mining engineer, moved the Jacobs family to Berkeley, California—into the very home where Wills had once lived. Jacobs began playing tennis while still a young child, learning the sport at the Berkeley Tennis Club. Pop Fuller, who was also Wills's coach, taught Jacobs the game and also organized the first duel between the Helens.

It was a practice set, played at the Berkeley Tennis Club, and it featured 14-year-old Helen Jacobs, eager and perhaps slightly intimidated, against 17-year-old Helen Wills, polished and perhaps a bit haughty. Seven minutes after the set began, it was over, as Wills demolished her younger opponent by a score of 6-0. Jacobs was hoping to play a second set, but Wills declined and left the court.

And so the pattern began. Throughout their careers the two players would meet eight more times, and in seven of those matches Wills would emerge triumphant. Fortunately, there were other rivals to play, and Jacobs made a habit of beating most of them as she worked her way up the tournament ranks. In 1928, Jacobs played in her first U.S. Championship final and found herself across the net from Wills. Jacobs, who had played brilliant tennis up to that point, fell apart against her older rival, and lost in straight sets, 6-1, 6-2. The next two times the Helens faced one another, in the 1930 French Open final and then the 1932 Wimbledon final, Wills triumphed both times without a struggle.

Although Jacobs at this point posed little on-court threat to Wills, it was evident to all observers that the older Helen could barely tolerate the younger one. "There was definite friction between them," Kay Stammers, a British player during the time, wrote of the two Helens, "particularly, I think, on Helen Wills's side." "Perhaps they were not enemies," added Billie Jean King in her 1988 book *We Have Come a Long Way,* but surely they were not friends. I think Helen Jacobs would have enjoyed being Helen Wills's friend; Jacobs liked everyone. But Wills could not tolerate a rival so close to home."

The two women both had superb shots, but on court they had opposing personalities. Jacobs was outgoing, open, and friendly, whereas Wills was contained, focused, and aloof. Whenever Jacobs and Wills played one another, the crowd always rooted for Jacobs, partly because she was easier to like, and partly because she was the eternal underdog.

In 1933 Wills and Jacobs played one another again, in the final of the U.S. Championships at Forest Hills (Queens), New York. Jacobs had spent a great deal of time preparing for the match and arrived on the court not only in superb physical shape but armed with a new strategy. Jacobs had asked Wills's former nemesis, the great Suzanne Lenglen of France (who had retired from amateur tennis in 1927), for advice. Lenglen had advised Jacobs to keep Wills on the run with sharp angled, short shots—today called "chips."

The strategy paid off early for Jacobs, who took the first set by an 8-6 score. Wills came back to win the second, 6-3, and then, as was customary before a third set, the two women walked to the sidelines for a 10-minute break. When they resumed play, Wills was having trouble moving; the inactivity had apparently stiffened her leg and back muscles. Jacobs took advantage of Wills's immobility and moved ahead, 3-0. Whether it was genuine injury or the fear of losing that motivated Wills will never be known, but after the third game of the set ended, she walked slowly to the umpire's stand and defaulted from the match. Jacobs, sorry to see Wills in pain, put an arm on her rivals' shoulder. The two Helens had a brief conversation. Then, without shaking hands, they separated. Wills left the court without further ado and returned to her hotel. Later that day, word leaked to the press that when Jacobs, the new U.S. champion, placed her hand on Wills's shoulder, the older Helen looked at her and snapped, "Take your hand off of me!"

Helen Jacobs, who won four consecutive U.S. Championships in the early 1930s, took top honors at Wimbledon in 1936.
(Library of Congress)

Later, it was disclosed that Wills, too injured to complete her singles final match, had wanted to play in the doubles final with Elizabeth Ryan later on that very same day. Ryan, knowing it would be a public relations fiasco should Wills play, persuaded her not to. Even so, there is little doubt that Wills suffered a legitimate injury during the final against Jacobs; Wills took an 18-month hiatus from tennis. After she returned, she would win more championships, but she never played at Forest Hills again.

The good news for Helen Jacobs was that defaults and injuries aside, she had won her first major title. It would be the first of four consecutive U.S. championships for her.

The next plateau Jacobs strived for was a Wimbledon title. She had reached the final round in 1932, and again in 1934, but both times fell short of victory. In 1935 Jacobs was in the final again, and on the other side of the net, back from her hiatus, was Helen Wills. Jacobs, determined to win, focused on Wills's weaknesses—a less-than-strong backhand and a lack of mobility. After splitting the first two sets, Jacobs found herself ahead in the deciding set by a score of 5-3, and serving for the match. The score reached 40-30—for the first time in her life, Jacobs had a match point against Wills. Jacobs put the ball in play, and after a brief rally Wills hit a weak lob. It could have been an easy overhand winner for Jacobs, but she either misjudged it or lost concentration. Jacobs allowed the ball to bounce and ended up hitting the ball into the net. Shaken by her fatal error, Jacobs lost concentration completely and let the match slip away from her. Wills won four consecutive games to take the final and the championship.

Jacobs recovered from the disappointment, and the following year she herself triumphed at Centre Court at Wimbledon, with a victory over Germany's Hilde Sperling. But in 1938, Wills once again faced Jacobs in the final at Wimbledon, and Jacobs, hobbling on a bad ankle, went down in straight sets. Although it was common and indeed expected for a player to express concern and sympathy for an injured opponent, Wills did not offer words of comfort or indeed any words of all to Jacobs. She merely accepted and acknowledged Jacobs's congratulations with a handshake and a smile directed at no one in particular, and she walked off the court. The two Helens never saw one another again.

In addition to her four U.S. championships and her Wimbledon title, Jacobs played team tennis for the United States for 11 consecutive years, competing for the Wightman Cup from 1927 to 1938. After she retired from the sport in 1939, she spent time in the U.S. Navy, and she then became a writer of children's books, historical fiction, and several books on the game of tennis. She died in 1997. Wills outlived Jacobs, by one year.

Further Reading

King, Billie Jean, and Cynthia Starr. *We Have Come a Long Way: The Story of Women's Tennis.* New York: McGraw Hill, 1988, pp. 45–48.

Layden, Joe. *Women in Sports: The Complete Book of the World's Greatest Female Athletes.* Santa Monica, Calif.: General Publishing Group, 1997, pp. 122–123.

JENNINGS, LYNN
(1960–)   *Middle-Distance Runner, Long-Distance Runner*

Lynn Jennings, winner of 39 U.S. cross-country national championships, is one of the best American middle- and long-distance runners in history. A competitor in three Olympics, Jennings took a bronze medal in the 10,000-meter event at the 1992 games in Barcelona.

Born in Princeton, New Jersey, on July 1, 1960, Lynn Jennings grew up in Harvard, Massachusetts. It was also in Harvard that young Lynn discovered cross-country running. Although Lynn initially ran purely for the joy of the activity, she soon developed a taste for competition as well. By the time she was a junior at the Bromfield School, she was competing on the boys' track team—and tearing up the track against all girl competitors. Jennings won three consecutive cross-country championships in high school. Already well known in her home state, Jennings became a national celebrity of sorts in 1977 when, after winning the Boston Bonne Bell 10K—one of the best-known races in the world—General Mills chose to put her photograph on the Wheaties cereal box. The following year, 17-year old Jennings raced in her first Boston Marathon and finished third.

After her impressive marathon performance, Jennings received many offers for full athletic scholarships from some of the most prestigious universities in the country. Instead, she chose to attend a college that did not offer athletic scholarships, and she headed to Princeton Unversity in the fall of 1978.

Once at Princeton, Jennings struggled to combine training and competing with her rigorous study schedule and social life. Having lost her competitive zeal for the time being, she began missing training sessions and gained weight. Finally after her junior year, she dropped out of Princeton and decided to quit running altogether. One year later, though, Jennings returned to the university, rejoined the track team, and graduated with a degree in history in 1983.

The following year, Jennings continued to train, with the goal of competing for the U.S. Olympic team. But at the 1984 Olympic trials, Jennings lost her focus completely and finished dead last in the 3,000-meter event. Devastated by her performance, Jennings decided, once again, to retire from the track. She moved back to her parents' house in Harvard, and for a few weeks did absolutely nothing.

One morning in the fall of 1984, Jennings finally stepped outside her parents' house and, as she had done when she was a little girl, went for a long, quiet run, purely for the joy of the activity. And once again, the joy eventually turned to fire. At the age of 24, Jennings decided to return to competitive running. She left Massachusetts and moved to a small town in New Hampshire, where she began an intensive training program.

Her dedication paid off quickly; Jennings won her first of six consecutive national cross-country championships in 1985. Jennings, who would win a total of nine national cross-country titles, became the first U.S. runner to win the world cross-country championship in 1990. She would add two more world titles to her résumé in 1991 and 1992, and at the Olympic Games in Barcelona, her bronze medal time of 31:19:89 in the 10,000-meter race set a U.S. record.

Jennings continued to train and compete throughout the 1990s. In addition to her national cross-country championships, she ran for the U.S. Olympic team in the 1996 games in Atlanta (finishing 10th in the 10,000-meter event). In 1999 she returned to Boston to run once again in the marathon. Jennings finished 12th overall in that race, but first among all U.S. entries. In 2000, she attempted to qualify for her third Olympic team, but came up short in the Olympic trial marathon race.

Jennings continues to race in many middle- and long-distance events. When asked in 1997 why she remains competitive, she replied, "What you see might look like a harmless 37-year-old woman, but I have the heart of a ferocious tiger."

Further Reading

BeMent, Cindy. "WMO Interviews Lynn Jennings," *Women's Multisport Online Cover Story*. Available online. URL: http://www.womensmultisport.com/wmo_interviews_lynn_jennings.htm. Downloaded on March 21, 2001.

CNN.com/SI For Women: 100 Greatest Athletes. "Lynn Jennings," *Sports Illustrated For Women Online*. Available online. URL: http://sportsillustrated.cnn.com/siforwomen/top_100. Posted on November 29, 1999.

Layden, Joe. *Women in Sports: The Complete Book of the World's Greatest Female Athletes*. Santa Monica, Calif.: General Publishing Group, 1997, pp. 125–126.

JONES, MARION
(1975–) *Sprinter, Long Jumper*

Marion Jones said she would win five Olympic gold medals. The she went to the Sydney games in 2001 and came back with three golds and two bronzes. Perhaps Jones's accomplishment was slightly tarnished by her prediction, but even so, winning five medals in one Olympic competition was a momentous achievement.

Born in Los Angeles, California, on October 12, 1975, Marion Jones always ran fast. During her childhood, her main goal was to beat her brother, Albert Kelly. "I never could," she said later. "Even now, it's a struggle." Young Marion also had to struggle with her parents' divorce. When she was five, her father left their house; Marion would not be in touch with him again. Marion's mother remarried when Marion was eight, and her stepfather, whom Marion adored, died when she was 12.

But through it all, she ran fast. When she was nine, she watched the Los Angeles Olympics, and fell in love with the games. "I'm going to be an Olympic champion," she announced to her family.

Marion Jones, winner of three gold medals at the 2000 Olympic Games, is also a gifted long jumper and basketball player.
(Stu Forster/Getty Images)

Though she did not make it to the 1984 games in her own back yard, she was invited, eight years later at the age of 17, to compete in the 1992 Barcelona games. Jones, who was asked to serve as an alternate on the 4 × 100 relay team, declined the invitation. "I wanted to earn a starting spot," she later explained. By that time, Jones was a standout at both track and field and basketball at Thousand Oaks High School. Her athletic prowess earned her a double athletic scholarship to the University of North Carolina at Chapel Hill, where she joined both the track and women's basketball teams. It was at Carolina that Jones earned her first national championship. In 1994, Jones, a freshman starter, was asked to play the point guard

position for the Carolina Tar Heels. The point guard is, in a way, the quarterback of the basketball team. It is the point guard who gets the ball first after an inbounds pass and then dribbles it up the floor looking for an open team member (and often signaling a set play). Although she had never played the position before, Jones quickly became an astute point guard, and she played a pivotal role in Carolina's ascent through the National Collegiate Athletic Association (NCAA) championships. In the final game, Jones's teammate Charlotte Smith shot a three-pointer as time drained from the clock to give the Tar Heels the title.

Jones was thrilled to be part of a championship team, but the next year she broke her foot playing basketball. The injury not only cost her the opportunity to compete for the Tar Heel basketball and track teams in 1995–96, but it prevented her from trying out for the Olympic team. In 1997, Jones made a pivotal decision: she retired from basketball in order to concentrate full time on sprinting and long jumping. Her efforts quickly paid off: During her first year on the professional track-and-field circuit in 1997, she recorded the best marks of the season in the 100-meter race, the 200-meter races, and the long jump. The following year Jones was even more impressive: she went through the entire season without losing a sprinting or long-jumping event. She captured the world championship in all three of her specialties, and she was awarded the prestigious Jesse Owens award as the world's top amateur athlete.

By 1999, it was obvious that Jones would be a favorite to win gold at the 2000 Olympics. But could she truly win five gold medals? Yes, she said, matter-of-factly, to all who asked. She had the talent and determination to win. And to prove her point, she repeated as champion in the 1999 World Championships, once again winning the 100-meter, 200-meter, and long jump events. In 2000, Jones was beginning to gain national attention, not only for her athletic gifts, but for her confident prediction. Not all of the publicity surrounding Jones was completely positive. Some journalists wondered in print why Jones, a young, attractive, and articulate athlete, had married C. J. Hunter, a heavyset shot-putter who had been an assistant track coach at Carolina. Hunter, who was sometimes surly with the press, was constantly at Jones's side, acting as her training partner and sometimes her protector.

More questions arose in the late spring of 2000, after Jones collapsed with a back injury at the World Championships in Seville. Would her injury heal in time? Did she have the stamina to survive the preliminaries and finals of five separate events? Did she have the proper technique to win a medal in the long jump? But when the games began in Sydney, a relaxed and smiling Jones sailed through the 100-meter race with spectacular style. When she broke the ribbon, far ahead of her nearest competitor, she burst into an ear-to-ear grin: yes, it seemed, she really could win five golds.

But only two days later, Jones was dealt a difficult blow when journalists discovered that Hunter, who had withdrawn from the Olympic shot-put team with an injury, had tested positive for steroid use earlier in the year. Denying any wrongdoing, a tearful Hunter and Jones appeared together at a press conference. Jones announced that she believed her husband was innocent, and she then left the conference to resume practicing for her next event, the 200-meter race. The controversy surrounding Hunter left some wondering if Jones would be able to concentrate on her next race. But Jones answered all questions decisively by winning the 200-meter race almost as easily as she had won the 100-meter event.

Jones's quest for gold ended two days later, when she fouled on her final attempt in the long jump. Her leap was long enough to give her the championship, but she had crossed the starting block on her leap, which disqualified her jump. Disappointed but gracious in defeat, Jones settled for the bronze medal. Three days later, she landed another third-place medal as she singlehandedly pulled the 4×100 relay team, crippled by injuries, into a third-place finish. Jones, running the anchor leg, received the baton in seventh place. During her leg, she passed three runners and almost chased down another.

In Jone's final event, the 4×400 race, she showed that if she truly wanted to, she could have excelled in yet another event. "I don't like the 400-meter race," Jones had said earlier, "it's too long for me. I get too tired." Even so, Jones, who ran the third leg for her team, ran her portion of the race as quickly as the Olympic champion, Australia's Cathy Freeman, ran hers. Jones's team took top honors, giving her her fifth medal, and third gold, of the Sydney games.

In June 2001 Jones and Hunter separated, citing irreconcilable differences. Jones continues to train, in pursuit of world records and excellence on the track. Chances are good that as the Olympics return to Athens, their city of origin, in 2004, Jones will be back, determined once again to do the unthinkable and capture those elusive five gold medals.

Further Reading

Clemmons, S. Jason. "Marion Jones: Catching Up with the World's Fastest Woman," Femsports, June 1999. Available online. URL: http://femsportmag.hypermart.net/fshtm/marion.htm. Downloaded on February 7, 2001.

Penner, Mike. "Just Do It," Los Angeles Times Magazine, August 9, 2000: 33–35.

Rapoport, Ron. See How She Runs. Chapel Hill, N.C.: Algonquin Books, 2000.

JOYCE, JOAN
(1940–)   Softball Player

Major League Baseball pitchers can fling a pitch to the plate at speeds approaching 100 miles an hour. Surely these men throw the ball harder than anyone in the world . . . or do they? One woman, the legendary softball pitcher Joan Joyce, could fling a softball 116 miles per hour.

Joan Joyce was born on August 1, 1940, in Waterbury, Connecticut. The daughter of a high school baseball coach, Joan grew up throwing balls, either to her father, or against the back wall of her parents' house. By the time she was 10, Joyce knew how to run bases, how to catch fly balls, and how to throw a mean-breaking fast ball.

At age 13, Joan took her prestigious talents to the Raybestos Brakettes, one of the best known amateur softball teams in the nation. By the time she was 17, in 1957, she had become the star pitcher for the Brakettes. Over the next 19 years, Joyce would lead the Brakettes to 12 national championships. During that time she won 507 games (against only 33 losses), and she threw 123 no-hitters. Her earned run average for her entire career was a measly 0.19. Hitters facing Joyce had to contend not only with her 116 mile-per-hour fastball, but with a "riser," a "drop," a screwball, a knuckleball, and a changeup. Women were not the only players who had trouble hitting a Joyce pitch. Facing Joyce in an exhibition, Ted Williams, who hit against major league pitchers exceedingly well during his prodigious career, managed to nub two or three foul balls and swung through many more before dropping his bat in disgust and walking away.

Joyce was a nearly unhittable pitcher, but she was a prodigious hitter as well, with a .327 batting average. Little wonder that during her 21-year career with the Brakettes Joyce was an Amateur Softball Association All-American 19 times, and she won the league's most valuable player award eight times.

In 1973, Joyce competed at the National Fast Pitch Championships, where she won nine games against no losses and tossed eight shutouts. Two years later, she played her final year with the Brakettes, winning all 36 games that she started and leading the team to yet another national title. After the 1975 season, Joyce left amateur baseball to help start a professional league. From 1976 through 1979, she owned and managed the Connecticut Falcons. Joyce also pitched for the team; few people were surprised that the Falcons won the Women's Pro League World Series in 1976, 1977, 1978, and 1979.

When Joyce finally retired from competitive softball after the 1979 season, she rapidly turned her attention to golf. Having already become a member of the Ladies' Professional Golf Association (LPGA) in 1977, she competed regularly in LPGA events during the early and mid-1980s.

Although she never won an event, she finished in the top 10 at several tournaments and was one of the tour's most respected players.

Joyce was inducted into the International Women's Sports Hall of Fame in 1989. Five years later, she returned to softball, this time as the head coach of the Florida Atlantic University team. Joyce continued to hold this post in 2001. During her tenure as head coach, she has turned the Florida Atlantic Owls into one of the most competitive teams in the nation.

Further Reading

Layden, Joe. *Women in Sports: The Complete Book of the World's Greatest Female Athletes.* Santa Monica, Calif.: General Publishing Group, 1997, p. 127.

Silas Bronson Library Waterbury Hall of Fame. "Joan Joyce." Available online URL: http://www.biblio.org/bronson/joan.htm. Downloaded on March 19, 2001.

JOYNER-KERSEE, JACKIE
(Jacqueline Joyner)
(1962–) *Heptathlete, Long Jumper*

Jackie Joyner-Kersee dominated the heptathlon, the most grueling of all athletic events for women, in two straight Olympic games, and she won a total of six Olympic medals in her glorious career. She is considered by many to be the finest woman athlete of the 20th century.

If Joyner-Kersee's achievements are impressive on their own, they become downright awe-inspiring when set against the context of her childhood, spent in the impoverished and often violent inner city. Jacqueline Joyner was born on March 3, 1962, in a tiny house in East St. Louis, Illinois. The oldest of four children, she was named for Jacqueline Kennedy by her grandmother, who predicted that "someday this girl will be the first lady of something." But first, Jackie, along with her siblings Al, Angela, and Debra, had to survive life in the ghetto.

For Jackie, that meant surviving in a neighborhood where death was a part of daily life. When she was 10, Jackie's dance teacher was killed. The following year, she watched a man get shot to death in front of her house. When she was 14, her grandfather murdered his wife with a shotgun. In the meantime, work in East St. Louis was slow—factories were boarded up and many families were unemployed—and drug use was abundant. By the time they were teenagers, many of Jackie's neighbors were hooked on crack or other substances.

But amid the chaos on the streets around them, something kept the Joyner kids moving forward. To begin with, Jackie's mother, Mary Joyner, was a guiding force for all four children. (Jackie's father was a railroad switchman who worked in Springfield, Illinois, and was home only on weekends.) Mary believed that the best way out of the neighborhood for her children was through hard work and discipline. She encouraged her children not only to stay in school but to work hard and earn good grades.

In addition, both Jackie and her brother Al were able to focus on sports, not only as a positive pastime, but as a possible ticket to success. When she was nine, Jackie tried out for her first track-and-field team, at the local community center. She made the squad as a middle-distance runner, but soon decided that her favorite event was the long jump. "I became a long jumper almost by accident," she said later. "The coaches were waiting for the girls to jump, and I just ran over and *leapt.*"

By the time she was 13, Jackie was leaping in state championships. The following year, she was competing in the Junior Olympics, not only in the long jump, but in the pentathlon, which consists of five events. By that time, she was in high school, and although Jackie played other sports as well—she was the captain of the volleyball team and the best player on the basketball squad—she was first and foremost a track star.

When she was 17, Joyner won state championships in both the long jump and the 400-meter events. She also set a new Illinois record with a jump of 22 feet, $4^1/_4$ inches. At the end of her senior year, she had a ticket out of East St. Louis, in the form of an athletic scholarship to the University of California at Los Angeles (UCLA).

But just as she thought that she had survived the tragedies of her childhood, another one came at her full force. In January 1981, in the middle of Joyner's freshman year at UCLA, her mother contracted a rare form of meningitis and lapsed into a coma. Summoned home to East St. Louis, Jackie learned that her mother was brain dead and was breathing only with the help of a respirator. Jackie and her brother Al instructed the doctor to remove the life-support system. During the ensuing days of profound grief (one of Jackie's sisters fainted during her mother's funeral; the other suffered a seizure), Jackie remained at home to provide strength for her family.

When she returned to UCLA, Jackie tried to turn her focus back to the track and to the classroom (Joyner had internalized her mother's determinations and remained a disciplined student throughout her school career), but she was coping with her own grief and diminishing inner strength. During this time she met Bob Kersee, an assistant women's track coach who had recently arrived at the UCLA campus. Like Joyner, Kersee had lost his mother when he was 18; he became her supporter and close friend.

Kersee also became Joyner's coach, which was a battle in and of itself. Joyner had initially come to UCLA to play basketball as well as compete in track and field, but Kersee believed that if Joyner devoted herself full time to the track and added some skills to her long-jumping and middle-distance running talents, she would be competitive in the most prestigious of track-and-field events, the heptathlon.

Unlike other track-and-field events, which usually demand only a single skill, such as strength, endurance, or speed, the heptathlon is a seven-part competition that demands all three of these talents. Heptathletes compete over a two-day period, and they are awarded points based on their finishes in seven events. On the first day, they run the 100-meter hurdles, then compete in the high jump, the shot put, and the 200-meter dash. On the second and final day, the athletes compete first in the long jump, and then in the javelin throw. The final event, at the end of the second day, is the grueling 800-meter event. Some of the athletes at this point are running for glory; others are merely trying to finish without collapsing in exhaustion.

Joyner initially resisted Kersee's grand idea; she loved playing basketball, and more important, she worried that spending valuable time learning and perfecting other skills, such as the high jump and javelin throw, which Joyner had never done before, would take away from precious training at her favorite event, the long jump. But Kersee prevailed, and soon Joyner was competing—and winning—heptathlon events on the collegiate level.

In 1983 Joyner was named a member of the U.S. World Champion track team. It was a double triumph for the Joyner family: Jackie's brother Al, who had gone to Arkansas State University to specialize in the triple jump, also made the team. Both Joyners traveled to Helsinki to compete. But Jackie Joyner struggled at the championships; early in the meet she suffered a pulled hamstring, and she withdrew from the event after the first day. "The Helsinki meet was the first time I ever encountered an injury that was so bad I couldn't compete," she said later. "I had never experienced anything like that before."

But Joyner would experience the same injury several months later, when she aggravated the hamstring during training. This time she was determined to finish her event; she was competing at the 1984 Olympic trials, and she had to finish first or second in order to qualify for the games. With her leg wrapped in heavy tape, Joyner not only finished the pentathlon but set a new world record of 6,520 points in the process. At the end of the trials, both Joyners had made the Olympic team, Jackie in the pentathlon and Al in the triple jump.

The Joyners went to Los Angeles as a living example of the triumph of hope and hard work over poverty and hard times. Al Joyner told the press that he and his sister were at the Olympics on a personal mission—"to prove that there were better things to come out of East St. Louis than crime." And at the games, both Joyners made their point. Surprisingly, though, it was Al—not a

favorite to medal in his event—who took gold back to Illinois, with top honors in the triple jump. Jackie was the pregame favorite to win the heptathlon, but her nagging hamstring injury kept her from competing well on the first day. On the second day, she was able to make up some ground; she needed a time of 2 minutes, 13 seconds, in the 800-meter race to take the gold. Bothered in part by an asthmatic condition she had battled on and off since childhood, Joyner ran the final event in 2:13:03, missing the gold by one-third of a second. She made no excuses for her performances, and she displayed her silver medal with pride.

After the Olympics, Joyner returned to training with a new intensity and new determination: she was aiming for gold in 1988. Kersee and Joyner spent countless hours working together, and eventually their relationship, which for several years had been strictly professional, became a romantic one. In January 1986 they married. Several months later, Joyner-Kersee's brother Al married FLORENCE GRIFFITH JOYNER, another athlete trained by Kersee.

In July 1986, Joyner-Kersee gave what was up to that time her most dominating performance in the heptathlon; at the Goodwill Games in Moscow, she set a world record with 7,148 points—shattering the old one by 200 points. It was the first world record in a multi-event competition by an American since BABE DIDRIKSON ZAHARIAS shattered the triathlon mark in 1936.

Less than four weeks after Moscow, Joyner-Kersee somehow managed to outdo her Goodwill Games performance, logging 7,161 points in the heptathlon. Joyner-Kersee was now head and shoulders above her competition and, it seemed, virtually unbeatable on the track and off. She was given the 1986 Sullivan Award, for top amateur athlete, as well as the Jesse Owens Award.

During the next summer, Joyner-Kersee continued her dominance, winning the world championships in both the pentathlon and the long jump. In addition, she was beginning to draw comparisons to historical sports figures. "Those calling her America's greatest athlete since Jim Thorpe may

Considered by many to be the best all-around athlete of the second half of the twentieth century, Jackie Joyner-Kersee was an Olympic champion in the heptathlon, the most grueling of all events, as well as the long jump.
(Mike Powell/Getty Images)

not be exaggerating," said the *Sporting News* in September 1987.

At the 1988 Olympic trials Joyner-Kersee fought her way through the heptathlon despite a painful hand injury she had sustained when she tore her thumb on her spike during the long jump. And in the individual long jump event she tied a world record at the trials with at leap of 24 feet, $5^1/_2$ inches. But her greatest performance came at the Olympic Games themselves, in Seoul, Korea, in September 1988.

It was not her easiest victory, but it was one of her most courageous. After a solid start with a victory in the 100-meter hurdle event, Joyner-Kersee struggled with the high jump—her old hamstring injury had flared up, and she scored poorly in the event. She finished the first day with a disappointing 22.56 time in the 200-meter event, and returned to the Olympic village that night, 103 points behind her world-record pace. But even so, Joyner-Kersee was in first place by 181 points.

On the second day, she performed splendidly in the long jump, but her javelin throw fell 11 feet short of her average distance, costing her precious points. More important, she was in considerable pain while throwing the spear and was unable to muster any leg strength behind her throw. And the race that would test her legs the most—the event that had cost her gold in Los Angeles four years earlier—the 800-meter race, was still to come.

Somehow Joyner-Kersee managed to finish the race, finishing fifth with a time of 2:08:51. It was enough for a new world record, giving Joyner-Kersee a total of 7,291 points. More important, it gave her the championship—she had won the Olympic gold medal in the heptathlon—and the title of the world's greatest female athlete. Joyner-Kersee also won gold in the long jump, becoming the first athlete, male or female, to win gold medals in both a multievent competition and an individual event.

Following the 1988 games, Joyner-Kersee returned to the streets of East St. Louis, this time as a world champion intent on giving something back to the community. That Thanksgiving she flew 100 children from her neighborhood to New York City to see the holiday parade, and the next year started the Jackie Joyner-Kersee Foundation in East St. Louis.

But Joyner-Kersee was not finished with track and field quite yet. She continued to train in both the heptathlon and the long jump, and in 1992 she once again won the Olympic heptathlon, becoming the first woman to win back-to-back gold medals in an individual event since WYOMIA TYUS. Her performance at those Barcelona games prompted another Olympic champion, 1976 decathlon gold-medalist Bruce Jenner, to label Joyner-Kersee the "greatest athlete on the planet." In 1996 Joyner-Kersee competed in her fourth and final Olympic competition. She had lost some speed and strength over the years, and this time was unable to overcome a leg injury suffered the first day of the pentathlon. She withdrew from that competition, and several days later found herself in sixth place in the long jump competition with one jump to go. The crowd in Atlanta grew silent; perhaps they realized it was the last jump Joyner-Kersee would make in Olympic competition. And then Joyner-Kersee, injured leg and all, took one final leap. She jumped 22 feet, $11^3/_4$ inches on that last attempt, good enough for a bronze Medal—a triumphant ending to a legendary Olympic career.

Joyner-Kersee returned to her other favorite sport, basketball, after the Atlanta games, playing for a season with the Richmond Rage of the American Basketball League (ABL). When the ABL folded the following year, she contemplated a comeback in track and field, and she began to train for the 2000 Olympic Games. But after a few jumps at the 2000 Olympic trials in Sacramento, California, Joyner-Kersee decided to call it quits, once and for all. Accompanied by her husband and coach, she left the track for the last time. After her retirement, Joyner-Kersee continued to work for her foundation, helping the children of East St. Louis reach their potential.

Further Reading

Davis, Michael D. *Black American Women in Olympic Track and Field: A Complete Illustrated Reference.* Jefferson, N.C.: McFarland, 1992.

Joyner-Kersee, Jackie, and Sonja Steptoe. *A Kind of Grace: The Autobiography of the World's Greatest Female Athlete.* New York: Warner Books, 1997.

Layden, Joe. *Women in Sports: The Complete Book of the World's Greatest Female Athletes.* Santa Monica, Calif.: General Publishing Group, 1997, p. 131.

Sugar, Bert Randolph. *The Sports 100: A Ranking of the Greatest Athletes of All Time.* Secaucus, N.J.: Citadel Press, 1995.

K

KAMENSHEK, DOTTIE
(Dorothy Kamenshek)
(1923–) *Baseball Player*

During World War II, when many of the great Major League Baseball players, including Ted Williams and Joe DiMaggio, left the diamond to serve in the armed forces, a new, all-girls' baseball league was formed. At its full inception, the All-American Girls' Baseball League (AAGBL) had 10 teams—all based in the Midwest—and 600 players. Of the women who played baseball for the AAGBL, the most gifted was Dorothy Kamenshek, who played first base for the Rockford Peaches.

Dorothy Kamenshek was born on December 21, 1925, in Cincinnati. The Kamensheks were not a wealthy family, and after her father's death when Dottie (as she was called) was nine, money grew even tighter. Dottie was an enthusiastic softball player as a child, and her love of sports continued as she grew older. When she learned in 1943 that a new all-women's professional baseball league was holding tryouts at Wrigley Field, she grabbed her glove and took a bus to Chicago. Dottie's mother was not enthusiastic about letting her daughter go to Illinois, but she had already turned down Dottie's request to let her make money by joining the army and, believing that her daughter had little to chance to be chosen by the league anyway, gave Dottie permission to go.

Rain was pouring down on Wrigley Field when Dottie arrived for the tryouts, and she found herself one of 250 women competing for 60 spaces on four teams. Scouts began cutting players after the first day of tryout, "You'd be afraid to answer the phone in your hotel room," Kamenshek remembered later. But Dottie was ultimately chosen by the Rockford Peaches, who put the five-foot, six inch player in the outfield.

After the first 12 games of that inaugural season in 1943, Peaches manager Eddie Stumpf switched Kamenshek to first base. Kamenshek trained religiously for her new position. Realizing that a first baseman had to be "as long as possible" in order to catch infielders' throws as quickly as possible, Kamenshek worked on her footwork, both during the season and in the winter. "I threw (a pillow) on the floor in front of a full-length mirror and pretended it was first base," she said about her off-season training, "I practiced shifting my feet. I stayed flexible all year round." Kamenshek not only improved her own abilities at first base, but she devised positions that men would later imitate at the major-league level; she is often credited with inventing "the stretch," in which the first baseman will extend as far as possible toward a thrown ball while keeping the side of his or her foot on the base. "Dorothy Kamenshek was the fanciest-fielding first baseman I'd ever seen," said Wally Pipp, who played first base for the New York Yankees in the 1920s.

Kamenshek also knew how to hit. She was, in fact, the league's leading hitter in 1946 and again in 1947. She rarely struck out; in 3,736 at-bats during her career, she fanned only 81 times. She was a line-drive hitter who could hit to all fields. She could also lay down a bunt with precision on either the first- or third-base line. Kamenshek's lifetime batting average of .292 was the highest of all the women who played in the AAGBL.

By the time Kamenshek retired from the league, in 1952, she had led the Rockford Peaches to four Shaugnessey Series championships, which were the equivalent of World Series titles. She played for nine full seasons in the league, which prospered in the mid 1940s but by the early 1950s was struggling. The AAGBL folded in 1954, and to date women have never again played professional baseball in the United States.

Kamenshek had begun taking classes at the University of Cincinnati while she was still playing with the Peaches. She majored in physical education, but when she injured her back during the 1949 season (she continued playing, wearing a back brace), she received physical therapy for the pain, and decided that after retiring, she would become a physical therapist.

In 1958, Kamenshek received her degree in physical therapy from Marquette University, and she began a successful career in that field. In 1961 she moved to California to become the chief of the Los Angeles Crippled Children's Services Department. Kamenshek had found a second career after baseball, and she realized that it was her years with the Peaches that had given her confidence to pursue her ambitions. "One thing about our league: it gave a lot of us the courage to go on to professional careers at a time when women didn't do that." Kamenshek retired from her post in the mid-1980s and continued to live in California.

Further Reading

Gregorich, Barbara. *Women at Play: The Story of Women in Baseball.* New York: Harcourt Brace, 1993, pp. 84–87, 90–95.

Smith, Lissa, editor. *Nike Is a Goddess: The History of Women in Sports.* New York: Atlantic Monthly Press, 1998, pp. 47–48.

KERRIGAN, NANCY
(1969–)   *Figure Skater*

Nancy Kerrigan never won an Olympic gold medal. She never captured a world championship title, and she took top honors at the U.S. championships only once. Yet Kerrigan is one of the most well-known female sports figures in the United States, and she is arguably the most successfully marketed skater since SONJA HENIE.

The story of Nancy Kerrigan began in Stoneham, Massachusetts, where she was born on October 13, 1969, the third and youngest child of Dan Kerrigan, a welder, and his wife, Brenda. When Nancy was about a year old, Brenda was stricken with a rare eye disease that left her almost completely blind. Nancy, a quiet, caring child, grew up taking care of her mother, choosing her clothes for her and helping with the housework and the cleaning.

The Kerrigans lived a block away from the Stoneham skating rink, and when Nancy was six, she began taking ice skating lessons there. Nancy's teacher immediately spotted her talent, and suggested to Nancy's parents that they might want to invest in private lessons for their daughter. The Kerrigans did not have a lot of money, but they saw that their shy daughter was happiest on the ice. Dan took a night job to make extra money, and the Kerrigans hired a private skating teacher for Nancy.

When Nancy was eight, she began skating in competitions. Her family always traveled with her, and they cheered eagerly from the stands. The Kerrigans had more and more to cheer about, as Nancy began to work her way up the junior national standings. In 1985 she took second place at the Eastern Junior Regionals, and two years later, she placed fourth at the National Junior Championships.

During this time Nancy remained a student at Stoneham High School. In order to fit her training in, she arose at 4 A.M. every weekday and practiced at the Stoneham skating rink. After graduating from high school, she enrolled at Emmanuel College, a women's college in Boston. In the winter of 1988, she won the National Collegiate Championships, which made her eligible to skate at the U.S. championships the following year.

Kerrigan was virtually unheard of when she entered the rink at the U.S. championships in the winter of 1989, but she impressed the judges with her graceful skating and her elegant outfits. She placed fifth in the competition; over the next five years she would work her way up though the national rankings, and in 1993, she won the title.

In 1992, Kerrigan qualified for the U.S. Olympics by placing second at the U.S. championships. Together with her teammates, KRISTI YAMAGUCHI, the national champion, and Tonya Harding, the third-place finisher, Kerrigan traveled to Albertville, France. The competition in Alvertville was billed as a showdown between Yamaguchi and Japan's Midori Ito, and true to form, Yamaguchi took the gold and Ito the silver. But Kerrigan, skating a superb short program and a solid free skate, surprised the skating world by taking the bronze. For Kerrigan, it was a fateful moment. Yamaguchi had stated that she would retire from competitive skating after the Albertville Olympics. Now, as the bronze medal winner, Kerrigan was Yamaguchi's heir apparent.

If Kerrigan was surprised and delighted by the results and aftermath of the Albertville Olympics, her teammate Tonya Harding, who had traveled to France with hopes of a medal herself, might have been disappointed and even galled by them. Harding was a superbly athletic skater—one of two women who has landed a triple axel in competition (the other is Midori Ito),—but she lacked the grace and artistry of Kerrigan and Yamaguchi. Even so, Harding had bested both Kerrigan and Yamaguchi in 1991, taking top honors at the U.S. championships, and she had taken a silver at the 1991 world championships, finishing below Yamaguchi but above Kerrigan, who had won the bronze.

But in 1993, Kerrigan eased to victory at the U.S. championships, while Harding failed to place. Now, not only was Kerrigan the undisputed top U.S. skater, but she was receiving endorsements as well. She was named one of *People* magazine's 50 most beautiful celebrities, and she was followed regularly by photographers and media. The attention and extra pressure was not always easy for Kerrigan; at the World Championships in Prague in 1993, where she was favored to win gold, she missed her first jump during her free skate, and then turned two triple jumps into singles. She placed fifth.

The 1993 world championships served as a wake-up call for Kerrigan, who knew she would have to practice and train with new intensity if she had any hopes to take a medal at the 1994 Olympics. She added several hours to her already intensive training program, and by the time the 1994 U.S. championships were set to begin in Detroit, she was skating smoothly and confidently.

Two days before the championships, Kerrigan was entering the Joe Louis Arena in Detroit on January 6, 1994, to practice her routine. All of a sudden, a man emerged from the shadows and hit Kerrigan on the leg with a lead pipe. In severe shock and pain, Kerrigan fell to the floor and screamed. Her father, who had accompanied Kerrigan to her practice session, lifted his daughter in his arms and carried her to a nearby hospital.

Fortunately, Kerrigan had no broken bones, but her thigh was badly swollen, and her knee was severely bruised. Kerrigan had no choice but to withdraw from the U.S. championships, which could have had severe ramifications for her. In Olympic years, the members of the Olympic team are determined by the top finishers at the United States Nationals. With Kerrigan sidelined by injuries, the gold medal went to Harding, and a young skater from California named MICHELLE KWAN took the silver. But shortly after the nationals ended, the Olympic committee announced that since Kerrigan had been unfairly prevented from skating in the Nationals—a tournament she was favored to win—she would automatically be selected for the Olympic team. This meant that Kerrigan and Harding, the new national champion, would be the skaters selected to represent the United States at the 1994 Olympics in Lillehammer, Norway.

In the meantime, Detroit police had tracked down Kerrigan's assailant. Through inquiries and interviews, authorities discovered that Tonya Harding's ex-husband, Jeff Gillooly, had hired the assailant. Even more shocking, Gillooly announced several days later that Harding had not only known about the attack, but that she had enabled it by letting the assailant know when Kerrigan would be at the arena. Harding denied the charge, however, and lacking any definitive proof, the Olympic committee did not remove Harding from the team.

Kerrigan recovered from her injuries, but she had a long road ahead to regain her confidence and her strength, and not much time to do so; the Olympics were to begin eight weeks after the U.S. championships. Kerrigan began skating again two weeks after the injury, and she used the remaining month before Lillehammer to skate as often as she could, both by herself and in front of live audiences. By the time she traveled to Lillehammer, Kerrigan was back to full strength.

The ladies' ice-skating competition does not begin until the second week of the Olympic games. Nevertheless, from the moment the games began in Lillehammer, all eyes were on the two U.S. figure skaters. The Kerrigan/Harding affair had become international news, and the arena was jammed with photographers and media every time Harding and Kerrigan took the ice to practice. The two skaters had not seen each other since the Detroit attack and the ensuing discoveries. How would they act toward one another? Harding and

Kerrigan did share the ice several times during pre-competition warm-ups, but they did not exchange a word or, it appeared, even a glance.

The publicity and pressures of the past eight weeks culminated on the night the competition began. Both Kerrigan and Harding were slated to skate short programs. Harding performed poorly, falling once and staggering during several of her jumps. But Kerrigan skated flawlessly. At the end of the short-program portion of the competition, Harding had fallen out of contention for a medal, while Kerrigan was in first place.

Two nights later, in front of a sold-out arena and an international TV audience of more than 3 billion viewers—the largest audience the event has ever drawn—Kerrigan skated her freestyle program. With an easy smile that belied the pressures of the past eight weeks, Kerrigan performed brilliantly and received high marks from the judges in both the artistic and technical categories. After a bizarre performance by Harding—who begged (and received) permission from the judges to restart her program because her laces were not properly tied—only one skater stood between Kerrigan and the gold medal. That skater, Oksana Baiul of Ukraine, performed a glorious free-skating program, and in one of the closest and most controversial decisions in figure skating history, took top honors over Kerrigan by one-tenth of a point.

Kerrigan had not won the gold, but she returned from Lillehammer a hero. Shortly after the games ended, she announced her retirement from competitive amateur skating and turned professional. In 1995, she married her agent, Jerry Solomon, and a year later the couple had a son, Matthew. Kerrigan continues to skate in exhibition tours, and she remains a role model for young skaters—a symbol of discipline, survival, and triumph.

Further Reading

Greenspan, Bud. *Frozen in Time: The Greatest Moments at the Winter Olympics.* Santa Monica, Calif.: General Publishing Group, 1997.

Kerrigan, Nancy, and Steve Woodward. *Nancy Kerrigan: In My Own Words.* New York: Hyperion, 1997.

KING, BETSY (Elizabeth King)
(1955–) *Golfer*

Betsy King, the all-time leading money winner on the Ladies' Professional Golf Association (LPGA) tour, has won 30 major championships, including three Grand Slam events. What makes these accomplishments all the more impressive is the amusing fact that as a child, King did not particularly like golf.

Born in Reading, Pennsylvania, on August 13, 1955, Betsy King was an excellent student and a terrific athlete. Although her father, Dr. Weir King, taught Betsy and her brother to play golf when Betsy was 10, she did not spend a great deal of time on the golf course. Instead, she started for her high school basketball team, and she battled .480 as the shortstop of the softball team. In the meantime, King found the time to become a semifinalist in the U.S. Golf Association Junior Girls' Championships. Even so, King ranked golf near the bottom of her activity list, and she rarely played the game competitively.

After graduating from high school, King went to Furman University in South Carolina, where she played field hockey as well as basketball. When she was a sophomore, King hurt her knee severely while playing hockey. The injury effectively ended King's basketball and hockey career. Reluctantly, she turned to golf.

In 1976, King and her Furman teammates—including future professionals Beth Daniel and Sherri Turner—led their university to the golf National Collegiate Athletic Association (NCAA) championships. Later that year King played in her first U.S. Women's Open, and she shot the best score of any amateur, finishing eighth overall. The following year, King decided to turn professional.

Her first years on the LPGA tour were difficult ones for King. In her first three seasons, she managed only two second-place finishes, and she floundered in the lower half of many tournament finishes. Finally in 1980, King decided to train with the renowned coach Ed Oldfield, who persuaded King to change her game drastically.

Working with Oldfield, King developed a much more powerful and accurate swing, and in 1984, she won her first LPGA tournament, taking top honors in the Women's Kemper Open. King won two more LPGA events in 1984, became the tour's leading money maker for the year, and was named player of the year. After winning one tournament in 1985 and in 1986, King decided to take a break from the tour in 1987, to finish some work she had committed to do for Habitat for Humanity. She returned to competition in time to win the Dinah Shore Women's Open, and she ended up winning the Vare trophy for maintaining the lowest on-course average for 1987.

King had her best year in 1989, when she won six tournaments, including the U.S. Women's Open and took home more than $650,000 in winnings. In 1990 she successfully defended her Open title and won her second Dinah Shore tournament. One of the greatest thrills of King's career came in 1995. The holder of 29 LPGA tournament championships, King had to win one more in order to gain entry into the elite LPGA Hall of Fame, an honor reserved for those who have won 30 or more titles in the tour. On June 25 of that year, King erased a two-stroke deficit to win the ShopRite LPGA Classic over her old college teammate Beth Daniel. With that victory, King became only the 14th player to join the Hall of Fame.

After suffering a poor year in 1996, King returned to form in 1997 to win her third Dinah Shore tournament. She continues to play golf on the LPGA. A devout Christian, she has donated a large percentage of her tournament earnings to religious charities.

Further Reading

Friend, Tom. "Finally, King Finds Peace on Fairway," *New York Times,* July 13, 1995, B13.

Layden, Joe. *Women in Sports: The Complete Book of the World's Greatest Female Athletes.* Santa Monica, Calif.: General Publishing Group, 1997, p. 133.

White, Nan. "Betsy King." *Great Athletes.* Hackensack, N.J.: Salem Press, 2001, pp. 1315.

KING, BILLIE JEAN (Billie Jean Moffitt)
(1943–)   *Tennis Player*

Perhaps the most visible leader in the fight for equality and respect for women athletes in the United States was a tennis player named Billie Jean Moffitt King. A record-breaking champion who changed the face of the women's game on the court, King was also an outspoken advocate who claimed that a woman could swing the racket just as well as a man—and then proved it when she beat Bobby Riggs in a highly publicized and nationally televised tennis match.

Billie Jean Moffitt was born in Long Beach, California, on November 22, 1943. Early in her childhood, Moffitt's first athletic love was for baseball. She played often with her brother Randy, who would grow up to pitch professionally for the San Francisco Giants. When she was 11, Moffitt began taking tennis lessons, and she quickly blossomed into an athletic and confident player. During her teens, she began talking about her goal of winning Wimbledon, the most prestigious and competitive tennis tournament in the world. And in 1961, Moffitt achieved that aspiration, when she and Karen Hantze became the youngest players ever to win the Wimbledon Ladies' Doubles Crown.

In the early 1960s, tennis was not the money-laden sport that it is today. The four major Grand Slam tennis tournaments—Wimbledon, the U.S. Championships, the French Championships, and the Australian Championships—were, like the Olympics, events for amateurs only. Players who hoped to make money in the sport did so in minor tournaments in which they were paid "under the table." All that changed, however, in 1968. That year, the four Grand Slam events, as well as all other major tennis tournaments, became "Opens," meaning that any player, whether professional or amateur, could qualify to play. In addition, prize money was now offered to the participants. Billie Jean King (she had married Larry King in 1966) was one of the most outspoken athletes during this transition. Lamenting the nation's view of tennis as a leisurely country-club activity rather than the competitive sport she knew it was, King observed that "we have to get this game off the society pages and on to the sports pages!"

Although tennis players had won the war for recognition and financial compensation in 1968, it was a tainted victory for women in the sport. The tournaments were now paying their champions, but the purses offered to female champions were far lower than those won by their male counterparts. In 1968, for example, when King won the first Wimbledon ladies' singles championship of the open era, her prize money totaled $3,000. Rod Laver, who won the men's singles event that year, took home $8,000. The following year, King earned $800 when she captured the Italian Open singles title. The winner of the men's championship at the same tournament claimed $3,500 in prize money.

But perhaps the greatest insult King and her fellow female players endured came at the hands of Jack Kramer, one of King's fellow activists in the battle for professional status. In 1970 Kramer organized and hosted the Pacific Southwest Open and offered a purse of $12,500 for the men's champion. The prize money for all women players, in the meantime, totaled $7,500, with no payments for women who failed to make the quarterfinals. King, who had been advocating the need for a separate women's professional tour since the early 1960s, then persuaded eight of the best women's players to boycott the Pacific Southwest Open. Several weeks later, those nine players competed in their own tournament in Houston. This fly-by-night event was organized by *Tennis World,* a tennis magazine, and was sponsored by Philip Morris, a cigarette company.

King and her fellow revolutionaries were quickly suspended by the U.S. Tennis Association (USTA) for participating in an event it had not sanctioned. In due course, however, the women won the battle; by 1971, they had their own professional tour, labeled the Virginia Slims All-Women's Pro Circuit. Two years later, more than 60 women were involved in the Virginia Slims tour, which then included 30 events, all awarding at least $10,000 in prize money.

In later years, some controversy would surround the fact that women's tennis allowed itself to be sponsored by Virginia Slims, one of the Philip Morris–owned cigarette companies; some argued that it was hypocritical and unethical for an athletic event to advertise and promote tobacco use by associating itself so closely with a cigarette brand. Eventually, Virginia Slims was replaced as the main sponsor of the women's professional tennis tour. Even so, King has never wavered in her support for Virginia Slims, who provided financial support and corporate sponsorship for female tennis palyers during their time of need.

Having helped establish a separate women's tour for her peers, King now set her sights on an even greater challenge. She meant to settle a score and, in doing so, show U.S. sports fans that women tennis players deserved the same respect and attention as their male counterparts.

The saga of Billie Jean King and Bobby Riggs began early in 1973 when Riggs invited any top-ranked woman tennis player to challenge him to a match. Riggs was eager to prove his claim that women tennis players lacked the physical endurance and the mental strength to beat a man. In May, the English player Margaret Smith Court, one of King's greatest on-court rivals and the holder of several Grand Slam championships, accepted Riggs's invitation and agreed to play him in a best-of-three-set match. Before play began, Riggs, a consummate showman as well as a self-proclaimed chauvinist, entered the court carrying red roses for his rival. Court accepted the flowers from a smiling Riggs, but her concentration was shattered. She lost to Riggs in straight sets, 6-2, 6-1.

Court's defeat added fuel to Riggs's fire. Claiming that it was his job to help "keep our women at home—with the babies, where they belong," he reissued his challenge and was delighted when King responded by inviting him to play her in a winner-take-all, $10,000, best-of-five-set match. "I want Billie Jean," he said. "She's the one I wanted in the first place!" King, in the meantime, felt compelled to play Riggs, in part to avenge the loss suffered by

Billie Jean King in action early in her career. Not only did King defeat Bobby Riggs in a highly publicized match in 1973, but she also played a key role in the establishment of a separate professional tennis tour for women.
(Library of Congress)

Court earlier that year. "Margaret opened the door, and I intend to close it," King said.

When King and Riggs entered the Houston Astrodome on the night of September 23, 1973, they came onto the court from opposite ends of the arena. And in truth, the two challengers were opposites in virtually every way. King was a passionate and earnest athlete, who strove to play competitive tennis, not only for the glory of winning, but for the chance to advance a cause. Riggs, better known as a showman than as a serious athlete, wore his "male chauvinist" label with pride. Moreover, having captured two consecutive Wimbledon titles, the 29-year-old King was the top-ranked woman player in the world. Riggs, at 55, was well past his prime as a player. Even so, he remained confident that a woman could not possibly defeat him, and media and oddsmakers alike appeared to believe his claim: Riggs was heavily favored to beat King in what was being called the "Battle of the Sexes" tennis match.

At the Astrodome that night, King quickly outserved, outvolleyed, outhustled, and plain outplayed her cocky opponent. It took King less than two hours to write a new chapter in the chronicles of women's sports, as she tore Riggs to shreds in straight sets, 6-4, 6-3, 6-3. At the end of the match, King flung her racket to the rafters victoriously. It is a moment still regarded as among the most pivotal in the history of women's athletics.

Contemporary women's tennis owes a tremendous debt to Billie Jean King, not only for the invaluable role she played as an advocate for equal rights, but for adding a new dimension to the game on the court. Before King's era, the vast majority of women tennis players were baseline specialists, meaning that they preferred to stay back and hit ground stroke after ground stroke, rather than attempting to run to the net and volley. King was one of the first women players to master the "serve and volley" strategy, a style of play that at the time was much more prevalent in the men's game.

King's style of play not only helped to make women's tennis a more exciting and flashy game, it also helped her to become one of the most prolific champions in the history of the sport. Throughout her career, King captured 35 Grand Slam titles, including a record 20 Wimbledon titles. King's final Wimbledon championship came in 1979, when she and MARTINA NAVRATILOVA won the women's doubles crown. That win propelled King ahead of Elizabeth Ryan, a tennis player who had won the bulk of her 19 Wimbledon championships during the 1920s. Upon hearing that King was about to break her record, Ryan, who had once said she didn't want to live to see her record broken, declared that ". . . if my (record) has to go, I would like Billie Jean to have it, because she has so much guts." (Ironically, Ryan died the night before King broke her record. She was 87 years old.)

After King retired from competitive tennis in 1980, she remained an active presence in women's tennis. She coached and advised such players as Martina Navratilova and JENNIFER CAPRIATI, and she continues to campaign for respect and equal pay for women tennis players. King's willingness to do battle for women's rights made her one of the great heronies of the feminist movement, both on and off the court.

Further Reading

Layden, Joe. *Women in Sports: The Complete Book of the World's Greatest Female Athletes.* Santa Monica, Calif.: General Publishing Group, 1997, p. 134.

Smith, Lissa, editor. *Nike Is a Goddess.* New York: Atlantic Monthly Press, 1998, pp. 64–68.

Markel, Robert, Susan Wagoner, and Marcella Smith. *The Women's Sports Encyclopedia.* New York: Henry Holt, 1995, pp. 54, 57–63.

Sugar, Bert Randolph. *The Sports 100: A Ranking of the Greatest Athletes of All Time.* Secaucus, N.J.: Citadel Press, 1995, pp. 355–359.

KING, MICKI (Maxine Joyce King)
(1944–)   *Diver*

How many people would, after breaking an arm on a difficult dive at the world's most prestigious tournament, attempt the very same dive at the same competition four years later? One person who did that very thing was Micki King. After shattering her left forearm on a reverse one-and-a-half somersault at the 1968 games, King came back at the 1972 Olympic Games, performed the dive flawlessly, and won the gold medal.

It was a courageous move, but then again, Micki King was always fearless. Born on July 26, 1944, in Pontiac, Michigan, Maxine Joyce King began diving when she was 10 years old. At this age, young Micki displayed a grace and daring that stunned spectators. After graduating from high school, King attended the University of Michigan. Although King was clearly an elite athlete, she often had to fight for the chance to train. King's years at Michigan—from 1959 to 1963—ended well before Title

IX, the legislation that compelled all universities to offer the same opportunities to female and male athletes, became a law in 1972. Fortunately for King, the women's water coach at Michigan, Don Kimball, recognized her talent. He made sure that King got the training she needed. At times, he helped her sneak into the men's locker room at the university swimming pool, because there were no similar facilities for women.

Kimball also arranged for specific practice times for King—again, something that women were not accorded, because they did not have varsity status. During these sessions, Kimball taught King a wide range of dives—many of which had never been done by a woman in competition before. Armed with a sophisticated diving repertoire, King won three National Collegiate Athletic Association (NCAA) diving titles. In 1965, when she was a junior at Michigan, King won the U.S. national outdoor title in the 3-meter springboard competition and the U.S. national indoor title in the 10-meter platform competition.

King graduated from Michigan in 1966, decided to join the U.S. Air Force, and the U.S. Air Force Academy that fall. But she continued to dive, and in 1968 she traveled to Mexico City to compete in the Olympics as a member of the U.S. women's diving team. One of the favorites to win a medal, King scored high marks in the early part of the springboard competition. With eight dives down and two to go, King was in first place. But then disaster struck. On King's ninth dive, she hit the diving board and broke her left arm. Somehow, King finished the competition. But the injury cost her a medal, and she ended up in fourth place.

After Mexico City, King remained at the air force academy as a diving coach and continued to compete. She won the U.S. outdoor title in the 3-meter springboard in 1969 and 1970, and in the 10-meter platform in 1969, and in 1971 she took top honors at the U.S. indoor championships, once again in both the 3-meter springboard and 10-meter platform events.

In 1972, King returned to the Olympics, which were held this time in Munich, West Germany. At 28, King was one of the oldest competitors on the entire U.S. Olympic team. She was determined to win a medal however, and her persistence and passion showed during the 3-meter springboard event. After seven dives, King was in third place. She knew that she did not have to be spectacular—if she completed the competition with solid dives, she would leave Munich with a bronze. But King decided to take the risk. On her ninth dive, she completed one and one-half revolutions in a reverse (meaning she left the diving board facing away from the water and then flipped forward) position, and ripped through the water cleanly. Her scores on that dive jolted her into first place, and on her 10th and final dive, she clinched gold. Normally a stoic presence in competition, King became emotional on the medal stand and wept openly during the national anthem.

The following year, King became the diving coach at the air force academy—the first woman ever to hold a faculty position at a military academy. Also in 1973, King joined DONNA DE VARONA, BILLIE JEAN KING, SHEILA YOUNG, and WYOMIA TYUS as cofounders of the Women's Sports Foundation, an organization designed to inspire young women to compete in athletics.

King left the air force academy in 1977 to become director of women's athletics at the University of California at Los Angeles (UCLA). Six years later, she returned to the air force as diving coach and assistant director of athletics. In 1990 she became the president of U.S. Diving, which serves as the national governing body of the sport, and held that post for four years. In the late 1990s, King became the special assistant to the director of athletics and senior women's administrator at the University of Kentucky.

Further Reading

Layden, Joe. *Women in Sports: The Complete Book of the World's Greatest Female Athletes.* Santa Monica, Calif.: General Publishing Group, 1997, p. 136.

Offen, Stephanie, "Break in Tradition: Female Athletes Had to Push "U" System," Michigan Daily Online. Available online. URL: http://www.pub.umich.edu/daily/1999/nov/11-12-99/news/news17.html. Posted on November 12, 1999.

Microsoft Encarta Online Encyclopedia 2001. "King, Micki." Available online. URL: http://encarta.msn. com. Downloaded on March 22, 2001.

University of Michigan online, "Michigan in the Olympics—1972-Munich." Available online. URL: http://www.umich.edu/~bhl/bhl/olymp2/ol1972.htm. Downloaded on March 22, 2001.

KRONE, JULIE
(1963–)   *Jockey*

When the jockey Julie Krone rode to victory at the 1973 Belmont Stakes, she became the first woman to win one of thoroughbred horse racing's prestigious Triple Crown races. Krone, who at 4 feet, $10^1/_2$ inches was small even in the diminutive world of race riders, went on to become the most successful woman jockey in history.

Julie Krone was born on July 24, 1963, in Benton Harbor, Michigan. Her mother, Judi, and father, Donald, were horse trainers. When Julie was three, Judi put Julie on the back of a horse to show a perspective buyer how gentle the horse was. To Judi's horror, the horse rode off with the toddler on the saddle. But Julie did not panic; she simply reached down, grabbed the reins, and guided the horse back to her mother.

Although Julie was first interested in equitation, in which a rider guides a horse through patterns and jumps, by the time she was 13 she had decided to become a jockey. She began her career as a groom, then worked her way up to exercise rider (one who rides horses during workouts and warm-ups), and finally to victory.

Krone's first race victory came at Tampa Bay Downs in 1983. During the next few years her winnings increased, and by the end of the 1980s she was among the top five jockeys in the country. In 1992 Krone became the first woman to claim the New York Racing Association title, and she also rode in the Kentucky Derby—the third woman to do so—and finished 14th. One year later, she was chosen to ride a horse named Colonial Affair, one of the top three-year-olds in the country. Krone and Colonial Affair did not compete in the Kentucky Derby or the Preakness, the first two legs of the Triple Crown, but they swept to victory in the final event, the Belmont Stakes.

Later in 1993, Krone was thrown from a horse and trampled during a race at Saratoga. Krone's injuries, including a shattered ankle, severely bruised chest, and punctured elbow, were so severe that doctors were not sure that she would ever race again. But her accident notwithstanding, the Women's Sports Foundation recognized Krone's pioneering achievement at the Belmont Stakes and awarded her the Sportswoman of the Year award in 1993.

Fortunately, Krone did recover from her injuries. After extensive rehabilitation, she returned to the track in late 1994. She rode a horse named Suave Prospect to an 11th-place finish in the 1995 Kentucky Derby, and on April 18, 1999, after winning three races, she retired. Krone claims the key to her success was in remaining in shape and knowing how each horse likes to be ridden. Krone's strategies worked well for her. With more than $53 million in earnings, she is the top moneymaker among woman jockeys.

Further Reading

Greenberg, Judith E. *Getting into the Game.* Danbury, Conn.: Franklin Watts, 1997, pp. 118–119.

Layden, Joe. *Women in Sports: The Complete Book of the World's Greatest Female Athletes.* Santa Monica, Calif.: General Publishing Group, 1997, pp. 140–141.

Smith, Lissa, editor. *Nike Is a Goddess: The History of Women in Sports.* New York: Atlantic Monthly Press, 1998, p. 216.

KUSCSIK, NINA
(1938–)   *Long-Distance Runner, Marathon Runner*

The first woman to officially win a Boston Marathon was Nina Kuscsik, who performed that feat in 1972. Kuscsik, one of the great pioneers of women's distance running, would go on to win two New York City Marathons and to set a U.S. record in the 50-mile distance.

Nina Kuscsik, who was born in Long Island, New York, in 1938, was a 30-year-old housewife with three children in 1968, the year she started training for long-distance running. She made that decision the day she ran a mile at a local track and clocked a rather inauspicious time of seven minutes and five seconds. She and two of her friends, Charlie Blum and Bob Muller, decided they would all start training to run in the 1969 Boston Marathon.

Kuscsik trained with her friends, but she was aware that unlike Blum and Muller, she could not officially run in the marathon; women were not allowed to compete in the race. In order to do so, she would have to hide at the start and then jump into the crowd at the beginning of the course. In addition, Kuscsik had torn ligaments in her arm several weeks earlier. Although her cast was removed shortly before the marathon, her arm was still weak and painful.

Unperturbed by her circumstances, Kuscsik traveled to Boston a few days before the race. She, Muller, Blum, and her then-husband, Bob, drove through the course to become familiar with it. On the day of the race, Kuscsik, wearing a tank top under a shirt and a sweater, waited on the sidelines until the starting gun sounded and then ran into the race. With her thumb of her sore arm hooked into a loop in her bra, Kuscsik ran the entire race and crossed the finish line with a time of three hours and 46 minutes. "Our goal was to finish under four hours," she said later, "and we did." Relieved to have met her goal, Kuscsik returned to Long Island. "I remember thinking, that's it, now I can become a normal person again."

But Kuscsik remained obsessed with distance running. She returned to Boston in 1970 and 1971, and then, in 1972, ran in the first Boston Marathon women's race. By this time, Kuscsik, a veteran of more than 25 marathon races, had become the top distance runner in the country, and she proved it with a winning time of three hours, 10 minutes, and 26 seconds. The second-place finisher, Elaine Pederson, crossed the finish line a full 10 minutes after Kuscsik.

Several months later, Kuscsik went to New York City to compete in that city's marathon. New York City had had its own marathon since 1970, but like Boston, it did not allow women to compete in an official capacity until the 1972 race. Before the race, Kuscsik and her fellow female racers all stood on the starting line with the men and waited for the starting gun to go off. But when the gun sounded, something interesting happened. Rather than beginning the race at the sound of the gun, every woman competitor sat down for a full ten minutes. The women had organized a sit-down strike in order to protest the ban on women marathon runners. After 10 minutes passed, the women got up and began to run. Twenty-six miles later, Kuscsik crossed the finish line to become the first woman winner of the New York City Marathon. Her winning time of 3 hours, eight minutes, and 41 seconds is misleading, because the 10-minute protest was counted as part of every woman's running time.

Kuscik continued to run competitively for another eight years. She returned to New York City to win the 1973 marathon and then began concentrating on even longer distances. Competing in an international competition in West Germany in 1977, she set a U.S. record for a 50-mile race, completing the distance in six hours, 35 minutes, and 53 seconds.

In addition to her remarkable competitive career, Kuscsik has played a major role as an advocate for women's distance running. She has initiated several changes in U.S. policies that have resulted in more women's distance events as well as a U.S. championship. Then, in 1984, it was Kuscsik who introduced legislation that would be adopted by the United States and the Amateur International Athletic Union (AIAU). This legislation allowed the women's marathon to become an official Olympic event. Thanks to Kuscsik's actions, the first women's Olympic marathon was run at the 1984 games in Los Angeles.

A journalist and broadcaster as well an advocate, Kuscsik has written several columns on running for *Track and Field* magazine, and she serves as a local radio commentator for the New York City Marathon.

Further Reading

Cimons, Marlene. "Four Who Dared," *Runner's World* 31, no. 4 (April 1996): 72–78.

National Distance Running Hall of Fame. "Nina Kuscsik," Distance Running Online. Available online. URL: http://www.distancerunning.com/induc_kuscsik.html. Downloaded on June 25, 2001.

⊞ KWAN, MICHELLE
(1980–) *Figure Skater*

Michelle Kwan, who has three world championships and four U.S. championships to her credit, has won virtually every title but the Olympic gold medal. This goal has eluded her twice—at the 1998 Games in Nagano, Japan, and at the Salt Lake City games in 2002.

Born in Torrance, California, on July 7, 1980, Michelle Kwan was the youngest of three children born to Estelle and Danny Kwan, who had immigrated to the United States from Hong Kong in 1970. Michelle became intrigued with the ice at the age of four—she and the Kwan family attended all of her brother's ice hockey practices—and soon both Michelle and her older sister Karen were taking figure skating lessons.

Michelle entered her first tournament at the age of six, and when she turned 10 she began training with Frank Carroll, who told the young skater that if she worked hard, she could become a champion. That was all it took for Kwan, who immediately began a rigorous training program. Before she was 11, Kwan was skating three hours a day, seven days a week. Soon, the work began to show results. At the age of 12, Kwan won her first major junior tournament, taking top honors at the Southwest Pacific Regionals. One year later she skated in her first non-junior U.S. Championships and finished sixth.

Kwan won consecutive silvers at the U.S. Championships in 1994 (the year of the infamous NANCY KERRIGAN/Tonya Harding inci-

dent) and in 1995, and she placed fourth at the World Championships in 1995. But it was in 1996 that Kwan truly came into her own. A 16-year-old skater who looked young and waiflike on the ice, she and her coach, Frank Carroll, devised a daring routine at the World Championships. Kwan, who had always dressed in conservative, modest outfits, skated onto the ice wearing a sophisticated costume. For her long program, Kwan had chosen to portray the biblical figure Salome, who performed a seductive dance for the Roman emperor Herod in exchange for the head of John the Baptist. It was an intriguing routine, filled with glamor and sophistication, but could Kwan, small, delicate, and formal at the age of 16, pull it off?

The answer was a resounding yes. The moment Kwan began her Salome routine, she captivated the crowd and the judges with a brilliantly realized artistic performance. "Michelle didn't skate the role of Salome," wrote author Edward Z. Epstein, "she lived it." Light on the ice, yet completely in command of her spins and jumps, Kwan blazed her way to her first World Championship.

In 1997 Kwan finished second at the U.S. Championships, behind TARA LIPINSKI, and she took the silver behind Lipinski at the World Championships as well. But in 1998, she bested Lipinski at the U.S. Championships with a dazzling performance in the long program that earned her five perfect scores from the judges.

Entering the 1998 Olympic Games at Nagano, Kwan had emerged as the favorite to win gold. Lipinski, her teammate and rival, was the top choice for second, and many experts thought Nicole Bobek, who had finished third to Kwan and Lipinski at the nationals, had a good chance at the bronze. Bobek performed poorly during the short program, however, and ended up finishing 12th. Lipinski skated a solid short program, but it was Kwan, showing confidence and artistic flair, who won the highest votes from the judges.

By the night of the long program, Kwan was ahead of both Lipinski and Chu Len of China, the bronze medalist from the 1994 games. But during the long program, Kwan seemed slightly tentative. Her routine was very good, but it lacked the spark that had made Kwan's routine at the nationals so special. Kwan received high marks, but she knew that a brilliant routine by Lipinski could cost her the gold.

Lipinski did indeed skate brilliantly, and she took top honors at the Nagano games. Kwan told reporters that she was happy for Lipinski, and that although her medal "was not the color" she had wanted, she was proud of the way she had skated. Shortly after the Nagano games ended, Lipinski and Chen Lu both left competitive skating, but Kwan continued her rigorous training program.

She won the U.S. Nationals in 1999, 2000, 2001, and 2002 and after finishing second at the World Championships in 1999, came back to take the gold once again in 2000 and 2001.

Sadly for Kwan, history repeated itself at the Salt Lake City games. As at Nagano, Kwan led the field after the short program. But like the games in Japan, she was surpassed in the free skate by a fellow American. In fourth place after the short program, young SARAH HUGHES skated a near perfect routine in the long program. Even so, the gold was Kwan's to lose. But on the ice, the four-time world champion could not find her rhythm, and fell once, during one of her triple combinations. The gold went to Hughes, and this time, Kwan had to settle for bronze. After Salt Lake City, Kwan remained undecided about her future. It could be that the young Californian will decide to stop competing, and enter the professional ranks. But it is also possible that, come 2006, a 26-year-old Kwan will be floating on the ice in Turin, Italy, still striving for that elusive gold.

Further Reading

Epstein, Edward Z. *The Michelle Kwan Story.* New York: Random House, 1997.

Greenspan, Bud. *Frozen in Time: The Greatest Moments at the Winter Olympics.* Santa Monica, Calif.: General Publishing Group, 1997.

LADEWIG, MARION
(1914–)   *Bowler*

Marion Ladewig was quite simply the greatest woman bowler in history. In addition, she was instrumental to the increased popularity and interest in bowling during the 1950s and early 1960s, when she was in her prime as a player.

Born in Grand Rapids, Michigan, on October 30, 1914, Marion Ladewig bowled once or twice during her early childhood, but she was more interested in other sports, such as softball. But one night, when she was a teenager, Ladewig accompanied her softball team for a night out at a bowling alley and fell in love with the sport. A few days later, Ladewig took a job at a similar alley, as a cashier and an occasional pinsetter (in the days before automatic pinsetting, it was done manually). Her salary was only $2.50 per week, during the height of the Great Depression, but Ladewig made the most of her free practice time at the alley and quickly became an accomplished bowler.

During the height of Ladewig's career, in the 1950s, there were no professional bowling championships for women. The closest thing to a tournament during those years was the Women's All-Star Tournament, an event now known as the U.S. Open that is organized each year by the Bowling Professional's Association. Ladewig won the Women's All-Star Tournament a total of eight times between 1949 and 1963. She also took top honors at the Women's International Bowling Congress (WIBC) All-Events competition in 1950 and 1955, the WIBC doubles tournament in 1955, and, as a member of the Grand Rapids Fanatorium Majors, helped her club win the 1950 WIBC team championship. It was also in 1950 that Ladewig became the first and only bowler in history to win All-Events titles at the city, state, and national levels in one year.

Ladewig was an endearing and charismatic figure on the lane. She took to chewing gum during competitions in an effort to keep herself calm. This action earned her the nickname of "the Chiclet-chewing lady." Her talent and personality made her a role model for thousands of women during the 1960s and helped lift the popularity of bowling. Ladewig herself was so popular that she finished third in the voting for the 1963 Associated Press Female Athlete of the Year—the highest placing ever for a bowler.

After winning the World Invitational tournament for the fifth time, in 1965, Ladewig retired from competitive bowling. She continued to be involved in the sport, writing a bowling column for a newspaper and playing in exhibition tournaments at her bowling complex in Grand Rapids.

Further Reading

Layden, Joe. *Women in Sports: The Complete Book on the World's Greatest Female Athletes.* Santa Monica, Calif.: General Publishing Group, 1997, pp. 142–143.

Rintala, Jan. "Marion Ladewig." *Great Athletes.* Hackensack, N.J.: Salem Press, 2001, p. 1375.

▪▪ LAWRENCE, ANDREA MEAD
▪▪ (1932–) *Skier*

Andrea Mead Lawrence is the first and only U.S. Olympic Alpine skier to earn two Olympic gold medals. She performed this feat in one Olympiad, at the 1952 games in Oslo, Norway.

Born on April 19, 1932, in Green Mountain, Vermont, Andrea Mead grew up on a ski slope. Andrea's mother, who named her daughter after the Italian artist Andrea del Sarto, managed the Pico Peak ski resort, and before she was a teenager, Andrea was navigating the trails there better than anyone else. In fact, she had become such an expert on the slopes that she was winning regional and statewide competitions.

In 1948, 15-year-old Mead qualified to ski in the Olympics, which took place that year in Saint Moritz, Switzerland. Mead skied a fast downhill race, but she fell just short of the finish line and was eliminated from the competition. Disappointed by her performance in Saint Moritz, Mead contemplated quitting the sport entirely. Instead, she began training under a new coach, Karl Acker, and then dropped out of high school to concentrate solely on skiing.

Her commitment paid off. Mead qualified to ski in both the slalom and giant slalom events at the 1952 Olympic games in Oslo. In the meantime, she had married David Lawrence, a fellow skier who would also be competing in Oslo. Two days after the games began, Lawrence began her quest for gold in the women's downhill competition. Snow had been light that year in Oslo, and members of the Norwegian army had had to collect snow from other mountains in the area and then shovel it onto the competition slopes. These conditions did not bother Lawrence in the least as she blazed down the slopes a full two seconds faster than the second-place finisher.

Lawrence had won the first U.S. gold medal of the Oslo games, an achievement duly noted by the *New York Times,* who called the new downhill champion "the little American housewife." But Lawrence still had another race to ski: the slalom competition, which took place on a steep and treacherous hill. During her first run, Lawrence slipped on the icy slope and fell. But she got up quickly and completed the run quickly enough to be in fourth place after the first run. A day later, Lawrence sealed her second gold of the game with a flawless run down the same slope.

With two gold medals, Lawrence was a full-fledged Olympic hero. She returned home to Vermont, where she was honored with daylong festivities, complete with a marching band. Lawrence and her husband retired from competitive skiing after the Oslo games. A few months after their return to Vermont, they moved to northern California, where they had five children. Several years later, Andrea Mead Lawrence embarked on a second career, as an environmental activist, which she continues to pursue today.

No other U.S. skier has ever won two Olympic gold medals. PICABO STREET did win two Olympic medals; she captured gold in the 1998 Giant Slalom event, but four years earlier, at the Lillehammer games, she had finished $17/100$ of a second behind the first-place finisher in the downhill race and had to settle for a silver.

Further Reading

Lerman, Josh. "The Greening of Andrea Lawrence," *Skiing,* January 1994, p. 18.

Smith, Lissa, editor. *Nike Is a Goddess.* New York: Atlantic Monthly Press, 1998, pp. 133–134.

LESLIE, LISA
(1972–)   *Basketball Player*

Perhaps the most recognizable player in the Women's National Basketball Association (WNBA) is the six foot, five inch Lisa Leslie. Long, lean, and completely dominating on the court, Leslie has not only provided topnotch offense and defense for the Los Angeles Sparks, but she was a leader in the United States' two consecutive gold medal Olympic triumphs in 1996 and 2000.

Lisa Leslie learned early how to be part of a team. Born on July 7, 1972, in Los Angles, California, she grew up with two sisters and a single mother, Christine Leslie. Christine did not have a great deal of money, but she refused to scrape by doing odd jobs or to go on welfare. Instead, Lisa's mother started her own trucking business, buying herself an 18-wheel vehicle when Lisa was still very young. Christine was on the road for several weeks at a time during Lisa's school years. Lisa and her sisters, who were cared for by a neighbor, missed their mother terribly when she was gone, but they helped one another out with both schoolwork and housework. "It made me grow up really fast," Lisa said later of her early independence.

Meanwhile, Lisa was growing physically too. By the time she finished junior high school, she was already six feet tall. Although Lisa's height would later make her one of the best basketball players in the country, it was not an easy thing for her to live with during her early teenage years. "It embarrassed me more than anything else," she said later. Toward the end of junior high school, however, a friend urged her to begin playing basketball. Lisa, who had never been interested in the sport before, began playing—and she never looked back.

By the time she was a senior in high school, Lisa Leslie was the most sought-after women's player in the country. With a scoring average of 27 points per game (including one contest in which she scored 100 points in the first half), she entertained several scholarship offers. Opting to go to a school close to her home, she chose the University of Southern California (USC).

At USC, Leslie earned All-America honors three times. In her senior year, she was named National Women's Player of the Year—one of the few times in history that the selection was unanimous. But perhaps Leslie's most memorable moment in college was not during a game, but in pregame warmups. Fully grown at six feet, five inches, Leslie would regularly dunk the ball at the end of her warm-up sessions. It was a move she refused to do during

Lisa Leslie celebrates the 1996 Olympic championship in style. During a high school game, the future WNBA all-star scored 100 points—in one half.
(Allsport Photography)

competition, however. Because slam dunks have never been a part of the women's game, she was worried about being accidentally injured by a player who remained under the basket.

After graduating from USC in 1994, Leslie played professionally in Europe for a season, and then joined Team USA, the Olympic squad that toured the country and then won gold at the 1996 Atlanta Olympics. During Team USA's victorious Olympic campaign, Leslie led all players with a 19.5 points-per-game scoring average. She saved her most impressive performance for the gold medal match, when she scored a masterful 29 points as the United States upended defending world champion Brazil to take the Olympic title.

The following year, Leslie began playing for the Los Angeles Sparks franchise of the WNBA. She quickly became the premier center in the league, leading all players in rebounding and earning a unanimous selection to the All-WNBA team. In 1998, Leslie added another gold medal to her résumé, sparking Team USA to a gold medal at the World Championships. But perhaps Leslie's greatest moment was two years later, when she led the U.S. team to a second consecutive gold medal at the Sydney Olympic games. This time, the team was playing away from home, and as the favorites to win the tournament, they often found the fans cheering for their opponents. Lesser players might have been disconcerted by the unfavorable crowds, but Leslie and her teammates rose to the occasion, dominating opponents through the early rounds. In the gold medal game, the United States played against Australia, the home team. Leslie scored 26 points, and the visitors prevailed. At the end of the game, a delighted Leslie ran around the gym and then allowed her reveling teammates to give her a spontaneous haircut.

Her Samson-like tresses grew back in time for the 2001 WNBA season, when Leslie led the Los Angeles sparks to their first league title. In the process Leslie seized most valuable player honors for both the regular season and championship series, and was also named the most valuable player at the annual WNBA all-star game.

Further Reading

Fisher, David. *Lisa Leslie.* Kansas City, Mo.: Andrews-McMeel, 2000.

Rutledge, Rachel. *The Best of the Best in Basketball.* Brookfield, Conn.: Millbrook Press, 1998, pp. 27–30.

⊞ LIEBERMAN, NANCY
(Nancy Lieberman-Cline)
(1958–) *Basketball Player*

Nancy Lieberman was denied a chance to play in the 1980 Olympics when the United States decided to boycott the Moscow games. She played in several collegiate championships, before women's teams were included in the National Collegiate Athletic Association (NCAA), and her professional basketball career was hampered by the fact that there were no successful paying leagues for women in the United States during her career. Even so, Lieberman has left her mark on the sport of women's basketball, and she is considered to be one of the great pioneers of women's sports.

Born in Far Rockaway, New York, on July 1, 1958, Lieberman fell in love with basketball when she was seven years old. Her mother, Renee, who had divorced Nancy's father several years earlier, tried hard to discourage Nancy from playing basketball. Renee constantly gave Nancy dolls to play with—to no avail. And in desperation, Nancy's mother even punctured her daughter's basketball with a screwdriver.

But Nancy was determined to play, and play she did—at all locations in New York City and at all hours. Nancy practiced constantly on her neighborhood courts, day and night; when she could no longer see the ball or the hoop, she played "radar" ball, because she could hear the sound of the ball clanging through the metal circle. She quickly learned where the best pickup games in the city were, and she regularly traveled from Far Rockaway into Harlem and downtown Manhattan.

Nancy took a lot of grief from the boys on the court and sometimes ended up getting into fistfights with them, but she held her own in the games and was eventually accepted and respected.

Nancy did not play against girls until she got to high school. She played for her school team, but she was by far the best player on the court and found the games unchallenging. During her sophomore year, she joined an all-women's amateur team called the Rockaway Seahorses and also played for an Amateur Athletic Union team. As a high school junior, Lieberman played for the U.S. national team in the Pan American Games. One year later, a few weeks after her high school graduation, she traveled to Montreal to play in the 1976 Olympics. At 17, Lieberman was the youngest member on the team, which won a silver medal.

After the Olympics, Lieberman attended Old Dominion University on a basketball scholarship. Lieberman played college ball for several years before the NCAA recognized and sanctioned women's sports. Playing in the Association of Intercollegiate Athletics for Women (AIAW), she was a four-time All-American at Old Dominion and twice led the school to national championships. Two years after Lieberman's graduation, women's basketball finally came under the NCAA umbrella; with that came better facilities for women, expanded media exposure (including television coverage), and, eventually, higher attendance at the games.

Lieberman left Old Dominion in 1980 with high hopes of leading the U.S. team to a gold medal in the Moscow games. Disappointed when the United States decided to boycott, she soon joined the newly formed Women's American Basketball Association, where she played with the Dallas Diamonds until the league folded in 1982. Lieberman then began playing with the Washington Generals, serving as point guard (and only female player) on the team, which toured with the Harlem Globetrotters. In the early 1980s she also became MARTINA NAVRATILOVA's personal trainer and helped groom the Czech athlete into the premier tennis player in the world.

In 1986, Lieberman became the first woman to play for a men's professional basketball league when she joined the Springfield Fame, a franchise in the United States Basketball League. When that league folded, she turned her time and attention to the business world. She bought two sporting goods stores, endorsed several products, and owned real estate in Texas and St. Croix.

Her business deals made Lieberman a wealthy woman, but basketball remained her true passion. In 1992 Lieberman married Tim Cline, a retired professional basketball player (they separated in late 2001), and during the early 1990s she worked as a television commentator for ESPN and Prime Sports, and she ran basketball camps during the summer. Heartened by the establishment of the WNBA in 1997, Lieberman-Cline returned to the court first as a player and then as head coach for the Detroit Sparks, one of the league's franchises. After four seasons at the helm for the Sparks, Lieberman-Cline resigned at the end of the 2001 season and signed a contract as an analyst for ESPN.

Further Reading

The Jewish Student Online Research Center, Seymour Brody. "Nancy Lieberman." Available online. URL: http://www.us-israel.org/jsource/biography/Lieberman.html. Downloaded on January 6, 2001.

Layden, Joe. *Women in Sports: The Complete Book on the World's Greatest Female Athletes.* Santa Monica, Calif.: General Publishing Group, 1997, pp. 149–150.

LIPINSKI, TARA
(1982–) *Figure Skater*

When 16-year-old SONJA HENIE won the gold medal at the 1928 Olympics, few believed that anyone would ever become an Olympic champion at a younger age. But then Tara Lipinski came along to grab gold at the 1998 Olympic Games at the age of 15, and just like that, Henie's mark was shattered. In the process of winning top honors at the Nagano Olympic Games, Lipinski also scored one of the major upsets in Olympic history, topping the heavily favored MICHELLE KWAN, Lipinski's teammate and archrival.

Tara Lipinski was born in Philadelphia on June 10, 1982. Her parents, Jack and Pat Lipinski, swear that they remember their 26-month-old daughter watching the 1984 Olympics and then climbing on top of an upside-down Tupperware box and pretending to accept a medal.

In fact, Tara was constantly on the move as a toddler. Her parents urged her to go outside and run off her excess energy, but their young daughter did not think running was fast enough for her. When Tara was three, her mother enrolled her in a toddler roller-skating class. At the age of five, Tara was the only girl on a youth roller hockey team, which suited her fine until one youngster skated over her fingers. Around that time, she noticed that people on ice skates could actually travel faster than those on roller skates. By the time she was six, Tara was taking ice-skating lessons at a local rink.

When Tara was seven, Jack Lipinski took a promotion in his company, and the Lipinskis relocated to Sugar Land, Texas. Tara was intent on continuing to ice-skate, and mother and daughter took to rising at 3 A.M. for Pat to drive Tara to her skating lessons in Houston. Tara would skate for two hours every morning, and then Pat would whisk her back in the car and back to Sugar Land in time for school. During the summer Tara would travel to Delaware to skate with Scott Gregory, the coach her parents had hired for Tara while they were still living in Philadelphia.

Eventually, the Lipinskis realized that Tara was determined to become an ice-skating champion, and with that goal in mind they decided that both Pat and Tara—then 10 years old—should move to Delaware so that Tara could train with her new coach, Jeff DiGregorio. Jack, in the meantime, stayed behind in Sugar Land, and the family spent the next five years living apart. Tara left school and began taking lessons from private tutors, and she and Pat began traveling around the country so that Tara could skate in competitions.

In 1994, the 12-year-old Lipinski competed at the Junior World Championships and finished fifth. The following year, the Lipinskis parted ways with DiGregorio and hired a coach whom they believed would bring Tara to her ultimate goal: a gold medal at the 2002 Olympic games. The new coach was Richard Callaghan, who had guided Nicole Bobek and Todd Eldredge to national championships. The Lipinskis were delighted to find Callaghan, but working with him meant that Pat and Tara would have to move again. They relocated to Bloomfield Hills, Michigan, and Lipinski began training with Callaghan every day.

In 1996 Lipinski skated at her first U.S. Championships, and although she was a bit awed by the atmosphere of a major competition, she did well enough to finish third, behind Michelle Kwan and Tonia Kwiatkowski. Lipinski's third-place finish earned her a trip to the 1996 World Championships, but at the tournament, in Edmonton, Alberta, she faltered in the short program and finished 15th overall.

Lipinski may have been overwhelmed by her first visit to the World Championships, but by her second time at the tournament, in Lausanne, Switzerland, in 1997, she was completely in her element. By that time she had seized the 1997 National Championships, and skating with a newfound confidence—and with several new triple jumps in her routine—she performed flawlessly to become, at the age of 14, the youngest world champion in ice skating history.

Back in the United States, Lipinski knew that although she had won the World Championship, she faced stiff competition from Michelle Kwan, who had captured the national title in 1996. At the National Championships in January 1996, Kwan skated a magnificent short program, but Lipinski fell during her own short program—a rarity for Lipinski, one of the sport's most technically proficient skaters. In the long program, Kwan once again soared, earning several perfect-six scores from the judges. Lipinski, knowing that a trip to the 1998 Nagano Olympics was on the line for the top three finishers, skated a solid long program to secure the silver. The bronze medal went to Nicole Bobek.

During the weeks between the National Championships and the Olympic Games, the trio of Kwan, Lipinski, and Bobek received a great deal of media hype. Most people assumed Kwan would win the gold. Could Lipinski and Bobek capture silver and bronze? If they did, they would become the first U.S. team in history to capture all three medals. The three were featured on magazine covers and made a commercial together as well.

But in Nagano, Kwan, Lipinski and Bobek went their separate ways. Bobek had suffered a bout of flu and was indoors for much of the early part of the Olympics. Kwan had elected to stay in the United States until the ice-skating competition began. But Lipinski decided to make the most of her experience in Nagano. "I wanted to win, but I also wanted to have fun," she later said. She attended the other ice-skating events, cheering on her training partner, Todd Eldredge, in the men's singles competition, and eating meals with athletes such as hockey player Wayne Gretzky.

When the competition began, Bobek, still under the weather from her illness, skated a poor short program and fell out of medal contention. Lipinski skated well, but Kwan floated through her program and received the highest scores. Going into the long program, most people believed that if Kwan skated solidly, she would clinch the gold medal. Lipinski's best hope, it seemed, was for silver.

Kwan did skate well in her long program, but she appeared tentative in her jumps. She landed shakily more than once, and her skating speed was not what it had been in her superb short program. Kwan's artistry and elegance earned her high marks, but she had left an opening. Lipinski would have to skate brilliantly, but if she did, she could win gold.

Lipinski was the final skater of the evening, and she performed the routine of her life, skating with precision, energy, and fire. By the end of her routine she knew she had a chance at the gold, and when her scores flashed on the boards, she jumped up and down. Lipinski, who had strived to win Olympic gold in 2002, had realized her dream four years early.

After Tara Lipinski upset Michelle Kwan to win gold in figure skating at the 1998 Olympics, she retired from competition–at the age of 16.
(Allsport Photography)

In April of 1998, Lipinski decided her training had taken enough of a toll on her family, and she retired from competitive skating. At that point, she and her mother moved back to Sugar Land to join Jack. After her retirement, Lipinski signed several endorsement contracts, and she began skating with Stars on Ice, a popular professional tour.

Further Reading

Famous Women. "Tara Lipinski: A Biography." Available online. ULR: http://www.three30.com/entertainment/photofamous/women/lipinski_tara/biography.shtml. Downloaded on December 13, 2000.

Lipinski, Tara, and Emily Costello. *Triumph on Ice.* New York: Bantam Books, 1998.

Sports Biographies: "Tara Lipinski Biography." Available online. URL: http://www.geocities.com/Colosseum/Park/6216/biography.html. Downloaded on February 3, 2001.

LOPEZ, NANCY
(1957–) *Golfer*

During the late 1970s, women's golf lacked a charismatic figure who combined charisma and talent in the way that BILLIE JEAN KING, for instance, had for women's tennis. Then along came Nancy Lopez to set the sport of golfing—and the world—on its ear.

One of the most charismatic players in women's golf, Nancy Lopez has won every major championship except for the U.S. Open.

(Allsport Photography)

Nancy Lopez was born in Torrance, California, on January 6, 1957. Her father, Domingo Lopez, an auto mechanic, and her mother, Marina, a homemaker, moved the family to Roswell, New Mexico, when Nancy was three. It was in Roswell that eight-year-old Nancy first started playing golf. Her parents were both passionate about the sport, and Domingo, in particular, noticed something special about the way Nancy held and swung the clubs. "Don't make her wash the dishes," he told his wife during Nancy's first year on the links. "Those hands were made for golfing."

Domingo became Nancy's first coach, and they proved to be a winning combination from the start. When Nancy was nine, she won her first tournament—a peewee competition—by the rather comfortable margin of 110 strokes. Three years later she set a course record to take top honors at the New Mexico Women's Amateur Championship. By the time she was 17, she had won the United States Golf Association (USGA) Junior Girls Championships twice.

In 1975, Lopez entered her first U.S. Women's Open as an amateur. At the robust age of 18, she finished second. After sorting through a cart full of collegiate scholarship offers, Lopez decided to attend Tulsa University, where she won All-American honors for two consecutive years and took top honors at the National Collegiate Athletic Association (NCAA) championships in 1976. But after her sophomore year, Lopez decided to forego the remainder of her collegiate career and turned professional in 1977. Lopez entered the tour with astonishing ease, placing second in her first three tournaments.

Lopez took time off in late 1977 to grieve for her mother, who had died suddenly during an appendectomy. In 1978 she returned to the tour and became a dominant force. On her way to winning nine tournaments—eight of them in a row—including the Ladies Professional Golf Association (LPGA) tournament, Nancy Lopez lit up the links, not only with a searing if unorthodox golf swing (she cocked her wrist at the beginning of her stroke), but with an easy charm, disarming manner, and million-dollar smile. Suddenly, women's golf had a charismatic champion.

She also knew how to treat her fellow players, who liked and admired her, and how to handle the media, who dubbed her "Nancy with the laughing eyes." In the fall of 1978 her smiling countenance graced the cover of *Sports Illustrated,* which compared her talent and star quality to that of BABE DIDRIKSON ZAHARIAS.

Aware that one spectacular season does not a hall-of-fame career make, Lopez continued to focus on perfecting her game. "After my first year I thought, 'I could be a flash in the pan,' and I was also determined to show I was not," she once said. To prove her point, Lopez kept winning. By the time she was 26, she had finished on top in 26 tournaments. And in 1987, when she won her 35th tournament, she became the youngest woman ever to qualify for the LPGA Hall of Fame.

In the meantime, Lopez was keeping busy off the course as well. She remained by far the women's tour's most sought-after figure, and she appeared in countless magazines and on television talk shows to promote the game. She also somehow made time for a personal life. In 1979 Lopez married the sportscaster Tim Melton, but the marriage did not last. Three years later, she wed Ray Knight, a Major League Baseball player. Lopez and Knight have two daughters.

Throughout marriage and motherhood, Lopez continued to play golf, and she proved to be one of the most consistent players in the history of the tour. By early 2002, she had won 48 professional tournaments, including three LPGA championships. She has taken home the Vare trophy (awarded annually to the golfer with the lowest course average) three times and in 1998 was the recipient of the prestigious Bob Jones Award, given to one golfer, male or female, each year for distinguished sportsmanship.

Lopez continues to play on the LPGA tour and remains a presence both on and off the links. Her one professional disappointment is that she has never taken top honors at the U.S. Women's Open; she has finished second four times, but so far the championship has eluded her. Not surprisingly, Lopez keeps this challenge in perspective. "I'd love to win the Open," she admitted once, "but I have enough good things in life that I won't be shattered if I don't."

Further Reading

Layden, Joe. *Women in Sports: The Complete Book on the World's Greatest Female Athletes.* Santa Monica, Calif.: General Publishing Group, 1997, pp. 153–154.

Smith, Lissa, editor. *Nike Is a Goddess: The History of Women in Sports.* New York, Atlantic Monthly Press, 1998, pp. 94–96.

Women's Sports Illustrated online. "Nancy Lopez," SI For Women: 100 Greatest Athletes. Available Online. URL: http://sportsillustrated.cnn.com/siforwomen/top_100/13/. Posted on December 6, 1999.

LOPIANO, DONNA
(1946–)   *Softball Player, Administrator*

It is said that success is often borne of failure, and in the case of Donna Lopiano, the adage holds true. Denied the right to play Little League at the age of 11, Lopiano went on to become an award-winning softball player, an innovative women's athletic director at a major university, and, ultimately, the president of the Women's Sports Foundation.

Donna Lopiano was born on September 11, 1946, in Stamford, Connecticut. A passionate athlete as a young child, Donna was the only girl in the neighborhood who played stickball with the boys. Her ambition at this time was simple: She wanted to be either an astronaut or a professional athlete. She was good enough at sports, not only to be accepted by her male teammates, but to be named the starting pitcher on the neighborhood Little League team.

It was 1957, and it did not occur either to Donna or to anyone on her team that her gender might keep her from playing. But while she was standing in line and waiting for her team uniform, Donna was approached by a league official, who informed her that "only boys" were allowed to participate.

For Donna, it was a life-changing moment. Intent on playing, she switched to softball, and at the age of 16, joined the Brakettes, a women's team based in nearby Stratford, Connecticut. While with the Brakettes, Lopiano had the opportunity to play with such softball greats as JOAN JOYCE. She also had the chance to see the world; at the age of 17, she traveled with the team for exhibition games played in Europe and Asia.

Lopiano was a passionate athlete, but she was also a dedicated student. A physical education major at Southern Connecticut State University, she decided after college to pursue a doctorate in that field at the University of Southern California (USC). By the time Lopiano entered USC, she had been a part of 26 national championships in four sports—softball, volleyball, basketball, and field hockey. In 1972, the same year she earned her doctorate at USC, she led the Brakettes to a national title.

Moving east after graduate school, Lopiano took a job at Brooklyn College, where she coached basketball, volleyball, and softball. Then in 1975, she relocated to Austin, Texas, to begin her tenure as director of Intercollegiate Athletics for Women at the University of Texas. During Lopiano's 17 years at Texas, Longhorn women's teams won 18 national championships in six sports. As dedicated to learning as she was to athletic success, Lopiano insisted on holding her students to strict academic standards.

As if her academic and athletic successes at Texas were not enough, Lopiano also achieved miraculous results in her efforts to raise salaries for coaches of women's sports at Texas, as well as in securing better equipment and facilities for the athletes. At the beginning of her tenure at Texas, the annual budget for women's sports at the university was $50,000. When she left in 1992, that funding had increased to $4 million.

Lopiano left Texas to continue her work on a more national level. The Women's Sports Foundation (WSF), founded in 1973 by several women atehtes, including BILLIE JEAN KING, MICKI KING, WYOMIA TYUS, and DONNA DE VARONA, was the perfect venue for Lopiano's talent and energy. As president of the WSF, Lopiano is one of the most influential women in sports. In that position she has played crucial roles in publicizing some of women's most pivotal contemporary athletic events, including the national women's basketball tour, which preceded the 1996 Olympic Games in Atlanta, and the Women's World Cup soccer match in 1999.

In addition, Lopiano has written countless articles about women in sports, and she frequently lectures about gender equality in athletics. Her overall mission at the WSF is to ensure that women in sports—on all levels—receive opportunities equal to those of their male counterparts.

Further Reading

Layden, Joe. *Women in Sports: The Complete Book on the World's Greatest Female Athletes.* Santa Monica, Calif.: General Publishing Group, 1997, pp. 62–63.

Sports Illustrated for Women. "Donna Lopiano," 100 Greatest Athletes, CNN/Sports Illustrated. Available online. URL: http://sportsillustrated.cnn.com/siforwomen/top_100/53/. Posted on November 29, 1999.

LUDTKE, MELISSA
(1951–) *Journalist*

In 1977 the journalist Melissa Ludtke successfully sued Major League Baseball for denying women reporters the right to enter players' locker rooms. It was a landmark case for female journalists, who up to that time had had to interview players either on the field or in the corridors of the dugout. Ludtke's law case brought up issues of privacy, journalistic ethics, and of course, women's rights.

Born in 1951 in Iowa, Melissa Ludtke was six months old when her father, a university professor, moved his family to Amherst, Massachusetts, to take a job at the state university there. Melissa and her four younger siblings grew up in Amherst and spent their summers on Cape Cod. After graduating from Wellesley College in 1973,

Ludtke became interested in news and journalism, and she interviewed for a researcher position at CBS News. Having no prior experience, she did not get the job. Ludtke also interviewed unsuccessfully at *Sports Illustrated,* where she had also hoped to work as a researcher. But Ludtke was intent on working at *Sports Illustrated;* she kept in touch with her contacts at the magazine and began taking low-profile sports reporter assignments for small publications in order to boost her résumé. Finally, the magazine had another opening for a researcher. Ludtke interviewed once again, and, this time, she got the job.

Ludtke worked her way up the ranks at *Sports Illustrated.* After a couple of years as a researcher, she began reporting sports events for the magazine. Always an ardent baseball fan (her parents were die-hard Red Sox devotees), Ludtke was thrilled to be put on the baseball beat. During the spring, summer and fall, Ludtke reported and wrote stories from Major League Baseball stadiums all over the country. After the season ended, she would switch gears and cover the National Basketball Association (NBA) for the magazine.

For the most part, Ludtke had little trouble gaining access to the locker rooms. The vast majority of NBA franchises allowed women in, and although it was the policy of Major League Baseball to ban female reporters from locker rooms, many teams allowed Ludtke in through the back door.

During the first game of the 1977 World Series, between the New York Yankees and the Los Angeles Dodgers, Ludtke was on assignment at Yankee Stadium. After speaking with both team managers about letting her in the locker rooms, Ludtke took her place in the press box and waited for the game to begin. Then she heard her name announced over the stadium public address system: she was being paged to the commissioner's office. The Dodgers' press secretary had alerted Bowie Kuhn, who was then the commissioner of baseball, that a woman had asked to gain access to the men's locker room. Citing Major League Baseball policy, the commissioner's representative informed Ludtke that she would not be allowed into either locker room. She would have to remain in the corridor outside the dugout, and a player representative would bring the players whom she wanted to interview out to her.

Ludtke stuck to the rules and interviewed all players after they had left the locker room. During the sixth game of the series, Yankee outfielder Reggie Jackson hit three home runs and then gave two hours of interviews in the locker room. By the time he was brought out to Ludtke in the corridor, he was exhausted. He begged off the interview, and Ludtke had to write her story without talking to the series' most valuable player.

In the meantime, Ludtke had been approached by several women sportswriters who suggested that she bring suit against Major League Baseball, the largest sports corporation in the United States. When she learned that *Sports Illustrated* would support her, she sued. Affidavits were sent by some of the leading sports journalists in the nation, including Mike Lupica, Pete Axhelm, Jane Gross, and Roger Angell.

As soon as the suit was filed, Ludtke's case became headline news. Ludtke took the attention in stride. "If you mix the ingredients of sex, sports, and the potential for the notion of nudity kind of in the middle of it, and women and men, you're sort of guaranteed that you're going to get an enormous amount of coverage in this country," she said.

It took the court only two months to rule in Ludtke's favor: By banning female reporters from players' locker rooms, Major League Baseball was guilty of sex discrimination. Kuhn's office appealed the decision, but the higher courts upheld the original decision. Ludtke had broken a barrier. During the 1978 World Series, Ludtke and the other women reporters went into the locker rooms—through the front door—along with their male counterparts.

In 1978, Ludtke married Eric Lincoln, also a sportswriter. The following year, she left *Sports Illustrated* to take a job as a researcher at *60 Minutes,* a television news program. In 1985, she took a job as a reporter at *Time* magazine and then left the magazine world for good in 1989 to become a freelance writer. Ten years later, her book about single mothers, *On Our Own,* was published. In 1996, Ludtke became a mother herself, when she traveled to China and adopted a baby girl. Ludtke, Lincoln, and their daughter, Maya, live in Cambridge.

Further Reading

Ritchie, Anne G. "Interviews with Melissa Ludtke," Washington Press Club Foundation, February 21, 1993; March 2, 1993; January 15, 1994; May 6, 1994. Available online. URL: http://npc.press.org/wpforal/lud.htm. Downloaded February 5, 2001.

M

MARBLE, ALICE
(1913–1990)   *Tennis Player*

In the early era of women's tennis, no female player had ever put together a complete offensive attacking game, combining serves, approach shots, and volleys that was comparable to the men's game—no one, that is, until Alice Marble, whose strength, diversity of shots, and sheer athleticism added a new dimension to the women's game.

The daughter of a logger and cattle rancher, Alice Marble was born in Plumas County, California, on September 28, 1913. When Alice was six years old, she moved with her father and three brothers (her mother had died the year before) to San Francisco. Shortly after that, Marble's father died, and Alice's older brother Dan became head of the household.

Marble loved playing sports with her brothers and their friends, and she often accompanied them to the baseball park to watch the minor-league San Francisco Seals play. One day in 1927, Alice, a ferocious tomboy, was mistaken for a boy by one of the Seals players and invited onto the field for a game of catch. Alice corrected the player's assump-

tion, but she accepted his invitation and played so well that she became the Seals' ball girl.

But two years later, when Marble was 15, her brother Dan told her it was time for her to stop playing baseball. "You've got to stop being a tomboy," he said. "Here's a racket I bought you . . . you must play a ladylike game." Alice was furious with her brother, but she took his gift and began to play on the public courts at Golden Gate Park. Tennis became her new passion, and by the time she was 17, she was competing on the national level.

Marble's first major tournament, the 1931 U.S. Championships at Forest Hills, New York, was over a bit too quickly for her—she was eliminated in the first round. But another player advised her to get some coaching and to simplify her game—Marble had a variety of spins and other trick shots but hadn't yet mastered the basic ground strokes. A few weeks later, Marble was working with a San Francisco coach, and by the following year her game had improved so much that she was the seventh-ranked player in the country.

It was also in 1932 that Marble met Eleanor "Teach" Tennant, one of the most ambitious and

Alice Marble overcame illness and injuries to win four major tennis championships in the 1930s. She would later play a key role in helping Althea Gibson become the first African American to play in tournaments sanctioned by the United States Lawn Tennis Association.
(Library of Congress)

successful tennis coaches in the country. Shortly after becoming Marble's coach, Tennant changed and expanded her training regimen. Playing five practice sets of tennis a day, Marble eventually developed a strong, powerful game, with crushing, deep ground strokes. Under Tennant's tutelage, Marble became the first woman to develop a sophisticated serve-and-volley game. Marble would serve a strong, twisting ball to her opponent, then rush to the net and put away the return. It was a strategy that had, up to that time, been seen only in the men's game.

Armed with what was dubbed the "fastest tennis ever played" by the Associated Press, Marble shot up the ladder, to the number-three slot in 1933. But just as her game was reaching its peak,

she was struck by illness. Marble longed to play for the U.S. Wightman Cup team, and in order to do that she was required to play in a three-day tournament. The chairman of that tournament, Julian S. Myrick, was also the head of the Wightman Cup Committee. Myrick requested that Marble play both singles and doubles in the tune-up tournament, which took place in Easthampton, New York, in blazing heat. Marble wanted to comply with Myrick's wishes, although doing so would mean playing nine matches in three days.

Marble got through the first two days of the tournament, but on the final day, after playing four matches in 100-degree temperatures, she collapsed. Marble had suffered a mild sunstroke and was also diagnosed with anemia.

Her collapse in Easthampton marked the beginning of an arduous time for Marble, who played a reduced schedule for the rest of 1933 and then traveled to Paris in the spring of 1934 to compete at the French championships. But early in her first French match—which was also played in extremely hot weather—Marble collapsed again, this time on the court. She returned home to the United States, where she was diagnosed with tuberculosis and told that she would never play tennis again.

Weak and devastated by the news, Marble entered a sanitarium. Teach Tennant, furious on Marble's behalf, tried unsuccessfully to force Myrick to pay her player's medical bills. After Myrick refused, Tennant paid the bills herself, taking on extra tennis students to help meet the costs.

Eventually, Marble recovered from her illness and was able to leave the sanitarium. She lived at Tennant's house and began a rehabilitation program to get herself back into playing shape. In 1936, two years after her collapse at the French championships, Marble won her first major tournament, beating HELEN JACOBS in the final of the U.S. championships. Then the floodgates opened. For the next few years, Marble dominated tennis, winning the U.S. championships for three years running and taking top honors in Wimbledon in 1939—not only in singles, but in women's and mixed doubles.

In 1940, still at the peak of her game, Marble made the decision to turn professional. She joined a tour of players that included Bill Tilden and Don Budge, and she traveled to 50 U.S. cities to show off her power game. The tour eventually failed however, and very quietly, Alice Marble retired from tennis. Although Marble no longer competed, she remained involved in tennis and played a pivotal role in the career of ALTHEA GIBSON. Marble wrote an editorial in the July 1950 edition of *American Lawn Tennis* in which she urged the American Lawn Tennis Association (ALTA) to allow Gibson, an African American, to play in ALTA-sanctioned events. Shortly thereafter, Gibson shattered the color barrier in women's tennis.

During her relatively short career, Marble changed the face of women's tennis. Her serve-and-volley game inspired later tennis pioneers, such as BILLIE JEAN KING and MARTINA NAVRATILOVA. King later wrote in her book *We Have Come a Long Way,* that with Alice Marble "women's power tennis had only begun." Marble died in California in 1990.

Further Reading

Davidson, Sue. *Changing the Game: The Stories of Tennis Champions Alice Marble and Althea Gibson.* Seattle, Wash.: Seal Press, 1997.

King, Billie Jean, and Cynthia Starr, *We Have Come a Long Way: The Story of Women's Tennis.* New York: McGraw Hill, 1988, pp. 50–52.

Layden, Joe. *Women in Sports: The Complete Book on the World's Greatest Female Athletes.* Santa Monica, Calif.: General Publishing Group, 1997, pp. 158–159.

⊞ McCORMICK, PAT (Patricia Jean Keller, Patricia Keller McCormick)
(1930–) *Diver*

Pat McCormick, the first U.S. diver to win gold medals in both the springboard and platform events at the same Olympiad, performed this feat not only once but twice. At the Helsinki games in 1952, McCormick made history when she seized top honors in the platform event, two days after taking gold in the springboard competition. Four years later in Melbourne, Australia, McCormick defended both titles successfully.

Patricia Jean Keller was born on May 12, 1930, in Seal Beach, California. Raised by her mother, a nurse, Pat and her younger brother often traveled to nearby Venice, California, where they both became fitness enthusiasts at an early age. Pat was a natural athlete who learned the basics of diving simply from watching others and imitating them. Although she had little formal training, she was talented enough to win several local diving meets. It was at one of those competitions that Pat was noticed by the coach of the Los Angeles Athletic Club, who invited the young girl to train with his team.

At the Los Angeles Athletic Club, Keller began a grueling regimen that included 100 dives every day, six days a week. She rarely broke this training pattern, enduring a number of injuries that ranged from the merely annoying—bruises—to the painful—broken bones. Although Keller was a highly disciplined athlete in her own right, she also found a great source of motivation in her training partners, which included such former Olympic champions as Sammy Lee and Victoria Draves.

In 1948, 18-year-old Keller participated in her first Olympic trials. Although she failed to qualify for the team, her fourth-place finish at the trials further served to increase her confidence. "All of a sudden," she said later, "I knew I could win the Olympics. I realized that at Los Angeles I was working with world class athletes every day." As if to prove her worth to the rest of the diving world, Keller won her first national championship in 1949 when she took top honors in the outdoor platform diving event. Later in 1949, she married Glen McCormick, a pilot, and began competing under her new surname.

In 1951, McCormick won the indoor national championships in both the springboard and platform competitions. The following year, she easily qualified for the U.S. Olympic team and traveled to the games in Helsinki, Finland. After winning two gold medals, McCormick returned to the United

States and easily won her third national indoor championship, once again seizing golds in platform and springboard events. All told, McCormick won five consecutive indoor national championships in the springboard and platform events in 1951–55, and she took top honors at the outdoor championships in 1949–51 and 1953–56.

After giving birth to a son in early 1956, McCormick returned to training and qualified for her second Olympic team. In Melbourne, Australia, McCormick again completely dominated both of her events; she left the games with two more gold medals. No other U.S. diver would win gold medals in both springboard and platform diving in two consecutive Olympic Games until Greg Louganis in 1984 and 1988. At the end of 1956, McCormick became only the second woman in history to receive the prestigious Sullivan Award, given each year to the top amateur athlete.

McCormick chose to retire after the 1956 diving season, and she opened a diving camp. She gave birth to a second child in 1960, a girl named Kelly who would follow in her mother's footsteps; Kelly McCormick won a silver medal in the springboard event at the 1984 Olympic Games in Los Angeles and a bronze in the same event at the 1988 Olympics in Seoul.

Further Reading

Layden, Joe. *Women in Sports: The Complete Book on the World's Greatest Female Athletes.* Santa Monica, Calif.: General Publishing Group, 1997, pp. 160–161.

McCormick, Pat. "An Olympian's Oral History," *Amateur Athletic Foundation of Los Angeles.* Available online. URL: http://www.aafla.org/6oic/OralHistory/OHmccormick.indd.pdf. Downloaded on December 28, 2001.

McCUTCHEON, FLORETTA
(Floretta Doty)
(1888–1967) *Bowler*

Who says that bowling champions have to roll a brilliant game during their first time on the lanes? Certainly not Floretta McCutcheon, who scored a less-than-stellar 69 in her first game. McCutcheon improved somewhat since that first game, bowling a total of seven perfect-300 games and becoming the first woman bowler to become a national celebrity.

Floretta Doty was born in Ottumwa, Iowa, on July 22, 1888. Although tenpin bowling had been invented and adapted by several U.S. clubs several years before Floretta was born, she herself did not even pick up a bowling ball until she was 35 years old. Married by that time to John McCutcheon, "Mrs. Mac" had decided to join a bowling league on a whim. Her first bowling game was an indication of how difficult her initial year in the league must have been; at the end of the season, she quit.

Three years later, though, she returned. This time, she stuck with the sport, and astonishing things began to happen. In 1927, McCutcheon stunned a local audience when she took on the reigning world champion, Jimmy Smith, in an exhibition match and beat him. Over a three-game series, McCutcheon outscored Smith by a series score of 704 to 697. The victory was so astounding that it earned McCutcheon a place in the famed "Ripley's Believe It or Not" book series.

Later that year, McCutcheon decided to travel around the country and bowl in similar exhibitions. Her tour was so successful that in 1930, she opened her own establishment, the Mrs. McCutcheon School for Bowling in New York City. Nine years later, she retired from the sport to teach full time at her school. By that time, she had amassed a total of 11 800-series scores, and more than 100 700-series scores. In 1944 McCutcheon moved to Chicago, where she continued to teach bowling for another 10 years. McCutcheon retired for good in 1954 and settled in California, where she lived until her death in 1967.

Further Reading

Layden, Joe. *Women in Sports: The Complete Book on the World's Greatest Female Athletes.* Santa Monica, Calif.: General Publishing Group, 1997, p. 248.

MEAGHER, MARY TERSTEGGE
(1964–) *Swimmer*

The champion swimmer Mary T. Meagher was so dominant in the butterfly that during her prime the press dubbed her "Madame Butterfly," and she earned that moniker by mastering the most difficult of all swimming strokes during her long and distinguished career.

Mary Terstegge Meagher was born in Louisville, Kentucky, on October 27, 1964. The Meaghers were a family with 11 girls and one son. There were in fact, so many daughters in the family that the Meaghers quite possibly ran out of girls' names; born 10 years apart, the oldest and youngest daughters were both named Mary. The baby of the family, Meagher was always called "T," for her middle initial, by her siblings and parents.

An enthusiastic and talented swimmer from the start, Mary T. was only 14 years old when she joined the U.S. national swim team. Swimming in her first international competition at the 1979 Pan American Games in San Juan, Puerto Rico, Mary T. was expected to perform solidly in the 200-meter butterfly event. The eighth-grader stunned the competition, not only by taking the gold medal in the event, but by breaking a world record in the process. Her time of 2:09:77 shattered the mark, which had been held jointly by Meagher's teammate TRACY CAULKINS and East Germany's Andrea Pollack.

It was an astonishing debut, but rather than rest on her laurels, Meagher continued to strive for faster times. One month after the Pan American Games, she did just that, swimming the 200 meters in a scorching 2:08:41 in the preliminary heat at the Senior National Swimming Championships in Fort Lauderdale, Florida. In the finals of the event, a few hours later, she was even faster, blazing through the water in 2:07:01. Meagher's time was the quickest ever by a woman swimmer in the 200-meter butterfly, and it was faster than many male swimmers at the time.

The inevitable next stop for Meagher was the 1980 Olympics. Along with the rest of the country's most elite athletes, she competed in the U.S. Olympic trials. By this time, Meagher owned world records in both the 200-meter and 100-meter butterfly events, having logged a time of 59.29 in the shorter race at the 1980 Indoor National Swimming Championships. Meagher easily earned a place on the team, but she was denied the opportunity to compete when the United States boycotted the Moscow Games.

Disappointed but still determined, Meagher went back to work, constantly aiming for faster times in the butterfly events. Few did it better. "In her prime," her coach, Dennis Pursley, said of Meagher, "Mary had no weaknesses. Motivation, technique, physical attributes, I don't know that I've seen an athlete who did not have a weakness on that list—except for Mary."

In 1981, Meagher showed off her strengths in dramatic fashion. At the U.S. Long Course Championships in Wisconsin, she set a new world record in the 100-meter event, swimming the race in 57.93. Two days later, she repeated the feat in the 200-meter race, lowering her own mark with a time of 2:05:96.

Three years later, Meagher once again qualified for the U.S. Olympic swim team, and this time she got to compete in the games. Swimming in front of a boisterous home crowd in Los Angeles, Meagher captured a gold medal in the 100-meter butterfly event. Several days later, she won a second gold, this one in the 4 × 100 medley relay.

After the 1984 games, Meagher decided to retire. But two years later, she changed her mind. Knowing that she had won her medals against a depleted field—several Soviet-bloc countries (including East Germany, traditionally a women's swimming powerhouse) had boycotted the Los Angeles games—she wanted to try her luck at an Olympiad that featured both Western and Eastern athletes. Although Meagher did not win gold at the 1988 games in Seoul, South Korea, she did snare a silver in the 4 × 100 medley relay, as well as a bronze in the 200-meter butterfly event.

In 1989, Meagher retired from swimming for good. She settled in Peachtree, Georgia, with her husband, the former Olympic speed skater Mark Plant, and their two children. Meagher's world record in the 200-meter butterfly lasted long after she had left the sport. It was finally broken by JENNY THOMPSON in August 1999.

Further Reading

Layden, Joe. *Women in Sports: The Complete Book on the World's Greatest Female Athletes.* Santa Monica, Calif.: General Publishing Group, 1997, pp. 138–139.

Sports Illustrated for Women. "Mary T. Meagher," 100 Greatest Athletes, CNN/Sports Illustrated. Available online. URL: http://sportsillustrated.cnn.com/siforwomen/top_100/38/. Posted November 29, 1999.

MEYER, DEBBIE (Deborah Meyer)
(1952–) *Swimmer*

Debbie Meyer was the first woman to win three individual swimming gold medals in one Olympiad. She achieved this feat at the 1968 games in Mexico City.

Born in Haddonfield, New Jersey, on August 14, 1952, Debbie Meyer spent her first 12 years on the East Coast. In 1964, her father, a marketing executive with the Campbell Soup company, received a transfer and a promotion, and the Meyer family moved across the country to Sacramento, California.

By then, Debbie, who had learned to swim as a young child and who had first begun racing when she was eight, was an accomplished swimmer. Even so, she was hardly prepared for the workouts her new coach at Sacramento's Arden Hills Swim Club would put her through. Sherm Chavoor, who was one of the best swim coaches in the country, demanded that his athletes swim 20 laps just as a warm-up. On her first day with Chavoor, Debbie began swimming the required distance, and became completely exhausted after four laps. Nevertheless, she kept her face in the water and her arms churning, and she eventually finished the laps.

Eventually, the workouts became easier, or perhaps Meyer just got better at them. In 1966—two years after the move to Sacramento—14-year-old Meyer, by now one of Chavoor's star swimmers, set a world record in the 400-meter freestyle event. One year later, she won the national title in the

same event, and then, in the summer of 1968, she qualified to swim the 200-meter freestyle, the 400-meter freestyle, and the 800-meter freestyle races at the Mexico City Olympics.

In Mexico City, Meyer swam almost flawlessly in all three events. She took top honors in the 200-meter freestyle race with an Olympic record time of 2:10:5, then grabbed the gold in the 400-meter event with a time of 4:31.8—another Olympic record. Then she set yet another Olympic mark with a time of 9:24 in the 800-meter race. Meyer, at the tender age of 16, became the first person—of either gender—to win three individual gold medals.

Meyer returned to the United States after the Olympics to national acclaim, and at the end of the year, she became the fourth woman in history to win the prestigious Sullivan Award. But after defending her national titles for three consecutive years, Meyers decided that for her, there was more to life than swimming. In 1972, just a few months before the Olympic Games, she retired from the sport at the age of 20. She later attended the University of California at Los Angeles (UCLA) and then she married and raised a family.

Further Reading

Layden, Joe. *Women in Sports: The Complete Book on the World's Greatest Female Athletes.* Santa Monica, Calif.: General Publishing Group, 1997, pp. 163–164.

Markel, Robert, Susan Wagoner, and Marcella Smith. *The Women's Sports Encyclopedia.* New York: Henry Holt, 1999, p. 79.

MEYERS, ANN
(1955–) *Basketball Player, Commentator*

Ann Meyers was the first woman to receive a basketball scholarship from a major university, the first captain of a U.S. Olympic women's basketball team, and the first woman to sign a contract with a National Basketball Association (NBA) team. After her playing days ended, Meyers continued her pioneering trend, becoming one of the first female sports broadcasters on television.

Born on March 26, 1955, in San Diego, California, Ann Meyers could always find a pickup basketball game in her own driveway. The sixth of 11 children, she learned the game from her older brothers. One of Meyers's siblings, Dave Meyers, had a distinguished college basketball career himself, at both the University of California at Los Angeles (UCLA) and in the NBA. Nevertheless, Meyers's first athletic love was for track and field. Her earliest athletic ambition, in fact, was to compete in the Olympics as a high jumper.

All that changed, though, in 1974, when Meyers became the first high school senior to play for the U.S. national women's basketball team. Although Meyers had excelled in seven sports in high school, she found the experience of competing in international competition so exhilarating that she decided to drop all the other activities and concentrate solely on basketball.

Meyers's decision came at a crucial time for women's sports. In 1972, Title IX, legislation that compelled U.S. universities receiving federal funds to offer equal opportunities to male and female students, became a law. All of a sudden, female athletes, who were once nearly invisible on university campuses, had the opportunity to attend college on fully funded athletic scholarships and to play for full varsity teams, rather than poorly funded clubs.

But although Title IX opened the doors for female athletes, most universities dragged their heels in upholding their legal obligations. For the first two years of the legislation's existence, in fact, the only universities willing to offer basketball scholarships to women were small schools that did not have high-profile men's programs. But Meyers was such a remarkable player that one university was willing to break that trend.

UCLA had long been a dominating force in men's basketball. Under Coach John Wooden, the vaunted UCLA Bruins men's team had won 10 National Collegiate Athletic Association (NCAA) championships, including seven in a row from 1967 to 1973. Fortunately for Meyers, UCLA made a decision to bolster its women's basketball

program, and ardently pursued and then signed the San Diego native to a full basketball scholarship.

UCLA's action was a crucial one for women's sports; soon after Meyers was signed, other major universities followed suit and began offering basketball scholarships to women. It proved fruitful for the university as well. Meyers, who combined speed and size (she was six feet, one inch tall) with a sound fundamental intelligence on the court, was named to the All-American women's basketball team (the equivalent of a collegiate all-star team) during each of her four years on campus, and during her senior year in 1978 she led UCLA to the national championship, winning player-of-the-year honors in the process.

In the meantime, Meyers expanded her international basketball résumé. She helped the U.S. national team win a gold medal in the 1975 Pan American Games and one year later made history again when she played for the first U.S. Olympic women's basketball team. For many years, advocates had been working to make women's basketball a more prominent international sport. Slowly, but surely, they made headway. In 1972 and again in 1974, special exhibition matches were set up between the United States and the Soviet Union. Even so, the most prestigious international event, the Olympics, did not have a women's basketball competition, and there were relatively few opportunities for the world's best women's basketball teams to play one another in any official capacity.

But all that changed when, in 1976, the Fédération Internationale de Basketball (FIBA) decided to add women's basketball to the Olympic Games, which were held in Montreal that summer. Meyers, who was named captain of the team, led the U.S. team to a silver medal (they lost a close game to the Soviets in the final). The following year, Meyers added another international medal to her collection when the U.S. team won gold in the 1977 Pan Am games.

Then, in the fall of 1979, Meyers once again played the role of pioneer. Bob Nassi, the owner of the Indiana Pacers of the NBA, signed Meyers to a $50,000 contract and asked her to attend the three-day team tryout. Meyers agreed to Nassi's challenge and became the first woman player to sign an NBA contract. Nassi's gesture met with mixed reactions from fans and media alike. Some thought the Pacers had invited Meyers to try out strictly for publicity. Others, such as Pacers coach Bob Leonard, did not think it was appropriate for a woman to try out for an NBA team. "He came from the old school where women were supposed to stay home and have babies," Meyers said of Leonard. "But I thought to myself, 'Hey, I've got bills to pay. I need a job, too.'"

Meyers played admirably in the tryout session, but she was cut from the team and never played in an NBA game. The Pacers did offer her a broadcasting contract, however, and she got her first taste of television commentating during the 1979–80 season, when she provided on-air analysis for several Pacers games. Later in 1980, she joined the New Jersey Gems of the Women's Professional Basketball League (WPBL). Meyers led the league in scoring and was named the league's most valuable player, but the WPBL folded one year later, and Meyers decided to hang up her uniform for good. She retired from the sport in 1982.

Her playing days behind her, Meyers returned to the broadcast booth, where she also had a distinguished career. In addition to providing commentary for Indiana Pacers games, she served as a broadcaster for CBS and ESPN, giving expert analyses of both women's and men's college basketball games. Meyers married Hall of Fame baseball player Don Drysdale in 1986. The couple had three children and lived together in southern California until Drysdale's death in 1993.

During her tenure on the court, Meyers helped bring women's basketball to a higher level. One reason she was such a pioneer was timing; her prime playing days coincided perfectly with the passage of Title IX, and with the FIBA's decision to make women's basketball an Olympic sport. But the bulk of the credit must go to Meyers herself, who proved that a woman can play the game of basketball—long considered a man's game only—with strength, grace, and pizzazz.

Further Reading

Layden, Joe. *Women in Sports: The Complete Book on the World's Greatest Female Athletes.* Santa Monica, Calif.: General Publishing Group, 1997, p. 164.

Macy, Sue. *Winning Ways.* New York: Henry Holt, 1996, pp. 136–138.

Markel, Robert, Susan Wagoner, and Marcella Smith. *The Women's Sports Encyclopedia.* New York: Henry Holt, 1995, pp. 10–12.

Smith, Lissa, editor. *Nike Is a Goddess.* New York: Atlantic Monthly Press, 1998, pp. 301–303.

MILLER, CHERYL
(1964–   )   *Basketball Player*

Anyone who might think that the game of women's basketball lacks excitement should take a look at some footage of Cheryl Miller, and then think again. A four-time All-American who led the University of Southern California (USC) to back to back National Collegiate Athletic Association (NCAA) championships and then the U.S. national team to Olympic gold in 1984, Miller is one of the most charismatic and gifted players in the history of the sport.

Born in 1964 in Riverside, California, Cheryl was the third child of Saul Miller, a jazz saxophonist, and his homemaker wife, Carrie. The five Miller children were all enthusiastic athletes; Cheryl's older brother Darryl grew up to become a major-league pitcher, and her younger sister, Jackie, excelled in volleyball. But it was Cheryl and her brother Reggie—now an all-star player for the Indiana Pacers—who tore up the neighborhood basketball courts. One of the duo's favorite tricks was for Reggie to challenge the neighborhood boys to a game of two-on-two—"the two of you against me and my sister," Reggie would say. Not knowing Cheryl, the challenged pair would eagerly agree to a game—and would inevitably suffer a trouncing.

Despite her obvious talent, Cheryl had a great deal of trouble finding a team to play on. During junior high school, she tried out for the boys' team. Although she outperformed many of the players, including the coach's son, she was denied a spot on the squad. Upset and insulted, Cheryl came home and announced she was quitting the sport. Instead, her father persuaded her to join the girls' team, "and be the best player out there."

In high school, Miller played for the girls' team and proved to be not only the best player on her team but in the entire state of California. At six feet, two inches tall, she towered over everyone else and had the statistics to prove it. In four years at Riverside Polytechnic High School, Miller scored a total of 3,405 points—an average of about 37 points per game. In one memorable performance, Miller poured in 107 points in a single game. Not suprisingly, she led her high school to four consecutive state championships.

Miller was heavily recruited by universities. Out of more than 250 offers, she elected to stay close to home and attend USC. At USC, Miller was about as dominant as she was in high school, dazzling teammates and opponents with marvelous ball handling and shooting skills. Miller also had a tremendous amount of on-court presence; her charisma, as well as her talent, helped USC break women's basketball attendance records during her tenure there.

In addition to leading USC to two consecutive NCAA crowns—and walking away with Final Four most valuable player honors in the process—Miller had joined the national team and put the world on notice with a 37-point performance at the World University Games that helped the United States seize the gold. After her sophomore year in 1984, Miller began to train with the national team for the Olympic Games, which were to be held on her own home turf, the city of Los Angeles. Miller put on a show in front of the hometown crowd, leading the United States to gold with an exuberant and dominant performance.

Despite her many moments of glory, Miller faced an unpleasant situation after graduating from USC in 1986. There were no professional leagues for women in the United States at the time, and Miller had little enthusiasm for playing in any of the European leagues. She opted instead to stay in the United States and keep playing for the national team, but in 1988 an injury kept her from playing in the Olympics. Deeply disappointed, Miller retired from playing basketball.

One of the top collegiate women's basketball players in history, Cheryl Miller led USC to back-to-back NCAA titles, and then helped the United States win gold at the 1984 Olympic Games.
(Rick Stewart/Getty Images)

Shortly after hanging up her uniform, Miller decided to take a job as an assistant coach at her alma mater, USC. She also served time in the broadcast booth at ABC, providing expert commentary when the U.S. national women's team played. In 1993 she became the head coach at USC, and the following year led the team to the Mideast Regional Finals. Two years later she took a job in the newly formed WNBA, as general manager and head coach of the Phoenix Mercury. She resigned as Mercury coach in 2001.

Further Reading

Biography Resource Center. "Cheryl Miller," *Contemporary Black Biography.* Volume 10, Detroit, Mich.: Gale Research, 1995.

Buell, Cathy M. "Cheryl Miller," *Great Athletes.* Hackensack, N.J.: 2001. p. 1723.

CNN.SI for Women. "Cheryl Miller," 100 Greatest Athletes. Available online. URC: http://sportsillustrated.cnn.com/siforwomen/top_100/15. Downloaded on December 1, 1999.

MITCHELL, JACKIE (Bernice Verne Mitchell, Jackie Gilbert)
(1914–1987)   *Baseball Player*

According to the score sheet, and to all who witnessed the event, Jackie Mitchell struck out Babe Ruth and Lou Gehrig, who batted back-to-back against her during a 1931 exhibition game in Chattanooga, Tennessee. But did she really elude Ruth and Gehrig with her left-handed sinker ball pitch, or was it just a publicity stunt? The question will never have a definitive answer, but all those involved in the planning of the exhibition game—including Mitchell herself—claimed that it was a legitimate feat, and it is very likely that they were telling the truth.

Born in 1914 in Chattanooga, Tennessee, Bernice Verne "Jackie" Mitchell weighted less than five pounds at birth and was a small and somewhat sickly child. All that changed, however, when her father, a doctor, prescribed baseball as an exercise to strengthen his daughter. "I was out at the sandlots with Father from as long as I remember," she said of her early diamond days. When she was about seven, Brooklyn Dodgers pitcher Dazzy Vance spotted the young girl throwing the ball in the sandlot, and he gave her an impromptu pitching lesson.

Whether it was Vance's instruction, Jackie's natural talent, or a combination thereof, Jackie developed a lethal sinker ball pitch that, delivered from her left hand, curved in on right-handed batters and away from left-handers. Using the pitch, Jackie began playing baseball in Chattanooga and, in one outing, struck out nine men. In March 1931 Jackie went to a baseball camp in Atlanta that was well known for honing future major-league players, such as Luke Appling. A few weeks after the camp ended, a former-pitcher-turned-manager named Joe Engel signed her to a minor-league contract with the Chattanooga Lookouts.

Mitchell was the second woman in history to sign a professional men's baseball contract (Lizzie Arlington, who signed a minor-league contract in 1898, was the first). She probably realized from the start that she had little chance of making it to the major leagues; asked what her goals were for her baseball career, Mitchell answered that all she wanted was "to stay in professional baseball long enough to buy a roadster." She later amended her statement and announced that her dream was to "get into a World Series."

Soon after Mitchell signed the contract, Engel decided to set up an exhibition game between the Chattanooga Lookouts and the New York Yankees, and he featured Jackie Mitchell in his press releases advertising the game. The press was somewhat skeptical of Engel—an agent who had previously sold out a stadium by raffling off a house—but the idea of Ruth and Gehrig facing a woman pitcher was nonetheless intriguing to media and fans alike.

On a cool, damp April day in 1931, the Yankees and the Lookouts faced each another in a sold-out stadium in Chattanooga. Things did not begin well for the home team; the first two Yankees hit Clyde Barfoot, the Lookouts' starting pitcher, hard, and the Yankees were leading, 1-0, with the heart of their batting order still coming up in the top of the first. The manager of the Lookouts strode to the mound and immediately removed Barfoot from the game. In came Mitchell, who threw a couple of warm-up pitches as the crowd buzzed. The next two batters were Babe Ruth and Lou Gehrig.

Ruth came to the plate and took the first pitch, a ball. Then Mitchell threw two straight sinker balls, which the Babe swung at—and missed. Two pitches later, a Mitchell pitch whistled past Ruth, for a called third strike. Babe kicked the dirt, cussed out the umpire, and marched back to the dugout, hurling his bat to the ground. Then Gehrig stepped into the batter's box, swung fruitlessly at three Mitchell pitches in a row, grinned and walked back to the

Posing here with her victims, Jackie Mitchell struck out Babe Ruth (right) and Lou Gehrig (left) at an exhibition game in 1931.
(Library of Congress)

dugout. The fans went wild—Ruth and Gehrig both fanned . . . by a woman? Incredible! The next hitter was the Yankee second baseman, Tony Lazzeri, a fine hitter in his own right. After swinging at Mitchell's first pitch, Lazzeri took four straight balls and walked to first. The Lookouts manager came out of the dugout and removed Mitchell from the game, to a standing ovation.

Mitchell's debut was over, and soon, too, was her minor-league career. Kenesaw Mountain Landis, then the commissioner of baseball, voided Mitchell's contract, on the grounds that baseball was "too strenuous a game" to be played by a woman. Devastated, Mitchell was left to find work pitching on exhibition teams. In 1933 she signed a contract to play for a barnstorming club called House of David. She would come in for an inning or so in each game, and for a while it kept her entertained. But after four years of touring with the team, she tired of the job, which sometimes entailed participating in publicity stunts—in one game she pitched while riding a donkey—and she retired from baseball for good in 1937.

After leaving the game, Mitchell worked in her father's office back in Chattanooga, and many people forgot about the girl pitcher with the mean curveball. When she was 53 she married Eugene Gilbert, whom she had known for most of her life. To her friends and neighbors, she was Jackie Gilbert, just another resident of Chattanooga.

But years later, in 1973, the *Chattanooga News Free Press* published a letter asking the question, "Whatever happened to the girl who struck out Babe Ruth?" Mitchell saw the letter and called the paper to identify herself. The exchange set off a new interest in Mitchell, who received hundreds of fan letters. Mitchell was back in the limelight, and she used the opportunity to express her wish that women would one day play professional baseball again. Referring to BERNICE GERA, she said, "There is one woman umpire in professional baseball now and maybe some day there will be a player in the big leagues." Mitchell died in 1987.

Further Reading

Gregorich, Barbara. *Women at Play: The Story of Women in Baseball.* New York: Harcourt Brace, 1993, pp. 66–72.

Smith, Lissa, editor. *Nike Is a Goddess: The History of Women in Sports.* New York: Atlantic Monthly Press, 1998.

MOORE, ELISABETH
(1876–1959) *Tennis Player*

Elisabeth Moore, an early U.S. tennis champion, is remembered most for a decision she had no part in making, and which she ardently disagreed with. After Moore defeated Marion Jones in a long and grueling five-set match in 1901, the all-male board at the United States Lawn Tennis Association (USLTA) decided to change the rules in women's tennis, limiting match play to a maximum of three sets, rather than five.

Born in Brooklyn, New York, on March 5, 1876, Elisabeth Moore came of age during the time that tennis was gaining enormous popularity in the United States. She first began playing the sport as a teenager, and she won her first U.S. championship title in 1896, when she took top honors in both the singles and doubles events. After a five-year drought, Moore was again at the top of her game for the 1901 U.S. championships.

At this time, all matches—both men's and women's—were a best-of-five-set format, meaning that the first to win three sets emerged victorious. The tournaments also had a format that differed dramatically from contemporary ones, in that the defending champion of a tournament earned an automatic entry into the final game. All the challengers played in the "all-comers" tournament, and the winner of that event would face the well-rested defending champion in the "challenge round" to determine the tournament winner.

Moore entered the 1901 U.S. championships as a challenger and dominated her early-round matches, but she then faced Jones in the all-comers final. The two women played what would become the longest women's final in history; after more than four hours, Moore emerged on the victorious end of a 4-6, 1-6, 9-7, 9-7, 6-3 match (there were no tie-breakers). Then Moore had to face the defending champion, Myrtle McAteer, and to make matters even more difficult for the challenger, the match took place on the very next day after her match against Jones. But Moore rose to the challenge, and in another five-set match, she defeated McAteer to take the tournament. The only woman ever to play five-set matches on consecutive days, Moore played 105 games of singles during that stretch.

But although Moore, who was in top physical shape, showed few ill effects from her marathon matches, Jones was not quite as fortunate. Her arduous loss to Moore in the all-challenge final had left her visibly exhausted. She limped through the final few games of the match, and evidently her fatigue caught the attention of the USLTA officials. A few days after Moore's victory over McAteer, the association announced a rule change: Women would no longer play best-of-five-set matches.

Angry about the decision and the fact that neither she nor Jones had been consulted beforehand, Moore made her displeasure known. "I do not think any such change should have been made without first canvassing the wishes of the women players," she wrote in an open letter in *Lawn Tennis,* the publication of the United States Lawn Tennis Association.

Moore would go on to capture two more U.S. singles championships, in 1903 and 1905, and she also won U.S. championships in doubles in 1896 and 1903 and in mixed doubles in 1902 and 1904. She died in 1959; the rule she so loathed has outlived her and exists to this day.

Further Reading

King, Billie Jean, and Cynthia Starr. *We Have Come a Long Way: The Story of Women's Tennis.* New York: McGraw Hill, 1988.

Layden, Joe. *Women in Sports: The Complete Book on the World's Greatest Female Athletes.* Santa Monica, Calif.: General Publishing Group, 1997, p. 171.

MULDOWNEY, SHIRLEY
(Shirley Roque)
(1940–) *Drag Racer*

A vision in pink in a wild and dangerous sport, the drag racer Shirley Muldowney became the first woman to be licensed by the National Hot Rod Association (NHRA). Competing during the late 1960s in a bright pink car, Muldowney had few fans on the virtually all-male circuit, but she did manage to win 17 titles—the second-highest total in NHRA history.

Shirley Roque was born on June 19, 1940, in Burlington, Vermont. Her father, Belgium "Tex" Roque first introduced his daughter to driving when she was 12. Three years later, Shirley, who never excelled as a student, dropped out of school completely and married her boyfriend, Jack Muldowney, an auto mechanic. Jack and Shirley became a dynamic duo of auto racing. With Jack building the cars and Shirley driving them, the Muldowneys won most of the amateur drag racing competitions they entered.

When Shirley turned 19 in 1959, she and Jack decided to turn professional. It was in many ways a daring move; Shirley was the only woman on the circuit and was often booed lustily by fans as she prepared to race. Rather than allowing herself to be disconcerted by these hostile reactions, Muldowney decided to flaunt her differences. She appeared at races dressed in vibrant pink outfits and drove a car of the same color. "The attitudes against me didn't bother me," she later told the *New York Times,* "trying to hold on to a 1,700-pound car with a 2,000-horsepower engine is hard work, and anyone that says different is out of his mind."

Muldowney not only held on to her cars but often steered them to victory. With several regional titles under her belt, she was on the brink of national stardom. Then, real life interfered. Beset by marital problems, she and Jack divorced in 1972. A year later, she had a serious car accident in which she suffered second-degree facial burns (her eyelids melted together during the crash). Muldowney recovered from her injuries and eventually returned to the circuit.

Although she won many events during the late 1970s and 1980s, Muldowney never made much money in car racing. Not only did she have few friends on the circuit—often her top rivals would work together to target her for defeat—but she found it exceedingly difficult to find corporate sponsorship. Her situation changed somewhat in 1983, with the release of *Heart Like a Wheel,* a documentary film about her life and career.

Heart Like a Wheel turned Muldowney into a celebrity of sorts; she gained new respect from her on-track rivals, and several women interested in pursuing a racing career contacted her for advice. But in 1984 Muldowney had the most severe accident of her career when her car hit a culvert while she was racing. Muldowney's right thumb and right foot were partially severed, and she also suffered a fractured pelvis, two broken fingers, compound fractures in both ankles, and torn cartilage in both knees. For months she lay in a hospital bed, and she underwent four operations that ran up a cost of more than a $150,000. Interestingly, one of Muldowney's chief track rivals, Don Garlits, helped finance her surgery.

Somehow Muldowney managed to come back after her near-fatal crash, and in 1989 she reentered the racing circuit. That same year she married Rahn Tobler, her former crew chief, and she entered a professional partnership with Garlits. In 1996, Muldowney began racing in IHRA (International Hot Rod Association) tournaments, then returned to the national tracks the following year. In 2002, Muldowney was still racing, at the age of 62. She has struggled with injuries and finances throughout her career. Still, she has no regrets. "Ninety-nine percent of drivers can't do what I do because there is no demand for them," she told *USA Today* in 1998. "I'm able to drive a car and have fun, and people pay to see it."

Further Reading

Garrett, Jerry. "Drug Queens," *Car & Driver,* July 1998, p. 151.

Muldowney Racing Enterprises. "Shirley Muldowney Official Website." Available online. URL: www.muldowney. com. Downloaded on March 27, 2002.

MURDOCH, MARGARET
(Margaret Thompson)
(1942–) *Shooter*

Margaret Murdoch chose to compete in a sport that pits women against men, and she emerged a champion several times over. The first woman to win a competition at a world championship, Murdoch was also the first woman to win a gold medal at the Pan American Games, and she came within a hair of becoming the first woman to win a shooting gold medal at the Olympics.

Born in Topeka, Kansas, on August 25, 1942, Margaret Thompson did not begin shooting competitively until several years after she had graduated from Kansas State University. But her competitive career began both literally and figuratively with a bang. At the Pan American Games in 1968, she came seemingly out of nowhere to capture a gold medal in the small-bore rifle competi-

tion. Perhaps even more impressive, Murdoch won the title with a world record score of 391. But although her achievement was noted by her competitors, it was hardly noticed outside of the shooting world. Shooting was not particularly popular with the media, most of whom mentioned it only in passing—if at all—so few people realized that the sport had its first female champion.

But Murdoch—who had married Mark Murdoch in 1966—was not overly interested in gaining media attention anyway. Her major goal was to continue to compete and win in her sport. She did just that in 1970, when she took top honors in the small-bore standing position competition at the world championships. Once again, Murdoch, who, incidentally, was four months pregnant at the time, did not gain much attention for this feat.

Six years later, Murdoch decided to compete at the Olympics. In the closest competition in Olympic shooting history, Murdoch finished the small-bore standing position event in a virtual tie with her U.S. teammate, Lanny Bassham. After nearly five hours of investigating every target, the judges determined that Bassham's shooting was slightly better than Murdoch's, and awarded him the gold. Murdoch had, of course, won the silver, but Bassham, who had expressed disapproval of the judges' decision, invited Murdoch to stand on the first-place podium with him during the playing of the national anthem.

Shortly after the Olympics, Murdoch retired from the sport and became a registered nurse. Acknowledged for her achievements at last, she was inducted into the International Women's Sports Hall of Fame in 1988.

Further Reading

Layden, Joe. *Women in Sports: The Complete Book on the World's Greatest Female Athletes.* Santa Monica, Calif.: General Publishing Group, 1997, p. 174.

Reith, Katherine. "Four of the Best Join the Greatest," vol. 11, no. 1. *Women's Sports and Fitness* (January–February 1989): 56.

N

NAVRATILOVA, MARTINA
(Martina Subertova)
(1956–   )   *Tennis Player*

The greatest female tennis player in U.S. history is a woman who was born and raised in a small Communist country on the other side of the Atlantic. Martina Navratilova, who defected to the United States at the age of 18, was more than a tennis champion. She was an outspoken athlete whose approach to competing changed the face of tennis and completely revolutionized women's sports in the United States.

Martina Navratilova was born on October 10, 1956, in Prague, Czechoslovakia. Her father, Miroslav Subert, was a professional skier. Her mother, Jana Subertova, a ski instructor, left Miroslav when Martina was three. Mother and daughter moved to Revnice, a small village near Prague. There, Jana met and married a professional tennis player named Mirek Navratil, who eventually adopted Martina. (Navratilova is the feminine form of Navratil.)

It was Navratil who first taught young Martina to play tennis. Six years old at the time, she fell in love with tennis at first sight. "The moment I stepped onto the crunchy red clay . . . felt the joy of smacking the ball," she said later, "I knew I was in the right place." Two years later, Martina entered her first tournament. At eight, she was the youngest player in the competition; the officials, in fact, tried to bar her from playing, claiming that she was too small, but Martina played anyway and reached the semifinals.

Encouraged by this success, she began playing competitive tennis regularly. During this early period, Martina played predominantly on red clay courts, which was the surface of most courts in the former Czechoslovakia. Of all tennis surfaces, clay, which allows for a slow, high-bouncing ball, favors players such as CHRIS EVERT, who have strong baseline games with deep, consistent ground strokes. But although young Martina initially learned the clay court game, from childhood she found the baseline game a dull one. For Martina, fun on the tennis court meant rushing the net.

Fortunately for Martina, she found someone who recognized that she was a natural serve-and-volley player. "George Parma," Navratilova said years later, "saw from the start that I was an attacking player, and he let me be that." As her fellow young Czech players learned to hit deep and consistent strokes from the baseline, Martina learned to hit a powerful serve and follow it to net. She learned to angle her volleys. And she learned how to whack an overhead. Parma encouraged his gifted protégée not only to play but to travel. "See the world, Martina," he told her. "Compete whenever you have the chance."

Martina did compete, in both singles and doubles tournaments throughout Czechoslovakia. She was in the midst of a tournament in Pilsen, about 40 miles from her hometown, on a fateful summer day in 1968. Eleven-year-old Martina had spent the night of August 20 at her doubles partner's home, near the tournament. The two girls woke up the next morning and saw Soviet tanks out the window. The Soviet Union had invaded Czechoslovakia. For Martina, life had changed forever. "I saw my country lose its verve, lose its productivity, lose its soul," she wrote years later.

Parma, who happened to be vacationing in Austria when the invasion occurred, never returned to his homeland. Heartbroken by her coach's departure, Martina nevertheless continued to play tennis, and in 1972, at the age of 16, she won the Czechoslovakian national championships.

The following year, 17-year-old Navratilova traveled for the first time to the United States. From her first moments in the United States, Navratilova was in love with America. She loved the language, the players, and the fans. She also loved the junk food. In two months on the tennis tour, she gained 25 pounds.

She also gained the respect of some of the top players on the tour. The year 1973 was a pivotal one for Navratilova, not only because it was the year that she first saw the United States, but because it marked the first meeting between the Czech player and the woman who would become her chief rival and close friend. Chris Evert was the top-ranked player in the game when she and Navratilova met for the first time. Although Evert prevailed in straight sets by a score of 7-6, 6-3, Navratilova was encouraged by her performance. "I said to myself, 'If I can do this against the best in the world, then maybe next time I can win the match,'" she recalled later.

Navratilova slowly began her ascent toward the upper echelon of the women's tour. After taking top honors at the Wimbledon junior tournament in 1973, she began playing on the adult circuit full time. In 1974 she won her first tournament, in Orlando, Florida, and the following year she reached the quarterfinals of the Australian Open, beating the legendary Australian player Margaret Court in the process. Later in 1975 Navratilova played for the Czech Federation Cup team, and she led her home nation to the title. The Federation Cup championship provided another first for Navratilova: Playing for the title, she beat Chris Evert for the first time.

Navratilova had brought the Federation Cup to Czechoslovakia, but she was not eager to be back in her home country. She missed the freedom of life in the United States; as important, she realized that in order to reach the number-one spot in tennis—and Navratilova was determined to do just that—she would have to compete in the major tournaments, the vast majority of which were held in the United States.

The Czech government was less than delighted with Navratilova's obvious affinity for all things American. Officials within the country declared that she was becoming "too westernized," and then threatened to prevent her from returning to the United States for the U.S. Open in August 1975. For Navratilova, this was the last straw. She did go to the United States for the U.S. Open, and after Evert defeated her in the semifinal round, she elected to stay for good, asking for political asylum.

Navratilova was now where she wanted to be, but the following years would prove challenging for her, not only on the court, where she battled to reach the top of the rankings, but in her adopted homeland, where she would struggle for citizenship and acceptance. Only 18 years old at the time of her defection, she began life in the United States truly alone. She could not return to Czechoslovakia to see her family, and they could not travel to Palm Springs, California, where she had settled, to see her.

Meanwhile, her increasing success on the tennis court had made Navratilova a wealthy woman. To ease the loneliness and the pressure, she would go on elaborate shopping sprees and would often drop thousands of dollars in a week on automobiles and designer clothes. The U.S. media was critical of what they perceived as extreme materialism and did not hesitate to pan her excesses on a daily basis.

Her immaturity also showed on the court; a highly emotional player, she would often let an error or a questionable line call destroy her concentration. Navratilova most likely reached the nadir of her early days in the United States during the 1976 U.S. Open. Ranked number three at the beginning of the tournament, she appeared out of shape and out of focus during her first round match with Janet Newbury, an unseeded player. After Newbury defeated her in the nationally televised match, Navratilova sat in her courtside chair and wept openly. Newbury crossed over to comfort her, as millions of Americans watched.

That match may well have served as a turning point for Navratilova. Earlier in 1976 she met Sandra Haynie, a golfer who became Navratilova's close friend and mentor. Under Haynie's guidance, Navratilova began to battle her weight problem through a rigid conditioning program. She also left southern California and moved to Dallas. Through a combination of diet, exercise, and psychological counseling, Navratilova got both her body and mind in shape. She shed 20 pounds in the course of a few months, and also became fluent in English. Navratilova's natural wit and intelligence could now be fully understood by her U.S. peers; she was a locker room champ at "Boggle," the word game.

Navratilova was beginning to dominate her opponents on the court as well. At Wimbledon in 1978, she defeated Evonne Goolagong, a top Australian player, in the semifinal round to advance to the championship match against Chris Evert. Navratilova played an inconsistent first set against Evert, netting an easy overhead on set point to give Evert the early lead. But she stormed back to take the second set, and then in the third, she turned the tables on her opponent. With the normally steely Evert serving at 4-2, Navratilova broke serve and then held to tie the set at 4. Then, in a sudden reversal of personality, it was Navratilova who stayed focused and Evert who lost concentration. The seasoned Wimbledon champion made a string of unforced errors, and Navratilova took advantage to seize 12 of the last 13 points to take the match and the title. It was Navratilova's first Grand Slam championship. In some regards it was a bittersweet day in her life—she told reporters that she "didn't know whether to laugh or cry." Here she was at Centre Court, holding the Wimbledon trophy above her head, and her parents were not there to see her win. Not only did the Czech government refuse to allow Jana and Mirek Navratil to travel to Great Britain for the tournament, but the Czech media refused to report Navratilova's victory, either on television or in the press.

Still, it was a moment to savor. And the following year, the Czech government loosened its restrictions on Navratilova's family. This time, Jana was in the stands to watch Navratilova once again face the player who was fast becoming her top rival—the newly married Chris Evert-Lloyd. When Navratilova triumphed, Jana jumped up and danced around her seat.

Centre Court and Wimbledon would become Navratilova's personal playground during her career. She went on to win nine singles titles there, including an unprecedented six in a row, from 1982 to 1987. In the 1980s Navratilova began to dominate play on other courts as well. She won titles at the Australian Open in 1981, 1983, and 1985, and took top honors at the French Open in 1982 and 1984. And at the U.S. Open, where she had so publicly grieved in 1976, she won four championships.

Although Navratilova was now a champion, she was in many ways a player without a following. Although she resided in the United States, she was not yet a U.S. citizen and did not feel completely acclimated. In addition, her adopted country had its own women tennis idols. Navratilova's top on-court rivals during the late 1970s and early 1980s were Evert and TRACY AUSTIN. Both Austin and Evert were ground-stroking baseline players with slender, traditionally feminine physiques. In contrast was Navratilova, with a much more muscular and athletic body, playing a more traditionally men's game, with a strong serve-and-volley style. Partly for these reasons, Navratilova had never felt much affection from U.S. audiences.

All that changed, however, at the U.S. Open in Flushing, New York, in 1981. Navratilova, who had never won at Flushing Meadows, took the court against Austin in the final, and lost in straight sets to the young Californian. At the end of the match she congratulated her young rival and politely walked

In addition to winning a record 18 Grand Slam singles titles, Martina Navratilova revolutionized women's tennis with her strength, speed, and superb serve-and-volley game.
(Allsport UK/Allsport)

off the court as the crowd applauded. But moments later, when Navratilova was presented with her runner-up plaque, the crowd stood up and gave her a thunderous standing ovation. They applauded Navratilova for her grace and sheer athleticism on the court, and they applauded to show the Czech player that they accepted her.

It was also in 1981 that Navratilova became a U.S. citizen. Now she was a full-fledged American, and she soon became one of the nation's more outspoken citizens when later that year she announced that she was homosexual. Navratilova's candor about her sexuality no doubt cost her millions of dollars in endorsements. Even so, she not only remained open and honest about it throughout her career but became a dedicated advocate for gay rights.

In 1983, Navratilova won her first U.S. Open, whipping Chris Evert-Lloyd in straight sets. During the match, it was clear that Navratilova, who had spent a considerable amount of time on physical conditioning under the watchful eye of her trainer, NANCY LIEBERMAN, had set a new precedent for athleticism in women's sports. She was quite simply stronger and faster, more so not only than Evert-Lloyd, but every woman on the tennis tour in the early 1980s.

Although Navratilova could win on all surfaces at at every location, there was one tournament that mattered more to her than all the others. "That court," Evert said of her rival and close friend's relationship with Wimbledon, "is her court."

It was fitting, then, that Navratilova won her 18th and final Grand Slam singles title on Centre Court's grass surface. She did so in 1990 in impressive fashion, dominating Zina Garrison in straight sets. Four years later, she played her final Grand Slam singles tournament there. After losing in the 1994 tournament final to Conchita Martinez by a score of 6-4, 3-6, 6-3, Navratilova acknowledged the warm ovation of the crowd with a gracious speech. Then, she walked fully around Centre Court—perhaps the only runner-up in the history of sport to take a victory lap. A full 75 minutes after the match had ended, the ovations were still thundering for Navratilova. With her runner-up trophy and flowers in hand, she finally departed Centre Court. But before leaving for good, she bent down and quietly picked a few blades of court grass as a simple memento.

Navratilova continued to compete in singles on an irregular basis until 1994, when she made her final appearance at the Virginia Slims tournament. At the time of her official retirement from tennis, she was the biggest moneymaker in the history of women's tennis. In addition to her 18 Grand Slam singles titles, she had won 31 Grand Slam women's doubles events. Navratilova's serve-and-volley game made her a natural doubles player, and her partnership with Pam Shriver proved to be the most successful doubles team in tennis history.

Although she had officially retired in 1994, Navratilova returned to Grand Slam events several times after that. She won the mixed doubles event at Wimbledon in 1995 with her partner Mark Woodforde, and in 2000 and 2001 she competed at the Wimbledon, French Open, and U.S. Open tournaments in both the mixed doubles and women's doubles competitions. She has also spent a considerable amount of time and energy working for charitable causes, and she has occasionally provided expert commentary from the broadcast booth.

Navratilova brought tennis up to a higher level on the court, and she did so with grace, humor, and honesty. Those attributes, together with her sheer athleticism on the court, make her one of the most important female role models in this country. "She has pushed the next generation to be better," Billie Jean King said of Navratilova, "and that is each generation's responsibility."

Further Reading

King, Billie Jean, and Cynthia Starr, *We Have Come a Long Way: The Story of Women's Tennis.* New York: McGraw Hill, 1988.

Smith, Lissa editor. *Nike Is a Goddess: The History of Women in Sports.* New York: Atlantic Monthly Press, 1998, pp. 70–73.

Sugar, Bert Randolph. *The Sports 100: A Ranking of the Greatest Athletes of All Time.* Secaucus, N.J.: Citadel Press, 1995.

NELSON, MAUD
(Clementina Brida, Maud Olson, Maud Dellacqua, Maud Nielson)
(1881–1994) *Baseball Player, Scout*

Maud Nelson was, quite simply, the most important person in the history of early women's baseball. For 40 years she played, managed, owned teams, and scouted for the Bloomer teams, which were all-women's clubs that played against one another in the early part of the 20th century.

Yet Maud Nelson is largely unknown today; few sports historians know much about her, and the vast majority of sports fans have never- heard of her. But in 1993 an author named Barbara Gregorich wrote a book entitled *Women at Play,* in which she chronicled Nelson's life in detail.

In order to write about Nelson, Gregorich did an enormous amount of digging in archives and libraries; there was very little written about Maud Nelson, even during her lifetime. One reason for this lack of information is that Nelson played under several different names. She was, at varying times during her career, not only Nelson but Nielson, Brida, Olson, and Dellacqua.

Born in northern Italy on November 17, 1881, Maud Nelson's original name was Clementina Brida. Her family immigrated to the United States when Clementina was very young. Where the Brida family settled is not known, but wherever it was, Clementina clearly found out about baseball because, by the time she was 16, she was playing baseball for a Bloomer team.

Fans today may be surprised to learn that at the turn of the 20th century in America, there was a thriving professional baseball league that included women on its rosters. This 1890s league—also known as the Bloomer teams or Bloomer Girls—was not an end-of-the-century phenomenon that disappeared soon after it lost its novelty. Rather, some teams in the league, such as the Boston Bloomer Girls, the Western Bloooomer Girls, and the Star Bloomers, stayed in business for more than 40 years. The public paid to watch the Bloomer teams play for the simple reason that the women on the field played top-notch baseball.

Of those women on those early fields, Nelson was probably the best player. She was, as Gregorich notes, the ace pitcher for the Boston Bloomer team. Pitching every day, Nelson would often start the game, and then, after dominating the opposing team for two or three innings (she often struck out all the players she faced), she would yield the mound to another pitcher. Nelson apparently survived this grueling schedule, for at the age of 27, she was still playing ball. Then pitching for the Cherokee Indian Base Ball Club, a team that featured both men and women, Nelson toured Canada with the Cherokee squad, and she later married its manager, John Olson.

In 1911 Maud and John Olson became co-owners and managers of the Western Bloomer Girls. (It is not known when she changed her name to Maud.) Not only did Olson pitch for the team, but after her stint on the mound was over, she would stay on the field to play third base. Of the infield positions in the game of baseball, third base is arguably the most frightening. Called the "hot corner," it is a mere 90 feet from home plate. Those who play third have to handle screeching line drives pulled by right-handed hitters. Likewise, ground balls hit to third usually get there very quickly. The third baseman has to be quick enough to field the ball quickly, then stand up and make a long, accurate throw across the diamond to first base, before the batter gets there. That Nelson played this position after pitching her two or three innings is a clear indication of her talent and flexibility, not to mention her courage. In addition, she was a reliable and productive hitter—something few pitchers in today's professional leagues can boast of.

Nelson also scouted for the Western Bloomer Girls. Most people who recruited players for Bloomer teams stuck to their home cities and regions; players chosen by Boston were usually from New England, for example. But Nelson, years ahead of her time, scouted players for the Western Bloomer Girls from all parts of the country.

Soon after John Olson died in 1917, Nelson must have left the Western Bloomer Girls. At this time she continued to play baseball—at the age of 36—with the Boston Bloomer Girls. During the off-season, she also managed a women's baseball team from the Chicago Athletic Club and played exhibition games in various cities in the South. According to Gregorich, Nelson married her second husband, Costant Dellacqua, in the early 1920s. Dellacqua's son by a previous marriage, Joe Dellacqua, said years later that Nelson turned to his father and said simply, "Let's start a baseball team." With little ado, the Star Ranger Girls were born.

The Star Ranger Girls lasted from 1922 until the mid-1930s. During that time Nelson, working as manager and scout, recruited some of the most talented women of the late Bloomer Girl era. But her modesty was such that her recruits did not know that she was a former player. Margaret Gisolo, who was recruited in 1929, played with the Star Ranger Girls for five years. During that time, she had no idea that her manager, then know as Maud Dellacqua, had ever been a player, much less the finest of her era.

With the nation in the midst of the Great Depression, interest in the Bloomer teams dwindled in the 1930s. The teams that Maud Nelson had played for, managed, and owned had all folded by 1935. Women would have to wait another eight years for an opportunity to play professional baseball. Some players, like Rose Gacioch, had a second chance to play professionally for the All American Girls' Baseball League (AAGBL); Gacioch had played for Nelson's Star Ranger Girls in 1934 and later became one of the key members of the Rockford Peaches, one of the best teams in the AAGBL. But for Nelson, the end of the Bloomer teams meant the end of her baseball career. Shortly after the leagues folded, she retired and moved to Chicago with Dellacqua. She died there in 1944. For three decades, Nelson was the cornerstone of women's baseball in the United States. As a player, she dominated opponents, both on the mound and in the batter's box. And later, as manager and owner, she proved to be an indefatigable figure, providing the opportunity for the finest women players in the United States to grab their gloves and take the field.

Further Reading

Gregorich, Barbara. *Women at Play: The Story of Women in Baseball.* New York: Harcourt Brace, 1993, pp. 2–11, 32–36.

NYAD, DIANA (Diana Sneed)
(1949–   )   *Marathon Swimmer*

Diana Nyad, one of the great U.S. woman marathon swimmers, was the first woman to swim around Manhattan Island when she performed the feat in 1975. Four years later, she notched another first when she set a record for long-distance swimming—for both men and women—with a 102.5-mile stint between the Bahamas and Florida.

Born in New York City on August 22, 1949, Diana Sneed (she changed her name to Nyad when she was an adult) was a natural athlete who learned to swim while still a toddler. When she was very young, Diana moved with her parents, William Sneed, a stockbroker, and Lucy Sneed, a homemaker, to Fort Lauderdale, Florida.

Diana was a serious and highly disciplined swimmer from a very young age. While still a teenager, she focused on earning a spot on the U.S. Olympic swim team in hopes of competing in the 1968 games in Mexico City. Her dream was a realistic one; at the age of 16, she was the top backstroker in Florida. But Nyad's ambition was shattered when, in 1966, she contracted a severe case of viral endocarditis, a heart infection. Nyad was confined to bed rest for a full six months, and she missed her opportunity to become an Olympian.

Nyad enrolled at Emory College in 1967, but she got into serious trouble with the school administration when she parachuted out of her 44th-floor dormitory window. Expelled from Emory, Nyad attended Lake Forest College in Illinois, where she graduated Phi Beta Kappa in 1973.

After college Nyad decided to pursue marathon swimming, a sport that had caught her interest several years earlier. In 1969, Nyad had competed in—and won—her first long-distance competition, a 10-mile race in Lake Ontario. Five years later, Nyad returned to Lake Ontario, determined this time to swim across it. That she did, crossing the 32-mile body of water in 18 hours and 22 minutes.

In 1975 Nyad decided to attempt a swim around Manhattan Island. On a September morning, she entered the East River to begin her journey but stalled when a southern storm swept through the city. Nyad swam in place under the Brooklyn Bridge and waited for the storm to pass, but after doing so for more than an hour, she decided to abandon the journey and try again another day. Two weeks later she made her second attempt, and this time she succeeded, not only in swimming around Manhattan, but in doing so in world-record fashion. It took Nyad seven hours and 57 minutes to circle the island; her time was several minutes faster than the old record, set by Byron Sommers in 1947.

Having made it in New York, Nyad now set her sights on Cuba. More precisely, Nyad aimed to become the first swimmer of either gender to swim the 103-mile distance from Cuba to Florida. After training for many months, Nyad made her attempt in May 1978. In order to protect herself from shark attacks, she swam in a shark-proof cage. Unfortunately, the cage trapped water, which rose in waves and pounded Nyad as she attempted to swim. Nauseated and exhausted from the countercurrent, which was so powerful during one four-hour period it had actually swept her backward two miles, she gave up the attempt, after spending 41 hours in the water.

In 1979, Nyad once again attempted a long-distance swim when, in her cage once again, she worked to navigate the waters between Bimini, in the Bahamas, and Jupiter, Florida. This time she was successful, as she knifed through 102.5 miles of ocean in 27 hours and 38 minutes. She retired from marathon swimming in 1980 and became a sports announcer for television as well as an author.

Further Reading

Biography Resource Center. "Diana Nyad," *Contemporary Authors.* Farmington, Mich.: Gale Group, 2000.

Layden, Joe. *Women in Sports: The Complete Book on the World's Greatest Female Athletes.* Santa Monica, Calif.: General Publishing Group, 1997, p. 179.

O

OAKLEY, ANNIE (Phoebe Ann Mosey)
(1860–1926) *Markswoman*

Without a doubt, the most celebrated shooter in the history of the United States is the legendary Annie Oakley, subject of tall tales, songs, and even a Broadway musical and Hollywood movie. For all the hoopla about Oakley, she was in truth a revolutionary figure—perhaps the first American woman to become a bona fide celebrity because of her athletic talent.

Phoebe Ann Mosey was born on August 13, 1860, in Darke County, Ohio, the fifth of eight children born to Jacob Mosey, a veteran of the War of 1812, and his wife, Susan, a former nurse. The Moseys lived in extreme poverty—a situation that grew dramatically worse when Jacob died in 1864. Susan went back to work, and several of her children eventually were removed from their mother's care. Young Annie (as her siblings called her) was sent to live in an orphanage at the age of nine and then with a farming family. At the age of 12, Annie ran away from her foster home and found her mother and siblings.

Already a sure hand with a rifle (she used to accompany her older brothers on hunting trips when she was six years old, and at the age of eight she killed a squirrel with a single shot), Annie became an accomplished hunter to help feed her family. As her skill became more polished, she began selling her game at local markets.

By the time she was 16, Annie had earned a reputation as a fine markswoman—so much so that when a vaudeville act traveled to Cincinnati looking for an accomplished shooter to participate in a challenge match, Annie was selected. The challenge match pitted Annie against the star of the vaudeville act, Frank Butler. Older than Annie by 10 years, Butler was undoubtedly favored to better the local teenager. But Annie astonished the crowd—and her opponent—by beating Butler in the match. Butler apparently recovered graciously from his loss; less than a year later, he married his defeater.

The Butlers traveled and performed together regularly, and soon became a premier attraction on the vaudeville circuit. Annie, who adopted the stage name "Oakley" shortly after her wedding, was a natural performer, exhibiting not only a terrific shooting ability but an appealing stage presence as well. In 1885, Butler and Oakley signed on with Buffalo Bill's Wild West Show, which was among the first traveling rodeos. Oakley quickly

The most celebrated markswoman in history, Annie Oakley never competed in her sport. Instead, she became a legend, through a combination of personality and talent.
(Library of Congress)

became the star of Buffalo Bill's show, and Butler, an astute business manager as well as a performer, was happy to show off his wife's formidable talents. In one of their favorite routines, Oakley would shoot a cigarette protruding from her husband's mouth. When word of this trick reached the ears of the Kaiser Wilhelm II of Germany, he became so entranced with Oakley that he asked her to perform the trick with him when the Wild West Show traveled to Germany. Oakley agreed to do it, but only if Wilhelm held the cigarette in his hand rather than his mouth. It was certainly a clash of cultures as the young woman from the impoverished rural areas of Ohio took aim at German royalty. As usual, her aim was true.

Oakley continued to perform in Buffalo Bill's rodeo until 1901, when she was injured in a train accident and was forced to retire. By then, she had become one of the best known women in the world. In 1922 Oakley was involved in another accident, this time in an automobile. She survived but was immeasurably weakened by the incident and never fully recovered. In 1926, Oakley died of pernicious anemia. Frank Butler, who was at his wife's bedside at her death, died three weeks later.

Further Reading

Annie Oakley Foundation. "Tall Tales and Truths About Annie Oakley." Available online. URL: http://www. ormiston.com/annieoakley/. Downloaded on May 2, 2001.

Layden, Joe. *Women in Sports: The Complete Book on the World's Greatest Female Athletes.* Santa Monica, Calif.: General Publishing Group, 1997, pp. 179–180.

Legends of the West. "Annie Oakley Dies Here Last Evening," November 4, 1926, *Greenville Daily Advocate.* Available online. URL: http://pages.prodigy.com/legends/annie.htm. Downloaded on March 27, 2002.

OBERG, MARGO (Margo Godfrey)
(1953–) *Surfer*

Margo Oberg, perhaps the most gifted woman surfer in history, won the first three professional world championships in her sport's history. A fearless competitor who racked up more than 100 trophies during her career, Oberg captured seven consecutive amateur championships as well.

Born on September 8, 1953, in La Jolla, California, Margo Godfrey rode her first waves at the tender age of 10. One year later, she made her competitive debut at the 1965 Western Regional Surfing Championships. The tournament had a special category for San Diego female residents, and since there was no age limit or minimum for its competitors, 11-year-old Margo eagerly joined the tournament. She may have been the youngest competitor at the championships, but she was so impressive on the board—surfers are judged by the difficulty and size of the wave they ride, as well as the maneuvers they perform and the power and speed they use—that she took first place in the tournament.

The next year, Margo accomplished something equally impressive when she competed in the 12-and-under division of the Menehune Championships and whipped her competitors—all of whom were boys—to capture her first national title. In 1968, at the age of 15, Margo became the top-seeded women's surfer in California. She sealed her ranking with her first world championship later in the year.

In 1969 Margo defended her world championship successfully but then retired from competition. Three years later, Godfrey married Steve Oberg, and the couple settled in Hawaii to teach surfing and manage a concession stand at a resort hotel in Kauai. Oberg returned to the circuit in 1975, when surfing became a professional sport. Oberg promptly won the first professional world championship that year and took top honors in the 1976 and 1977 world championships as well. She took a year off from the tour in 1979, and then she returned once more to claim two more world championships in 1980 and 1981.

Oberg once again took time off from surfing, this time to have a child in 1982, but then came back in 1983 to win the Women's World Cup. She would compete in that tournament several more times, claiming second place in 1984 and 1988, then finishing fourth in 1991, her final year as a competitive surfer.

After retiring from her sport for good, Oberg spent some time in the broadcast booth, providing commentary for surfing events for such programs as ABC's *Wide World of Sports*. But her biggest passion since leaving competitive surfing has been teaching. She owns and operates Margo Oberg's Surfing School in Maui, Hawaii, where she lives. Early in her career, Oberg summed up her ambition simply and concisely. "There are 10 famous men in surfing, and one really famous woman. That's me," she told *Sports Illustrated* in 1976. "I want to ride the biggest waves any woman has ever ridden."

Further Reading

CNN.SI for Women, 100 Greatest Female Athletes. "Margo Oberg," *Sports Illustrated for Women*. Available online. URL: http://sportsillustrated.cnn.com/siforwomen/top_100/99/. Posted on November 29, 1999.

Layden, Joe. *Women in Sports: The Complete Book on the World's Greatest Female Athletes*. Santa Monica, Calif.: General Publishing Group, 1997, pp. 180–181.

⊞ OUTERBRIDGE, MARY EWING
(1852–1886) *Tennis Player*

Did she or did she not? Although plenty of detractors deny that Mary Outerbridge was indeed the person who first introduced tennis to the United States, she is officially credited as "the mother of tennis" in this country.

Not much is known about this athletic and intelligent woman. Records do show that Mary Ewing Outerbridge was born in Philadelphia on March 9, 1852, and that she died 34 years later in New York. It is also a fact that when she was almost 22, Outerbridge took a trip to Bermuda. There she saw British officers who were stationed on the island playing a game on a grassy lawn with rackets, a net, and a ball. She found out that the game, known as lawn tennis, was a popular sport in Great Britain and other parts of Europe.

Experts differ on what happened after Outerbridge noticed the game in Bermuda. Some claim that she bought balls, a net, and a few rackets, packed them up with her, and brought them back to Staten Island, New York, where she lived for most of her life. According to this version of the story, Outerbridge introduced the game at the Staten Island Cricket and Baseball Club. It did not take long for tennis to catch on, and within months tennis had swept the nation.

Skeptics argue, however, that Outerbridge could not possibly have been the person who first brought tennis to the United States. Some claimed that she did not visit Bermuda until 1875, and by that time, tennis was already a popular sport in America. There is documentation, however, that Outerbridge's trip to Bermuda occurred in January 1874, which makes it technically possible for her to have discovered the sport. Then there are arguments stating that tennis did not become an organized sport until February 1874, so Outerbridge could not have purchased equipment in Bermuda in January of that year.

In his book *The Modern Encyclopedia of Tennis,* tennis commentator Bud Collins states that although it might be true that Outerbridge did introduce the game to her club in Staten Island in 1874, the first documented tennis match actually occurred that same year in Arizona. Still another school of thought gives credit to a Bostonian named James Dwight. A graduate of Harvard, Dwight may have played the game with his cousin, Fred Sears, in Nahant, Massachusetts, in 1874. What is known is that Dwight won the first tennis tournament played in this country, in 1876, and that he would go on to organize several important tennis competitions.

The claim that Mary Ewing Outerbridge was the original founder of tennis in the United States does have a strong following. In 1981—almost 100 years after her death in 1886—Outerbridge was inducted into the International Tennis Hall of Fame. Visitors who pass her bust can note the inscription on her plaque: "Mary Ewing Outerbridge," it reads: "The Mother of American Tennis."

Further Reading

International Tennis Hall of Fame. "James Dwight," tennishalloffame.com. Available online. URL: http://www.tennisfame.org/enshrinees/james_dwight.html. Downloaded on June 25, 2001.

King, Billie Jean, and Cynthia Starr. *We Have Come a Long Way: The Story of Women's Tennis.* New York: McGraw Hill, 1988.

Layden, Joe. *Women in Sports: The Complete Book on the World's Greatest Female Athletes.* Santa Monica, Calif.: General Publishing Group, 1997, pp. 182–183.

New York City Women's Biography Hub, "Mary Outerbridge," CUNY Libraries Online. Available online. URL: http://www.library.csi.cuny.edu/dept/history/lavender/386/mouter.html. Downloaded on June 24, 2001.

P

PEPPLER, MARY JO
(1940–)   *Volleyball Player*

The gifted athlete Mary Jo Peppler founded and played for a world championship volleyball team, and she was the first great U.S. volleyball player.

Mary Jo Peppler was born on October 17, 1940, in Rockford, Illinois, and when she was very young, she moved with her family to Long Beach, California. Peppler began playing volleyball while at Long Beach High School, and when she was a senior she tried out for and made the local volleyball team, the Long Beach Shamrocks. Peppler proved to be a valuable asset, helping the Shamrocks win a national championship in the early 1960s.

After she graduated from high school, her parents moved to San Francisco, but Peppler elected to stay in southern California, which boasted the finest volleyball teams in the nation. Peppler played whenever she could, and she earned money doing odd jobs, including selling encyclopedias. In 1964 Peppler made the Olympic volleyball team and traveled to Tokyo to compete in the games. The U.S. team did not fare well in the Olympics, however, failing to advance past the qualifying rounds.

Peppler played Olympic volleyball again at the Mexico City games in 1968, and two years later, she joined the U.S. national team, which played in tournaments all over the world. Peppler's play for the national squad was so dominating that although the United States finished 11th in the world championships that year, she was named the tournament's most valuable player.

In 1972 Peppler moved to Houston, where she founded, coached, and served as captain on a volleyball team called E Pluribus Unum. Peppler's digs, serves, and spikes led the squad to national championships in 1972 and 1973, but then the team disbanded in 1974 when a new international volleyball league was formed. The new league, known as the International Volleyball Association, consisted of several co-ed teams. Peppler eagerly signed on to play for the team from El Paso-Juarez, but the league folded after only one season.

Peppler suffered another disappointment in 1976. Outspoken and blunt off the court, she had angered the United States Volleyball Association (USVBA) with some comments she had made about gender inequality in the sport. As a result, the USVBA informed her that she would not be welcome on the U.S. Olympic team that would travel to Montreal for the 1976 games.

Bruised by the rejection, Peppler turned to another activity completely when she was invited to compete against other top women athletes on an ABC sports program called *Women's Superstars.* The program, a spin-off of the popular *Superstars* program which pitted top male athletes against one another, featured such prominent figures as BILLIE JEAN KING, MICKI KING, and CATHY RIGBY competing with one another in a series of sports that included cycling, swimming, and running. Peppler came in and completely dominated the field, walking off with the $50,000 cash prize. It was the most money she would ever earn as a player in sports.

In 1977, Peppler retired from playing competitive volleyball in order to concentrate on coaching. She has coached both court and beach volleyball and has also authored a book on playing competitive volleyball. In 1993 she moved back to California, where she took a job as director of coaching for Coast Volleyball in San Diego.

Further Reading

Layden, Joe. *Women in Sports: The Complete Book on the World's Greatest Female Athletes.* Santa Monica, Calif.: General Publishing Group, 1997, p. 186.

Markel, Robert, Susan Wagoner, and Marcella Smith. *The Women's Sports Encyclopedia.* New York: Henry Holt, 1999.

Volleyball Hall of Fame. "Mary Jo Peppler," 1990 Entries. United States Volleyball Online. Available online, URL: http://www.volleyhall.org. Downloaded on December 27, 2001.

⊞ **PICKETT, TIDYE** (1913–1971), and
LOUISE STOKES (Louise Stokes Fraser)
(1914–1978)
Track Athletes

At the 1932 Olympic Games in Los Angeles, California's own Buster Crabbe succeeded Johnny Weismuller as the United States' favorite swim-

ming champion by grabbing the gold in the men's 400-meter freestyle. And on the track, a young Texas tornado by the name of BABE DIDRICKSON ZAHARIAS won two gold medals in Herculean fashion, placing women athletes on the U.S. radar once and for all. But the 1932 games were also noteworthy for a far less heroic reason: Louise Stokes and Tidye Pickett, two athletes who had earned places on the U.S. women's track team, were denied the right to compete, for one simple reason—they were African American.

Tidye Pickett was born in Chicago in 1913. Louise Stokes was born a year later, in 1914, in Malden, Massachusetts. Both Tidye and Louise made their marks in track and field while in college; Pickett dominated track-and-field events at Illinois State (later Northern Illinois) University, where she competed with and against future Olympian Mary Terwilliger, setting several college records. Stokes did her early training in Boston, where in 1930 she competed in the first women's indoor track meet held in that city. At the Boston meet, Stokes set a new U.S. record in the broad jump, and in 1931 she was elected—over local favorite Mary Carew, a white runner—the recipient of the Curley Cup, the trophy for the best women's track performance of the year.

Both Pickett and Stokes went to Evanston, Illinois, to compete in the Olympic trials in July 1932. The trials featured a dominating performance by Babe Didrikson, who won a total of six events in a three-hour time span. Stokes and Pickett, in the meantime, quietly sealed their place in history with solid runs in the 100-meter finals (Pickett finished sixth; Stokes, in a dead heat with her hometown rival Carew, tied for fourth) and became the first African Americans to earn places on the U. S. women's track team.

But even though Pickett and Stokes were legitimate team members, they were sometimes made to feel like outsiders. Their troubles began on the two-day train journey from Evanston to Los Angeles. All team members traveled to the Olympics together, but during a one-night stay in a Denver hotel, Stokes and Pickett were not allowed to eat with the rest of the team, because the hotel's dining room was restricted to whites. The rest of the team shared a jovial dinner hour, while Pickett and Stokes, confined to their room, ate quietly together.

The following day, another distressing incident occurred. On the way from Denver to Los Angeles, Pickett and Stokes were resting in their shared Pullman Car compartment, Stokes in an upper berth and Pickett in the lower berth. What happened next might have been meant as a amusing prank, but it was hard for Pickett or Stokes to laugh when Babe Didrickson, walking past the reclining Pickett, threw a pitcher of ice-cold water on her. The two women confronted one another; harsh words were exchanged, and no apologies were issued.

Once in Los Angeles, Pickett and Stokes felt less isolated as they practiced daily with their teammates. But then the U. S. Olympic Committee decided, after a lengthy meeting, to pull Stokes and Pickett from the team. The officials claimed that two white runners—both of whom had been bested by Stokes and Pickett at the Evanston trials—were actually faster than the two African-American runners and that they should be the ones running in the relay. With little further ado, Stokes and Pickett had been replaced. They were invited to remain in Los Angeles, and they watched the Olympics from the sidelines.

Four years later, however, both runners were back, hoping for a chance to compete in the 1936 Olympics in Berlin. Both runners competed in the 1936 Olympic trials. Pickett took a silver in the finals of the 80-meter hurdles, clinching a spot on the U.S. team. Stokes did not perform as well; in her events she was pitted directly against HELEN STEPHENS, the Missouri-born athlete who dominated the trials that year. Whether Stokes was overwhelmed or intimidated by Stephens is not known, but she did not qualify for the team on the merits of her performance at the trials. Given her sub-par outing at the trials, and of course the incident at Los Angeles four years earlier, it must have been downright shocking for Stokes when she was

informed that the U.S. Olympic Committee had decided to make her a member of the team. When Stokes joined her teammates on the ship to Germany, "there was," reported the *Chicago Defender,* "no happier athlete on the boat."

Once in Europe, Stokes and Pickett participated in team training and, this time, attended all team events. Stokes recalled a banquet in Berlin for all the Olympic athletes. Adolf Hitler was in attendance at the dinner, and the U.S. team was seated so close to the dictator that, Stokes remembered, "I could have reached out and touched his neck."

The 1936 Berlin games are best remembered for Jesse Owens's achievements; in the cradle of the Nazi regime he won four gold medals and broke nine Olympic records. But it is also important to know that the Berlin Olympics marked the first time in history that an African-American woman competed in any even for the U.S. team. Although Tidye Pickett's Olympic career was a brief one—she was disqualified in the semifinal heat of the 80-meter hurdle race—her presence on the track did break a barrier. Stokes, in the meantime, was once again delegated to the sidelines. Although she had trained regularly in preparation for the 400-meter relay, it was decided, again behind closed doors by the U.S. Olympic Committee, that she would not run.

After the 1936 Olympics, Stokes was invited by the Polish runner Stella Walsh to join her athletic club in Cleveland and continue competing, but she declined Walsh's offer and retired from track and field. After working as an elevator operator, Stokes eventually became a professional bowler. She was a founding member of the Colored Women's Bowling Association in 1941, and she won many titles over the next 30 years. In 1944 she married Wilfred Fraser, a Caribbean cricket player. Louise Stokes Fraser died on March 25, 1978.

Pickett's track career also ended after the 1936 games. Returning to her home state, she became a teacher and then the principal at a school in Ford Heights, Illinois. After her death in 1971, the Ford Heights school was renamed in her honor.

Further Reading

Davis, Michael D. *Black American Women in Olympic Track and Field: A Complete Illustrated Reference.* Jefferson, N.C.: McFarland, 1992.

Plowden, Martha Ward. *Olympic Black Women,* illustrated by Ronald Jones. Gretna, La.: Pelican Publishers, 1996.

POSTEMA, PAM
(1954–   )   *Baseball Umpire*

Pam Postema was the most illustrious woman umpire in the history of baseball. She also came tantalizingly close to becoming the first woman ever to umpire on the major league level. That she was not chosen for that position, and ended up suing Major League Baseball for sexual discrimination, is either an asterisk on a stellar career or a telling statement about the level of gender inequality that remains in sports.

Pam Postema was born in 1954, the daughter of Philip Postema, a farmer, and Phyllis Postema, a housewife. The Postemas lived in Willard, Ohio, and Pam, the youngest of three children, was an enthusiastic baseball player from early childhood. She learned the game from her older brother, and by the time she was in high school she was the regular third baseman for a local baseball team.

After graduating from high school, Postema worked in a series of blue-collar jobs. In 1976 her mother told her about Christine Wren, who was at the time the only female umpire in professional baseball. Inspired by Wren, Postema traveled to Florida and applied to the Al Somers Umpire School. Somers encouraged Postema to go elsewhere; he explained to her, as he had almost 30 years earlier to BERNICE GERA that there were no proper facilities for women in the leagues' baseball parks. But Postema persevered, and Somers eventually accepted her.

Postema not only studied at Somers's institute, she also excelled there, graduating high in her class. After leaving the school, she spent three months working semipro and amateur games, and then she signed a contract to work as an umpire in the rookie division of the Gulf Coast League. The first woman signed by the league, Postema was paid a salary of $550 a month. Her first year in the rookie leagues was eye-opening for Postema, who for the first time witnessed (and was often the object of) angry outbursts by players and managers. "I could never believe anyone could be that loud or that rude," she said of one encounter, in which a manager stood nose-to-nose with her and shouted at the top of his lungs, "I had never experienced anything like that before."

Eventually Postema got used to the volatile baseball personnel, and she became a respected umpire in the rookie leagues. She began working her way up the minor-league ladder; she was promoted to the single-A level, then to the double-A leagues. And in 1982, with six years of minor-league experience under her belt, Postema became the first woman to umpire on the triple-A level—the highest ranking in the minor leagues—when she accepted a post with the Pacific Coast League.

During her years as a triple-A umpire, Postema tolerated very little verbal abuse, either from managers and players, or virtually anyone who challenged her authority. Postema once ejected a batboy and even came close to tossing a mascot out of a game. She admitted that her short tolerance on the field was largely due to what she perceived was the lack of respect for women umpires on the part of players, managers, and fans. In addition, Postema noted that her fellow umpires were not nearly as supportive of her on the field as they were with one another. "The attitude of the other umpires," Postema said of her colleagues, "was, if you have to, work with her, but don't help her. Don't make it easy."

Despite her feelings of isolation, Postema remained in the league for six years. For any umpire, six years on the triple-A level is a long tenure. Most of Postema's peers had already been promoted to the major league or had left professional baseball for other careers. But Postema continued to work triple-A games, hoping that eventually she would be promoted to the major leagues.

Indeed, Postema was considered a prospect for Major League Baseball in 1988, and in the spring of that year she was invited to work an exhibition game between the Pittsburgh Pirates and the Houston Astros. By this time Postema was garnering a great deal of publicity; her attempts to become the first female umpire in the major leagues put her on the cover of *Sports Illustrated.* The Astros-Pirates game itself was uneventful, and Postema, working behind the plate, earned high marks from the Houston manager, who said he thought Postema "called a good game."

But at a press conference shortly after the game, the Houston relief pitcher Bob Knepper, after acknowledging that Postema was in fact a decent umpire, made a statement that would become infamous: "I just don't think a woman should be an umpire. There are certain things a woman should not be and an umpire is one of them. It's a physical thing. God created women to be feminine. I don't think they should be competing with men. It has nothing to do with her ability. I don't think women should be in any position of leadership. I don't think they should be presidents or politicians. I think women were created not in an inferior position, but in a role of submission to men. You can be a woman umpire if you want, but that doesn't mean it's right. You can be a homosexual if you want, but that doesn't mean that's right either." Knepper went on to say that if Postema did continue her campaign to umpire in the major leagues, he would not "condemn her. But if God is unhappy with her, she's going to have to deal with that later."

Knepper received a great deal of negative publicity for his comments, and the National Organization for Women threatened to boycott Houston home games. But no one from either the Houston Astros organization or Major League Baseball penalized or chastised him, and Postema, in the meantime, languished as another season in the minor leagues got under way. The following year,

Bart Giamatti, who was then commissioner of baseball, invited Postema once again to umpire spring training, but when Giamatti died in the summer of 1989, Postema realized that her chances to make the major leagues had all but disappeared.

Sure enough, in December 1989 Postema received a letter informing her that her umpiring services were no longer required. Her 13-year career in the minor leagues had ended. But Postema was not ready to leave without a fight. She filed a sexual discrimination suit against Major League Baseball, stating that "I believe I belong in the Major Leagues. If it weren't for the fact that I'm a woman, I would be there right now." Postema did not return to baseball again, and the suit was settled out of court.

In 1992, Postema, working in a factory in Ohio, wrote a book about her experience, entitled *You've Got to Have Balls to Make It in This League.* In her book, Postema stressed that she eagerly awaited the day that the first female umpire works in the major leagues. As of 2002, that day had not arrived; in 1998 two female referees gained employment in the National Basketball Association, but on baseball's highest level, a woman has yet to shatter the glass ceiling.

Further Reading

The Baseball Reliquary Inc. "The Shrine of the Eternals/2000 Nominees: Pam Postema." Available online. URL: http://www.baseballreliquary.org/postema.htm. Downloaded on December 15, 2000.

Gregorich, Barbara. *Women at Play: The Story of Women in Baseball.* New York: Harcourt Brace, 1993, pp. 191–196.

Pickett, Al. "Remembering a Lost Scoop," *Abilene Reporter-News,* October 30, 1977. Available online. URL: http://www.texnews.com/sports97/alcol103097.html. Downloaded on December 21, 2000.

Postema, Pam, and Gene Wojciechowsky. *You've Got to Have Balls to Make It in This League: My Life as an Umpire.* New York: Simon & Schuster, 1992.

R

RAWLS, BETSY (Elizabeth Rawls)
(1928–)   *Golfer*

During her early years on the course, Betsy Rawls regularly competed against the likes of BABE DIDRICKSON ZAHARIAS, PATTY BERG, LOUISE SUGGS, and MICKEY WRIGHT. By the time her playing career ended, Rawls had made her own mark on the sport, finishing with 55 major victories—the fourth highest total in history.

Born in Spartanburg, South Carolina, on May 4, 1928, Elizabeth Rawls did not even venture onto the golf course until she was 17 years old, when her father first taught her the game. Even then, Rawls had other things in mind. She attended the University of Texas at Austin as a math and physics major. Unlike many of her contemporaries, Rawls did not leave college early to turn professional. In fact, Rawls did not even play golf in college; more than 20 years before the passage of Title IX, there were no competitions for women athletes in the Southwest Conference.

Although Rawls did play some golf during her college years—she won the 1949 Texas Amateur, and a year later, finished second to Babe Didrickson Zaharias in the U.S. Women's Open—she was also quite serious about academics. In 1951, she graduated Phi Beta Kappa from Texas. Later in 1951, Rawls turned professional, and she promptly won three tournaments, including the U.S. Women's Open. It would be the first of four U.S. Open championships for Rawls—only Mickey Wright has won as many. Rawls played a consistent game—she would win multiple championships every year between 1951 and 1962 and at least one annually from 1951 to 1966.

Although Rawls's strength was always her short game, she worked tirelessly at her swing as well. As countless amateur links fanatics will gladly attest, the golf swing is one of the most difficult motions in sports to master. Rawls, a physics major, found the mechanics so difficult to understand that she begged her coach, Harvey Pennick, not to "throw too much" at her when he worked on it with her. Although Rawls never did attain the tour's best swing (that honor goes to Mickey Wright), she conquered it well enough to lead the tour in victories in 1952, 1957, and 1959.

Rawls had her finest year in 1959, when she won 10 titles, including her first Ladies' Professional Golf Association (LPGA) championship. That year she not only claimed the Vare Trophy, awarded annually to the player with the lowest course average, but set a record for earnings, with $27,000—an impressive total in the days before major sponsorships and endorsements, Perhaps Rawls's most cherished accomplishment on the course occurred 10 years later, in 1969. At age 41, Rawls had slowed down considerably. She had not won a major event since 1966 and, as important, had lost a great deal of confidence in her ability. But Rawls upset a field of younger players to capture her second LPGA tournament. It was the last major championship she would win.

In 1975, Rawls hung up her golf clubs, retiring from a 24-year playing career in which she had amassed 55 victories. But Rawls remained actively involved in the game; soon after her retirement, she served a six-year stint as a tournament director for the LPGA Championships, and in 1980, became the first woman to officiate at the Men's U.S. Open Championships. A year later, Rawls left her LPGA position to take over the reins as executive director of the McDonald's LPGA Championships. During Rawls's tenure, the McDonald's tournament would become one of the most prestigious championships on the tour.

Rawls won the Bob Jones Award for her sportsmanship, dedication, and service to the sport of golf in 1996. Later that year she retired from her post on the McDonald's tournament. Always gracious, Rawls looked back on her career with fondness. "Anybody who can make a living in golf is lucky," she said after she retired. "Then to receive all the benefits accorded to me in the process . . . well, it makes me feel fortunate. It's more than I could possibly deserve."

Further Reading

Four Women Golfers. "Betsy Rawls," Reeds Web. Available online. URL: http://www.reedsweb.com/drtbird/golf/html/brawls.htm. Downloaded on May 7, 2001.

Layden, Joe. *Women in Sports: The Complete Book on the World's Greatest Female Athletes.* Santa Monica, Calif.: General Publishing Group, 1997, pp. 195–196.

Smith, Lissa, editor. *Nike Is a Goddess: The History of Women in Sports.* New York: Atlantic Monthly Press, 1998, pp. 89–90.

World Golf Hall of Fame Profile. "Betsy Rawls." Available online. URL: http://www.wgv.com/wgv/library.nsf/news/F9E45DABA1D9B1338525687E00734B86. Posted on January 17, 2001.

⊞ RETTON, MARY LOU
(1968–)   *Gymnast*

Mary Lou Retton is the first and only U.S. gymnast to win the all-around gold medal in an Olympic gymnastics competition. Retton's achievement came in front of a home crowd at the Los Angeles games in 1984.

The youngest of five children, Mary Lou Retton was born on January 24, 1968, in Fairmont, West Virginia. An active and focused child, Mary Lou began taking tap dancing and ballet lessons at the age of four. The following year, her parents enrolled her in a gymnastics class at the University of West Virginia. When she was eight years old, Mary Lou watched Nadia Comaneci become the first gymnast to receive perfect scores of 10 on her way to winning three gold medals at the 1976 Olympics in Monteral. Comaneci's performance filled Mary Lou with a sense of purpose. More than anything, she wanted to be an Olympic gymnastics gold medalist.

Recognizing their daughter's unbridled enthusiasm and talent, the Rettons decided to hire Comaneci's former coach, Bela Karolyi, to train Mary Lou. This was a major decision for both Mary Lou and her parents; Karolyi lived and worked in Houston, and in order to train with him, Mary Lou would have to move there. Mary Lou was determined, and her family did not stand in her way. On New Year's Day of 1983, Mary Lou Retton, 23 days shy of her 15th birthday, moved from West Virginia to Houston, Texas, to pursue her Olympic dreams.

Under Karolyi's tutelage, Retton became an aggressive and daring gymnast. But the road to success was not an easy one. The practice sessions were endless and exhausting. Once Retton came home from a session so exhausted that she slept through a tornado that damaged her home. Karolyi put Retton on a strict diet to tone her muscular, sturdy body. He also helped her develop some highly acrobatic routines on the uneven parallel bars; Retton perfected some of the most difficult moves in the sport and invented a few of her own.

Late in 1983, Retton suffered a broken wrist during practice. In a cast for four weeks, she missed the 1983 World Championships. But the following year, completely healed and hungry for glory, she was the top-place finisher at the U.S. Olympic trials. The path to gold had been set: now Retton had to walk that path with perfection.

The 1984 Los Angeles games were a perfect venue for Retton, for several reasons. In the first place, she would be performing in front of a home crowd, always an advantage for an athlete. Second and perhaps as important, one of the traditional powerhouses in gymnastics would not be present. Four years after the United States boycotted the Moscow Olympics for political reasons, the Soviet Union in turn boycotted the Los Angeles games, as did several other Iron Curtain countries, among them East Germany, Czechoslovakia, and Bulgaria. This meant that several of the world's top gymnasts would not be competing in Los Angeles.

Despite the Iron Curtain boycott, one Communist country did decide to participate in the Olympics. Romania, the home nation of both Comaneci (by this time living in the United States) and Karolyi, had decided to forgo the Soviet order to boycott and sent an Olympic team to Los Angeles. Romania's gymnastics team, led by Ecaterina Szabo, was a formidable opponent for the U.S. squad. And Szabo, the reigning all-around world champion, was favored to win the all-around Olympic gold medal.

Retton knew that in order to beat Szabo she would have to be nearly flawless during all four events. She piled up a host of high scores on the balance beam, in the floor exercise, and on the uneven parallel bars. Szabo also performed exquisitely, and with one event to go, Retton was leading by a mere $2/100$ of a point. Retton's final event, the vault, was one of her strongest. She stood at the starting line, knowing that she needed a score of

9.8 or better to clinch the all-around gold. Retton sprinted down the mat, leaped on the board, and sprang off the vault. Twisting and turning high in the air, she came down solidly on both feet, stood straight, and beamed a winning smile at the crowd. Seconds later, the electric scoreboard made it official. Retton had not only won gold, but she had done so with a perfect score of 10.

The all-around gold was not Retton's only medal of the 1984 Olympics. She also won a team silver as the United States finished second to Romania in the team competition, and then added a silver in the individual vault competition and bronze medals in both the uneven parallel bars and the floor exercises. Her total of five Olympic medals remains a record for a U.S. gymnast of either gender.

After the Olympics, Retton became one of the most popular athletes in the United States. She endorsed numerous brands and appeared in many commercials. "Watch out, big boys!" she warned in a well-known cereal advertisement. After sharing the 1984 Sportsperson of the Year honors with gold-medal hurdler Edmund Moses, she retired from gymnastics and became a highly sought-after motivational speaker.

Retton wrote a gymnastics column for *USA Today* during the 1992 and 1996 Olympics. She has also served as a commentator in the television broadcast booth, providing useful explanations and thoughts during Olympic and World Championship gymnastics competitions. She married Shannon Kelly, a football player, in 1996. The couple have two daughters, Kayla and McKenna.

Further Reading

Biography.com. "Mary Lou Retton." Available online. URL: www.biography.com/magazine/biomag/marylou.html/. Downloaded on December 28, 2001.

Christian Speakers.com. "Mary Lou Retton." Available online. URL: http://www.christianspeakers.com/speakers/retton.htm. Downloaded on February 15, 2001.

Layden, Joe. *Women in Sports: The Complete Book on the World's Greatest Female Athletes.* Santa Monica, Calif.: General Publishing Group, 1997, pp. 195–196.

RICHARDSON, DOT
(Dorothy Richardson)
(1961–)   *Softball Player*

Dot Richardson was the star shortstop for the U.S. women's softball team during the gold-medal campaigns in the 1996 and 2000 Olympic Games. Off the diamond, she was and is an orthopedic surgeon with a thriving practice.

Dorothy Richardson was born in Orlando, Florida, on September 22, 1961. Her father, Ken, was an air force mechanic, and Dot, along with her three siblings and her mother, Joyce, lived on several military bases during her childhood. Although Dot showed an affinity and a passion for baseball when she was very young, it was hard for her to find a team to play on. Little League teams did not allow girls to play during the late 1960s and early 1970s, and Dot, who had as much talent as any of the boys in her area, was confined to neighborhood games. The situation was so outlandish that once, when Dot was playing the boys in a street contest, a Little League coach approached her. "Honey," the coach said, "I'd love for you to play for me. If you don't mind, we'll just cut your hair and call you Bob." Dot, insulted by the incident, refused the offer.

When Dot was 10, she was spotted by another coach. This time, it was a happier meeting, as the coach told Dot that he would like her to try out for his team, a softball squad called the Union Park Jets. Dot, who had never considered softball as an alternative to her beloved baseball, was thrilled. She was even more delighted when she made the team—a rather astonishing achievement, given the fact that she was 10 and the average age of her teammates was 26. But Dot earned her place on the diamond, playing a stellar shortstop and batting well enough to make the league's all-star team.

Richardson played several sports at Orlando's Colonial High School, including tennis, track and field, and softball. She then went to Western Illinois University, where she played softball for a year and led the nation with a .480 average. A year later, in the fall of 1980, she transferred to the University of California at Los Angeles (UCLA) and played for the Bruins. During her first season in a Bruins uniform, she led the team to the first National Collegiate Athletic Association (NCAA) women's softball championship. Voted an All-American for each of her three years at UCLA, Richardson won the NCAA women's softball Player of the Decade honor for the 1980s.

But as talented as Richardson was on the field, she had another passion as well. A premed student at UCLA, she intended to continue her medical training after college and become a doctor. In 1983, she went to medical school at the University of Louisville, and after completing her degree there in 1986, she returned to California to take a residency at the University of Southern California (USC). It was hard for Richardson, who was training to become an orthopedic surgeon, to continue her softball career while she was at Louisville and USC, but she kept in shape on her own time. While at Louisville she would fly on weekends to Stamford, Connecticut, to play for the Raybestos Brakettes, an amateur softball team. And at USC, she would return from long hours at the hospital to practice hitting the ball in her room, where she had installed her own pitching machine and net.

Somehow Richardson managed to stay sharp on the diamond as well as in the classroom. In 1995, she discovered that for the first time in history, the 1996 Olympic Games in Atlanta would feature women's softball as a medal sport. Competing in the Olympics was a lifelong ambition for Richardson, who applied for—and received—permission from the American Medical Association to take exactly one year off in order to play in Atlanta. Then she tried out for and made the national softball team.

Richardson and her teammates played superb ball in front of the home crowd at the 1996 Olympics. After cruising through the early rounds with only one loss, the team faced China in the gold-medal game. It was a close game from the start as both teams played stellar defense. In the top of the third inning, Richardson threw a runner out at the plate to keep the game scoreless, but her really heroic moment came in the bottom of the third. With a runner on third and nobody out, Richardson came to the plate. After taking a strike from China's ace pitcher, Liu Yaju, Richardson swung and hit the ball down the left field line. The ball wrapped around the foul pole in fair territory and landed in the bleachers for a home run. Richardson's blast gave the United States a lead they would never relinquish, as they beat the Chinese 3-1 to win gold.

Elated with the championship, Richardson celebrated with the team, but then packed her things. Her one-year leave ended the day after the Olympic victory, and she was due back at USC. She flew back to the Los Angeles campus, where she was greeted by the school marching band.

Four years later, Richardson, now a practicing orthopedic surgeon, returned to the softball team to help the U.S. team defend its title at the 2000 Olympic Games in Sydney, Australia. The team was not as strong as it had been in 1996, but it did get through some early-round defeats to qualify for the medal games. In the semifinal, Richardson smacked two hits and drove in the winning run as the U.S. team defeated the hometown Australians to earn a ticket to the gold-medal game against Japan. One day later, Richardson contributed to the winning U.S. effort with remarkable defense and a timely walk as the United States beat Japan by a score of 2 to 1 to earn a second gold medal.

Richardson has a successful orthopedic practice in southern California. "I just love orthopedic surgery," she said in 1996. "Whether it's a child with a birth defect whom I'm able to help walk better or an athlete working to get back on the field, it's very rewarding." Her other love, of course, is softball, which she continues to play in her spare time. The game still fills Richardson

While Dot Richardson was still in medical school, she was granted a one-year leave by the American Medical Association so she could play softball for the Olympic team in 1996. Her home run in the gold-medal game helped give the Americans the first Olympic women's softball Championship.
(Andy Lyons/Getty Images)

with delight. "When you watch me play," she told the *Oregonian* in 1997, "I hope you see an expression of pure joy."

Further Reading

"Dot Richardson." Dot Richardson Enterprises, Inc. Available online. URL: http://www.dotrichardson.com/home.htm. Downloaded on December 28, 2001.

Smith, Lissa, editor. *Nike Is a Goddess: The History of Women in Sports.* New York: Atlantic Monthly Press, 1998, pp. 252–255.

RIDDLES, LIBBY
(1956–)   *Dogsled Racer*

Libby Riddles is the first woman ever to win the Iditarod, the 1,000-plus-mile dogsled race through the heart of Alaska.

Not surprisingly, Libby Riddles always loved the outdoors. Born in St. Cloud, Minnesota on April 10, 1956, her first ambition was to become a cowgirl. But by the time she was in high school, Riddles knew that she wanted to live in Alaska. She had fallen in love with the idea of living in a frozen northern wilderness. After graduating from high school, Riddles took a job as a bank teller, saved most of her money, and soon had enough cash to buy a plane ticket.

Shortly after settling in a small town near Anchorage, Riddles learned how to train and race dogs. Beginning with small races that covered short or middle distances, she worked on her technique and endurance. Finally, in 1981, she decided she was ready to compete in the Iditarod. In that race, Riddles finished 20th, and she met a fellow racer named Joe Garnie. Riddles and Garnie teamed up romantically and professionally. The couple moved to Teller, Alaska, and opened a kennel, where they bred and trained more than 60 dogs.

In the meantime, Riddles continued to race. In 1985, she entered her fifth consecutive Iditarod, but few on the scene viewed her as a major contender. Most experts predicted that if a woman emerged victorious that year, it would be SUSAN BUTCHER, who had been among the top 10 finishers the previous two years. But Butcher had to withdraw midway through the event, when her dogs were attacked by a moose in the middle of the wilderness.

Riddles, meanwhile, had driven a sure and steady course. Eight hundred miles into the race, she decided to take a major gamble. As her fellow racers spent the night in an Inuit village, Riddles arose in the middle of the night. While a major snowstorm blanketed the course and lowered visibility dramatically, she got on her sled and resumed the race. As 40-mile-per-hour winds blew, Riddles made steady, if sometimes slow, progress. Conditions were so poor that at times she could not see the next marker on the trail. "I'd put my snowhook in and walk up ahead of the dogs until I could see the next marker," Riddles explained later. "And we repeated that process. It was very slow. For some idiot reason the dogs trusted that I knew what I was doing." Her patience and perseverance paid off. At the end of the race, she crossed the finish line well ahead of the nearest competitor.

The victory made national news. A woman had won the grueling Iditarod race! Suddenly dogsled racing, formerly delegated to the back pages of sports sections, was a front-page story. Riddles was invited to the White House, where she met President Ronald Reagan. She was interviewed by *Vogue* magazine, and the Women's Sports Foundation named her the Professional Woman Athlete of 1985. For Riddles, the victory had its own dividends. "Now every time I ride a cab in Nome," she said of the city where the Iditarod race completes its run, "it's free."

Riddles has yet to win another Iditarod. She finished 16th in 1989 and 32nd in 1995. She continues to race however, and in addition, she gives motivational speeches, produces independent films, and writes about her life as a champion dogsled racer.

Further Reading

Anchorage Daily News Iditarod Hall of Fame: "Libby Riddles," *Anchorage Daily News.* Available online. URL: http://www.adn.com/iditarod/hallfame/riddles.html. Downloaded on February 17, 2001.

Freedman, Lew. *Iditarod Classics: Tales of the Trail from the Men and Women Who Race Across Alaska.* Fairbanks, Ak.: Epicenter, 1992.

Layden, Joe. *Women in Sports: The Complete Book on the World's Greatest Female Athletes.* Santa Monica, Calif.: General Publishing Group, 1997, p. 200.

"Libby Riddles," Copyright Elizabeth Beckett and Sarah Teel. Available online. URL: http://library.thinkquest.

org/11313/Iditarod/libby.html. Downloaded on February 17, 2001.

"Meet Libby Riddles," Female Frontiers. Available online. URC: http://quest.arc.nasa.gov/space/frontiers/riddles. html. Downloaded on February 17, 2001.

RIGBY, CATHY
(1952–) *Gymnast*

The first U.S. gymnast to place in the top 10 at an Olympic competition, Cathy Rigby overcame a host of illnesses and personal pressures to become a successful entertainer.

Cathy Rigby was born on December 12, 1952, in Long Beach, California. A premature baby who weighed only four pounds at birth, Cathy suffered from chronic bronchitis and pneumonia as a young child. Nevertheless she was extremely active and flexible, so much so that when she was 10, her father hired Bud Marquette, then the coach of the Southern California Acro Team, a local gymnastics team, to give Cathy lessons in gymnastics. Cathy's strength and courage impressed Marquette from the start. "You can't teach fearlessness," he said of his young student. "It has to be inborn. And you can't be a gymnast without it."

Not only was Rigby fearless, but she was talented as well. In 1968, at the age of 16, she qualified for the U.S. Olympic team. At the games that year in Mexico City, the U.S. women placed sixth overall. Rigby proved to be the top gymnast on the national squad, finishing 16th in the competition at Mexico City. It was an impressive finish; in the late 1950s, 1960s, and 1970s, competitive gymnastics was completely dominated by teams from Eastern Europe, particularly those from the Soviet Union and Romania. Placing in the top 20 at an international competition was an impressive feat for a U.S. gymnast, and Rigby's achievement did not go unnoticed by the gymnastics community.

When she returned from Mexico City, Rigby suddenly represented the best hope for U.S. glory in gymnastics. It was a great burden for anyone to bear, and Rigby responded to the pressure admirably. She began training relentlessly, and the effort paid off handsomely. At the 1970 world championships, she won a silver medal in the balance beam event—the first U.S. gymnast ever to win a medal in an international competition.

As Rigby ascended the international gymnastics rankings, the publicity surrounding her increased exponentially. Rigby, who had decided to enroll at California State University in Long Beach after graduating from high school, dropped out of college to devote herself fully to training. Feeling the pressure to keep her weight down, she developed bulimia—a condition she would later defeat and then talk about openly.

Rigby was expected to dominate the 1972 Olympic trials completely, but she fell off the high bar during her dismount. She escaped injury, but lost valuable points in the process. Two days later she twisted her ankle in the floor exercise competition and had to withdraw from the competition. Although Rigby did not place in the top three— ordinarily an achievement a gymnast must accomplish in order to make the Olympic team—the judges decided to exercise a special privilege and placed Rigby on the team.

Once in Munich, the site of the 1972 games, Rigby moved fearfully on each apparatus, she appeared tentative and performed without the spontaneity that had graced her performance at the Mexico City games. Nonetheless, she performed solidly in a competition dominated by an up-and-coming Soviet gymnast named Olga Korbut. Rigby led her squad to a fourth-place team finish—the highest a U.S. team had ever placed up to that time—and she took 10 place in the individual all-around competition.

Although she failed to win a medal, Rigby returned to the United States a hero. She appeared on countless magazine covers and talk shows, as well as on television commercials, endorsing various products. Rigby was a gracious and willing participant in all of this publicity, but when she began to face pressure to train for the 1976 Olympics, she elected to retire from competition instead.

Rigby did travel to Montreal for the 1976 Olympic Games but as a media correspondent rather than a competitor. She sat comfortably in the broadcast booth and provided expert commentary as Romania's Nadia Comaneci turned in the first perfect scores in Olympic history. The following year, Rigby married Tom McCoy, a marketing consultant.

In addition to her commentary, Rigby embarked on an entirely new career when she agreed to play the title role in a Broadway revival of the musical *Peter Pan*. She would perform the role semiregularly during the next six years, and in 2000, she played the part in a cable television broadcast of the play.

Further Reading

Layden, Joe. *Women in Sports: The Complete Book on the World's Greatest Female Athletes.* Santa Monica, Calif.: General Publishing Group, 1997, pp. 201–202.

Biography Resource Center. "Cathy Rigby," *American Decades CD-ROM.* Gale Research, 1998.

Biography Resource Center, "Cathy Rigby," *Great Women in Sports.* Detroit: Visible Ink Press, 1986.

RIGGIN, AILEEN
(Aileen Young, Aileen Soule)
(1906–)   *Diver, Swimmer*

When Aileen Riggin won the springboard diving event at the 1920 Olympics in Antwerp, Belgium, she was only 14 years old—at the time the youngest athlete of either gender to win an Olympic championship. Four years later, at the Paris games, Riggin would become the first athlete in history to win Olympic medals in swimming and diving when she took the bronze in the 100-meter backstroke race.

Born in New York City on May 2, 1906, Aileen Riggin was a competitive swimmer from an early age. She was also a passionate diver; although she never had formal training in the sport, she had a natural talent, and absolutely no fear when flying off the springboard. In early 1919, Aileen, an eighth-grader who competed on weekends for the Women's Swimming Association of New York, learned that the Antwerp Olympic Games would have aquatic events for women.

Aileen Riggin, who won a gold medal in springboard diving at the 1920 Olympic Games, became the first athlete to win a medal in both swimming and diving when she took a bronze in the 100-meter backstroke at the Paris games in 1924.
(Library of Congress)

The U.S. Olympic Committee was strongly opposed to sending women to Antwerp, believing that competing in such an intense environment was not suitable for the "gentler" of the genders. Nevertheless, Aileen began training seriously for this potential opportunity. Conditions in the United States were far from ideal for women divers; there were no swimming pools with diving boards that women could use. Aileen practiced by diving off the side of the pool, and she made the Olympic team.

Although she had earned the right to go to Antwerp, Aileen still faced dissension and disapproval, this time because of her age. The Olympic Committee argued that both 14-year-old Riggin and her diving teammate, Helen Wainwright, who was also 14, were too young to represent the United States. Fortunately for both divers, the manager of the Women's Swimming Association convinced the officials that the two girls would not embarrass their home nation, and eventually Wainwright and Riggin sailed to Antwerp with the rest of the team.

Teammates and friends on their home turf, Wainwright and Riggin became top rivals once the springboard diving competition got under way in Antwerp. Far and away the most powerful competitors, the two girls challenged each other throughout the compulsory dives and through the early portion of the free-diving segment. They were in a virtual tie near the end of the competition, but then Riggin, the final diver of the day, executed a near-perfect running forward layout somersault to capture top honors. The diminutive New Yorker stroked to the victory stand to receive her prize and stood all of four feet, eight inches tall as she accepted her medal. Not only was Riggin the youngest athlete at the time to win an Olympic gold, but she was also the smallest.

Four years later, Riggin once again qualified for the U.S. diving team and also earned a place on the swim squad. This time no one questioned her right to compete in the Olympics, which were held that year in Paris. When the springboard diving competition got under way, Riggin again found herself in a tight race for the gold with a U.S. diver. However, Riggin's effort fell short, as she took second place behind the gold medal efforts of her teammate Elizabeth Becker. But three days later Riggin made history again, when she won a bronze medal in the 100-meter backstroke race. Not only is Riggin the first athlete to win medals in both swimming and diving, but she remains the only U.S. Olympian of either gender to compete in both events.

Riggin returned to the United States after the Paris games. Two years later she retired from amateur competition and began to spread her sporting wings in dramatic fashion. She appeared as a featured performer in the first coaching movie for aspiring swimmers, served a stint as a sportswriter for a newspaper, skated in a SONJA HENIE movie, and performed, along with her friend ELEANOR

HOLM, in the first Aquacade, produced by Holm's husband, Billy Rose.

As of early 2002, Riggin is in her 10th decade. Married to Howard Soule since the mid-1950s (her first husband, Dwight Young, was killed in World War II), she lives in Hawaii, where she still competes in master swimming events.

Further Reading

Layden, Joe. *Women in Sports: The Complete Book on the World's Greatest Female Athletes,* Santa Monica, Calif.: General Publishing Group, 1997, pp. 202–203.

Rabalais, Scott. "Stories about USMS Swimmers—Aileen Riggin Soul," *SWIM Magazine,* May/June 1996. United States Masters Swimming. Available online. URL. http://www.swimgold.org/55/sto/sou06eb.htm.

Wulf, Steve, "She Has Done Just Swimmingly," *Time,* Summer Special Issue, vol. 148, no.1, p. 96.

RILEY, DAWN (Wendy Riley)
(1964–   )   *Sailor*

Dawn Riley, the first woman to work as a crew member for an America's Cup winner, is also the first woman to captain an all-women's entry in the America's Cup, where she took command of a boat that raced in the 1995 competition.

Born Wendy Riley in Detroit, Michigan, on July 21, 1964, Dawn Riley (she changed her first name when she was 12) first became intrigued with sailing when she was 13. That year her father, Chuck, a marketer, and mother, Prudence, a massage therapist, took their three children out of school to go on a family sail. The sail, which lasted a full year, took the Rileys from Detroit to New York, then southward to the Caribbean, and then back again. On the day they got back, Dawn got a call from someone looking for a crew member. "We're having a race and we need someone to help out," the person said. "Know anyone?" Dawn joined the race, and became hooked on the sport once and for all.

The next year, Dawn joined the North Star Sailing Club, where she became commodore of the junior sailing program. After earning a degree from Michigan State University in 1987, Riley

Dawn Riley, who became the first woman ever to crew for an America's Cup champion yacht in 1992, skippered the first all-women's yacht to compete in this most prestigious of yacht races when she took the helm of the America 3 in 1995.
(Getty Images)

turned her full attention to sailing. Three years later she worked as the watch captain and engineer on the *Maiden,* which sailed with an all-women's team in the 1989–90 Whitbread, which is a year-long, round-the-world race.

In 1992, Riley decided to focus more fully on match races, and she promptly gained a spot on the crew on the *America3,* which took top honors at the America's Cup that year. The most prestigious event in yacht racing, the America's Cup is either a best-of-seven or a best-of-nine regatta that pits the finest sailors in the world against one another. In the 1992 race, Riley worked as pitman—meaning that she worked in the cockpit of the ship and han-

dled the sails—for Bill Koch's *America3* yacht, which entered the race as an underdog to the Italian and New Zealand entries. After enduring eight grueling months of qualifying races, the *America3* defeated Dennis Connor's *Stars and Stripes* entry to reach the finals. Racing against the Italian entry in the final, Koch, Riley, and company took the *America3* to victory by a 4-1 score.

Three years later, Riley returned to the America's Cup, this time as skipper of the *America3.* By this time, Riley was a highly experienced sailor, having skippered the *Heineken* and an all-woman crew in the 1993–94 Whitbread race. For the 1995 America's Cup, Riley had once again chosen an all-female crew, making the ship the first all-woman boat to race in the America's Cup. Riley and company competed gamely, but they lost in the challenging round to Dennis Connor's ship, the *Young America.* Connor and his crew would reach the final, only to lose to New Zealand by a score of 5-0. With two America's Cups under her belt, Riley took a position as crew member on the Maxi Yacht *Morning Glory,* which set the all-time course record in the 1996 Sydney-to-Hobart ocean race.

In 1995, Riley started her own foundation. Called America True, Riley's organization promotes and teaches the sport of sailing to young people. The America True foundation also sponsored its own yacht, *America True,* for the 2000 America's Cup. Riley and her co-ed crew participated in the challenger races in 1999, but lost out to the eventual finalist, the *Prada.* After those challenge rounds, Riley stayed in Auckland, New Zealand, where she has a home. A motivational speaker and author as well as the finest woman sailor in the history of the sport, Riley will prepare the *America True* for the next America's Cup, in 2003.

Further Reading

Larson, Paul C. *America's Cup: The Women's Team.* Los Angeles: Summit Publishing Group, 1997.
Noonan, Peggy. "Dawn Riley: Women to Watch," Women. com. Available online. URL: http://www.women.com/ career/riley.htm. Downloaded on July 10, 2001.

⊞ ROBERTS, ROBIN
(1960–)   *Commentator*

Robin Roberts has served as the voice of the Women's National Basketball Association (WNBA) on ESPN since the league's inception in 1997. The first African-American broadcaster ever hired by ESPN, Roberts brings not only good on-air presence but tremendous intelligence and knowledge to the broadcast booth.

Born in Pass Christian, Mississippi, on November 23, 1960, Robin Roberts inherited her strong will and pioneering talent from her parents. Her father, Lawrence Roberts, served as a member of the Tuskegee Airmen during World War II, and her mother, Lucimrian, was for many years an active member of the Mississippi Board of Education. Robin was a natural athlete who won the state junior bowling championships at the age of 10 and later starred for her high school basketball team.

Roberts enrolled at Southeastern Louisiana University on a basketball scholarship in 1978, and she became the third leading rebounder and scorer in school history. But Roberts was just as interested in school as she was in sports. Inspired by her older sister, Sally-Ann, who was an on-air local news anchor, in college Robin decided to major in communications with the hope of becoming a television sports reporter.

After graduating from Southeastern Louisiana State University in 1982, Roberts took a job as a sportscaster for a local television station in Hattiesburg, Mississippi, and several years later moved to Nashville to take a similar job. In 1987, a recruiter for ESPN noticed Roberts's work, and offered her a job for the network. Interestingly, Roberts turned down the offer; she thought she needed more experience in a large market, so she ended up taking a job at an Atlanta station.

Three years later, ESPN beckoned again. This time, she was offered a job as an anchor on the network's late-night edition of *SportsCenter.* Roberts accepted the offer, and two months after arriving at the station she became the anchor of *NFL Prime Time* and *Sunday Sports Day.*

During her tenure at ESPN, Roberts has served as commentator for the National Collegiate Athletic Association (NCAA) women's basketball tournament final, as well as lead broadcaster for the WNBA games. In addition, Roberts has produced her own series, *SportsLight,* a program that examines the influence of sports on successful people.

In addition to assignments for ESPN, Roberts has served as host of ABC's *Wide World of Sports* since 1996. Working for both networks, Roberts has become one of the leading figures—of either gender—in sports broadcasting. As comfortable discussing sports issues as she is giving play-by-play, Roberts is one of a growing number of African-American female role models. She relishes this role and happily notes that opportunities for women in sports have steadily increased during her career. "It's a little easier today for a woman to find a place in a mostly male industry, thanks to the accomplishments of so many women athletes," she said in 2001. Those who find rewarding jobs in television also owe a debt of gratitude to Robin Roberts, who helped blaze the broadcasting trail.

Further Reading

Hellmann, Carrie Lutes. "Robin Roberts Obeys Mom, Steps up to Mike," Presbyterian News Service, May 22, 2001. Available online. URL: http://www.pcusa.org/pcnews/01175.htm. Downloaded on June 29, 2001.

Biography Resource Center. "Robin Roberts," *Contemporary Black Biography.* Volume 16. Detroit: Gale Research, 1997.

⊞ RUDOLPH, WILMA
(1940–1994)   *Sprinter*

What are the chances that a child who could not walk at the age of four would one day run faster than any woman in the world? Call it a long shot or a miracle, but Wilma Rudolph, a sickly child, grew to up to win three gold medals in the sprinting events in the 1960 Olympic Games in Rome.

Rudolph, who was born on June 23, 1940, in Clarksville, Tennessee, was the 17th child born to her father, a railroad porter named Ed Rudolph, during two marriages. Wilma was born prematurely and was a small and disease-prone toddler. Bouts with double pneumonia and then with scarlet fever left her so weak that her left leg was virtually paralyzed. Rudolph would drag herself around her house but could not put any pressure whatsoever on the soles of her feet. Fortunately for Rudolph, her mother, Blanche Rudolph was intent on seeing Wilma walk. Once a week for two years, Blanche would take her daughter—in the back of the Greyhound bus—to Nashville to see a specialist. The Nashville doctor put heavy orthopedic shoes on Wilma's feet and a brace on her left leg. At home, Wilma's mother or one of her 16 older siblings would give her long leg massages every day.

The family slowly but surely saw their tireless work begin to pay off. At the age of six Wilma began hopping on one foot. At eight she was able to walk without help for the first time. At 10 she had shed all the heavy devices the Nashville doctor had prescribed for her but one orthopedic shoe, which she wore on her left foot. And in a memorable moment, when Wilma was 11, her mother watched dumbfounded as Wilma went outside and played basketball in her bare feet. She would never need the orthopedic shoe again.

It did not take Rudolph long after that to begin excelling at sports. At Burt High School she was a star basketball player, earning all-state honors twice. On the basketball floor Rudolph must have been quite a sight; she was a tall, skinny (89 pounds) young woman who was constantly buzzing around the court. Her coach, amused by his young player's constant energy, nicknamed her "Skeeter," and the name stuck.

But it was on the track that Rudolph was destined to make her mark. In 1955, when she was a sophomore, her high school coach recommended that Rudolph attend Ed Temple's summer track-training program. Temple, who was the track coach at Tennessee State University, held the program every summer to recruit promising high school athletes and also to keep his college runners in top shape. At Temple's camp, Rudolph met some of the nation's fastest runners. Mae Faggs,

already a veteran of two Olympic Games, was one of the athletes on campus. Another was Isable Daniels, who like Rudolph was a high school student, but she had several junior sprinting records under her belt.

Temple trained his athletes to compete in the National Amateur Athletic Union (AAU) outdoor meet in Ponca City, Oklahoma. True to form, Faggs won the 100-yard and 220-yard events at the meet. Rudolph, by contrast, distinguished herself not at all in her national competition debut, finishing fourth in the 75-yard dash.

Rudolph left Temple's camp discouraged. The Olympics were a year away, and she had very little confidence in her ability. At one point she even considered quitting track completely, even though she was improving markedly during practices. It was Mae Faggs, the surrogate mother on Temple's team, who encouraged Rudolph to keep training—"Stick close to me," she told the younger runner. Rudolph heeded her words. In races when both runners competed, Rudolph would look up from her starting blocks, spot Faggs, and remind herself to stay close.

The strategy worked; Rudolph finished second to Faggs in the 200-meter race at the 1956 AAU meet in Philadelphia. One week later, at the Olympic trials in Washington, D.C., she repeated her second place 200-meter finish, behind Faggs again, to earn a place on the U.S. Olympic squad.

The U.S. track team that competed in Melbourne in 1956 traveled to Australia with high hopes of Olympic glory. But reality set in soon after their arrival. It was cold and rainy in Melbourne, and the weather seemed to bog down the U.S. competitors. Margaret Mathews, a long jumper expected to win gold for the United States, fouled out early in her event and did not qualify for the finals. Rudolph also performed poorly; she did not survive the trial heats for the 200-meter race. Even Faggs, the leader of the U.S. women's team, did not make the finals of the 200-meter event, losing in the semifinal heat of the competition.

The U.S. women's team entered the relay portion of the Olympic competition with no medals and low spirits. One of the runners on the 4×100 team, in fact, was so depressed and nervous that she refused to compete and had to be replaced. By the time the qualifying heats began, the team included three Tennessee State veterans—Faggs, Mathews, Isabel Daniels—and one high school junior, Wilma Rudolph.

The relay team did not perform smoothly during the qualifying heats, but the runners did do well enough to get to the finals. In the championship race, the U.S. runners finished third, a mere $^2/_{10}$ of a second behind the first-place, world-record-setting Australians. Wilma "Skeeter" Rudolph had helped the U.S. women win their only medal at the Melbourne Olympics. The achievement did wonders for her confidence.

Rudolph returned to the United States from Melbourne in late 1956, and the following summer, at age 16, she again attended Temple's summer camp. Competing in the girls' division, she set new AAU records in the girls' 75-yard and 100-yard events, and she also ran on a record-breaking 300-yard relay team. Rudolph began to set her sights on the next Olympiad, to be held in 1960 in Rome.

But in 1958, something unexpected happened. At the age of 17, Rudolph became pregnant. Raised in a devout Baptist family, Rudolph was uneducated in the facts of life and had very little idea what the consequences of having unprotected intercourse were. Fortunately for Rudolph, her family was fairly understanding. They told Wilma to have the child (although they forbade her to continue to see her boyfriend, whom they held responsible for the pregnancy), and they would help her care for the baby.

In the fall of 1958, Rudolph had a baby girl, whom she named Yolanda. One of Rudolph's older sisters, Yvonne, who was married and living in St. Louis, cared for the infant while Rudolph returned to training and to school—she was now a freshman at Tennessee State. In the meantime, however, she had taken a full year off from training. Her road to Rome would be a difficult one.

Rudolph divided her time at Tennessee State by working at the school post office, which helped

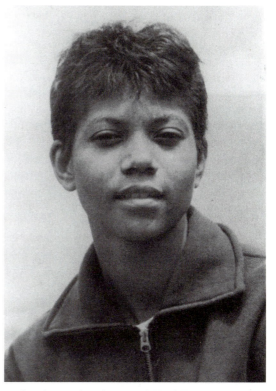

Stricken with polio as a child, Wilma Ruldolph would grow up to become one of the most decorated sprinters in track and field history. Rudolph won three gold medals at the 1960 Olympics.
(Library of Congress)

pay her room and board; studying to stay afloat in her classes; and, of course, training with Coach Temple. During this time Temple taught her the important elements of sprinting—the long scissoring stride, the lean at the finish—that would become closely associated with Rudolph after she became Olympic champion. She enjoyed the training, and it paid off for her.

In 1959 Rudolph won the AAU outdoor national championships in the 100-meter race, and the following year she completely dominated the AAU indoor championships at Chicago University, with victories in the 50-meter race, the 100-yard dash, and the 220-yard dash. In July of

1960 she competed in the AAU outdoor championships, claiming gold in 100- and 200-meter races and setting meet records in the process.

Rudolph easily made the 1960 Olympic team, but despite her achievements over the past two years, she was not the favorite to win gold in Rome. Barbara Jones, Rudolph's Tennessee State teammate, had missed the Melbourne Olympics because of injury but had captured gold in the 1952 Helsinki Games. She had also excelled at the Pan American Games in 1959 and had finished a very close second to Rudolph in the 100-meter race during the Olympic trials. Lucinda Williams, another Tennessee State runner, had won the 200-meter events at the 1958 AAU outdoor championships and at the Pan American Games in 1958 and 1959.

Both women posed a threat to Rudolph not only because of their physical talent, but because they were older and more confident runners. Jones and Williams were intent on winning gold. Rudolph, on the other hand, had no such clear goals in mind. "I remember talking to my mother before I left," Rudolph said later, "I said, 'Well, I am in three events. Maybe I can bring one medal back.'"

The U.S. team members were much more comfortable in Rome than they had been four years earlier in Melbourne. One major reason for the added confidence was that Ed Temple, coach not only to Rudolph but to Jones and Williams at Tennessee State, was named the coach of the U.S. track team and was on the premises the entire time.

Rudolph found a great deal of comfort in Temple's presence and eased her way through the early heats of the 100-meter event. But Jones, feeling the pressure of being favored, fell short in the semifinals. Rudolph quite simply blew away her competitors in the final of the event, beating her rivals by four yards. Her time of 11 seconds flat was a new world record. More important, perhaps, Rudolph had won gold—the first U.S. runner to do so in the 100-meter event since HELEN STEPHENS in 1936.

The 200-meter event was in many ways a carbon copy of the 100-meter race. Rudolph once

again easily made the finals—setting a world record in her first heat—and then stood on the sidelines while the event's favorite, this time Lucinda Williams, was disqualified in the semifinals. In the final, Rudolph breezed to victory for her second gold medal of the games.

Rudolph was slated to run in one more race—the 4 × 100 race. Running with teammates Williams, Jones, and Martha Hudson, Rudolph was chosen to anchor the race, meaning that she would run the fourth (final) leg. The relay is a competition that depends not only on the speed of the participants but also on the passing of the baton. Handing a stick off in a race may seem like a simple concept, but in fact it must be done precisely and quickly. Moreover, this handoff happens in the relay while both runners are in motion. Many relay races have hinged on the delicate maneuvering of the baton pass. And if it is done poorly, it can be costly. In 1996, for example, the U.S. men's 4 × 100 relay team, favored to win a medal, dropped the baton and failed to finish the race.

The U.S. women's relay team in 1960 was a speedy quartet, but they had fierce competition in the teams from the Soviet Union and Poland. The first three U.S. runners ran well, and Lucinda Williams, running the third leg, was in the lead as she prepared to hand the baton to Rudolph. But the handoff was a bad one—both racers bobbled the stick, and Rudolph had to slow down considerably to ensure that her grasp on the baton was secure. In the meantime, the Polish anchor, Jutte Heine, flew past her.

With the baton tucked safely in her hand at last, Rudolph put her head down and sprinted. With long, scissorlike strides, she caught Heine, and leaned into the tape in first place to clinch her third gold medal of the Rome games. Rudolph was now an Olympic hero.

Rudolph returned to Clarksville a celebrity. She was toasted in her hometown with a parade; people lined the streets to catch a glimpse of her, and her picture was in virtually every window. The following month she was seen by 300 million television viewers on *The Ed Sullivan Show,* and she made more than 100 personal appearances over the following few months. She met President Kennedy, who said, "It really is an honor to meet you and tell you what a magnificent runner you are." In December 1960, European sportswriters named her Sportswoman of the Year—the first time a U.S. athlete had won the honor—as did the Associated Press.

But fame and glory aside, Rudolph was still a student at Tennessee State. She continued to work at the post office for room and board—Olympic glory in 1960 did not lead, as it can today, to million-dollar endorsement contracts. Rudolph had left Rome a hero, but not a millionaire. She continued to train and to compete. She won the 100-meter event and was on the top-finishing 4×100 relay team (she chose not to compete in the 200-meter event) at the 1961 AAU outdoor championships.

By 1962, however, Rudolph was becoming world-weary. She realized that no matter what she did on the track, she would be hard-pressed to top her own prior performances. With that in mind, she retired from track and field and completed her degree in education at Tennessee State. After graduating, she became an elementary school teacher and coach in Tennessee, and several years later she headed a community center in Indiana.

Rudolph also spent time with her daughter, Yolanda. In 1963 she married Robert Eldridge, Yolanda's father, and the couple had four more children before divorcing in 1976. Rudolph spent a great deal of time in the late 1970s and 1980s working as the head of the Wilma Rudolph Foundation, which worked to motivate children through sports. Sadly, Rudolph was diagnosed with an inoperable brain tumor in 1993, and died a year later, at the age of 54.

Wilma Rudolph will be remembered as a top athlete—the first sprinter to win Olympic gold since 1936, and the first African-American female sprinting champion. But her legacy includes not only excellence on the track but generosity off it. Through her work as a coach and teacher she reached thousands of children. Moreover, her athletic achievements are a lasting inspiration, reminding us all that if a young girl can shed her leg braces and sprint to Olympic gold, perhaps anything is possible.

Further Reading

Davis, Michael D. *Black American Women in Olympic Track and Field: A Complete Illustrated Reference.* Jefferson, N.C.: McFarland & Co., 1992.

Layden, Joe. *Women in Sports: The Complete Book on the World's Greatest Female Athletes.* Santa Monica, Calif.: General Publishing Group, 1997, pp. 209–210.

Rathbun, Elizabeth. *Grace and Glory: A Century of Women in the Olympics.* New York: Triumph Books, 1996.

S

ST. JAMES, LYN (Evelyn Cromwell)
(1947–)   *Race Car Driver*

Lyn St. James, the first woman to record a 200-miles-per-hour time on an oval track, was the second woman to race in the Indianapolis 500 and the first woman to win a professional race driving solo. A successful entrepreneur as well a racer, St. James has succeeded in a field that has always posed a challenge for its women participants.

Evelyn Cromwell (she changed her last name when she began racing) was born in Willoughby, Ohio, on March 13, 1947. An only child, Lyn first became interested in cars as a young child. Her father, Alfred, was a sheet metal worker who inspired Lyn's fascination with machines, and her mother, Judy, was crippled when she was a child—"the only way she could get around was in a car," Lyn remembered later.

Although Lyn was a talented athlete, her main focus at the Andrews School for Girls, where she attended high school, was music. Lyn diligently studied the piano at Andrews, but she also found another passion. One night Lyn went to the drag races with a group of friends. One of her cronies was racing that night, and after he lost the heat, he

gave Lyn a challenge: "If you think you can do better," he said, "go ahead." Lyn hopped in his car, entered a heat—and won. The next day, however, it was back to school and back to the piano.

After graduating from Andrews, Cromwell went to the St. Louis Institute for Music, where she earned a piano-teaching certificate. Lyn returned to Ohio after graduating from the institute, took a job as a secretary, and taught piano on the side. She also began racing on a regular basis. It was at the track that she met her first husband, John Caruso, whom she married in the early 1970s. Caruso and Cromwell began racing in local Sports Car Club of America (SCCA) events. Cromwell's car spun out of control and landed in a pond during her first SCCA race, but she soon mastered the courses. After winning back-to-back SCCA Florida Regional Championships in 1976 and 1977, and then advancing to the SCCA National Runoffs the following year, she decided to pursue sponsors and turn professional.

Always an assertive entrepreneur, Cromwell changed her name officially to Lyn St. James (inspired by the television actress Susan St. James) and promptly talked the Ford Motor Company into sponsoring her. In 1981 she won the Top

Woman Driver award in the International Motor Sports Association Kelly American Challenge series. Four years later, she became the first woman to win a North American Professional road race driving solo when she took top honors at an event in Watkins Glen, New York. Later in 1985 she achieved another first when she averaged more than 200 miles per hour on the oval track at Alabama's Talladega Superspeedway. She also won back-to-back titles at one of the most prestigious races, the Daytona 24 Hours marathon, when she and a male team of drivers took top honors in 1987 and 1988.

By this time St. James was by all accounts a successful race car driver. Moreover, she had achieved her success in one of the most difficult sports that a woman can compete in. In theory, women should be as competent as men when it comes to driving a car; it does not, after all, demand superior strength or manual speed, only perfect timing and fearlessness. In truth, however, the sport is one of the most difficult for a woman to excel in; the vast majority of drivers have always been male, and the few females who have tried to smash the glass ceiling have been ostracized by their peers and often rejected both by fans and potential sponsors.

St. James did run into some trouble on the sponsorship front in 1991 when Ford decided to drop St. James, along with some other drivers. But always the diligent entrepreneur, St. James sought other sponsors immediately, and the following year, she was able to persuade Goodyear, JC Penney, Agency Rent-A-Car, and Danskin to cosponsor her latest endeavor: Using a million-dollar car, St. James was planning to enter the 1992 Indianapolis 500 race.

In the vaunted history of the event, only one woman had ever qualified for the Indianapolis 500. That was JANET GUTHRIE, who became the first woman on the Indy track in 1976. St. James easily qualified for the 1992 event and then finished a respectable 11th. The effort was good enough to earn St. James, by then a 45-year-old veteran, Rookie-of-the-Year honors.

St. James, who has also competed in the Indianapolis 500 in 1993, 1994, and 1995, continues to race. Married since 1993 to Roger Lessman (she divorced her first husband in 1987), her goal is to ultimately set a new land speed record (the current mark is 413 miles per hour). It is a challenging goal, but as her record shows, St. James has a knack for getting what she pursues.

Further Reading

Biography Resource Center. "Lyn St. James," *Great Women in Sports*. Detroit: Visible Ink Press, 1996.

Indianapolis 500: Meet the Drivers, "90—Lyn St. James," CBS Sportsline. Available online. URL: http://poll.sportsline.com/u/racing/auto/indy/1997/drivers/stjames.htm. Downloaded on June 30, 2001.

SAUNDERS, TRICIA
(Patricia McNaughton)
(1966–) *Freestyle Wrestler*

The freestyle wrestler Tricia Saunders is one of the world's top competitors in the relatively young sport of woman's wrestling. A three-time world champion, Saunders gained experience wrestling against boys, and at one point she had to sue for the right to compete.

Patricia McNaughton was born into a family of wrestlers in Ann Arbor, Michigan, on February 21, 1966. Tricia's father, grandfather, and older brothers had all competed in wrestling, so Tricia began practicing moves and flips when she was very young. At the age of nine, she entered her first tournament. Competing only against boys, Tricia won seven of her first nine matches. In 1976, at age 10, she took the Michigan title in the 50-pound-and-under weight class—the first girl ever to win that state tile.

By that time, Tricia had already seen her share of controversy. Scheduled to compete in the 1975 Amateur Athletic Union (AAU) Eastern National Age Group tournament—the only female to qualify—she was banned from the competition on the basis of her gender. Tricia's parents sued the AAU. Although the ruling was in her favor, it came too late for Tricia to compete in the tournament.

After winning the state title in 1976, Tricia decided—at the ripe old age of 12—to retire from the sport. She felt that she had gone as far as she could as a female freestyle wrestler. Tricia enrolled at the University of Wisconsin at Madison in 1984 and graduated four years later. Diploma in hand, Saunders decided to return to wrestling, which by then was officially recognized as a sport for women as well as men.

It did not take Saunders long to regain her form. In 1990 she became the first U.S. champion and then went on to win three world championships, in 1992, 1996, and 1998. Saunders, who became the first recipient of the U.S. Wrestling Woman of the Year award, has been married to Townsend Saunders, who won a silver medal in wrestling at the 1996 Olympic Games, since 1997. The couple lives in Phoenix and has two children.

The holder of nine national wrestling champions, Saunders hopes to compete at the Olympics in 2004, when women's freestyle wrestling will become an official medal sport.

Further Reading

CNN/SI-SI For Women. "Spotlight: Tricia Saunders," United States Wrestling Online. Available online. URL: http://sportsillustrated.cnn.com/siforwomen/news/1999/04/26/sportlight. Posted on April 21 1999.

Longman, Jere. "Women Move Closer to Olympic Equality," *The New York Times* (August 20, 2000): 1, 22.

⊞ SEARS, ELEONORA (Eleo Sears)

(1881–1968) *Squash Player, Tennis Player, Equestrian*

Many athletes excel at one sport or another, but few reach elite heights in more than one event. That Eleonora Sears won championships in both squash and tennis and was also one of the finest equestrians of her time is a tribute to her talent, her tenacity, and above all, her versatility.

"I began exercising the moment I fell out of my crib," Sears once told a friend, and in truth, Eleonora "Eleo" Sears, who was born into a world of privilege on September 28, 1881, in Boston, remained in action all of her life. She was also a member of one of America's aristocratic families: Her father, Frederick Richard Sears, was a shipping executive; her mother, Eleonora Randolph Coolidge Sears, descended from a most prominent American family—she was the great-granddaughter of Thomas Jefferson.

Frederick Sears was a tennis enthusiast (he allegedly played on the first tennis court ever built in the United States), and his daughter inherited his love of the game. Tennis in the early part of the 20th century was an elegant game for the upper class. Eleo's contemporaries would appear on the court dressed in formal tennis clothes—full dresses with long sleeves—and would spend an easy hour patting the ball over the net. Eleo, by contrast, ran around the court in short sleeves—appalling some aristocratic audiences—and smacked every shot as though she were competing in a tournament.

Sears brought the same level of energy to every sport she played—of which there were many. During her early years, Sears would become an accomplished player of baseball, football (she played quarterback), polo, and skeet shooter. She also excelled at water sports; Sears once swam the five-mile distance between Newport and French Beach, Rhode Island, with ease, and she beat the America's Cup holder, Harold Vanderbilt, in a one-on-one sailing race. In addition, Sears became one of the first women to fly a plane, when she piloted a small aircraft in 1910.

Sears won the great bulk of her 240 championship trophies in three sports: tennis, squash, and horseback riding. In 1911, at the age of 30, she won the U.S. Open Doubles Tennis Championship with her partner, Hazel Hotchkiss. The next year she reached the finals of the singles event at the same tournament, and in 1915, 1916, and 1917 she repeated as doubles champion. Sears was equally successful at squash; she won the first U.S. women's championship in 1928, was named the captain of the United States International Squash Racquets team the following year, and eventually served as president of the National Women's Squash Racquets Association.

Racquet sports obviously had some appeal for Sears, but equestrian events truly held her passion. An expert rider and jumper, she owned a stable full of both show horses and racers. Competing in an event shortly before World War I, Sears caused a bit of a media furor when she refused to ride her horse sidesaddle, as was customary for women then, and entered the arena sitting astride the horse and wearing men's trousers. But despite the controversy, she was a serious equestrian whose horses (many of which she rode herself) won blue ribbons at national events almost every year for several decades.

One of the earliest proponents of women's fitness, Sears was also a dedicated walker who enjoyed long hikes—not only in the countryside but between major cities. In the 1920s she once again attracted media attention with several major walking expeditions, including hikes between Providence and Boston and between Fontainebleau and Paris, France.

Athletic prowess aside, Eleanora Sears remained a supremely social aristocrat whose name appeared in the society columns just as often as on the sports pages. She was well acquainted with (and reportedly one of the favorite dancing partners of) the future King Edward VIII, and despite her open resistance to traditional clothes on the tennis court, she was listed as one of the nation's best-dressed women for several years running.

Although Sears was reportedly briefly engaged to Harold S. Vanderbilt in 1911 (whom she had beaten in a yacht race one year earlier), she never married. During her later years she had residencies in both Boston and Palm Beach, Florida. She also continued to own horses and remained a steady presence at equestrian events. Eleanora Sears died of leukemia in 1968. She was 87 years old.

Further Reading

Layden, Joe. *Women in Sports: The Complete Book on the World's Greatest Female Athletes.* Santa Monica, Calif.: General Publishing Group, 1997, pp. 216–217.

LeFrenz, Marie. "The Queen and I—Profile of Eleonora Sears," The Equestrian Network. Available online.

URL: http://www.equijournal.com/equijournal/mcl4.shtml. Downloaded on May 2, 2001.

SELES, MONICA
(1973–   )   *Tennis Player*

If guts and grit alone could determine a sports figure's place in history, Monica Seles would be at the top of every list. Seles, who holds nine Grand Slam titles, was the victim of a violent assault in 1993 that left her physically injured and in severe emotional turmoil. Not only did Seles survive the incident, but she returned to competitive tennis and remained one of the top players on the professional tour.

Monica Seles was born in Novi Sad, Yugoslavia, on December 2, 1973. Her father, Karojl, was a cartoonist, and he and his wife, Esther, a computer programmer, encouraged both Monica and her brother, Zoltan, to play sports. Karojl was his children's first tennis coach, and Monica in particular enjoyed his teaching style, which consisted of drawing cartoon characters on tennis balls and then asking Monica to smash them.

By the time Monica was eight, she was playing in junior tennis tournaments. She won the Yugoslav 12-and-under championship at the age of nine, and the following year took the top prize at the European 12-and-under championships. In 1985 Monica was playing in a tournament in Florida when her free-swinging style of play caught the eye of Nick Bollettieri, who offered her a scholarship to his tennis academy in Bradenton, Florida. It was a big decision for the Seleses, but one they agreed to do. Monica moved to Bradenton in late 1985 and was soon joined by her brother and her parents, who quit their jobs.

Seles happily worked long hours on the blazing Bradenton courts at Bollettieri's academy. She hit the ball so hard that soon the other girls refused to play with her. Fortunately for Seles, there were plenty of boys willing to play with her—at least initially. Fellow Bollettieri student (and future French Open champion) Jim Courier played her once, and then reported the following to *Sports Illustrated:* "First ball, whap! She smacks a winner. Next, whap! A winner. After fifteen minutes I walked off. I told Nick, never again."

In 1989, Seles joined the professional circuit. She defeated CHRIS EVERT in the finals of the second tournament she played, and she reached the finals of the U.S. Open that September, but she lost to Evert in straight sets. Four months earlier, Seles lost in the semifinals of the French Open, to the top-seeded player, Steffi Graf of West Germany. It was the beginning of a red-hot rivalry, one that would include superb tennis on the court and some tragic drama off of it.

In 1990, Seles took her first Grand Slam event, defeating Graf in the finals of the French Open. Then, after losing in the quarterfinals of the U.S. Open, she begin a streak of torrid play in which she did not lose before the finals in any tournament she played in. Seles's game featured blazing two-handed ground strokes on both her forehand and backhand sides. Hitting with strength and tremendous accuracy, Seles could pin her opponents on the baseline or pass them at the net. The streak, which lasted from October 1990 to March 1992, helped make Monica Seles the number-one-ranked tennis player in the world, a position she held on March 30, 1993.

On that day, she faced Magdelena Maleeva on a court in Hamburg, Germany. During a changeover, which is the three-minute breather that players enjoy after every other game, Seles was getting ready to walk back onto the court when a stranger walked up behind her and stabbed her in the back. Her assailant, a 38-year-old German named Guenter Parche, later confessed to authorities that he had stabbed Seles because he wanted his favorite player, Graf, to be the top player in the world again.

The attack landed Seles in the hospital, where she was visited by a stunned Graf, who was terribly upset by the incident. Seles did not sustain life-threatening injuries, but she did suffer an acute case of post-traumatic stress syndrome. Making matters worse for Seles was the fact that Parche

received a light sentence from the German courts—possibly because Seles refused to testify against him. Instead of going to prison, he was placed on court probation. Seles stayed away from tennis for two years, battling her own emotional demons and intense fears that Parche would some day attack her again. "The one place I felt safe," she told *Sports Illustrated* in 1994, "was on the tennis court—now, this is the place I feel least safe."

After many months of physical and emotional therapy, Seles made her professional tennis comeback in 1995. After beating Martina Navratilova in an exhibition tournament, Seles returned to the tour and promptly won the first tournament she entered, the Canadian Open. Then, in September 1995, she reached the finals of the U.S. Open, where she met Graf in the final. Having taken over the top spot in women's tennis during Seles's absence, Graf drew first blood by winning the first set. Then, to the surprise of everyone at the stadium, Seles won the second set by a score of 6-0. Although she lost the third set, Seles was delighted to be back in the limelight, and her exuberance showed. "One of the reasons I came back was to feel this excitement," she told *Sports Illustrated.* "The crowd was great. I wish I could take them with me everywhere I went."

In January 1996, Seles won her ninth Grand Slam title, beating Anke Huber, another German player, in straight sets in the final of the Australian open. In May 1998, Seles suffered another setback when she lost her beloved father to cancer shortly before the French Open. Seles elected to compete in the tournament anyway. Wearing her father's wedding ring around her neck, she clawed her way to the semifinal round of the French Open, where she met the new number-one player in the world, Martina Hingis of Switzerland. Hingis was heavily favored to win the match, but Seles, playing in front of an enthusiastic crowd, stunned her young opponent, defeating her in straight sets. Although Seles lost the final to Arantxa Sanchez-Vicario, her performance in the 1998 French Open will be remembered, like Seles herself, as spirited and gutsy.

Seles continues to play tennis on the professional tour. She has remained in the top 10 among women players, but has not reached a tournament final since the 1998 U.S. Open, when she lost to Graf in straight sets.

Further Reading

Biography Resource Center. "Monica Seles," *Great Women in Sports*. Detroit, Mich.: Visible Ink Press, 1996.

Seles, Monica, and Nancy Richardson. *Monica: From Fear to Victory*. New York: Harper Mass Market, 1996.

⠿ SHAIN, EVA
(1908–1999)   *Boxing Judge*

On January 6, 1975, a middle-aged woman by the name of Eva Shain walked into a hearing room and applied for a license to judge professional boxing matches. The following day, the New York State Athletic Commission chairman informed Shain that her application had been approved. As simply as that, Shain became the first woman granted the authority to judge a men's boxing match.

Born in New Jersey, in 1908, Eva Shain did not attend a boxing match until she started dating her future husband, a ring announcer. Eva married Frank Shain in 1938 and began accompanying her husband to the matches he announced. Eventually she learned to keep score of the fights; as her husband announced the names of the athletes, Eva would sit at ringside, keeping track of the jabs and punches thrown by such renowned boxers as Rocky Graziano and Eddie Gregory.

It was at one of these boxing matches in 1967 that Shain caught the eye of Johnny DeFoe, the head boxing coach of the Police Athletic League. "[DeFoe] asked me, 'Who did you give that fight to?'" Shain told *Sports Illustrated* years later. "I told him who and why, and he said, 'How'd you like to be judge?' That was it. I was hooked."

Shain began judging amateur bouts, and as the years progressed, she became a valuable and respected judge. After she received her professional license, Shain was initially viewed with hesitation and some condescension, from both the boxers and her judging peers in the ring. But she proved herself to be a fair and discerning judge.

In 1977 Shain was asked to judge her first title bout. The fight, between Ernie Shavers and Muhammad Ali, might have intimidated a lesser personality, particularly since the fight took place at New York City's Madison Square Garden, a prestigious boxing venue. But Shain was calm and collected, even as her name was called out. "When they announced the judges," Shain remembered, "everyone was yelling, 'My gosh, she's a woman!' It was like I was a freak!" Still, Shain kept her presence of mind. Along with her fellow judges, she scored the fight in Ali's favor.

Over the course of her career Shain judged more than 4,000 professional fights. She kept working in the ring—up to 25 bouts a year—until she was diagnosed with cancer in 1998. She died, in Englewood, New Jersey, the following year.

Further Reading

WBAN, Women's Boxing Archive Network. "Historical Events," Women's Boxing Online. Available online. URL: http://www.womenboxing.com/historic.htm. Downloaded on June 22, 2001.

Wertheim, Jon L. "One Tough Grandmother," *Sports Illustrated*, August 5, 1996, p. 5D.

⠿ STALEY, DAWN
(1970–   )   *Basketball Player*

Dawn Staley is a basketball veteran of one National Collegiate Athletic Association (NCAA) finalist team, two professional leagues, and two gold medal Olympic efforts. A natural passer and ball handler, Staley has always been a leader on the floor.

Born in Philadelphia on May 4, 1970, Dawn Staley was the youngest of five children born to Clarence and Estelle Staley. The Staleys lived in a housing project in the inner city, and Dawn learned early on that she wanted something better. "You can learn a lot from a bad environment," she said of her childhood neighborhood. "The main thing is that you learn what it means to be down and out and have no place to go. It gives you the incentive to get out."

Dawn learned how to play basketball from her three older brothers. As the only girl playing on the neighborhood courts, she soon discovered that it was better to give than receive. Realizing that if she could pass well, it would give her more playing time, she decided to concentrate on ball-handling skills. Soon Dawn was passing so well that she was among the first picked in every pickup game.

At Dobbins-Randolph Vocational-Technical High School, Staley led her team to three consecutive city championships. By her senior year, she had become one of the top players in the country. With a scoring average of 31 points a game, she was named the national player of the year by *USA Today.* Although Staley received a large number of scholarship offers, she had already made up her mind about where she would go to college. Debbie Ryan, the coach of the University of Virginia Cavaliers, had seen Staley play when she was still in junior high school. Impressed by her ball-handling skills and natural talent, Ryan began writing letters to Staley, encouraging her to keep playing and asking her to keep Virginia in mind when it came time to consider college basketball.

During her freshman year at Virginia in 1988–89, Staley earned Atlantic Coast Conference (the collegiate league Virginia plays in) rookie-of-the-year honors with an average of 18.5 points and 4.5 assists a game. The following year, she was named a first-team All-American, as her 17.9 points and 4.4 assists per game led the Cavaliers into the NCAA title game. It was the first time the Cavaliers had made it to the national finals, and although they lost to Stanford, Virginia had put the nation on notice.

In the following season, Virginia was the preseason favorite to win the title. Staley, who would win Naismith Player of the Year honors, again led the Cavaliers to the NCAA championship game, but Virginia lost the title to Tennessee. Even so, Staley, was named the Final Four's most valuable

player. Next year was Staley's fourth and final year for the Cavaliers, and she once again took Naismith Player of the Year honors. Staley, who averaged 14.5 points per game and 6.1 assists during the regular season, led Virginia to the Final Four. This time, they lost in the semifinal game to Stanford, who would go on to win the title.

Although she did not claim an NCAA final, Staley set a school record for scoring at Virginia, with 2,135 total points. Even more impressive, she set a new NCAA record for steals, with 454. After graduating from Virginia, Staley played for two years in France, Italy, Spain, and Brazil. Then in 1996, she returned to the United States to join the national team. On the way to the Olympics, the national squad embarked on a grueling, nine-month national tour. It was a challenging time for the team, which boasted the finest players in the nation, but who were just learning to play together for the first time. Staley, who backed up TERESA EDWARDS as point guard, played well for the crew, which posted a perfect 52-0 record during the national tour and then went on to claim the gold medal at the 1996 Atlanta Olympic Games.

After the Olympics, Staley was happy to stay in the United States; in early 1996 the announcement came that not one but two professional leagues for women would be starting up. The Women's National Basketball Association (WNBA) which had the backing of the National Basketball Association, was one of those leagues, but Staley chose to play with the other organization, which was called the American Basketball League (ABL). Staley spent two seasons with the Richmond Rage of the ABL, but then decided to join the rival league when she realized the ABL was floundering. "It was a tough decision, considering that I was a founding member of the league," she told a newspaper in 1998, "but at the same time I had to look at women's basketball as a business like everyone else."

Staley joined the Charlotte Sting of the WNBA, and as the starting point guard, she led the team to the tournament semifinals in 2000. One month later, Staley once again played for the U.S. team as it traveled to Sydney to defend its title in the 2000 Olympic Games. This time Staley started at point guard for the team, which swept to its second consecutive gold medal.

In the fall of 2000, Staley began a different endeavor. By now a seasoned player, she believed that it was time to become a mentor as well as a player. With this goal in mind, she signed on as head coach of the women's basketball team at Temple University, which is in her hometown of Philadelphia. Staley spends the academic year in Philadelphia, and then goes to Charlotte during the summer to run the floor for the Sting. In 2001, Staley led the Sting into the finals of the WNBA Championships, but they lost the title to the Los Angeles Sparks.

Further Reading

Araton, Harvey, "Staley the Icon Leads Her 'Little Sisters,'" *New York Times,* February 18, 2001, sect. 8, p. 2.

Rutledge, Rachel. *The Best of the Best in Basketball.* Brookfield, Conn.: Millbrook Press, 1998.

USA Basketball. "Dawn Staley," USA Basketball.com. Available online. URL: http://www.usabasketball.com/ Women/staley_bio.html. Downloaded on June 28, 2001.

▦ STEPHENS, HELEN
(1918–1994) *Sprinter, Weight Thrower*

The sprinter Helen Stephens captured gold medals in the 100-yard dash and the 4×100 yard relay at the 1936 Olympic Games in Berlin, Germany. Stephens's story is remarkable enough for the simple reason that she was reportedly the sole U.S. athlete at those games who was invited to meet Hitler. But even more intriguing is the bizarre twist of fate that unfolded after Stella Walsh, one of Stephens's top rivals, accused her of being a man and demanded that she take a test to prove her gender.

Helen Stephens was born on February 3, 1918, in Fulton, Missourri. The daughter of a farmer and a homemaker, Helen was a gifted natural athlete, not only on the sprint track, but in the broad jump

and shot put as well. The woman known as the "Fulton Flash" was a high school freshman when, according to legend, she ran a 50-yard dash in a practice heat with a time that matched the current world record. Stephens also tied the world record in the broad jump while in high school, and by the time she was 17, she was competing in American Athletic Union (AAU) track-and-field events.

It was at Stephens's first AAU tournament, in St. Louis in 1935, that she first competed against Stella Walsh, the defending Olympic gold medalist in the 100-yard dash. Born in Poland, Walsh had grown up in Cleveland; her parents had immigrated to the United States when she was an infant. The holder of 30 national championships as an American, Walsh decided to switch her citizenry and represent Poland in the 1932 Olympics in Los Angeles. Walsh was unequivocally the top sprinter in the United States—and then, in 1935, she came face to face with Helen Stephens.

The 17-year-old, six-foot-tall Stephens was a virtual unknown to most of the veteran athletes at the AAU tournament. But by the end of the competition, she was the most talked-about athlete on the track. Stephens had entered four events—the 50-meter dash, the 200-meter dash, the shot put, and the broad jump—and had taken top honors in each of them. Competing against Walsh in the 50-meter dash, Stevens triumphed easily—and then insulted her rival even more intensely by declaring that she had never heard of her. An outraged Walsh began referring to Stevens as "that greenie from the sticks."

Walsh's dander was up, and she began training for the 1936 Olympic Games determined to defend her 100-yard medal at any cost. Stephens, in the meantime, had gone back to the AAU competition in 1936 and won all five of the events she entered. Not only was Stephens now a worldrecord holder, having smashed the mark at the 200-meter event at the 1936 AAU games, but she had never been defeated in a sprint event in her entire career. For those reasons, Stephens emerged as the clear favorite to take the gold medal at the 100-meter event at the 1936 Olympic Games in Berlin.

If anyone thought that Stephens could be beaten, it was Walsh, who had clung to her belief that she, not Stephens, was the finest female sprinter in the world. But the oddsmakers had chosen correctly, as Stephens triumphed easily over Walsh to take top honors in the event. It proved to be the first of two gold medals for Stephens. Several days after her first victory, Stephens ran the 4 × 100 meter event. The United States fielded a strong team for the relay, featuring two gold medal winners—Stephens was joined by Elizabeth Robinson, who had taken top honors in the 100-meter event at the 1928 games. Nonetheless, the U.S. team was trailing the British and German teams by several meters at the race's halfway mark. But then the Germans, who had set a world record in the event during the qualifying rounds, inexplicably dropped the baton. The U.S. team and the British were left to fight it out for the gold, and thanks to an inspiring anchor run by Stephens, the United States took first place.

Stephens was now a double-medal winner. She had impressed the host nation with her speed and her blonde looks, and one German in particular insisted on meeting her face to face. A nonplussed Stevens recalled their visit several years later:

Helen Stephens, who never lost a competitive race, won the 100-meter event at the 1936 Berlin Olympics. In the process, she impressed Adolf Hitler and angered her chief rival, 1932 sprint champion Stella Walsh. (Library of Congress)

"Hitler comes in and gives me this Nazi salute. I gave him a good old Missouri handshake. He shook my hand, put his arm around me, pinched me, and invited me to spend the weekend with him." She respectfully declined.

But if Stephens had a humorous encounter with Hitler, her subsequent association with her Polish rival in Berlin was less amusing. Not only was Walsh outraged that she had been beaten so soundly in her attempt to defend her 100-meter gold medal, but she was determined to prove that Stephens had done so under false pretenses. Several days after the race, Walsh began a whispered campaign among her fellow Polish athletes, and eventually, the Polish media, that Stephens was actually a man. Over the course of a few days, the Polish press published several articles that stated, among other things, that "Helen was better off named Henry." Otherwise, the articles went on to say, there was little explanation for her outlandishly speedy times on the track.

In the midst of the accusations, a dazed Stephens was told to take a physical test to prove her gender. The results came back quickly: Stephens was undoubtedly female. The sporting world accepted the results calmly, and Stephens kept her gold medals. She went on to win the 1937 AAU championships in the 200-meter, 50-meter, and shot put events, and then, without further ado, hung up her track cleats for good. Stephens had retired from competition with a flawless record in the sprints: She had competed in 100 races, and she had won every single one.

For Walsh, however, the 1936 Olympics proved to be only the beginning of her obsession with Stephens. She was determined to prove, to the end, that Stephens was indeed a male, and she spent the next 44 years of her life trying to convince the press, and virtually anyone else who would listen, of her cause. Then, in 1980, Walsh was shot and killed during a robbery in Cleveland. The victim of a senseless murder, Walsh underwent a mandatory autopsy. The physical examination ended with a stunning disclosure: Stella Walsh had no female sex organs. She was, in fact, a man.

After retiring from competitive track and field, Stephens continued to compete in exhibitions, running against such exalted competition as her compatriot Jesse Owens. During World War II she joined the U.S. Marine Corps, and in later years she came back to the track, first as a college coach and then as a competitor in senior events. In her second competitive career, as in her first, Helen Stephens never lost a race. She died in St. Louis in 1994.

Further Reading

Layden, Joe. *Women in Sports: The Complete Book on the World's Greatest Female Athletes.* Santa Monica, Calif.: General Publishing Group, 1997, pp. 226–227.

Shell, Pat. "Three Ring Circus: The Twisted Tale of Stella Walsh," ABC Olympics.com. Available online. URL: http://www.abc.net.au/olympics/s177264.htm. Downloaded on January 10, 2001.

Women in American History, by Encyclopedia Britannica. "Stephens, Helen." Available online. URL: http://www.women.eb.com/women/articles/Stephens_Helen.html. Downloaded on January 11, 2001.

STONE, TONI
(Marcenia Lyle, Toni Stone Alberga)
(1921–1996)   *Baseball Player*

During her two-year stint with the Indianapolis Clowns of the National Negro Leagues, Toni Stone, the only woman to play in the Negro Leagues, shared a field with the likes of Satchel Paige and Oscar Charleston. She also endured countless insults about her gender, yet survived and thrived in a league that—as she was told countless times—was definitely not one of her own.

Toni Stone, whose original name was Marcenia Lyle, was born in St. Paul, Minnesota, in 1921. Her father, a barber, and her mother, a beautician, were greatly surprised when Marcenia fell in love with baseball at an early age. Despite their objections, Marcenia would often skip school and peruse the neighborhood for pickup baseball games. Although Marcenia became a regular presence on St. Paul's inner-city diamonds, she was not always accepted by her fellow players—all of whom were boys. The locals labeled her "Tomboy," but they let her play.

In 1932, Gabby Street, a former manager for the St. Louis Cardinals, lost his job in the major leagues and moved to Minnesota to manage the minor-league St. Paul Saints. Street also established a baseball school for boys, which many of Marcenia's cronies joined. Determined to be included, Marcenia asked Street for a chance to play. Street turned down the 11-year-old girl's request, but Marcenia simply asked again—and again and again. By now Street considered Marcenia to be a major-league pest, but he finally said he would watch her play ball—once. When Street saw Marcenia's talent, he went out and bought her a pair of cleats. The next day Marcenia enrolled at his school.

During World War II, Lyle moved to San Francisco, where her sister, a nurse in the military, was stationed. Arriving in California with little money and no place to stay (it took her several weeks to locate her sister), she found herself a job and an apartment. Then she found a baseball league to play in. Under a new name—she rechristened herself "Toni Stone" because Toni sounded like her St. Paul nickname, Tomboy—she showed up at a tryout for the American Legion League, which was a group of semipro barnstorming teams. Playing center field during tryouts, Toni Stone impressed the owners and coaches, and soon she won a place on the San Francisco Sea Lions, an all-African-American barnstorming team.

Stone had found a way to get paid for doing what she loved best. Baseball was not only a passion for the young African-American woman from St. Paul, it was also a means of identity and a point of pride. "In baseball," she said later, "I was accepted for who I was and what I could produce." And for the San Francisco Sea Lions, Stone began producing right away. In her first at-bat for the team, she smacked a hit that drove in two runs. But as delighted as Stone was to be playing semiprofessional baseball, she was less than pleased with the Sea Lion management, which was not paying her what it had promised they would. During a road trip to New Orleans, Stone received an offer to play for the New Orleans Creoles, for $300 a month. Without hesitation Stone accepted the bid and moved to Louisiana.

Strictly a barnstorming squad during MAUD NELSON's playing days, the Creoles had become a team in the minors of the Negro Leagues in the 1940s. When Stone joined them in 1949, she received a fair amount of publicity and hype. Sports journalists wondered in print whether Stone might one day reach the highest level of the Negro Leagues and kept track of her performance on the field. Stone responded well to the increased attention; playing second base, she proved to be a nimble and sure-handed infielder. At the plate, her average improved during each of her four years with the Creoles, and in her final season there, in 1953, she batted a highly respectable .263.

By the time Stone was playing for the Creoles, the Negro Leagues had entered their final phase of existence. In 1947 Jackie Robinson had broken the racial barrier and joined the Brooklyn Dodgers. Over the next few years, many of the finest players in the Negro Leagues followed suit. In 1951, Hank Aaron, a second baseman for the Indianapolis Clowns, left the Negro Leagues to play for the major-league Boston Braves. That left an opening in the Clowns infield, and two years later, Indianapolis hired Toni Stone to fill the void.

Many fans in Indianapolis wondered if Stone's hiring was a publicity stunt—and indeed, the league, having lost its best players to major-league franchises, was in dire financial straits. But the reason did not matter to Stone, who showed up in Indianapolis with her glove and her baseball shoes. "I've come to play," she announced. Syd Pollack, the owner of the Clowns, insisted that he had chosen Stone because of her talent, not her gender. But others on the team were not so sure. And Stone herself questioned Pollack's motives when he requested that she play in shorts. She refused.

The manager of the Clowns, Buster Haywood, had few complaints about Stone's talent or desire to play. And he allowed himself to say that in "women's baseball, she would be a top player." (Stone was not permitted to play in the All American Girls' Baseball League because of her race). But

Haywood also contended that Stone "couldn't compete with the men to save her life."

Perhaps Stone was not the strongest or the fleetest player on the team, but she did play solidly at second base for the Clowns, and her average of .243 was respectable as well. Even so, her teammates never accepted her presence on the team and were not shy about letting her know their feelings. "They didn't mean any harm, and in their way they liked me," Stone would say of her fellow Indianapolis players, "[It was] just that I wasn't supposed to be there. They'd tell me to go home and fix my husband some biscuits or any damn thing. Just get the hell away from here."

But there were lighter moments as well. After Haywood left Indianapolis, the Clowns hired a new manager. Oscar Charleston, the new skipper of the Clowns, was one of the Negro Leagues' best players and biggest superstars. Stone was not only in awe of Charleston, but she appreciated his decency and kindness. "He was the greatest, he was fair," she said of Charleston, "he'd let me get out there and hit." Then there was her one at-bat with the legendary pitcher Satchel Paige, who took the mound against her in an exhibition game in 1953. "He threw me a fastball," she later recalled, "and I got a hit . . . right out over second base. Happiest moment of my life."

In 1954 Stone was traded to the Kansas City Monarchs, one of the finest franchises in the Negro Leagues. Stone was delighted to be playing for the Monarchs, but soon after she arrived she realized that she was spending more time on the bench than on the field. She badly wanted to play but realized after protesting several times that her situation was not about to change. Stone, who had married Aurelium Alberga in 1950, retired from the Negro Leagues after one season with the Monarchs.

Although she no longer competed professionally, Toni Stone Alberga continued to play baseball with neighborhood teams until she was 60. Living in Oakland, California, with her husband, she worked as a nurse for several years. Her husband died in 1988, but Stone Alberga continued to live in their Oakland home. In 1990, she traveled to

St. Paul, Minnesota, where the "Tomboy" attended "Toni Stone Day." During a daylong celebration, Toni Stone Alberga, the girl who fought to play baseball during her entire career, had returned to her old stomping grounds a hero. At 79, she had come full circle.

Further Reading

Gregorich, Barbara. *Women at Play: The Story of Women in Baseball.* New York: Harcourt Brace, 1993, pp. 169–176.

Markel, Robert, Susan Wagoner, and Marcella Smith. *The Women's Sports Encyclopedia.* New York: Henry Holt, 1999.

STREET, PICABO
(1971–) *Skier*

The superstar skier Picabo Street not only has one of the best names in sports, but she owns downhill skiing medals in consecutive Olympic games—the only U.S. skier to achieve that feat. Street scored a silver medal at the 1994 winter Games, and four years later, won a gold in Nagano.

Born on April 3, 1971, in Triumph, Idaho, the baby girl born to Stubby and Dee Street was named just that—Baby Girl Street. But when her parents had trouble securing a passport for their infant daughter (the U.S. government was not amused by the generic name) they changed her name to "Picabo," a Native American word that means "shining waters." Picabo traveled a great deal with her family. During her childhood she and her parents spent time in Central America, and they made several trips across the United States. At home, just outside of Sun Valley, Idaho, the Streets lived in a house with no television, and they grew their own food.

Picabo also spent a great deal of her childhood on the ski slopes. By the time she reached high school, she had learned to blaze aggressively down mountains at dazzling speeds. But although Picabo had an abundance of talent, she considered skiing to be a fun activity, and not much more. As much as she loved conquering the slopes, she hated the training and conditioning that accompany being a world-class athlete. She was a member of her high school ski team, but an undisciplined one at that.

Even so, Street's natural ability carried her quite far in high school. At the age of 16, she was the western junior champion. The following year, she took top honors in the national junior downhill and super giant slalom competitions. And at the age of 19, Street was the national junior champion.

But championships and trophies aside, Street remained an undisciplined athlete. Her poor training habits got her in trouble on the U.S. ski team. Two years after making the team, Street was kicked off in 1990 when she showed up for training in poor shape. Fortunately for Street, she learned her lesson, and began following a more grueling training regimen. She rejoined the team in 1991 and began to compete in World Cup competitions.

Street's star ascended steadily over the next two years, and in 1993, she finished second in the combined event at the World Championships. Then came her silver medal in the downhill event at the 1994 Olympics in Lillehammer, Norway. Street followed those up with a string of World Cup victories during the 1994–95 World Cup season. But in 1997, Street's career was put on hold when she fell during a training run and severely tore a ligament in her knee. Street's injury was so severe that many predicted she would never compete again. But Street underwent an aggressive rehabilitation regimen that got her back on the slopes by the end of the year.

Then, two months before the Olympics, Street suffered another injury when she lost consciousness after a fall in Sweden. A lesser athlete might well have hung up her poles after two such severe accidents, but Street was intent on competing in the 1998 Olympics. She arrived in Nagano, Japan, feeling relatively healthy and promptly won a gold medal in the super giant slalom event.

The 1998 Olympics sealed Street's celebrity. She returned to the United States a hero and was honored in Idaho with a key to her home city of Triumph—the mayor even named a street after her. She signed several endorsement deals and became wealthy.

In the weeks leading up to the 2002 Salt Lake City Olympics, Street announced that she would be retiring from skiing after the games. She failed to make the Olympic team in the super giant slalom but qualified in the downhill. Street did not win a medal in Salt Lake City, but she shared a moment with the crowd. After completing her second and final downhill run, she bowed graciously to the crowd, who applauded her triumphs, and her career, enthusiastically.

Street has not made an official decision about her next move, but there is reason to believe she will remain in the public eye. Outgoing and vivacious, she has considered a career in television, either as a broadcaster or as a talk-show host. "Every time I watch Rosie O'Donnell, I think about [having my own television program]," she confided to *Time* magazine in 1998. "I want to do that with athletes so the world can see all these powerful and funny personalities."

Further Reading

Layden, Joe. *Women in Sports: The Complete Book on the World's Greatest Female Athletes.* Santa Monica, Calif.: General Publishing Group, 1997, pp. 229–230.

Smith, Lissa, editor. *Nike Is a Goddess: The History of Women in Sports.* New York: Atlantic Monthly Press, 1998, pp. 150–151.

STRUG, KERRI
(1977–) *Gymnast*

The most physically painful moment in Kerri Strug's life to date was also her most famous. At the Atlanta Olympics in 1996, Strug, competing on an injured ankle, completed a solid vault. After her landing, she crumpled to the floor in horrific pain as the home crowd cheered. Strug's vault had lifted the United States to its first team gold in Olympic history.

Kerri Strug was born on November 19, 1977, in Tucson, Arizona. By the time she was six, she was taking gymnastics lessons from Jim Gault, a gymnastics coach at the University of Arizona. Six years later, Strug, a motivated and outgoing child, begged her parents to let her train with Bela Karolyi, the legendary gymnastics coach who had guided Nadia Comaneci to four gold medals in the 1976 Olympics. The problem for the Strugs was that Karolyi lived and worked in Houston. Young Kerri would have to move there in order to train with him. Kerri's parents initially said no, but their daughter asked them to reconsider, again and again, and they finally gave their consent.

Under Karolyi, Strug blossomed into a sure-footed and confident gymnast. At the age of 14, she earned a place on the national team, and the following year she was the youngest member of the Olympic squad that took a bronze medal at the 1992 Barcelona Olympic Games. In 1993 Strug finished fifth in the all-around competition at the World Championships, and two years later she won a scholarship to the University of California at Los Angeles (UCLA).

Strug deferred her entrance to UCLA in order to train full time for the 1996 Olympics. By that time the U.S. gymnastics team had become one of the best of the world. It featured a blend of such mature performers as Shannon Miller and such young and energetic talent as Dominique Moceanu. Strug was a solid member of the team, but she was often overlooked by her teammates, some of whom were favored to win medals in individual events at the Olympics.

As it happened, the U.S. gymnasts got off to a splendid start in the team competition; after the first day, they had a comfortable lead. But on the final day Moceanu began to struggle. At age 14 the youngest member of the team, she had been hampered by injuries throughout the games and possibly rattled by the pressure as well. Moceanu fell twice during the team vaulting competition. In team competition the judges drop the lowest scores, which of course meant that Moceanu's scores would automatically be thrown out. But this meant that Strug, who had severely sprained her ankle during the first day of competition, would not only have to vault, but she would have to do so well enough to clinch the gold.

Strug knew she had two jumps to play with—judges take the higher score of the two vaults—but she also knew that her ankle might not be strong enough to sustain two landings. She took off on her first jump hoping that she would land cleanly. But although Strug turned a clean vault in the air, she landed hard on her feet and fell on the landing. Strug sat on the mat, wincing in pain. Then she got to her feet and hobbled back to the starting line. Somehow she ran down the mat, turned a sterling jump, and landed cleanly. The fans erupted. It was one of the most exciting moments at the 1996 Olympic Games.

It was also a heroic moment for Strug, who had heard her ankle crack on the landing of that last jump. Her final vault had broken her ankle and eliminated her from the individual competitions still to come. At the medal ceremony, Karolyi carried Strug, her ankle taped, to the medal podium, where she and her teammates received their gold medals.

Strug had to take several months off after the Olympics to allow her ankle to heal. In 1997 she enrolled at UCLA, where she graduated in 2001. She no longer competes in gymnastics, but she performs in several exhibitions every year.

Further Reading

"Kerri Strug Biography," USA Gymnastics Online. Available online. URL: http://www.usa-gymnastics.org/athletes/bios/s/kstrug.html. Downloaded on February 14, 2001.

"Kerri Strug, Olympic Gold Medalist." Available online. URL: http://www.sportsplacement.com/Strug.htm. Downloaded on February 14, 2001.

Layden, Joe. *Women in Sports: The Complete Book on the World's Greatest Female Athletes.* Santa Monica, Calif.: General Publishing Group, 1997, pp. 231–232.

SUGGS, LOUISE (MacLouise Suggs)
(1923–) *Golfer*

Louise Suggs, one of the great legends of women's golf, won eight major championships during her long and illustrious career. Just as impressive, Suggs, who had a long and fluid natural swing, beat several top male players during her prime, including Sam Snead and Gardner Dickinson. Little wonder that the comedian and avid golfer Bob Hope, after seeing her hit a 300-yard drive, said dryly, "I'm going to the clubhouse to get me a skirt."

Born in Atlanta, Georgia, on September 7, 1923, Suggs learned golf at an early age. Her father, John Suggs, who played semiprofessional baseball for the Atlanta Crackers (a team owned by Louise's maternal grandfather), managed a golf course after retiring from baseball. Louise, who worked at the club as a caddie, got lots of practice playing, not only with her father, but with the other caddies—all of whom were boys. "We played a game called 'short knocker'," Suggs said much later. "Whoever hit the shortest ball had to pick up all the others." Incited by the competition, Louise learned to stroke the ball far; she rarely had to pick up anyone's ball.

In 1940, 16-year-old Suggs won her first tournament, the Georgia Amateur Championship. She would win 11 more amateur titles over the next eight years, including the U.S. Amateur Championships in 1947 and the British Amateur crown in 1948. With those titles under her belt, Suggs decided to turn professional. She won her first major professional title, the U.S. Women's Open, in 1949, and followed that up with a victory at the Western Open that same year. After completing the 1950 season without a tournament victory, Suggs won her second U.S. Women's Open in 1951. Two years later, she seized her second Western Open, and after winning the Titleholders championship in 1954 and 1956, took her first and only Ladies' Professional Golf Association (LPGA) championship in 1957.

Unfortunately for Suggs, she played golf during the same period that BABE DIDRIKSON ZAHARIAS, perhaps the most famous woman golfer (and athlete) of all time, reached her prime on the links. Suggs was quieter and less emotional than the exuberant and charismatic Didrickson, and for that reason, garnered fewer headlines and less fan support. Even so, Suggs was the sport's leading money winner in the late 1950s, and she continued to earn top dollars on the course through the 1960s.

Suggs's greatest season was in 1953, when she won nine tournaments. That year she also wrote a book called *Par Golf for Women*. In his foreword to the book, the legendary golfer Ben Hogan wrote that Suggs's swing "combines all the desirable elements of efficiency, timing, and coordination. It appears to be completely effortless."

Suggs continued to play golf until 1984, when she was 61. She remained involved in the game, and in the late 1990s donated $500,000 to the LPGA efforts to promote junior golf. Suggs was honest about why she made such a generous donation. "Frankly, I want my name remembered," she said. As the first member ever to be inducted into the LPGA Hall of Fame, Louise Suggs will not likely be forgotten.

Further Reading

Becker, Debbie. "Living Legend Louise Suggs," LPGA Golfonline. Available online. URL: http://www.golfonline.com/womensgolf/lpgagolf/suggs0800.html. Downloaded on July 10, 2001.

Layden, Joe. *Women in Sports: The Complete Book on the World's Greatest Female Athletes*. Santa Monica, Calif.: General Publishing Group, 1997, p. 232.

SUMMITT, PAT HEAD (Patricia Head)
(1952–) *Basketball Coach*

Ever since 1981, when women's basketball became an official National Collegiate Athletics Association (NCAA) sport, one team has stood out as a dynasty. That team, the University of Tennessee Lady Volunteers ("Lady Vols"), has won six national championships, often in spectacular fashion. The players, of course, have come and gone, but Pat Head Summitt, the coach and spiritual leader of the Tennessee team, has remained on the sidelines to guide the team every year.

Patricia Head was born on June 14, 1952, in Henrietta, Tennessee. Her parents, Richard and Hazel Head, were impoverished farmers. Pat, along with her three older brothers, spent a good part of every day completing house and farm chores, but they always had time to play basketball. Young Pat learned the game from her brothers, and from her father she gained firsthand knowledge of hard work. On her 16th birthday, Pat was eager to go to a party at a local club. It had rained the previous evening, and hundreds of bales of straw had been blown to the ground. Pat's father told her that she had to help pick up the straw. She ended up spending most of her birthday working, but learned what she would later call a "valuable lesson" about discipline.

Head attended the University of Tennessee at Martin, where she earned a degree in physical education in 1974. Two years earlier she had suffered a serious knee injury playing basketball, and her orthopedist told her that she would probably never play the sport again. Head's father, though, urged his daughter to undergo knee surgery and continue training; it had been Pat's lifelong ambition to play in the Olympics, and the 1976 games in Montreal would be the first to feature women's basketball. Head made a successful recovery from surgery, and she went on to serve as a cocaptain of the first U.S. Olympic basketball team, which won a silver medal in Montreal.

In the meantime, Head had taken a job as assistant head coach of the women's basketball program at the University of Tennessee at Knoxville, where she had enrolled in the fall of 1974 to pursue a master's degree in education. Soon after she arrived, the head coach resigned, and Head was offered the job. Although she had never intended to coach full time, Head eventually found her rhythm on the sidelines. In the 1977–78 season, two years after she had become head coach, she guided the Lady Vols to a 28-5 record and a Final Four finish in the American Intercollegiate Athletic Women's (AIAW) tournament.

Over the next three years, Tennessee boasted a top-rated team that would earn a stellar record during the regular season but then fall short during the postseason tournament. In 1979, the Lady Vols lost in the semifinals, and in 1980 and 1981, they lost in the championship game. Nineteen eighty was also the year Head married R. B. Summitt, a banker.

In 1982, the first NCAA women's basketball tournament was held. Pat Head Summitt and her team reached the Final Four of this prestigious championship but failed to win their semifinal game. Although Tennessee continued to field top-notch teams over the next five years, they failed to bring home the NCAA crown, falling short at various points in the tournament.

Although Summitt had yet to win a collegiate title, she brought home an even larger prize when, in 1984, she coached the United States to a gold medal at the Los Angeles Olympic Games. Summitt finally gained the top prize in collegiate sports when Tennessee took the NCAA crown in 1987, beating Louisiana Tech in the final. The Lady Vols have won five other titles, taking top honors in 1989, 1991, 1996, 1997, and 1998.

Summitt has been called a "high-intensity" coach and with good reason. She had always demanded that her players attend classes—insisting that they sit in one of the first three rows—and, on the court, has kept team members after practice to run extra sprints. Summitt herself had an intense experience when, while experiencing labor pains in her ninth month of pregnancy in 1990, she elected to go on a recruiting trip to Allentown, Pennsylvania. She visited the potential player, made a successful pitch for her to join the Lady Vols, and then flew back to Knoxville. Her son, Ross Tyler Summitt, very nearly was born several thousand feet up on that return flight.

The second most successful coach in the history of women's collegiate basketball, Summitt has taken her team to the Final Four a record 15 times. She was inducted into the Women's Sports Hall of Fame in 1990 and into the National Basketball Hall of Fame in 2000.

Further Reading

Layden, Joe. *Women in Sports: The Complete Book on the World's Greatest Female Athletes.* Santa Monica, Calif.: General Publishing Group, 1997, p. 233.

Smith, Gary. "Eyes of the Storm," *Sports Illustrated.* March 2, 1998, 90–106.

Summitt, Pat, with Sally Jenkins. *Raise the Roof: The Inspiring Inside Story of the Tennessee Lady Vols' Undefeated 1997–98 Season.* New York: Broadway Books, 1999.

SWITZER, KATHERINE
(1947–)   *Marathon Runner*

In 1968, Katherine Switzer ran in and finished the Boston Marathon. That alone would not necessarily make Switzer a pioneer. After all, thousands of women have run and completed the traditional 26-mile route around the great New England city. But when the qualifier is added that she was the first woman to run officially in the marathon, and that in order to do so she had to register as a man, it is clear that Switzer belongs on any list of great U.S. women sports trailblazers.

Breaking down barriers was always a priority for Katherine Switzer, who was born in 1947 in Falls Church, Virginia. After graduating from high school, Switzer enrolled at Lynchburg College, a conservative Christian institute in Virginia. Frustrated that Lynchburg did not have a women's track team, Switzer decided to compete in the mile event on the men's team. Switzer's actions were highly controversial; she received hate mail from local residents and college students alike. Even so, Switzer ran one event for the Lynchburg men's track team and finished the race.

In 1967, after completing her sophomore year, Switzer left Lynchburg and transferred to Syracuse University in upstate New York. An English and journalism major, she wrote an article for the school newspaper in which she stated her intention to one day run in the Boston Marathon. The world's oldest annual marathon, the Boston race was first staged in 1897. Run every spring, the race annually drew the finest long-distance runners from around the world. Every one of those runners was male, since the rules of the Boston Marathon stipulated that no women were allowed to compete.

Determined to change history, Switzer began training for the 26-mile journey while still at Syracuse. Like Lynchburg College, Syracuse did not have a women's track-and-field team. Undaunted, Switzer received permission from the men's track coach to train with the university's cross-country squad. During the winter of 1967, she befriended Arnie Briggs, a volunteer coach for Syracuse who had been a top-10 finisher in the 1952 Boston Marathon. Working with Switzer, Briggs became convinced that she could finish the course, and he encouraged her to submit an official application for entry into the marathon.

For Switzer, the question was how to fill out that application. She and Briggs were both aware that the marathon forbade women from competing. They also knew that in May 1967, a woman did run in, and finish, the race. Her name was ROBERTA GIBB, and she had completed the event well ahead of more than half of her male competitors. But Gibb had run much of the race in disguise—most people on the scene did not realize that the sweatshirt-hooded runner was actually a female.

In the weeks before the 1968 race, Switzer decided to fill out an application for the race that left her gender ambiguous; under "name," she wrote "K. V. Switzer." Before the race, Briggs, who had also entered the race, picked up Switzer's number for her. But Switzer, with her hair tied back in a ponytail and wearing a running suit and a hoodless tunic, pinned the number on her shirt front and walked to the starting line. When the race began, Switzer ran between Briggs and her boyfriend, Thomas Miller, a hammer thrower on the Syracuse team.

Before very long, spectators and photographers noticed that a woman was running in the race, and that she was wearing a number, signifying that she had officially registered for the event. Reporters and fans were surprised; no one had mentioned that the rule banning woman had been overturned. The Boston Athletic Association (BAA) officials were stunned as well. Four miles into the race, two BAA representatives, Will Cloney and Jock Semple, leaped from their post on the press bus and ran into the street, trying to catch up with Switzer. Cloney got into the race first, but he could not keep up with Switzer, who outran him. Running into the race from the sidelines, Semple did manage to reach Switzer. Shouting "Get the hell

227

out of my race and give me back my number!" he grabbed Switzer and tried to pull the number off her shirt. Tom Miller caught up to Semple, pulled him away from Switzer, and shoved him to the ground. Shocked by the episode, Switzer nevertheless continued to run, and she finished the event in four hours and 20 minutes.

It was not a terribly impressive time (the top 1967 finisher, Dave McKenzie, had broken the tape in a course-record two hours and 15 minutes) but Switzer had made history. In the weeks that followed the marathon, she became a national celebrity. Nevertheless, the BAA refused to acknowledge her finish or her achievement. They claimed that Switzer had entered the event under false pretenses. Even so, the BAA could not refute the evidence made not only by Switzer but by Gibb and other women who had run the course, unnumbered and under cover: Women belonged in the Boston Marathon.

Despite Switzer's achievement, the marathon did not officially admit women until the 1972 race. That year, the 25-year-old Virginian barrier breaker signed her application "Katherine Switzer" and received her number herself. She ran the race without incident and finished the course in 3:29:51— good for third place among women. The following year, Jock Semple once again caught up with Switzer. This time she was standing on the starting line, and instead of trying to grab her number, Semple kissed her on the cheek and wished her luck.

Switzer retired from competitive running in the mid-1970s. In 1978 she convinced Avon, one of the major manufacturers of women's cosmetics, to sponsor a series of women's races. Switzer served as director of the Avon series from 1978 until 1985. In addition to her role as advocate for women's running, Switzer took full advantage of her college training in journalism. She worked as a television sports broadcaster for several years and provided insightful commentaries during many Boston Marathons.

Further Reading

Jabbour, Kamal. "Katherine Switzer, Still Running Through Obstacles," *Syracuse Post Standard,* February 9, 1998, p. 8–9.

Layden, Joe. *Women in Sports: The Complete Book on the World's Greatest Female Athletes,* Santa Monica, Calif.: General Publishing Group, 1997, pp. 232–235.

SWOOPES, SHERYL
(1971–) *Basketball Player*

Sheryl Swoopes is one of the most successful women basketball players in history. She has won two Olympic gold medals and four consecutive Women's National Basketball Association (WNBA) championships. Even before these glories, Swoopes made a name for herself as one of the finest players in the college game, as a leader and superstar guard for Texas Tech University.

A Texas girl through and through, Sheryl Swoopes was born on March 25, 1971, in Brownfield, a small farming town in the southwestern part of the state. Sheryl's father, Billy, left the family when she was a baby. Her mother, Louise, worked two jobs in order to support Sheryl and her two brothers, James and Earl.

From early childhood Sheryl was a natural basketball player, with a shooting eye that made her a regular presence on neighborhood playgrounds, where she was the only girl but one of the most highly regarded players. When Swoopes played only with girls, she was always the finest player on the court. By the time she was in high school, Swoopes was six feet tall and was drawing comparisons to some of the finest men's players in the game. Describing her talent, some college scouts referred to her as "the next Michael Jordan."

At age 16, Swoopes was named the Texas state player of the year. The following year she was offered a full basketball scholarship to the University of Texas at Austin, and Swoopes, realizing that college ball was the next logical step, accepted. But after arriving in Austin, she felt overcome by homesickness and loneliness. Three days into her college career, Swoopes packed her bags and left the Texas capital. She returned to Brownfield briefly and then enrolled in South Plains Junior College, only a few miles away from her hometown.

Swoopes quickly dominated play at South Plains. Averaging 25 points and more than 10 rebounds a game, she was named Junior College Player of the year after her sophomore season. Now Swoopes felt more prepared to play for a full-fledged university, but rather than returning to Austin, she selected Texas Tech University, a smaller school located in Lubbock. Swoopes quickly became the leader at Texas Tech, where she played for the Lady Raiders. With a scoring average of 21.6 points per game, she helped her team clinch the Southwest Conference Championships.

The following season was an even more impressive one for Swoopes, who led the Lady Raiders to the National Collegiate Athletic Association (NCAA) championship. In the final of that tournament, against Ohio State, Swoopes scored 47 points. To this day, no college basketball player of either gender has scored as many points in an NCAA tournament final.

After graduating from Texas Tech in 1993, Swoopes yearned to continue playing basketball. But because there were at the time no professional women's basketball leagues in the United States, her only option was to move to Europe to compete in a league there. Swoopes moved to Italy, but once again, she became terribly homesick. After only three months and 10 games, she returned to her home country.

Fortunately for Swoopes, women's basketball was beginning to gain momentum in the United States. Shortly after she returned home, she learned that the National Basketball Association (NBA) would be sponsoring a national women's team that would go on a countrywide tour, playing against college teams. The team's tour would culminate with the 1996 Olympics, which would be taking place in Atlanta. Both the tour and the Olympics were a smashing success, and the national team dominated every opponent on its way to the Olympics. On the court, Swoopes averaged 13 points a game and shot 60 percent from the field in Atlanta.

After the Olympics, Swoopes had a decision to make: Not one, but two professional leagues for

One of the most colorful figures in the WNBA, Sheryl Swoopes has also played on two Olympic championship teams. Here she celebrates after scoring in the gold-medal game at the 2000 Olympics.
(Andy Lyons/Getty Images)

women were about to be formed in the United States. As an Olympic and collegiate star, she was being courted by both the American Basketball League (ABL) and the Women's National Basketball Association (WNBA). Swoopes finally agreed to play in the WNBA when league president VALERIE ACKERMAN promised her that she could play for the Houston Comets. Now a national celebrity, Swoopes remained true to Texas.

Swoopes and Houston turned out to be a winning combination. The Comets dominated the first four WNBA seasons, winning every championship. For the first three years, Swoopes's teammate CYNTHIA COOPER was the unquestioned on-court leader for the Comets. But in 2000, Swoopes was as formidable a presence as Cooper, winning regular season most valuable player (MVP) honors as Houston captured its fourth straight WNBA crown. Swoopes also played a major part in the women's national team's second consecutive Olympic gold medal campaign, this time at the 2000 games in Sydney, Australia.

Swoopes, who married Eric Jackson in 1993, continues to play for the Comets, although she suffered an injury in 2001 and spent the season on the sidelines. The couple live in Houston with their son, Jordan.

Further Reading

Layden, Joe. *Women in Sports: The Complete Book on the World's Greatest Female Athletes.* Santa Monica, Calif.: General Publishing Group, 1997, pp. 235–236.
Rutledge, Rachel. *The Best of the Best in Basketball.* Brookfield, Conn.: Millbrook Press, 1998, pp. 56–61.

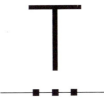

THOMPSON, JENNY
(1973–) *Swimmer*

The most decorated Olympic woman athlete of all time is Jenny Thompson, who has won 10 medals, eight of them gold. A gifted swimmer who specializes in freestyle and butterfly sprinting events, Thompson has also won 22 world championships during her long and distinguished career.

Born in Georgetown, Massachusetts, on February 26, 1973, Jenny Thompson is the youngest of four children—and the only daughter—in her family. When she was two years old, her parents divorced, and Jenny and her three older brothers were raised by their mother, Magrid Thompson, a medical technologist. "Jenny was going to be either the meekest person in the world or the most outspoken," one of her brothers confided to *Sports Illustrated*. Early on, Jenny was most definitely outspoken about her love of swimming. After trying out for a local team—and not making the cut—at the age of seven, she spent a year taking swim lessons every day, and the following year she not only made the team but became the best swimmer on it.

Over the next few years Thompson trained every day at the Seacoast Swimming Association in Dover, New Hampshire. The club was an hour away from Georgetown, so when Jenny was 12, the family moved to Dover to be closer to her practices. Two years later, Thompson swam in her first national competition and premiered with a bang as she won the 50-meter freestyle sprint at the 1987 Pan American Games. By this time a high school All-American, Thompson tried out, but failed to qualify for, the 1988 Olympic team. Disappointed, Thompson moved on and finished fourth in the 50-meter race at the World Championships. Her performance did not earn her a medal, but it did win her a scholarship to Stanford University.

At Stanford, Thompson quickly became the premier sprinter not only in the United States, but in the world. In 1991 she took top honors at the National Collegiate Athletic Association (NCAA) championships in the 50-meter and 100-meter freestyle events, and then, at the 1992 Olympic trials, set a world record in the 100-meter race and a U.S. record in the 50-meter event (needless to say, this time she qualified for the team). The world record left Thompson in tears. "It was the first time I've cried because I'm happy," she told *Time* magazine after the trials. "Other people get world records. Not me."

At the 1992 Olympic Games in Barcelona, Thompson took the silver medal in the 100-meter events, finishing second to Zhuang Yong of China, but finished fifth in the 50-meter freestyle race. Shaking off her disappointment, Thompson returned to the pool for the 100-meter freestyle relay and swam the anchor laps to lead the U.S. team to the gold medal. Days later she performed the same role in the 100-meter medley relay and, once again, helped her team win gold—and set a world record in the process.

Thompson's three-medal performance in Barcelona made her a national superstar, but she was personally disappointed, not only in her own performance, but in that of the Americans. Laden with talent, the U.S. women's Olympic swim team had gone to Barcelona favored to win as many as 11 of the 15 swim events, but ended up taking the top slot in only five races. Thompson herself had been favored to win both the 50-meter and 100-meter events, but she had come up short in both these individual races.

Nevertheless, Thompson returned to the United States a superstar, and the following year, she enhanced her reputation with six gold medals at the Pan Pacific Championships, as well as five national titles and five NCAA championships. That year Thompson was named the Swimmer of the Year by USA Swimming (the governing body for competitive swimming in the United States).

Thompson graduated from Stanford in 1995— one of the rare swimmers to complete her college degree. During her tenure at Stanford she won 19 NCAA titles and led her team to four consecutive all-around NCAA championships. Thompson elected to keep training with her college coach, Richard Quick, and set her sights on the 1996 Olympics. She entered the 1996 trials favored to win the 100-meter and 50-meter events, but in an upset, failed to qualify for either event. Thompson did qualify to swim in the relay events, however, and at the Atlanta games she helped the U.S. team win gold medals in both the 100-meter freestyle and the 100-meter medley relays. Then she swam the anchor leg for the U.S. team in the 200-meter freestyle race and won her third gold of the 1996 games.

Had Thompson chosen to retire after the 1996 Olympic Games, she still would have gone down in history as the most decorated swimmer in Olympic history—her Atlanta performance alone made her the first woman swimmer to win three relay gold medals, and her five gold medals put her in elusive company; BONNIE BLAIR was the only other American woman in history to win five gold medals. But Thompson chose to continue swimming, looking ahead to the 2000 games in Sydney, Australia.

In 1998, Thompson won the 100-meter freestyle and the 100-meter butterfly events at the U.S. National Championships. Those victories made her the 16th swimmer in history to win 20 or more national titles. The leading national title holder is TRACY CAULKINS, who holds 48 national championships. At the end of 1998, Thompson was once again named swimmer of the year by USA Swimming, and two years later, she qualified for her third Olympic contest. This time, Thompson had performed well enough at the trials to make the team, not only for the three relay races, but in the 100-meter freestyle and butterfly races.

At the Sydney games, Thompson failed to win a gold medal in an individual race, although she did pick up a bronze in the 100-meter freestyle. But in the relays, Thompson once again proved an invaluable part of the U.S. team, as she swam in the finals of the 100-meter freestyle, 200-meter freestyle, and 100-meter relays, helping her team win gold in all three races. Thompson retired from competitive swimming after the 2000 Olympics. She was a biology major at Stanford and plans to go to medical school and eventually become a doctor.

Further Reading

CNN/SI for Women. "Jenny Thompson," 100 Greatest Athletes, CNN/Sports Illustrated online. Available online. URL: http://sportsillustrated.cnn.com/siforwomen/top_100/62/. Posted on November 29, 1999.

Layden, Joe. *Women in Sports: The Complete Book on the World's Greatest Female Athletes.* Santa Monica, Calif.: General Publishing Group, 1997, pp. 227–228.

TORRENCE, GWEN
(1965–)   *Sprinter*

Gwen Torrence, winner of three Olympic gold medals, was one of the world's most natural athletes and one of the most hesitant as well. A lover of junk food and soap operas, Torrence had to be coaxed into training seriously for her sport. Once she did, however, she became a champion.

Born in Atlanta, Georgia, on June 12, 1965, Gwen Torrence was the youngest of five children. The Torrences lived in a housing project when Gwen was born, but by the time she got to high school they had moved into a house in the Atlanta suburb of Decatur. Gwen was a quiet high school student who made, as it turned out, a great deal of noise on the track. Spotting what he thought was an extraordinary natural talent, Ray Bonner, the physical education teacher at Decatur High School, asked Gwen to run for the school team. Gwen agreed to run for Bonner, but refused to wear either shorts or track shoes. "The spikes were too hot for my skinny legs," she explained to *Sports Illustrated* about her hesitations.

Torrence was equally hesitant when it came to training; Bonner had to drag her onto the track for team practice. Nevertheless, Torrence's talent shone through. When she was in 10th grade, Torrence ran a 220-yard dash wearing low-heeled patent leather pumps—and set an unofficial state record. After the race, Bonner approached her, and spoke plainly. "God will be angry with you if you waste such a natural talent," he reportedly said. Torrence finally relented and devoted herself more fully to her sport.

After graduating from Decatur, Torrence attended the University of Georgia on a track and field scholarship. At Georgia she won two National Collegiate Athletic Association (NCAA) championships in 1987, taking golds in the 100-meter and 200-meter events. By that time, Torrence had already made a national name for herself, having defeated Olympic champion EVELYN ASHFORD in the 55-meter dash at the 1986 Milrose Games. The next year, she married Manley Waller, and in 1988 Torrence competed in her first Olympic Games, in Seoul, South Korea, but failed to win a medal.

In 1989 Torrence left running altogether when she became pregnant and suffered complications that kept her confined to her bed for several months. Fortunately, she gave birth to a healthy son, Manley Waller Jr., in September of that year. Torrence returned to the track in 1990, but she had a difficult transition; the year away from the sport had left her out of practice and out of shape. But although Torrence did not win a single race in 1990, she did gain a new sense of ambition. She became determined to compete in the 1992 Olympic games and to win a gold medal.

In 1991 Torrence competed in the World Championships, picking up silver medals in the 100- and 200-meter events. The woman who beat her in both races, Germany's Katrin Krabbe, later tested positive for steroid use. Filled with a new sense of confidence, Torrence won the 100- and 200-meter sprints at the 1992 Olympic trials, and she went to Barcelona favored to win both races. But in her first race, the 100-meter dash, Torrence finished a disappointed fourth. She then made the mistake of telling the media that she believed three of her competitors in that race had taken performance-enhancing drugs. The other runners were offended by Torrence's remarks (no one tested positive), and she later issued a formal apology.

Amid this controversy Torrence prepared for the 200-meter race. This time Torrence lived up to expectations and won the event with a time of 21.81 seconds. Several days later she ran anchor for the 4 × 100 meter relay and helped the U.S. runners win gold. Now a double Olympic champion, Torrence had fulfilled her ambitions. Nevertheless, she decided to keep training; the 1996 Olympic Games would be held in Atlanta, her hometown, and Torrence wanted to win on her own turf.

In 1995 Torrence competed in the World Championships in Goteborg, Sweden. Although she won the title in the 100-meter race, she once again became embroiled in controversy when she easily beat the competition in the 200-meter final.

Gwen Torrence, winner of three Olympic gold medals, once set a state sprinting record in Georgia—while wearing a pair of patent leather pumps.
(Jed Jacobson/Getty Images)

After hearing several complaints from her opponents, the judges reviewed a tape of the race, and determined that Torrence had run out of her lane. She was disqualified from the race, and Merlene Ottey of Jamaica was awarded the gold. Ottey initially said publicly that Torrence was "cheating. She ran about two meters shorter than everyone else"—a quote that left Torrence in tears. But she later admitted that Torrence was far ahead of the others when she inadvertently crossed the lane, and that she would have won the race anyway.

At the 1996 Olympic trials, Torrence finished fourth in the 200-meter race and failed to make the team for that event, but she did qualify to run both the 100-meter individual and 4 × 100 meter relay races. In Atlanta, Torrence won a bronze medal in the 100-meter race and then, in front of her home crowd, helped the team take top honors in the 4 × 100 meter relay. She continued to compete in 1997, but she suffered a severe injury in 1998 and retired from the track for good. Divorced from Waller in 1997, she and Manley Jr. moved to Lithonia, Georgia. "Everyone wants to be the world's fastest woman," Torrence told *Sports Illustrated* in 1992. For a brief, shining time, Torrence was just that.

Further Reading

Biography Resource Center. "Gwen Torrence," *Great Women in Sports.* Detroit: Visible Ink Press, 1996.

Layden, Joe. *Women in Sports: The Complete Book on the World's Greatest Female Athletes.* Santa Monica. Calif.: General Publishing Group. 1997, pp. 239–240.

USATF Biographies. "Gwen Torrence," USATF.org, 2001. Available online. URL: http://www.usatf.org/athletes/bios/oldBios/2000/torrence.html. Downloaded on June 30, 2001.

TRASON, ANN
(1960–)   *Ultramarathoner*

The world's best female super-distance runner is Ann Trason. Not challenged enough by the basic 26-mile marathon courses, Trason has set her sights on longer distances. In so doing, she has set 20 world records in courses ranging from 50 to 100 miles.

Born in Albuquerque, New Mexico, on June 30, 1960, Ann Trason loved to run middle and long distances from an early age. She ran cross-country for her junior high team, and in high school, she ran at the U.S. Track Championships' 10-kilometer race and finished sixth. That performance won Trason a track-and-field scholarship to the University of New Mexico. But days before she was to run in her first competition, she suffered a serious injury and underwent knee surgery. Told by her doctor that she would never run again, Trason elected to concentrate on her studies.

Transferring to the University of California at Berkeley before her sophomore year, Trason earned an A-minus average as a biochemistry major. Meanwhile, she stayed off her knee—and off the track—for the remainder of her college years. After graduating from Berkeley, Trason stayed in the Bay Area, and took a job as a microbiology instructor. In the fall of 1985—a full seven years after she had injured her knee—Trason decided to go back to running. She began training for marathon races, and when she entered her first competition, she completed the course in an impressive time of two hours and 40 minutes.

Trason could have remained on the marathon circuit, and more than likely would have earned a lucrative living doing so. But another event had caught her eye in 1986, when she and a friend ran on a portion of the Western States Trail, near Lake Tahoe, California. "I just immediately fell in love with it," she told *Runner's World* of that experience. "I fell down—of course I fell down. And this great billowing cloud of dust rose up. But instead of choking me, it felt like a cloud was lifting me up."

In 1988 Trason traveled to France with her then fiancé, Carl Anderson (the two married in 1991). She was there to run a marathon, which she won with a time of two hours and 45 minutes, but she also knew that the World 100K (kilometer) Championships were happening in Spain. On a whim—"We're so close to Spain anyway," Anderson remembers her telling him—Trason decided to run in the race. She not only completed the course with ease, but she won the event and set a world record for women in the process.

The following year, Trason set records in the 100-mile races on both road and track courses, and she then went on to win the U.S. 24-Hour Race. Running for a full 24 hours in that event, Trason traveled a total distance of 143 miles, 132 yards. In 1990, she set a record on her favorite trail, the Western States, a 100-mile course that begins in Squaw Valley, Idaho, and ends in Auburn, California. Later that year she was upset

in the World 100K Cup by the British runner Eleanor Adams, but she came back in 1991 to win that title as well.

Trason had a serious setback in 1996 when she suffered another severe knee injury. Once again she underwent surgery (after running 10 miles on the treadmill the morning of the operation), and the doctor who performed the procedure informed Trason that the tendon and muscle of her knee had become completely separated from the bone.

For most athletes this would have been a career-ending injury, but Trason, who seems at times to possess superhuman strength, returned to training several months later. In 1997 she returned to competition, in time to post her ninth consecutive victory on the Western States Trail. Trason, who lives with Anderson in Oakland, California, continues to race in ultramarathon events. She took her 10 straight Western States title in 1998, and she took top honors in that event again in 1999, 2000, and 2001.

Further Reading

Brant, John. "One of a Kind," *Runner's World* vol. 32, no. 11 (November 1997): 92–99.

Cooper, Bob. "Running Circles Around the Boys," *Women's Sports and Fitness* vol. 12, no. 3 (April 1990): 62–66.

Milroy, Andy. "Profile: Ann Trason," Ultramarathon World. Available online. URL: http://fox.nstn.ca/~dblaikie/m02oc99a.html. Downloaded on June 25, 2001.

TYUS, WYOMIA
(1945–) *Sprinter*

At the 1964 Olympic Games in Tokyo, Wyomia Tyus blazed through the 100-meter final to capture gold in world-record fashion. And as if that were not enough glory for Tyus, she did it again four years later in Mexico City. In doing so, Tyus became the only woman to win gold medals in the 100-meter contest in two consecutive Olympic Games.

Unlike many other world-class sports figures, Tyus did not grow up in a family that paid a great deal of attention to athletics. She was born in

Griffin, Georgia, on August 29, 1945, the youngest of four children. Her mother was a laundry worker, and her father, who died when Wyomia was 15, worked in a dairy. Young Wyomia was the only one of her brothers and sisters who demonstrated any interest in sports, and her interest was, from the beginning, focused on track and field. It was the only sport in which she participated in high school, and the teenaged Tyus was such an impressive sprinter that she caught the eye of Ed Temple, who was WILMA RUDOLPH's teacher and coach.

Like Rudolph, Tyus went to college at Tennessee State University, where she worked not only with Temple but occasionally with Rudolph, who was five years older than Tyus and eager to help the younger runner reach her potential. Rudolph and Temple's training paid off very quickly for Tyus, who was touring Europe and demonstrating her speed and talent when she was barely 18.

Early in 1964, Tyus broke a world record when she ran the 70-meter indoor event in 7.5 seconds. But although Tyus had run the fastest indoor 70-meter race, she was not as impressive outdoors. Although it may not seem to make much difference whether a race is run outside or inside, in reality there are factors that separate the two types of races. The most important of these is weather. A race run inside is never influenced by natural forces such as sun, rain, or wind. For that reason, runers in races inside usually have faster times than those in races of the same distance that take place outside. Many, like Tyus early in her career, find they focus better inside because there are fewer distractions.

Because Tyus was a much more impressive runner inside than outside, few expected her to excel at the 1964 Tokyo Summer Olympics track events, which, as always, were held outdoors. But Tyus silenced the skeptics in dramatic fashion, not only by coasting to victory, but by shattering the world record in the process. A few days after her 100-meter individual triumph, she ran in the U.S. 4 × 100 relay and added a silver medal to her winnings.

Wyomia Tyus returned to the United States an Olympic hero, and she continued her sprinting dominance at Tennessee State, winning the 1965 and 1966 collegiate outdoor 100-meter championships. In 1966, Tyus and Edith McGuire, the 100-meter silver medalist in Tokyo and Tyus's Tennessee State teammate, were among several African-American athletes sent by the U.S. State Department on what was called a "goodwill tour of African nations." Tyus and McGuire traveled to several towns in Ethiopia, where they held a teaching demonstration for schoolchildren on the fundamentals of running. At the end of the tour, Tyus and McGuire were praised by the U.S. ambassador to Ethiopia as "a great inspiration who personified the freedom from reticence to which these young Ethiopian athletes aspire."

Back in the United States in 1967, Tyus began training for the 1968 Olympic Games. But she was no longer as dominant in the sprint events as she had been the previous two years. Two prominent sprinters, Irena Kirszenstein of Poland and fellow U.S. runner Barbara Ferrell, were beginning to challenge Tyus. Ferrell beat Tyus in the 100-meter event at the All-American International in July of 1967, and Kirszenstein matched Tyus's world record in a 100-meter event at an all-European event that same year.

To make matters more difficult for Tyus, after winning the indoor national championships in the 60-meter event (beating Ferrell by inches), she discovered a wound on her leg. The infection worsened and became more painful, and it was finally diagnosed as a black widow-spider bite. The infection was so painful that Tyus missed several weeks of training and entered the 1967 outdoor national championships at far less than full strength. The wound severely hampered Tyus's performance; she finished a disappointing fourth in the 100-meter race, as Barbara Ferrell matched Tyus and Kirszenstein's world record time of 11.1 seconds in the final.

Happily for Tyus, she recovered in time to regain her winning form for a meet between European and U.S. athletes. Pitted against Kirszenstein and Ferrell, Tyus sped to a first-place finish in the 100-meter race, finishing in 11.31 seconds, just $^2/_{10}$ of a second off the world-record time. Kirszenstein finished an eyelash behind, also with a time of 11.32, and Ferrell, coming in third, clocked a time of 11.4 seconds. Describing the race, the *New York Times* said that "Miss Tyus leaned so hard to the tape to hold off her rivals that she fell and was stretched out on the track." Tyus had won the race, but the stage was set for an Olympic showdown.

The 1968 Olympics in Mexico City remain one of the most talked-about games in the history of the event. There were several athletic high points, including long jumper Bob Beamon coming out of nowhere to shatter the world record with a leap of 8.90 meters, a mark that would remain untouchable for 20 years. But perhaps the most enduring images of the games occurred on the medal stand during medal ceremony following the men's 200-meter event. Two of the figures on the medal stand, gold medalist Tommy Smith and third-place finisher John Carlos, thrust their gloved fists in the air in a gesture that became known as the Black Power salute and stood that way, without moving, throughout the playing of the U.S. national anthem. It was a silent protest by Carlos and Smith of the way they believed African Americans were treated in the United States.

Smith and Carlos's gesture was the climactic moment in what had been an ongoing controversy. During the tumultuous year leading up to the Mexico City games, several African-American athletes had become angered by what they expressed as an ongoing "oppression and injustice" imposed on blacks in the United States. There was some talk and speculation that these athletes might boycott the Olympic Games as a form of protest, but all of the athletes ended up making the journey to Mexico City. The U.S. Olympic Committee was outraged by what it determined was unsportsmanlike behavior by Smith and Carlos on the medal stand and immediately expelled both athletes from the Olympic village.

In the midst of this controversy, Tyus quietly prepared to defend her championship in the 100-meter event. She knew the competition would be much fiercer than what she had seen in Tokyo; Ferrell and Kirszenstein were both capable of wresting the title from her. And the field of finals included not only these sprinters but three other runners who had at one time or another held the world record in the 100-meter event.

Tyus's jitters showed at the beginning of the race; she left her blocks before the starting gun went off and was charged with a false start. According to Olympic rules, every athlete is entitled to one false start before a given race without penalty. But a second false start results in immediate disqualification. Tyus returned to her blocks and this time, the start was true. She burst onto the track and sprinted to the finish line ahead of all of her competitors, and when she touched the tape she had set a new world record, finishing the event in 11 seconds flat.

Ecstatic that she had defended her title of "world's fastest woman" successfully, but also sympathetic to the plight of Carlos and Smith, Tyus decided to dedicate her second gold medal of the games, which she and Ferrell won as members of the U.S. 4 × 100 relay team, to the two expelled athletes. It was a gesture of great empathy by Tyus, who having grow up in the South, was well acquainted with the inequities endured by African-American athletes.

One year after the 1968 games, Tyus retired from amateur athletics. "After the Olympics," she later said, "I didn't even run across the street." Unfortunately for Tyus, she competed during a time when top amateur athletes were unable to reap any financial reward whatsoever from their endeavors. Tyus earned free travel and tremendous accolades from her fans, but in the face of all of her triumphs, she was unable to help her mother make ends meet. When Marie Tyus applied for welfare, the agents suggested that she seek financial assistance from her famous daughter. Mrs Tyus replied that "my daughter don't get paid for that. Don't get it wrong now. My daughter don't get money for that."

In 1971 Tyus married Art Simone. The couple had a daughter, Simone, and a son, Tyus Tillman. In 1973 a new professional organization called the International Track Association was formed. Tyus returned to competition, and for the first time in her career, she earned money for her winnings. After turning in her track shoes for good in 1975, she became a part-time television commentator, as well as an outdoor education teacher in Los Angeles.

Further Reading

Davis, Michael D. *Black American Women in Olympic Track and Field: A Complete Illustrated Reference.* Jefferson, N.C.: McFarland & Co., 1992.

Layden, Joe. *Women in Sports: The Complete Book on the World's Greatest Female Athletes.* Santa Monica, Calif.: General Publishing Group, 1997, p. 244.

V

VARE, GLENNA (Glenna Collett)
(1903–1989)   *Golfer*

Glenna Collett Vare, the leading women's golfer of the 1920s and 1930s, was one of the most influential athletes of her era. A master of several sports as a youngster, she grew up to win a record six national titles, as well as several of the most major championships of the time.

Born in New Haven, Connecticut, on June 20, 1903, Glenna Collett was raised in an intensely athletic family. Her father, Edwin Collett, was a national cycling champion, and her mother was an avid tennis player. Growing up with her brother, Edwin, Glenna's favorite sport was baseball. She was often the only girl playing in neighborhood games, but she was gifted enough with the bat and glove to play on her brother's team.

When Glenna was 14, her mother suggested that she try tennis. Glenna enjoyed the sport and played it well, but she discovered her true passion when she accompanied her father to the Metacomet Country Club in Providence, Rhode Island (the Colletts had moved to Rhode Island when Glenna was six). Watching her father and his cohorts hit golf balls on the course, she became

fascinated with the game and began playing that very weekend.

Soon after her initial golfing experience, Glenna began taking lessons with Alex Smith, a teacher who had himself won two U.S. Open championships. Smith helped Glenna develop a long, fluid swing as well as consistent putting and short-driving skills. At the age of 17, Glenna dropped out of high school to compete full-time on the amateur circuit. Later that year, she won her first golfing championship.

By 1922, Collett had become one of the most consistent players in women's golf. Her long drives had become her defining feature; she regularly hit 200 yards off the tee, and during one tournament in 1921, she hit a 307-yard shot, at the time the longest drive in the history of the women's game. Her strength, along with her accuracy, made Collett the favorite to win the 1922 U.S. Women's Amateur Championship. Collett found the pressure from the media difficult to handle, but she adjusted graciously to life in the spotlight. In a close tournament final, she outplayed four previous tournament winners to claim the title.

After winning the championship, Collett became the most popular player in the sport.

Beloved by media and fans alike, Collett proved to be a gracious presence on the links, in both victory and defeat. And there were plenty of victories for the five foot, six inch New Englander. In addition to her six Women's Amateur titles—she repeated as tournament champion in 1925, 1928, 1930, and 1935—Collett won the Canadian Ladies Open in 1923 and 1924, and she took top honors at the French Ladies Open in 1925. The one major championship that Collett never won was the British Ladies Open, although she finished second twice.

In 1931 Collett married Edward H. Vare. The couple had two children, Glenna and Edwin. Vare took the 1933 and 1934 seasons off to care for her babies, but returned to the links in late 1934 to compete for the Curtis Cup. The following year, she won her final U.S. Women's Amateur title, defeating a 17-year-old newcomer named PATTY BERG to take top honors.

Vare was one of six charter members of the Women's Golf Hall of Fame in 1950, and two years later, a prestigious award was named in her honor. Every year, the Vare Trophy is given to the player with the lowest course average. Vare continued to play competitively through the 1950 and her final appearance at the U.S. Women's Amateur competition was in 1958. After that she played sporadically in senior competitions, and in 1986 competed in the Point Judith (Rhode Island) Invitational Tournament for the 62nd consecutive year. She died three years later, of heart failure.

Further Reading

Cross, Thomas S. "Glenna Collett Vare," *Great Athletes.* Hackensack, N.J.: Salem Press, 2001. p. 2646.

Layden, Joe. *Women in Sports: The Complete Book on the World's Greatest Female Athletes.* Santa Monica, Calif.: General Publishing Group, Press, 1997.

W

WADE, MARGARET
(Lily Margaret Wade)
(1912–   )   *Basketball Player, Basketball Couch*

When she was a student at Delta State University, Margaret Wade was a pretty good basketball player. As coach of the Delta State women's basketball team, 41 years later, Wade became one of her sport's legendary figures. Under her guidance, the Delta State team became the first great dynasty in women's basketball.

Lily Margaret Wade was born in McCool, Mississippi, in 1912. When she was 17, Wade entered what was then called Delta State Teachers College, in Cleveland, Mississippi. During her first three years, she was a starter for the Delta State varsity team. In those days, women's basketball was played with six people on each side. The defending three players were confined to the back half of the court, while the front three, in the scoring court, were the only players allowed to shoot the ball. Wade, a forward in the scoring court, was one of the better shooters on her team. Delta State boasted a good team, but right before Wade's senior year, in the fall of 1932, the players were informed that the

administration had decided not to continue their women's basketball program. The sport of basketball, it had decided, was too strenuous a game for girls to play.

Devastated by the decision, Wade and her teammates protested passionately. The even burned their uniforms in public to show their distress, but their complaints fell on deaf ears. Wade stayed at Delta State despite the decision and completed her degree in 1933. Eager to play basketball again, she joined the Tupelo Red Wings, a semi-professional team. But when Wade was 24, she suffered a severe knee injury that effectively ended her playing career.

Her on-court days behind her, Wade remained determined to stay involved in basketball. In 1936, she began her career as a coach. For the next 21 years, she coached at the Mississippi scholastic level, leading teams from Marietta, Belden, and Cleveland high schools. During that tenure Wade compiled a dazzling 453-89 win-loss record.

In 1959, Wade decided to leave high school coaching. Then 47, Wade was lured back to her alma mater; Delta State hired her as an assistant professor of health, recreation, and physical education. Wade took the position, determined to restore women's basketball to the university. It took her 14 years to do it, but in 1973, Delta State fielded its first basketball team in 41 years. At the age of 60, Wade served as the team's head coach and, with her humor, passion, and profound knowledge of her beloved sport, promptly built a dynasty.

In 1974 Delta State compiled a record of 16 wins and two losses. The following year, the school won its first Association of Intercollegiate Athletics for Women (AIAW) championship. Delta State would defend its title successfully in 1975 and 1976; during that three-year span, the team had a win-loss record of 93 to 4, and in one phenomenal stretch, the team won 51 consecutive games.

In 1979, Wade retired from Delta State. Five years later, she was inducted in the National Basketball Hall of Fame—the first woman in history to be accorded that honor. Wade led a quiet life in Mississippi until her death in 1995. Her name lives on in college basketball; each year, the top player in women's collegiate basketball is given an award in recognition of excellence. That award is the Wade Trophy, named for the Mississippi native who took the sport of women's basketball to a higher level.

Further Reading

Basketball Hall of Famers Web Site. "Margaret Wade," Basketball Hall of Fame Online. Available online. URL: http://www.hoophall.com/halloffamers/Wade.htm. Downloaded on May 14, 2001.

Layden, Joe. *Women in Sports: The Complete Book on the World's Greatest Female Athletes.* Santa Monica, Calif.: General Publishing Group, 1997.

⊞ WASHINGTON, ORA
(1898–1971) *Tennis Player*

If ALTHEA GIBSON is the Jackie Robinson of women's tennis, then Ora Washington is the Josh Gibson. Althea Gibson, like Robinson, broke the color barrier to become champion, and she showed the world that African Americans belonged on the tennis court with their white counterparts. Like Josh Gibson, who hit more home runs in his career than Babe Ruth, Washington was possibly the best player of her time, but she was never allowed the opportunity to prove it. Washington won the all-black American Tennis Association (ATA) championship seven years in a row, between 1929 and 1935, and so thoroughly dominated the sport—which she could play competitively only against other African-American women—that she went completely undefeated during several seasons.

Born in Philadelphia, Pennsylvania, in 1898, Ora Mae Washington first began playing tennis when she was in her early twenties. Grieving over the loss of a sister, Ora was advised to take up tennis by some friends, who thought that the new activity would provide some diversion. Ora immediately showed talent on the court, and months after first picking up the racket, she began competing. In 1924, Washington defeated the top-ranked African-American player, Dorothy Radcliffe, to win her first national championship. For the next 12 years, Washington would not lose a match, either in the ATA circuit or in the other all-African-American tennis league, the African American National Tennis Organization.

Washington, who never had an official tennis lesson, developed her own form and her own routines. Rather than holding the racket at its grip, she would clutch it about halfway up the handle and hit balls all over the court. Unlike virtually every other tennis player who has ever competed, Washington disdained warming up. "I'd rather start from scratch and warm up as I went along," she said later. It may have been somewhat bizarre, but her formula and style was extremely successful. A champion in doubles as well as singles, Washington won a total of 14 ATA crowns during a seven-year stretch.

Like Josh Gibson, whose career parallelled Ruth's, Washington had a white counterpart who earned much more fame and fortune simply on the basis of her color. While Washington was beating every woman in sight in the ATA, Helen Wills was dominating the U.S. Lawn Tennis Association (USLTA) tournaments. Like Washington in the ATA Wills held her championship for seven consecutive years. But although Washington expressed her desire to play Wills several times, the two never played; Wills refused the challenges each and every time.

As dominating a player as Washington was, tennis was not the only sport she excelled at. As the starting center for the *Philadelphia Tribune* girls' basketball team for 18 years, Washington toured the country with her teammates during the 1930s and 1940s. The team offered clinics and exhibitions, also playing any team that would challenge them.

Washington retired from tennis in 1935, but she was coaxed back into playing by one of her rivals, Flora Lomax, who had won the ATA title in Washington's absence in 1936. Lomax challenged Washington to try to regain the title, and Washington, taking the bait, came back onto the court in 1937 to whip Lomax and reclaim the ATA championship. Washington stayed on the ATA tour until game officials asked her to retire—she was, they claimed, spoiling the hopes of younger players, who would rather not play at all than face the prospect of playing her.

After her second retirement, Washington went into domestic service. It might seem like an inauspicious ending to a splendid sporting story, but Washington made her second career a successful one. By 1961 she had earned enough money to buy her own building, where she prospered as a landlord until her death in 1971.

Further Reading

Biography Resource Center. "Ora Washington," *Great Women in Sports.* Detroit, Mich.: Visible Ink Press, 1996.
Biography Resource Center. "Ora Washington," *Notable Black American Women, Book 2.* Detroit, Mich.: Gale Research, 1996.

⊞ WHITE, NERA
(1936–) *Basketball Player*

In the 1950s and 1960s—long before the Women's National Basketball Association (WNBA), when women's basketball was not yet an Olympic sport

and the game was played with six players on a team—a lanky, six-foot-tall woman dominated the courts of Nashville, Tennessee. Her name was Nera White, and according to some, she may have been the best all-around player in women's basketball history.

Born on a farm in Oak Knob Ridge, Tennessee, in 1936, Nera White was the oldest of seven children. A natural athlete, White grew up playing basketball for fun with her siblings. As a student at Peabody College for Teachers in Nashville, White began playing for Nashville Business College (of which Peabody was a subsidiary), and she received full room and board for her efforts. During the 1950s and 1960s, women's collegiate basketball fell under the governance of the Amateur Athletic Union (AAU), which gave its players unlimited eligibility. So even after White graduated from Peabody in 1959, she was allowed to continue playing for the Nashville team.

This she did for another full 10 years. In the fall of 1959, White took a job in a printing shop, run by H. A. Balls, a wealthy businessman who owned the Nashville Business College team. White worked hard at the shop and was paid one dollar per hour for her efforts. Fortunately, every hour she spent playing or traveling for the team was counted as time working, so she was, in a sense, paid for playing basketball.

White, however, so loved the game of basketball that she probably would have played without financial compensation. During her day on the court, the rules for the women's game was very different from those for the men's game. There were six players on each side, with three players roaming the back court, and three on the otherside end who had the right to score. A talented guard who could both pass and shoot, White could also rebound when she was positioned under the basket, and she was equally effective driving through the lane for a layup or shooting a jumper from the perimeter.

Her inspired and ingenious play helped the Nashville team win 10 AAU championships, including eight consecutive titles between 1962 and 1969. White was the undisputed leader of the squad and so dominated play that she was named AAU Tournament MVP (most valuable player) 10 times. She could seemingly do just about anything on the court—including dunking.

In 1969, White decided to leave the Nashville team. One of her teammates had mothered a son, and that player, who was not married but already had another child, could not afford to keep him. White decided to adopt the boy, whom she named Jeff. She stayed with the printing shop and lived with Jeff in Nashville. Then, in 1982, H. A. Balls died, and his two nephews took over the shop. White lost her job and decided to become a farmer. She moved back to her old stomping grounds of Oak Knob Ridge to do so. Although White became something of a recluse after leaving Nashville, she did make the trip to Springfield, Massachusetts, in 1992, to become one of the first two women, along with Lucy Harris, to be inducted into the National Basketball Hall of Fame.

Further Reading

Marantz, Steve. "A Good Life Regretted," *The Sporting News,* March 4, 1996, pp. 32–36.

Lannin, Joanne. *A History of Basketball for Girls and Women: From Bloomers to Big Leagues.* Minneapolis, Minn.: Lerner Sports, 2000.

WHITE, WILLYE
(1939–) *Sprinter, Long Jumper*

Long jumper and sprinter Willye White is the only U.S. woman to compete in five Olympic Games. During her long and illustrious career, she rose from an impoverished childhood in the segregated South to win 12 national long jump championships and two Olympic silver medals.

Born in Money, Mississippi, on January 1, 1939, to Johnnie White, a disabled World War II veteran, and his wife, Willie, White grew up on a plantation in the Mississippi Delta. During much of her childhood, Willye, along with her three younger siblings, was raised by her maternal grandparents. Money was scarce in the family, and

by the time she was eight, Willye was working in the cotton fields for eight dollars a day. Willye's rare athletic gifts also came early to her; she often competed against older children and could beat them regularly at a variety of sports.

At the age of 10, White, who at the time attended a segregated elementary school in the town of Greenwood, tried out for the varsity track team at the community high school. White promptly outran all of the older girls and made the team.

After leading her high school team to area track championships for three consecutive years, White was recommended in 1956 by her high school coach to attend Tennessee State University's summer track-and-field training camp—the same program that WILMA RUDOLPH and WYOMIA TYUS would later attend. At the age of 17, White performed impressively in the program and was selected as a member of the Tennessee State varsity team—known as Ed Temple's Tigerbelles—which competed at the Amateur Athletic Union (AAU) championships in Philadelphia at the end of the summer.

White performed brilliantly in Philadelphia, posting a broad jump of 18 feet, six inches—a new U.S. girls' division record. Willye also competed in the women's division, and competing against several track-and-field veterans, she finished second in the long jump to Margaret Matthews.

The following week, the young upstart from Mississippi found herself at the Olympic trials in Washington, D.C., vying for a spot on the team that would travel to Australian, Melbourne, that September.

During the trials, White and Matthews dominated the long-jumping competition, and at the end of the competition she had finished second, with a leap of 19 feet, four inches, a mere $5^1/_2$ inches behind Matthews's winning (and record-setting) jump of 19 feet, $9^1/_2$ inches. White had made the team, and the next month, she was bound for Australia.

Matthews, a 19-year-old from Atlanta who was White's teammate not only in Melbourne but at Tennessee State, was a gifted long jumper, but she could not find a rhythm in Melbourne. Distracted at the games, perhaps because of the cold weather, and possibly because the Tennessee State coach, Ed Temple, did not make the trip to Australia with his athletes, Matthews jumped poorly in the qualifying rounds and failed to make the finals. White, by contrast, kept her concentration through the competition and qualified for the finals. In the medal rounds she leaped an impressive 19 feet, $11^{1}/_{2}$ inches, good enough for the silver medal and a new U.S. record.

The following year Matthews set a new U.S. record with a leap of 20 feet, one inch, becoming the first jumper from the United States to break the 20-foot jumping record. Matthews's new mark lasted precisely four days, until White shattered it with a 20 foot, $2^{1}/_{2}$ inch effort in Warsaw. White went on to hold her record for a glorious 48 hours; then Matthews, competing in Budapest, jumped 20 feet, $3^{1}/_{2}$ inches.

In 1960, Matthews and White graduated from Tennessee State. Matthews retired from competition, but White continued to compete and became the premier long jumper in the United States, winning the national championship that year and then qualifying for the Rome Olympics in September. Unfortunately, White lost her rhythm during the Olympics and performed poorly. She said later, "I was overconfident, and this is as bad as no confidence. In Rome, I was the first to jump and I had no excitement and no butterflies—and that was bad." White finished in 16th place.

Next year, White began sprinting competitively and, true to form, she soon became one of the fastest runners on the national team. Running in the 100-meter event in Stuttgart, Germany, she finished second to Wilma Rudolph, who set a world record with a time of 11.2 seconds. But White, running close behind Rudolph, clocked an 11.4 seconds time—equal to the old world record.

In 1964, White once again qualified for the Olympics in both the long jump and as a member of the 4 × 100 relay team. At the Tokyo games, she finished a disappointing 12th in the long jump—her leap of 19 feet, 11 inches was more than a foot

shorter than her best performances—but her luck improved in the 4 × 100 relays. Running on a team anchored by gold-medal winner Wyomia Tyus, White helped her team to a second-place finish, earning her second and final Olympic medal.

Willye White went on to compete in two more Olympic Games—in Mexico City in 1968 and in Munich in 1972—but her luck in the long jump did not improve. She finished 11th in the event in both Olympiads. After the Munich Games she retired from competition and took a job as a health administrator in Chicago. She was named to the President's Commission on Olympic Sports in 1976. After White left the commission in 1980, she returned to Chicago, when she became the director of health fitness for the Chicago Department of Public Health. In this capacity, White runs sports programs for underprivileged young people. When asked if she was disappointed that she never won Olympic gold, White smile and shrugged. "I won the gold medal of my life," she said.

Further Reading

Lamb, Yannick Rice. "Olympic Legends." *Essence* vol. 26, no. 9 (January 1996), pp. 93–94.

Layden, Joe. *Women in Sports: The Complete Book on the World's Greatest Female Athletes.* Santa Monica, Calif.: General Publishing Group, 1997, p. 256.

Davis, Michael D. *Black American Women in Olympic Track and Field: A Complete Illustrated Reference.* Jefferson, N.C.: McFarland & Co., 1992.

WHITWORTH, KATHY
(Kathryne Whitworth)
(1939–) *Golfer*

Kathy Whitworth's 88 Ladies' Professional Golf Association (LPGA) titles make her the most successful woman golfer ever to play the sport professionally.

Born in Monahans, Texas, on September 27, 1939, Kathy Whitworth was the shy, gentle daughter of Morris Whitworth, a hardware store owner, and his homemaker wife, Carol. Growing up in Jal, New Mexico, Kathy first picked up a golf club at the age of 15. Morris was his daughter's first teacher, and during those first years on the course, Kathy used her deceased grandfather's clubs.

Whitworth attended Odessa College in Texas, and as a student there she took top honors in the New Mexico State Amateur Open in 1957 and 1958. When she was 19, she left college to turn professional, and she traveled to Augusta, Georgia, home of the Titleholder's Championships—at the time one of the major tournaments in women's golf—to compete in the 1958 tournament.

The world of women's sports is full of miraculous stories—young athletes who stunned the nation or the world by finishing near the top of their very first competition or coming out of nowhere to claim a major championship. Not so with Kathy Whitworth, who played plainly and even poorly in her first few tournaments. She finished near the bottom of the list at the 1958 Titleholders Championships and did not win a championship until 1962—her fifth year on the tour.

In the meantime, Whitworth kept competing and kept improving. Shortly after joining the tour, she began training with the renowned coach Harvey Penick, who would later work with the golfers Ben Crenshaw and Tom Kite. Under Penick's tutelage, Whitworth, who already had a superb short game, learned to stand straighter over the ball and to turn her shoulder more fully during her swings. She also dropped about 50 pounds and began winning. In 1963, Whitworth won eight tournaments. The next season, however, she slumped badly, finishing the year with only one win. Penick scolded her for becoming too cocky. Whitworth did not enjoy the rebuke, but she took it seriously. In fact, she would later call it the "grandest lesson [she'd] ever learned."

Back on track, Whitworth won seven tournaments in 1965. By the end of the 1960s, her championships totaled 56. Unlike many of her peers, who competed in the major tournaments and in competitions close to their homes, Whitworth traveled extensively to play and usually strode off the course carrying the trophy. Even so, she was never a big celebrity—there were more outgoing golfers on the course, as well as figures who naturally attracted more attention.

In the mid-1970s, Whitworth suffered a severe depression and almost quit the game. Although she was still winning tournaments, she was not dominating golf the way she had in the 1960s. But Whitworth stayed on the links, and in 1981 she became the first woman player to earn $1 million in career winnings. Three years later, she won three tournaments—enough to best Sam Snead's record of 82 career titles and to make Whitworth the champion of champions.

Whitworth also contributed to the sport of golf off the links. She served four separate stints as president of the LPGA, the last one in 1989, when she guided the organization through some difficult financial times.

In 1990 Whitworth retired from the tour. Throughout her playing career she had not only won a record number of tournaments, but she had reaped many other prizes as well. Whitworth captured the Vare Trophy, named in honor of GLEN-NAVARE and awarded to the player with the lowest course average, seven times. Whitworth was named LPGA player of the year seven times as well, and in 1975 she was inducted into the LPGA Hall of Fame. In 1985 Whitworth became only the third woman (PATTY BERG and BABE DIDRIKSON ZAHARIAS were the others) to win the prestigious William Richardson award, bestowed on a player who has made "consistent contributions to the game of golf."

Since her retirement, Whitworth has remained an active presence in the golfing world. She is a contributor to *Golf for Women* magazine, provides televised instructional segments for The Golf Channel and serves as Chief Executive Officer (CEO) and manager of the Kathy Whitworth Golf School for Women, in Orlando, Florida.

Further Reading

GolfWeb. "Kathy Whitworth," PGATour.com. Available online. URL: http://www.golfweb.com/u/ce/feature/pgatour/0,1977,839844,00.html. Posted on March 23, 1999.

Layden, Joe. *Women in Sports: The Complete Book on the World's Greatest Female Athletes.* Santa Monica, Calif.: General Publishing Group, 1997, pp. 256–257.

Smith, Lissa, editor. *Nike Is a Goddess: The History of Women in Sports.* New York: Atlantic Monthly Press, 1998, pp. 91–93.

Women's Sports Illustrated online. "Kathy Whitworth," SI for Women: 100 Greatest Athletes. Available online. URL: http://sportsillustrated.cnn.com/siforwomen/top_100/35/. Posted on November 29, 1999.

WILLIAMS, ESTHER
(Esther Jane Williams)
(1923–)   *Swimmer*

Esther Williams became a much bigger name in Hollywood than she ever was in the sporting world. As a competitive swimmer she never won an Olympic medal or even competed in an international competition. But thanks to terrific timing and Williams's own special brand of charisma, she may well be the United States' most famous—and certainly its most financially successful—swimmer.

Given her future stardom in movies, it is fitting that the life of Esther Jane Williams began in Los Angeles, California. Born there on August 8, 1923, Esther grew up swimming and surfing on the beaches of her hometown. When she was nine, she attended the 1932 Olympic Games, which took place in Los Angeles. Witnessing U.S. heroes Buster Crabbe and ELEANOR HOLM swim to Olympic gold put ambitious thoughts in Esther's head. She began taking swimming more seriously, and by the age of 16 she had won three national championships in both the breaststroke and backstroke events.

Williams trained rigorously for the 1940 Olympics, and had those games taken place she very likely would have been an international champion. But fate intervened; World War II caused the cancellation of the Olympics, and Williams, at the top of her form but without a competition to prove it, ended up signing on as a swimmer with Billy Rose's Aquacade.

Rose was at the time the husband of Eleanor Holm, and several years earlier he had devised the showy and splashy swimming revue with Holm in mind. But Holm was ready to move on in 1940, leaving a star-sized hole in his production. Rose immediately recognized in Williams a charisma similar to that of his wife, and he built his 1940 show around her.

The Aquacade folded in 1941, but Williams was by then a star. On the lookout for a new celebrity, Metro-Goldwyn-Mayer (MGM), the most prestigious movie studio of its era, set its sights on Williams and signed her to a long-term contract. The studio executives were hoping that Williams would become a kind of water-borne SONJA HENIE, an exquisitely feminine athlete who could perform at her sport and, as important, turn a hefty profit.

Williams, given full star treatment from the moment she arrived on the set of her first movie, did not disappoint. In 15 years, she made more than 20 movies. With titles such as *Bathing Beauty, Million Dollar Mermaid,* and *Neptune's Darling,* most of her movies featured Williams doing what she did best—performing in, and often under, the water. Thanks to what was then state-of-the-art camera work and creative direction by Busby Berkeley, one of MGM's top directors, Williams splashed, spun, and shot through the water in lavish musical numbers that cost a fortune to produce and made a mint at the box office. Williams, a consummate athlete as well as a movie star, used her talent and strength to pull off elaborate dances underwater. By doing so, she unwittingly invented a new sport. Participants in synchronized swimming, now a fully sanctioned Olympic sport, have Esther Williams to thank.

After more than a decade at MGM, Williams left the studio in 1955. She continued to appear in a variety of movies, but she kept her feet on dry land for the remainder of her film career. In the meantime, she spent time with her family, including her third husband, Fernando Lamas; her stepson, Lorenzo Lamas; and her three children (from her second husband, Ben Gage) Benjamin, Susan, and Kimball. Williams had married Leonard Kovner in 1940. A year after she divorced in 1944, she had wed Gage. Divorced from Gage in 1959, Williams married Lamas in 1962. He died in 1987.

Now a Hollywood icon, Williams still occasionally appears in television and movie roles. In 1998 she wrote a successful memoir of her life, *The Million Dollar Mermaid*. She lives in Hollywood with her fourth husband, Edward Bell.

Further Reading

The Official Esther Williams Website. "A Short Bio of Esther Williams." Available online. URL: http://www.esther-williams.com/bio.htm. Posted on March 29, 1999.

Perry, Pat. "Esther Williams: Still in the Swim," *Saturday Evening Post*. Available online, URL: http://www.findarticles.com/m1189/n1_v270/20112865/p1/article.jhtml. January–February 1998. Downloaded on April 5, 2001.

Smith, Lissa, editor. *Nike Is a Goddess: The History of Women in Sports*. New York: Atlantic Monthly Press, 1998, pp. 188–189.

WILLIAMS, VENUS (Venus Ebonestar Williams) (1980–), and SERENA WILLIAMS
(1981–) *Tennis Players*

Two of the most talented players in contemporary women's tennis happen to be sisters who were born 15 months apart. Venus and Serena Williams are both Grand Slam winners and Olympic champions. They are also barrier breakers in their own right, the first two African Americans to win the sport's major championships since ALTHEA GIBSON.

Venus Ebonestar Williams and Serena Williams were the fourth and fifth children in a family of daughters born to Richard Williams, a security company owner, and his wife Oracene, a nurse. Born respectively on June 17, 1980, in Lynwood, California, and on September 26, 1981, in Saginaw, Michigan, Venus and Serena both grew up in Compton, California.

Richard Williams, who became fascinated with tennis after watching a young woman win a $30,000 purse in an afternoon, decided to steer all of his daughters toward the sport. The oldest three

had no interest, but Serena and Venus were natural athletes who showed an early knack for the game. Richard, who had taught himself tennis, was his young daughters' teacher, and he began playing with four-year-old Venus and three-year-old Serena on the neighborhood public courts.

It was in many ways an unusual setting for future tennis champions. Traditionally known as a "country club" sport, tennis has long been played on well-tended courts in affluent neighborhoods. Compton, an impoverished and dangerous suburb of Los Angeles, is a neighborhood more known for its gangs than for its courts. The park in Compton where the Williams girls practiced every day was not protected from any of the neighborhood's problems. There were days that the Williams girls heard gun shots as they hit their forehands and backhands; in addition to tutoring them on the game, Richard taught the girls how to drop, roll, and run, should they be shot at.

Nevertheless, Richard's daughters played relentlessly and splendidly. By the time they were nine and 10, they were playing on a competitive level. But Richard decided not to enter them in the junior circuit. Instead, he moved his clan to Delray Beach, Florida, and sent the girls to be coached by Rick Macci at his tennis academy.

Macci, who had coached future champions JENNIFER CAPRIATI and Mary Pierce, was used to teaching tennis to young prodigies. Nevertheless, several insiders were surprised by the fact that neither Williams would be competing on the junior circuit. Richard defended his decision by explaining that he wanted both girls to receive a full education without being distracted by the pressures of competition. Despite this admirable goal, the Williams sisters both turned professional at the age of 14. Richard reportedly wanted his daughters to wait, but when Serena and Venus pressed him, he agreed—on the condition that they get good grades on their report cards. Both Serena and Venus finished high school with B averages.

In the meantime, the tennis world was waiting to see how the Williams sisters would fare on the circuit. Word was out that they were supremely talented, but since they had never competed, there was little proof of their overall gifts. Venus made her debut in 1994, beating her first opponent and then losing in three sets to Arantxa Sanchez-Vicario, who was the second-ranked player in the world at the time. Serena played her first tournament a year later but premiered less auspiciously than her sister, losing in the first round.

At this time, Richard Williams boasted that the two sisters would one day become each other's top rival and that both would become top-ranked stars. Although neither girl had yet won a tournament, Williams's prediction did not seem to be completely unrealistic. Both girls had swift and strong ground strokes, terrific volleys, and supremely powerful serves. Although they did not have classic form or orthodox strategies, they also had few weaknesses, other than sheer inexperience.

Venus made her Grand Slam debut at the 1997 French Open, advancing to the second round, but she lost in the first round at Wimbledon that year. At the 1997 U.S. Open the 16-year old was ranked 66th in the world and was unseeded in the tournament. Nevertheless, she seared through her opening round matches and found herself in the semifinal against Irina Spirlea of Romania. Venus, who had become only the second player to reach the semifinals in her first U.S. Open appearance (Pam Shriver achieved it in 1977), defeated Spirlea and became the first African American since Althea Gibson to reach the tournament final. Although Martina Hingis defeated her in straight sets, Venus Williams had left her mark on the tournament and on the sport.

Even so, it was Serena, not Venus, who would win the first Grand Slam title in the Williams family. Playing in mixed doubles at Wimbledon in 1998, Serena teamed with Max Mirnyi of Belarus to take home the title. By this time, both sisters were receiving plenty of press coverage. Most of the publicity centered on how close the two were. They might be potential rivals on the court (the sisters had at this point faced each other twice in match play, with Venus winning both matches in three sets), but at home they were best friends and

Venus (left) and Serena Williams (right), one of the most potent doubles teams in contemporary tennis, are both Grand Slam singles champions as well.
(Clive Brunskill/Getty Images)

confidantes. Some reports, however, were less than complimentary, commenting on how aloof the sisters were on the circuit, and how, at times, some felt that their conduct on the court was less than sportsmanlike. Angered over the negative print, Richard Williams made several suggestions that the world of tennis was fraught with racism and that both his daughters had been somewhat ostracized as a result.

In 1999, both Serena and Venus advanced through the early rounds of the U.S. Open. Since they were on opposite ends of the ladder, it became increasingly possible, as the tournament progressed, that they would face one another in the championship game. That prospect ended when Venus lost in the semifinals to Martina Hingis, but Serena defeated Lindsay Davenport to advance to to the finals. In front of an enthusiastic crowd—including her sister—the youngest of the Williams sisters defeated Hingis in straight sets to become the first African American to win a Grand Slam since Gibson.

It was a great victory for Serena Williams, but fans and media wondered how Venus would react. At six feet, one inch tall and 169 pounds, Venus was taller and bigger than Serena, who packed 145 pounds on her five-foot-10-inch frame. Moreover, Venus was the older one and the first to make her debut. Would she be overshadowed by Serena?

The answer, as revealed at the 2000 Wimbledon tournament, was a resounding no. Once again both women powered their way through their beginning rounds. On the same end of the ladder this time, the sisters did meet one another, in a highly publicized and extremely tense semifinal game. Venus beat her sister in straight sets and then embraced her younger sister at the net. "Let's get out of here," Venus told the weeping Serena. The two left the court quickly. A day later, Venus came back to sweep Lindsay Davenport in straight sets. Now each Williams had her own Grand Slam title.

Venus Williams would go on to take top honors at the 2000 U.S. Open, to win a gold medal at the 2000 Olympic Games in Sydney, Australia, and to defend her Wimbledon title successfully in 2001. Serena, in the meantime, has fared less successfully as a singles player, but has won two Grand Slam doubles crowns—as well as the 2000 Olympic women's doubles gold medal—with her sister.

At the U.S. Open in September 2001, the two sisters came face to face for the first time in a Grand Slam final. In front of a sold-out stadium—and a national, prime-time television audience—Venus defeated her sister in straight sets. Venus and Serena Williams may play competitive tennis for years to come. It is also clear, however, that, at least for Venus, there is more to life than tennis. "Maybe when I'm 25," the future champion said in 1995, "I'll go to college and become a paleontologist or an archaeologist. But I need to catch up on biology first."

Further Reading

Biography Resource Center. "Serena Williams," *Newsmakers 1999* (updated 2000), Issue 4. Detroit, Mich.: Gale Group, 1999.

Biography Resource Center. "Venus Williams," *Newsmakers 1998* (updated 2000), Issue 2. Detroit: Gale Group, 2000.

Smith, Lissa, editor. *Nike Is a Goddess: The History of Women in Sports.* New York: Atlantic Monthly Press, 1998, p. 76.

"Venus Williams," *Sports Stars,* Series 1–4. Chicago: U*X*L, 1994–1998.

WILLS, HELEN (Helen Wills Moody, Helen Wills Roark)
(1905–1998) *Tennis Player*

In the 1920s and early 1930s, women's tennis had a true renaissance, both in Europe and the United States. In France, a player named Suzanne Lenglen would revolutionize the game, not only because of her spectacular play on the courts, but because she was a stylish and charismatic presence off the courts. And in the United States, a California socialite named Helen Wills would in her own way make just as great an impact on the game as Lenglen.

Helen Wills was born in Berkeley, California, on October 6, 1905, the only daughter of Clarence Wills, a physician, and Catherine, a homemaker. Young Helen, who had grown up swimming and riding her family's horses, took a passionate interest in tennis almost right away. When she was 14, Helen's father bought her a membership to the posh and socially prestigious Berkeley Tennis Club, where she began taking lessons from the club professional, the renowned teacher William "Pop" Fuller.

It did not take Helen long to master the game. When she was 15, she was so impressive on the court that Hazel Wightman, a champion player who made annual visits to the Berkeley Tennis Club, spotted Helen's talent. For six weeks, Wightman worked privately with Helen, teaching her volleys and approach shots. A year later, in 1921, Wills won the U.S. junior championships in Forest Hills, New York.

At those same U.S. championships, Wills sat in the stands to witness the finals of the women's tournament. Suzanne Lenglen, one of the players vying for the championship, had not lost in two years. But down a set to her opponent, the U.S. player Molla Mallory, and losing by a score of 0-2 in the second, Lenglen suddenly defaulted, complaining of ill health. The fans in the stand were displeased by what they interpreted as poor sportsmanship; some of them hissed as Lenglen was escorted off the premises. But Wills was thrilled by the match and by the talent of the players. It was there and then, she wrote later, that she "knew the goal for which I hoped to aim, the kind of tennis I wanted to play."

The kind of tennis Wills did play was a game of precision, anticipation, and control. She was not the most versatile or mobile of players, and she spent most of her time on the backcourt. But she always seemed to know where the ball would be hit, and her returns were consistent, deep, and powerful. She took those attributes to the courts of the U.S. championships in 1922, and used them to reach the final, where defending champion Mallory held her off in straight sets.

But the following year Wills was triumphant at Forest Hills, and during the next few years she would completely dominate the women's game. Between 1927 and 1933, in fact, she won every set she played—more than 150 consecutive matches. In the meantime, she attended the University of California at Berkeley and excelled there, too, earning a Phi Beta Kappa key.

Wills was also a prominent socialite—her circle of friends included George Bernard Shaw and Lady Astor—and a trendsetter in her own right. While Lenglen, who wore designer outfits and a debonair bandeau on her head during matches, is credited with turning tennis into a more stylish game, Wills made her own contribution: she was the first player to wear a visor on the court. She often showed up for matches wearing a combination of white and regal red, topped off by her white visor.

Her choice of attire was one reason that Wills earned the nicknames "Queen Helen" and "Imperial Helen," but she was also somewhat aloof; she never showed any emotion whatsoever while playing and was often cool and unapproachable off the court as well.

Manners and personality aside, Wills became the most prolific champion of her time. During her career she captured eight Wimbledon championships, seven U.S. titles, and four French crowns. She also led the U.S. team to several Wightman Cup victories. But as impressive as Wills's résumé is, she could have been even more prolific. An injury kept her from competing in all major tournaments in 1926, while she was at the peak of her game, and after her controversial default against HELEN JACOBS in the U.S. championship final, she stayed away from all competitive tennis for a year and a half, and she stopped playing at Forest Hills altogether.

Still, Wills was without a doubt the top-caliber player in the United States for the greater part of two decades. Her only rival in all of tennis during much of this time was Suzanne Lenglen. In today's age of year-round tournaments and media-hyped rivalries, there is little doubt that Lenglen and Wills would have opposed one another dozens of times. But before the modern age of tennis, great opportunities for classic matchups were fewer and farther between. In addition, there was little doubt that Lenglen, the older of the two players and the one with more to lose, was probably less than eager to test her talents against the upstart California.

In 1924, Wills made her first journey to Wimbledon, where she moved through the early rounds with ease. It was her great ambition to play Lenglen, perhaps with the championship on the line. But Lenglen, who had battled jaundice earlier in the year, arrived at the tournament out of shape and overweight. In her quarterfinal match against Elizabeth Ryan, she struggled tremendously. Although she pulled out a victory over Ryan in three sets, she left the court extremely agitated and upset, and the next day defaulted from the tournament on the advice of her doctors. The day after her withdrawal Lenglen went on a shopping spree, sparking rumors that her default was perhaps a result not only from nervous fatigue but from a desire to avoid confronting the fresher and sharper-hitting Wills. The young U.S. player went on to the final of the tournament that year, where she lost in three sets to Kitty McKane. It was the only defeat Wills would suffer at Wimbledon in her career.

Lenglen managed to avoid Wills for another year and a half, but in the winter of 1926 Wills decided to force the issue. Aware that Lenglen was competing on the French Riviera, Wills withdrew from her studies at Berkeley for a semester and traveled to Europe. The official reason Wills gave for her trip was to study art; but tennis followers were aware that what Wills really longed for was to play Lenglen. The French player was a bit taken aback by Wills's assertive move—she labeled it "cheeky." Nevertheless, there was little she could

do to avoid the confrontation without appearing threatened.

In the middle of February, both women entered a tournament in Cannes, and as they both moved easily through the early rounds, it became clear that they were headed for a showdown. Sure enough, as the tournament reached its conclusion, Lenglen and Wills were slated to meet each other in the final.

In her book *We Have Come a Long Way,* BILLIE JEAN KING states that the buildup for the Lenglen-Wills match was remarkably similar to the one that led up to her 1973 "Battle of the Sexes" match with Bobby Riggs. Indeed, the attention the event gathered was extraordinary, even by today's standards. The final round was publicized relentlessly by promoters and generated an unprecedented 800,000 francs in ticket sales. It is reported that U.S. film company offered $100,000 to film the event but was denied. And as the two competitors entered the court, a standing-room-only crowd of 4,000—well beyond the arena's capacity—jammed the premises.

The players, not surprisingly, were tense as the match began. Lenglen, who began the match playing passively and without her usual flair, left the court frequently in between points for a quick sip of brandy—to calm her nerves, she said later. Wills played tentatively as well. Used to the powerful and flat ground strokes of her U.S. American opponents, she was unaccustomed to Lenglen's style of tennis, which featured soft, short, accurately placed shots that would land practically anywhere within the boundaries.

Wills lost the first set but found her rhythm in the second. Then, with Wills serving at 4-3 and up by 30-15, Lenglen hit a shot that looked wide. Assuming that the shot was out, Wills did not pursue it and was stunned when the linesman motioned that it was good. She protested but the call stood. Rattled by the controversial call, Wills lost the game, and Lenglen regained the momentum.

Then, as if one controversial call was not enough for both players another situation arose

The most successful American tennis player of her day, Helen Wills helped turn the sport into a popular pastime for the nation's privileged class.
(Library of Congress)

with Lenglen up 6-5 and serving for the match. It was double match point at 40-15 when Wills hit a ball toward the back of Lenglen's side of the court. A male voice roared "Out!" and the two players strode up the net and graciously shook hands. As they were exchanging pleasantries, however, the court official was desperately motioning that the match had not ended; Wills's shot, he exclaimed, had hit the line; the male voice had belonged to an audience member, not an official. Lenglen and Wills turned around and play resumed. Wills came back to take the game, and the set was tied, 6-6.

But Lenglen, summoning all her strength, pulled out the next two games and triumphed, 8 to 6. With the match truly over and her reputation secure, Lenglen left the court and promptly collapsed. Wills had lost the match, but she did not leave France empty handed. After her loss to Lenglen, she was standing on the court by herself when a young man whom she had met earlier in the week jumped down from the grandstand and ran over to her. "You played awfully well," Wells's admirer told her. Wells and her fan, a San Francisco stockbroker named Frederick Moody, married in 1928.

The defeat to Lenglen was a rare one for Wills, who played tennis for another 12 years. Her final victory came at Wimbledon in 1938, when she defeated Helen Jacobs to capture her 19th and final major singles championship. After the match, Wills saluted Lenglen, who was then quite seriously ill with leukemia. "[Lenglen] was the greatest player who ever lived," Wills announced as she held her Wimbledon plate on July 1, 1938. Three days later, Lenglen died at the age of 39.

Wills retired right after the 1938 Wimbledon championships. She divorced Moody that same year, and married Adam Roark in 1939. The Roarks spent a great deal of time traveling during 1940. Helen Wills Roark became a freelance journalist, reviewing fashion shows and gallery openings for a San Francisco newspaper, as well as an artist in her own right. Later on, she also published books, authoring several mystery novels as well as her autobiography. She died in 1998.

Further Reading

Engelmann, Larry. *The Goddess and the American Girl: The Story of Suzanne Lenglen and Helen Wills.* New York: Oxford, 1988.

King, Billie Jean, and Cynthia Starr. *We Have Come a Long Way: The Story of Women's Tennis.* New York: McGraw-Hill, 1988, pp. 31–35.

Layden, Joe. *Women in Sports: The Complete Book on the World's Greatest Female Athletes.* Santa Monica, Calif.: General Publishing Group, 1997, pp. 169–170.

WOODARD, LYNETTE
(1959–   )   *Basketball Player*

Despite playing the heart of her career during a time when there were no professional basketball leagues for women in the United States, Lynette Woodard managed to make a tremendous statement for women in sports through one spectacular achievement: When she was 25, she became the first woman ever to play for the world-famous Harlem Globetrotters.

Born in Wichita, Kansas, on August 12, 1959, Lynette Woodard started playing basketball with her older brother, Darryl, when she was nine years old. The following year, the Woodard siblings began playing at Piatt Park, the public playground in their neighborhood. Lynette was the only girl on the local court, and not surprisingly, she got teased a lot—at first. "At first it was like 'get out of here.' And then they needed an extra player and they really needed me out there," she said.

By the time she got to high school, Lynette was definitely needed on the basketball court. At the age of 15, the five foot, 11 inch guard led North High School to the state championship. Among the spectators at that tournament was Marian Washington, the head coach of the women's basketball team, the Lady Jayhawks, at the University of Kansas. Although Woodard was only a sophomore, Washington placed her at the very top of her recruiting list. "When I saw how good she was," Washington said of Woodard, "I was scared to death."

Woodard did indeed play for Washington at Kansas, and she spent her four years in a Lady Jayhawk uniform scaring the wits out of her opponents. By the time Woodard graduated from Kansas in 1981, she had scored a record 3,649 points. A four-time All-American player, Woodard was named the collegiate player of the year during her senior season in 1981.

After leaving Kansas, Woodard played basketball for a year in Italy and then returned to Kansas to work as an assistant coach. She had her eye on a greater prize, however: named a member of the U.S. Olympic women's basketball team in 1980, Woodard lost her chance to play for a gold medal that year when the United States boycotted the Moscow games. Woodard set her sights on the 1984 Olympic Games in Los Angeles; this time, the United States came to play, and Woodard led the home team to a gold medal.

After the Olympics, Woodard faced a decision: She could go abroad to play professional basketball again, she could return to an assistant coaching post at Kansas, or she could retire from the game and pursue another career. Woodard chose something entirely different: she elected to audition for a spot on the Harlem Globetrotters. Woodard had been a Globetrotter fan since early childhood. One of her basketball mentors, in fact, was her cousin, Hubert "Geese" Ausbie, a Globetrotter who would visit the Woodards whenever the team was in Wichita. Woodard remembered how Geese could spin the basketball on his finger. Many years later, she had taught herself all of his tricks, and she had picked up his love for showmanship.

In the fall of 1985, Woodard outplayed 25 other women competing for the spot on the Globetrotters, and she earned a place on the team. Although some critics thought the Globetrotters had employed a woman solely as a publicity stunt, Woodard soon quieted the naysayers by playing terrific ball. And she loved every minute of it. "Playing with the Globetrotters is like playing jazz," she said of her time on the team. "You get to be as creative as you want to be."

Unfortunately, Woodard's stay with the Globetrotters ended after her second year with the team, when a change in management led to a contract dispute. Woodard left Harlem and flew to Japan, where she played professional basketball for eight years. After the 1993 season, she retired from the sport and returned to the United States. After more than two decades on the basketball court, Woodard decided to pursue a completely new profession, becoming a professional stockbroker.

In 1997, Woodard was lured back onto the floor when the Cleveland Rockers of the newly formed Women's Natural Basketball Association (WNBA) recruited her. After playing for Cleveland for a year, Woodard was traded to the Detroit Shock, where she played in 1998, 1999, and 2000. Although she had returned to the court, Woodard kept her day job; during the off-season, she continued to work as a stockbroker in New York City.

Further Reading

Herbst Diane. "Growing Up with Lynette Woodard," The Official Page of the Detroit Shock. Available online. URL: http://sportsillustrated.cnn.com/siforwomen/top_100/81. Downloaded on March 20, 2001.

Kansas State Historical Society. "Lynette Woodard Reached for the Hoops in Kansas." Available online. URL: http://www.kshs.org/people/woodard.htm. Downloaded March 20, 2001.

Layden, Joe. *Women in Sports: The Complete Book on the World's Greatest Female Athletes.* Santa Monica, Calif.: General Publishing Group, 1997, pp. 260–261.

WRIGHT, MICKEY
(Mary Kathryn Wright)
(1935–) *Golfer*

Ask virtually any golfer to name the sport's most difficult technical aspect, and most will tell you off the bat that it is the swing. Timing and form have to be perfect—one small error in technique can send the ball hooking or slicing wildly off course. But there is one golfer, Mickey Wright, to whom the swing came naturally. It was that swing—

described by Ben Hogan as the best he had ever seen—along with her tenacity, determination, and natural ability, that made Mickey Wright one of the most dominant players in the history of women's golf.

Born on February 14, 1935, Mary Kathryn Wright grew up in San Diego, California. Wright's father, an attorney, nicknamed her Mickey—short for Michael, the name he would have given her had she been born a boy. At age nine, Mickey received her first pair of golf clubs, a gift from her father. By that time she had already been hitting golf balls for five years; she began practicing that great swing—taught to her by her father—at the age of four.

When she was 11, Mickey began taking golf lessons at the La Jolla Country Club. Three years later, she won her first local tournament in style, posting a score of 70 in one of the rounds. Clearly, it was only a matter of time before Mickey Wright would become a national champion. This she accomplished in 1952, when at the age of 17 she took top honors at U.S. Golf Association (USGA) Girls' Junior Championships. Two years later, she won the World Amateur, title and played at her first U.S. Women's Open.

At this time, Wright was a psychology major at Stanford University. But she decided to leave college after her freshman year, so she could play golf full time. In 1954, Wright finished fourth at the U.S. Women's Open—which turned out to be BABE DIDRIKSON ZAHARIAS's final championship. In 1956, Wright began her own championship legacy, collecting her first tournament trophy. For the next 14 years, Wright won at least one championship, giving her a career collection of 82—the second highest total in the women's game, behind only KATHY WHITWORTH. She won the U.S. Women's Open title in 1958—a feat she would repeat in 1959, 1961, and 1964. She took top honors at the Ladies Professional Golf Association (LPGA) event four times as well, in 1958, 1960, 1961, and 1963. By the mid-1960s, Wright was the top player in the game. Her rivalries with not only Whitworth but also with BETSY RAWLS made

A picture-perfect swing helped make Mickey Wright the most dominant women's golfer in the early 1960s. Wright won the Vare trophy five consecutive years between 1960 and 1964.
(Library of Congress)

for a compelling era in women's golf. Of those three players it was Wright who commanded the most attention from media and fans alike. At the peak of her game, Wright had a complete arsenal of talents. Armed with an intelligent short game as well as that classic swing, Wright was the most natural player on the course.

But Wright's popularity was double-edged. The fledgling women's league during the 1960s had few annual events. Rather, the players would travel from one hastily arranged tournament to another. Wright was easily the player most in demand; when competition sponsors heard that she was not planning to participate in their event, they would threaten to cancel. Knowing that the livelihood of others depended on her, Wright gamely competed in dozens of tournaments throughout the 1960s. She won many of them—10 of 33 in 1962, 13 of 30 in 1963, and 11 of 27 in 1964—and she took home the Vare Trophy in five consecutive years, between 1960 and 1964.

At the same time, however, Wright was beginning to show signs of exhaustion. In addition to her packed playing schedule, Wright had been chosen as president of the LPGA in 1962—a position that demanded regular public appearances to promote the game. Never comfortable in that role, Wright began dreading her responsibilities. "I'm not good as far as wanting to be in front of people, glorying in it and loving it," Wright said later. "I think you have to love that to make that kind of pressure tolerable."

By 1969, Wright was suffering not only fatigue but also a severe foot condition that hampered her ability on the course. Citing those conditions, along with a severe fear of flying that made virtu-ally every travel day stressful, she announced her retirement from the game, at the age of 34. But although she had left the tour, she made sporadic appearances over the next decade. The most memorable of those came in 1979, when Wright, wearing tennis sneakers, finished second to NANCY LOPEZ at the Coca-Cola Classic. Wright's most recent appearance was at the 1993 Sprint Classic, where she finished fifth. She lives in Port Saint Lucie, Florida.

Further Reading

Layden, Joe. *Women in Sports: The Complete Book on the World's Greatest Female Athletes.* Santa Monica, Calif.: General Publishing Group, 1997, pp. 261–262.

Smith, Lissa, editor. *Nike Is a Goddess: The History of Women in Sports.* New York: Atlantic Monthly Press, 1998, pp. 89–91.

World Golf Hall of Fame. "A Profile of World Golf Hall of Famer Mickey Wright." Available online. URL: http://www.wgv.com/wgv/library.nsf/news/5C597B6E4A1D D277852567180072677B. Posted on February 14, 1999.

Y

(1971–) *Figure Skater*

In 1992, a U.S. skater named Kristi Yamaguchi captured gold at the Albertville Olympic Games, ushering in a new era of figure skating dominance for the United States.

Kristi Yamaguchi was born on June 12, 1971, in Fremont, California, one of three children born to Jim Yamaguchi, a dentist, and his wife, Carole, a medical secretary. Like several notable athletes, Kristi had to overcome a physical disability in her childhood; she was born with two clubfeet. For the first three years of her life, she wore corrective shoes to straighten her feet. When she was four, she was able to throw away the shoes, but her legs and feet were weak. To strengthen her legs, she began taking dance lessons.

At the age of six, Kristi fell in love with ice-skating and was soon struggling to maintain her balance on the ice. "She had a difficult time because she was very small and not very strong," her mother later said. But within a few months, she had gained strength and confidence, and at the age of eight she began training with a private coach, Christy Kjarsgaard-Ness.

Training meant getting out of bed at four o'clock every morning and practicing for two hours before school. Kristi also took one dance class every week; Kjarsgaard-Ness strongly believed that dance was an integral part of skating, and indeed, the movement and grace Kristi gained from those lessons helped make her one of the most artistic skaters in history.

During her early years in competition, Yamaguchi skated in both pairs and singles contests. In 1985, in she skated in her first national junior event, finishing fifth in the pairs event at the U.S. junior nationals with her partner, Rudy Galindo. Although Yamaguchi still trained with Kjarsgaard-Nees for her singles events, she and Galindo were coached by Jim Hulik for their pairs competitions.

It was a grueling schedule for Kristi, but her hard work was began to pay off. In 1986, she and Galindo won the gold medal at the U.S. junior nationals, while Kristi took fourth place in the singles competition. In 1988 she won two gold medals at the same tournament, taking top honors both in the singles and with Galindo in the pairs.

In 1989 Yamaguchi skated at the U.S. nationals for the first time, and finished second to Jill Trenary in singles. She and Galindo also competed in the pairs competition, and they surprised their older and more established rivals by taking the gold. Yamaguchi's double medal performance at the nationals made her the first woman to capture two medals at that competition in 35 years. Later in 1989, Yamaguchi went on to skate at the World Championships, finishing sixth in singles and fifth in pairs.

But if 1989 was a breakthrough year for Yamaguchi on the skating rink, it was also a difficult one off the ice. In April, Kjarsgaard-Ness moved to Alberta, Canada, and Yamaguchi relocated there to keep training with her coach. Galindo and Hulik traveled to Alberta as much as they could, but then, in December, Hulik died suddenly—and five days later, Kristi's grandfather died. "They were two big influences on me as a skater," Yamaguchi later said. "They were the happiest to see me go on. They made me work harder."

Yamaguchi realized in 1990 that she would have to make a choice between singles and pairs skating, in order to devote the time necessary to become an Olympic and world champion. After the 1990 World Championships, where she took fourth place in singles and fifth once again in pairs, she made her choice, and she and Galindo went their separate ways. Rudy Galindo would go on to become a successful singles skater in his own right, but Yamaguchi, despite her accomplishments, would always question her decision. "I miss pairs terribly," she told DONNA DE VARONA of ABC Sports after the Albertville Olympics. "There is something about working with someone out there on the ice and having the same goals together."

But Yamaguchi had her own goal: the 1992 Olympics. Along the way she captured her first World Championship in 1991, and then she took top honors at U.S. nationals in 1992. Finishing second and third to Yamaguchi at that competition were NANCY KERRIGAN and Tonya Harding, and all three skaters arrived in Albertville with hopes for a medal.

For Yamaguchi, the road to gold would not be an easy one. Although she was undoubtedly one of the favorites, she also knew she faced stiff competition from Midori Ito of Japan. Ito did not skate with the artistry that Yamaguchi had, but she did have a powerful weapon in her arsenal: Ito was, along with Tonya Harding, one of only two women in history who had landed a triple axel in competition. The axel is the most difficult of the jumps in figure skating, because it is the only one that the skater performs while in the forward position. In addition, because the skater takes off from the forward outside edge of the front foot and then lands on the back outside edge of the opposite foot, turning a triple axel actually means spinning for three and one-half revolutions, rather than merely three.

Yamaguchi realized she did not have a triple axel in her repertoire, but she also knew that she had an artistic flair which Ito and the other skaters lacked. In addition, she was aware that Ito would have to land the triple axel cleanly in competition in order for it to count. If she had trouble on the landing, it could in fact work against her. "I see a lot of misses on jumps in competition," she said shortly before the games, "and a clean program will beat them every time."

As it turned out, Ito did fall on the triple axel during her short program, and Yamaguchi skated the routine of her life. Her elegant program won first-place votes from all nine judges, and two days later, Yamaguchi skated to victory, despite falling on one of her triple jumps in her long program. Ito landed a triple axel during her long program and won the silver. Kerrigan took the bronze.

Two months after the Olympics, Yamaguchi successfully defended her World Championship title, and then she retired from competitive skating. She signed several lucrative endorsement deals and began skating in professional exhibitions and tournaments.

Further Reading

Greenspan, Bud. *Frozen in Time: The Greatest Moments at the Winter Olympics.* Santa Monica, Calif.: General Publishing Group, 1997.

Kim, Stuart. "Kristi Yamaguchi: A Biography" Available online. URL: www.polaris.net/~shanhew/biography/biography.html. Downloaded on November 18, 2000.

YOUNG, SHEILA
(Sheila Young-Ochowicz)
(1950–) *Speed Skater, Cyclist*

It is impressive enough that Sheila Young won three Olympic medals and three world championships in the sport of speed skating. But the fact that Young also won two cycling world championships—and that she was competing in both sports during the same time span—puts Young in a special category that few athletes aspire to and even fewer achieve.

Born in Birmingham, Michigan, on October 4, 1950, Sheila Young grew up in a large, athletic family. Both her parents enjoyed cycling and skating, and they encouraged their children to participate in both sports. Ironically, Sheila was the most hesitant of the Young children when it came to hitting the ice; the first few times she went skating, she had to be coaxed and even bribed. But Sheila's natural ability soon overcame her initial hesitations, and she eventually became an expert on the ice.

Sheila's life took a pivotal turn in 1962, when her mother died of ovarian cancer. At that point, 12-year-old Sheila moved with her family to Detroit, where her father had taken a new job. The change was painful for Sheila, and to compensate for her feelings of isolation, she devoted more and more time to speed skating. As Sheila became more serious about her sport, the entire Young family began accompanying her to her training sessions. Because there were no indoor facilities for speed skating, Sheila could practice her sport only during the colder months. During the spring and summer, she would supplement her training by hopping on her bicycle and hitting the roads. Her training might have been a bit unorthodox, but it was effective; by the time she was in her early twenties, she was one of the elite speed skaters in the United States.

In 1972, Young competed at the Winter Olympics in Sapporo, Japan. Although she was not considered a favorite for a medal, Young came within .08 seconds of winning the bronze. The fol-lowing year, Young became the uncontested number-one speed skater in the nation when she won national titles in the 500-meter, 1,000-meter, and 1,500-meter events. One month later, she won her first international championship when she took top honors in the 500-meter event at the speed skating world championships. But it was in the spring of 1973 that Young made history.

Although Young had cycled all her life, she had used the sport mainly as a training vehicle for her speed skating. But after winning her speed skating world title, she decided to test her talent and began entering world-class cycling competitions. Through sheer will and determination, she logged enough road time to qualify for the world championships in the sprints. Many people in the cycling world admired Young for practicing two sports at the same time, but no one thought she had much business entering the world championships. Young herself was anxious and uneasy during the early part of the competition, crashing twice in the early heats of the sprint preliminaries. But she pulled herself together, and then proceeded to shock the cycling world by upsetting the Soviet champion, Galina Ermalasva, to take the gold medal.

Not only was Young the first U.S. cyclist of either gender to win a world title, but she was the first U.S. athlete to take world championships in separate events during the same year. Even BABE DIDRIKSON ZAHARIAS, an Olympic champion track-and-field athlete, waited a full decade before becoming a champion in a second sport, golf.

After winning the cycling title, Young returned to the ice. She won top honors once again in the 500-meter event at the World Championships in 1975, and in the following year, she had one of the finest years any athlete has enjoyed in the history of U.S. Sports. In February, Young traveled to Innsbruck, Austria, to compete in all three speed skating events in the Olympics. Although she was primarily a sprinter on the ice, Young was athletic enough to excel at the longer distances as well. The favorite to take gold in the 500-meter event, Young won that race easily and then went on to win a bronze in the 1,000-meter race and the silver in the 1,500-meter event. In March, Young successfully defended her title in the 500-meter race at the world championships. Young put an exclamation point on her splendid year by grabbing her bicycle and riding to her second sprint world championship in the summer of 1976.

At the top of her game in two sporting events, Young decided to retire from both activities at the end of 1976. Two years later she married Jim Ochowicz, a businessman. The couple had a daughter, Kate, in 1980, and one year later, Young-Ochowicz returned to competition in both of her sports. After winning a remarkable third cycling world championship, she retired for good. Young-Ochowicz had two more children, Alex and Elizabeth. After completing a degree in physical education and health from the University of Wisconsin at Milwaukee, Young-Ochowicz became her daughter Elizabeth's personal speed skating coach. A member of the national speed skating team since 1998, Elizabeth "Elli" Ochowicz is a top prospect for a medal at the 2004 Olympic Games. Her mother, Sheila Young-Ochowicz, left coaching in 1998, and became a physical education teacher at an elementary school in Waukesha, Wisconsin.

Further Reading

CNN.com/SI For Women. 100 Greatest Athletes: "Sheila Young," *Sports Illustrated for Women Online.* Available online. URL: http://sportsillustrated.cnn.com/siforwomen/top_100/86/. Posted on November 29, 1999.

Layden, Joe. *Women in Sports: The Complete Book on the World's Greatest Female Athletes.* Santa Monica, Calif.: General Publishing Group, 1997, pp. 264–265.

RECOMMENDED SOURCES ON AMERICAN WOMEN IN SPORTS

■ ■ ■

Books

Baldwin, David. *Track & Field Record Holders: Profiles of the Men and Women Who Set World, Olympic, and American Records.* Jefferson, N.C.: McFarland Publishers, 1996.

Birrell, Susan, and Cheryl Cole. *Women, Sport and Culture.* Champaign, Ill.: Kinetics Publishers, 1998.

Daddario, Gena. *Women's Sport and Spectacle.* Westport, Conn.: Greenwood Publishing Group, 1998.

Da Silva, Rachel. *Leading Out: Women Climbers Reaching the Top.* Seattle, Wash.: Seal Press, 1993.

Davidson, Sue. *Changing the Game: The Stories of Tennis Champions Alice Marble and Althea Gibson.* Seattle, Wash.: Seal Press, 1972.

Freedman, Lou. *Iditarod Classics: Tales of the Men and Women Who Race Across Alaska.* Anchorage, Alaska.: Epicenter, 1992.

Glenn, Rhonda. *The Illustrated History of Women's Golf.* Dallas, Tex.: Taylor, 1991.

Greenspan, Bud. *Frozen in Time: The Greatest Moments at the Winter Olympics.* Santa Monica, Calif.: General Publishing Group, 1997.

Gregorich, Barbara. *Women at Play: The Story of Women in Baseball.* New York: Harcourt Brace, 1993.

Guttmann, Alan. *Women's Sports: A History.* New York: Columbia University Press, 1991.

Johnson, Susan E. *When Women Played Hardball.* Seattle, Wash.: Seal Press, 1994.

King, Billie Jean, and Cynthia Starr. *We Have Come a Long Way: The Story of Women's Tennis.* New York: McGraw Hill, 1988.

Langley, Dorothy. *A View from the Red Tees: The Truth About Women and Golf.* New York: Birch Lane Press, 2001.

Lannin, Joanne. *A History of Basketball for Girls and Women: From Bloomers to Big Leagues.* Minneapolis, Minn.: Lerner Sports, 2000.

Larson, Paul C. *America's Cup: The Women's Team.* Los Angeles: Summit Publishing Group, 1997.

Layden, Joe. *Women in Sports: The Complete Book on the World's Greatest Female Athletes.* Santa Monica, Calif.: General Publishing Group, 1997.

Lewis, Linda. *Water's Edge: Women Who Push the Limits in Rowing, Kayaking, and Canoeing.* Seattle, Wash.: Seal Press, 1992.

Longman, Jere. *The Girls of Summer: The U.S. Women's Soccer Team and How It Changed the World.* New York: HarperCollins, 2000.

Lumpkin, Angela. *Women's Tennis: A Historical Documentary of the Players and Their Game.* Long Beach, Calif.: Whitson Publishers, 1981.

Macy, Sue. *Winning Ways.* New York: Henry Holt, 1996.

Markel, Robert, Susan Wagoner, and Marcella Smith. *The Women's Sports Encyclopedia.* New York: Henry Holt, 1999.

Miller, Marla. *All-American Girls: The US Women's National Soccer Team.* New York: Archway Paperbacks, 1999.

Nelson, Mariah Burton. *The Stronger Women Get, the More Men Love Football: Sexism and the American Culture of Sports.* New York: Avon Books, 1995.

Phelps, Shirelle, editor. *Contemporary Black Biography*, Volume 24. Detroit, Mich.: Gale Group, 2000.

Plowden, Martha Ward. *Olympic Black Women*. Gretna, La.: Pelican Publishers, 1996.

Postema, Pam, and Gene Wojciechowsky. *You've Got to Have Balls to Make It in This League: My Life as an Umpire*. New York: Simon & Schuster, 1992.

Rathbun, Elizabeth. *Grace and Glory: A Century of Women in the Olympics*. New York: Triumph Books, 1996.

Rutledge, Rachel. *The Best of the Best in Basketball*, Brookfield, Conn.: Millbrook Press, 1998.

Ryan, Joan. *Little Girls in Pretty Boxes: The Making and Breaking of Elite Gymnasts and Figure Skaters*. New York: Warner Books, 1993.

Simons, Minot. *Women's Gymnastics: A History: 1966–1974*. Carmel, Calif.: Welwyn Publishing Company, 1995.

Smith, Lissa, editor. *Nike Is a Goddess: The History of Women in Sports*. New York: Atlantic Monthly Press, 1998.

Sugar, Bert Randolph. *The Sports 100: A Ranking of the Greatest Athletes of All Time*. Secaucus, N.J.: Citadel Press, 1995.

Turco, Mary. *Crashing the Net: The U.S. Women's Olympic Hockey Team and the Road to Gold*. New York: HarperCollins, 1999.

Wimmer, Dick, editor. *Women's Game*. Short Hills, N.J.: Burford Books, 1988.

Woolum, Janet. *Outstanding Women Athletes: Who They Are and How They Influenced Sports in America*. Phoenix: Oryx Press, 1992.

Websites

CNN.SI for Women. "100 Greatest Female Athletes," Available online. URL: http://sportsillustrated.cnn.com/siforwomen/top_100/1. Downloaded on December 28, 2001.

Hickok Sports Biographies. Available online. URL: http://www.hickoksports.com. Downloaded on December 28, 2001.

Ladies Professional Golf Association. Available online. URL: http://www.1pga.com. Downloaded on December 28, 2001.

U.S. Figure Skating Online. Available online. URL: http://www.usfsa.org. Downloaded on December 28, 2001.

U.S. Soccer Federation. Available online. URL: http://www.ussoccer.com. Downloaded on December 28, 2001.

Women's Sports Legends. Available online. URL: http://www.wslegends.com. Downloaded on December 28, 2001.

ENTRIES BY SPORT

Administrator and Coach

Ackerman, Valerie
Bell, Judy
Berenson, Senda
DeFrantz, Anita
Jackson, Nell
Lopiano, Donna
Summitt, Pat Head
Wade, Margaret

Baseball and Softball Player

Borders, Ila
Croteau, Julie
Fernandez, Lisa
Houghton, Edith
Joyce, Joan
Kamenshek, Dottie
Lopiano, Donna
Mitchell, Jackie
Nelson, Maud
Richardson, Dot
Stone, Toni

Basketball Player

Blazejowski, Carol
Cooper, Cynthia
Driscoll, Jean
Edwards, Teresa
Holdsclaw, Chamique
Leslie, Lisa

Lieberman, Nancy
Meyers, Ann
Miller, Cheryl
Staley, Dawn
Swoopes, Sheryl
Wade, Margaret
White, Nera
Woodard, Lynette

Bobsledder

Flowers, Vonetta

Bowler

Ladewig, Marion
McCutcheon, Floretta

Boxer and Wrestler

Ali, Laila
Saunders, Tricia

Commentator and Journalist

Carillo, Mary
De Varona, Donna
Ludtke, Melissa
Meyer, Ann
Roberts, Robin

Cyclist

Carpenter-Phinney, Connie
Young, Sheila

Diver and Swimmer

Babashoff, Shirley
Bauer, Sybil
Bleibtrey, Ethelda
Caulkins, Tracy
Chadwick, Florence
Curtis, Ann
de Varona, Donna
Ederle, Gertrude
Evans, Janet
Holm, Eleanor
King, Micki
McCormick, Pat
Meagher, Mary Terstegge
Meyer, Debbie
Nyad, Diana
Riggin, Aileen
Thompson, Jenny
Williams, Esther

Dogsled Racer

Butcher, Susan
Riddles, Libby

Figure Skater

Albright, Tenley
Fleming, Peggy
Hamill, Dorothy
Heiss, Carol
Henie, Sonja
Hughes, Sarah

Kerrigan, Nancy
Kwan, Michelle
Lipinski, Tara
Yamaguchi, Kristi

Golfer

Bell, Judy
Berg, Patty
Didrikson Zaharias, Babe
Gregory, Ann Moore
Inkster, Juli
King, Betsy
Lopez, Nancy
Rawls, Betsy
Suggs, Louise
Vare, Glenna
Whitworth, Kathy
Wright, Mickey

Gymnast

Retton, Mary Lou
Rigby, Cathy
Strug, Kerri

Hockey Player

Granato, Cammi

Jockey and Equestrian

Krone, Julie
Sears, Eleonora

Markswomen

Murdock, Margaret
Oakley, Annie

Race Car Driver

Guthrie, Janet
Muldowney, Shirley
St. James, Lyn

Referee, Umpire, and Scout

Clement, Amanda
Gera, Bernice
Houghton, Edith
Nelson, Maud

Postema, Pam
Shain, Eva

Rock Climber

Hill, Lynn

Rower, Sailor, and Water-Skier

Cook, Willa McGuire
DeFrantz, Anita
Riley, Dawn

Snow Skier

Fraser, Gretchen
Golden, Diana
Lawrence, Andrea Mead
Street, Picabo

Soccer Player

Akers, Michelle
Chastain, Brandi
Hamm, Mia

Speed Skater

Blair, Bonnie
Carpenter-Phinney, Connie
Young, Sheila

Squash Player

Sears, Eleonora

Surfer

Andersen, Lisa
Oberg, Margo

Tennis Player

Austin, Tracy
Brough, Louise
Capriati, Jennifer
Carillo, Mary
Connolly, Maureen
Evert, Chris
Gibson, Althea
Hansell, Ellen Ford

Jacobs, Helen
King, Billie Jean
Marble, Alice
Moore, Elisabeth
Navratilova, Martina
Outerbridge, Mary Ewing
Sears, Eleonora
Seles, Monica
Washington, Ora
Williams, Serena
Williams, Venus
Wills, Helen

Track-and-Field Athlete

Ashford, Evelyn
Benoit Samuelson, Joan
Brisco-Hooks, Valerie
Coachman, Alice
Decker Slaney, Mary
Devers, Gail
Didrikson Zaharias, Babe
Dragila, Stacy
Driscoll, Jean
Gibb, Roberta
Griffith Joyner, Florence
Jackson, Neil
Jennings, Lynn
Jones, Marion
Joyner-Kersee, Jackie
Kuscsik, Nina
Pickett, Tidye
Rudolph, Wilma
Stephens, Helen
Suggs, Louise
Switzer, Katherine
Torrence, Gwen
Trason, Ann
Tyus, Wyomia
White, Willye

Volleyball Player

Hyman, Flo
Peppler, Mary Jo

Weightlifter

Haworth, Cheryl

ENTRIES BY YEAR OF BIRTH

1850–1899

Berenson, Senda
Clement, Amanda
Hansell, Ellen Ford
McCutcheon, Floretta
Moore, Elisabeth
Nelson, Maud
Oakley, Annie
Outerbridge, Mary Ewing
Sears, Eleonora
Washington, Ora

1900–1909

Bauer, Sybil
Bleibirey, Ethelda
Ederle, Gertrude
Jacobs, Helen
Riggin, Aileen
Shain, Eva
Vare, Glenna
Wills, Helen

1910–1919

Berg, Patty
Chadwick, Florence
Didrikson Zaharias, Babe
Fraser, Gretchen
Gregory, Ann Moore
Henie, Sonja
Holm, Eleanor

Houghton, Edith
Ladewig, Marion
Marble, Alice
Mitchell, Jackie
Pickett, Tidye
Stephens, Helen
Suggs, Louise
Wade, Margaret

1920–1929

Brough, Louise
Coachman, Alice
Cook, Willa McGuire
Curtis, Ann
Gibson, Althea
Jackson, Nell
Kamenshek, Dottie
Rawls, Betsy
Stone, Toni
Suggs, Louise
Williams, Esther

1930–1939

Albright, Tenley
Bell, Judy
Connolly, Maureen
Gera, Bernice
Guthrie, Janet
Kuscsik, Nina
Lawrence, Andrea Mead

McCormick, Pat
White, Nera
White, Willye
Whitworth, Kathy
Wright, Mickey

1940–1949

de Varona, Donna
Fleming, Peggy
Gibb, Roberta
Heiss, Carol
Joyce, Joan
King, Billie Jean
King, Micki
Lopiano, Donna
Muldowney, Shirley
Murdock, Margaret
Nyad, Diana
Peppler, Mary Jo
Rudolph, Wilma
St. James, Lyn
Switzer, Katherine
Tyus, Wyomia

1950–1959

Ackerman, Valerie
Ashford, Evelyn
Babashoff, Shirley
Benoit Samuelson, Joan
Blazejowski, Carol

Butcher, Susan
Carillo, Mary
Carpenter-Phinney, Connie
Decker Slaney, Mary
DeFrantz, Anita
Evert, Chris
Griffith Joyner, Florence
Hamill, Dorothy
Hyman, Flo
King, Betsy
Lieberman, Nancy
Lopez, Nancy
Ludtke, Melissa
Meyer, Debbie
Meyers, Ann
Navratilova, Martina
Oberg, Margo
Postema, Pam
Riddles, Libby
Rigby, Cathy
Summitt, Pat Head
Woodard, Lynelle
Young, Sheila

1960–1969

Akers, Michelle
Andersen, Lisa
Austin, Tracy

Blair, Bonnie
Brisco-Hooks, Valerie
Caulkins, Tracy
Chastain, Brandi
Cooper, Cynthia
Devers, Gail
Driscoll, Jean
Edwards, Teresa
Golden, Diana
Hill, Lynn
Inkster, Juli
Jennings, Lynn
Joyner-Kersee, Jackie
Kerrigan, Nancy
Krone, Julie
Meagher, Mary Terstegge
Miller, Cheryl
Retton, Mary Lou
Richardson, Dot
Riley, Dawn
Roberts, Robin
Saunders, Tricia
Torrence, Gwen
Trason, Ann

1970–1979

Ali, Laila
Borders, Ila

Capriati, Jennifer
Croteau, Julie
Dragila, Stacy
Evans, Janet
Fernandez, Lisa
Flowers, Vonetta
Granato, Cammi
Hamm, Mia
Holdsclaw, Chamique
Jones, Marion
Leslie, Lisa
Seles, Monica
Staley, Dawn
Street, Picabo
Strug, Kerri
Swoopes, Sheryl
Thompson, Jenny
Yamaguchi, Kristi

1980–1989

Haworth, Cheryl
Hughes, Sarah
Kwan, Michele
Lipinski, Tara
Williams, Serena
Williams, Venus

INDEX

■ ■ ■